Instructional Design: Case Studies in Communities of Practice

Michael J. Keppell
Hong Kong Institute of Education, Hong Kong

Information Science Publishing
Hershey • New York

Acquisition Editor:	Kristin Klinger
Senior Managing Editor:	Jennifer Neidig
Managing Editor:	Sara Reed
Assistant Managing Editor:	Sharon Berger
Development Editor:	Kristin Roth
Copy Editor:	Alana Bubnis
Typesetter:	Cindy Consonery
Cover Design:	Lisa Tosheff
Printed at:	Yurchak Printing Inc.

Published in the United States of America by
Information Science Publishing (an imprint of IGI Global)
701 E. Chocolate Avenue
Hershey PA 17033
Tel: 717-533-8845
Fax: 717-533-8661
E-mail: cust@idea-group.com
Web site: http://www.idea-group.com

and in the United Kingdom by
Information Science Publishing (an imprint of IGI Global)
3 Henrietta Street
Covent Garden
London WC2E 8LU
Tel: 44 20 7240 0856
Fax: 44 20 7379 3313
Web site: http://www.eurospan.co.uk

Library of Congress Cataloging-in-Publication Data

Instructional design : case studies in communities of practice / Michael J. Keppell, editor.
p. cm.
Summary: "This book explains the strategies and heuristics used by instructional designers when working in different settings, articulates the sophistication of communication strategies when working with subject matter experts, and provides insight into the range of knowledge, skills, and personal characteristics required to complete the tasks expected of them"--Provided by publisher.
Includes bibliographical references and index.
ISBN 978-1-59904-322-7 (hardcover) -- ISBN 978-1-59904-324-1 (ebook)
1. Instructional systems--Design--Case studies. I. Keppell, Michael J., 1961-
LB1028.38.I557 2007
371.3--dc22

2006033765

British Cataloguing in Publication Data
A Cataloguing in Publication record for this book is available from the British Library.

All work contributed to this book is new, previously-unpublished material. The views expressed in this book are those of the authors, but not necessarily of the publisher.

Instructional Design: Case Studies in Communities of Practice

Table of Contents

Preface

Introduction

Instructional designers play a significant role in enhancing teaching and learning in cross-cultural international settings, universities, faculties, departments and school settings. Instructional designers enter these communities of practice and attempt to understand the context and achieve legitimate participation in each community. This book examines how instructional designers work across these diverse communities of practice, and illustrates the different methods with a range of heuristic, communication, and other unique strategies. This book consists of a number of peer-reviewed chapters that document real-world cases of instructional designers who work in diverse communities of practice.

The Target Audience

This book will be useful for instructional designers who want to improve their understanding of the knowledge, skills, strategies, heuristics and principles that are required to complete projects in challenging contexts and content areas. Instructional designers who work in universities, teaching and learning centres, educational technology centres, distance education providers, multimedia and online learning centres and business corporations will find this book useful for their professional practice. Moreover, this book will provide insights and principles to support instructional design departments who teach undergraduate and postgraduate students to become instructional designers. Other professionals, such as academic staff developers, human resource consultants, psychologists and knowledge management coordinators, will also benefit from this book.

How This Book is Organised

This book is divided into five sections: Section I. Professional Practice; Section II. Cross-Cultural Context; Section III. University-Wide Context; Section IV. Faculty and Departmental Context; and Section V. School Context.

Section I: Professional Practice

Section I examines general perspectives in relation to professional practice of instructional designers, educational designers and academic developers. The first four chapters examine the role of the instructional designer in organizational change as social change agents, challenges to the profession, heuristics for designers and how designers translate across communities of practice.

In Chapter I, *Richard A. Schwier, Katy Campbell* and *Richard F. Kenny* suggest that instructional designers act as social change agents in the design and development of instruction. They draw on the stories of instructional designers to develop a model of change agency that includes interpersonal, professional, institutional and societal dimensions. The model provides guidance for the development of new skills in instructional design, for serious reflection by instructional designers about their own influence as agents, and for graduate programs in instructional design to address agency.

In Chapter II, *Jenny Bird, Chris Morgan* and *Meg O'Reilly* continue the theme by presenting some of the major challenges faced by the profession. They explore the tensions arising when current practices are pushed by institutional agendas including quality assurance, technology and flexible learning imperatives, student demographics and the emerging models of educational design practice across national contexts. The chapter also discusses the current status of the profession itself, debates and trends towards professionalisation and accreditation, and the manner in which designers and developers operate as a community of practice.

In Chapter III, *Min Liu, Coco Kishi* and *Suzanne Rhodes* suggest that universities increasingly expect faculty to integrate technology in their teaching in innovative ways. In this chapter, they describe the development process they have used in training and working with student developers and guiding faculty-student project development teams. They outline critical issues instructional designers face when working with faculty content experts, and provide suggestions for becoming effective designers and overcoming the challenges in this academic setting.

In Chapter IV, *Michael J. Keppell* suggests that instructional designers broker across communities and provide new possibilities for innovative practice in professional settings. By acting as brokers, instructional designers translate between different communities of practice similar to a language translator, and coordinate multi-disciplinary projects and collaborations that foster connections across and within communities of practice. The unique vantage point of being on the borderline between communities of practice allows new possibilities for innovative design and professional development. This chapter provides insights into the nature of instructional designers as brokers.

Section II: Cross-Cultural Context

Section II examines a number of cross-cultural contexts. The first two chapters in this section examine the way that unique contexts in China and Papua New Guinea influence instructional design. The third chapter examines cross-cultural communication across professional cultures or academic tribes.

In Chapter V, *Susan Crichton* suggests that designers working on international development projects require culturally sensitive ways to create resources and provide training for individuals who have different cultural backgrounds. The "western" assumptions of instructional design are not universal principles and may pose particular challenges as project participants work together to find solutions to teaching and learning problems. This chapter provides a number of insights about the field of instructional design within a Chinese context.

In Chapter VI, *Lalen Simeon, Gwyn Brickell* and *Brian Ferry* suggest that the increasing emphasis on the use of ICT for research and teaching can be threatening for lecturers in the academic community. They suggest that these fears can be eased if professional development is supportive and ongoing, and provided in flexible, appropriate and adaptable ways. This chapter focuses on the results of two case studies and describes the roles that the two instructional designers played in facilitating the professional development of lecturers that were constructing e-learning environments. This study developed a team collaboration model for planning and designing e-learning resources that will be piloted in tertiary institutions in Papua New Guinea.

In Chapter VII, *Cathy Gunn* and *Beth Cavallari* suggest that the work of instructional designers in the current higher educational context is part of a complex process that traverses a range of professional relationships and communities of practice. The requisite professional skills include the ability to operate and communicate effectively across these different professional cultures. The term "culture" is used in a novel way to reflect the "academic tribes" concept described in Becher and Trowler (1989), and to highlight the complexity of working relationships in teams that are often transitory. This chapter presents a model that situates the instructional designer's role within the process of educational design and development.

Section III: University-Wide Context

Section III examines a number of university-wide contexts. These five chapters examine educational design practice, social constructivist approaches to instructional design, online professional development, the fostering of educational technology champions and a learning designer community.

In Chapter VIII, *Chris Morgan, Jenny Bird* and *Meg O'Reilly* describe a case study that provides an overview of educational design practice in a relatively small regional Australian university. In its 15-year history at Southern Cross University, educational design practice has been significantly shaped by its context, and has evolved continuously to meet the changing needs of the University and its student profile. This case study charts educational design evolution over the 15 years, the impact of online learning upon roles and practice, the current institutional "footprint" of the educational designers, the convergence of roles with academic staff development, and its current research agendas.

In Chapter IX, *Jacqueliné McDonald* and *Terry Mayes* present a case study that reflects on the changing approach of an instructional designer at an Australian university. The designer moved from one-to-one interactions with subject matter experts in the design of traditional print-based distance learning courses, to adopting a pedagogical framework that guides the use of technology in hybrid course design. This encourages the subject matter experts to design their courses in a way that emphasises what Wenger (2005) has called the "horizontalisation" of learning. The study contrasts the traditional approach to design with a social constructivist framework.

In Chapter X, *Stephen Quinton* describes two strategies for delivering educational design expertise and online professional development via the Internet. The issues and difficulties pertaining to the design and application of online staff development are examined in terms of the factors and needs that were observed during the implementation phases. The professional development initiative focuses on staff development Web sites. These sites aim to inspire instructional design staff to understand the implicit teaching and learning goals used by lecturers, and to assist lecturing staff to increase their awareness of instructional design methodologies. This approach allows participants engaged in online developments to share a common pool of understanding and expertise.

In Chapter XI, *Samuel Ng Hong Kok, Tang Buay Choo* and *Myint Swe Khine* examine an initiative to create Educational Technology (ET) Champions and leaders within a higher education institution in Singapore. It examines how the concept of communities of practice was applied to an initiative for transforming teaching and learning through educational technology. Instructional designers coached ET Champions in the principles of creating learning objects. The ET Champions later returned to their respective colleges to work with other lecturers. ET Champions progressed through five stages, which included peripheral, legitimate, core, strategic and transformational membership. Each stage required support and guidance within the community.

In Chapter XII, *Sarah Lambert* and *Christine Brown* highlight the importance of developing and sustaining a knowledge base among designers to enable the collective sharing of strategies and tools for communication within project teams. This chapter identifies and discusses the need to capture collective wisdom of designers who work in close proximity within the same university. It examines a case study of a project that illustrates changes in the design context in relation to types of projects (CD-ROM, Web-based, learning management systems), and discusses these trends through the eyes of two designers. It also discusses the trend away from large stand-alone projects to networked learning objects. It examines these trends in relation to a number of strategies that support the learning design community and its work.

Section IV: Faculty and Departmental Context

Section IV examines a number of faculty and departmental contexts. These four chapters examine a discipline-specific instructional design unit, the introduction of e-learning to a group of language teacher-educators in a traditional Chinese context, the advantages and disadvantages of a team approach to instructional design and the need for effective communication in the management of a project.

In Chapter XIII, *Len Webster* and *Patricie Mertova* tell a story of a discipline-specific instructional design unit located in a Faculty of Law of a large university. This unit is engaged in the instructional design and development of a variety of units/subjects, courses and projects for undergraduate, postgraduate and professional practice programs, and also a Graduate Certificate in Law Teaching. Other activities in this specific community of practice include assisting staff with new approaches to their teaching, developing longer-term relationships with teaching staff and fostering reflective practice.

In Chapter XIV, *Pamela Pui Wan Leung* describes how she introduced e-learning to a group of language teacher-educators in a traditional Chinese context. This chapter reports the strategies adopted in a one-year teaching development project, responses of participants, typical instructional designs generated and the causes for innovation-decision. It argues that, even in a context with a strong transmission tradition, an ordinary academic staff member can still function as a change-agent by diffusing innovative teaching. By revealing the process and results of the attempt, the author hopes that practitioners in the same field can continue to explore feasible ways of stimulating active learning in both teachers and students.

In Chapter XV, *Sue Bennett* examines how instructional designers work together in teams to solve problems. It examines the advantages and disadvantages of a team approach to instructional design. This case explores how a team of instructional designers worked together to create "Exploring the Nardoo," a multi-award winning CD-ROM developed by the University of Wollongong's Educational Media Laboratory (emLab). The case describes key issues related to the design and development of the package from the perspective of a faculty-based multimedia unit, which was established with a strong emphasis on advancing research through innovations in design.

In Chapter XVI, *Elspeth McKay* and *Jennifer Martin* suggest that project management is a pivotal tool that underpins the successful design of information systems. The authors argue that the strength of the human-dimension of human-computer interaction (HCI) is often omitted by system designers. It discusses some of the issues that arise when dealing with a multi-disciplined project team. These include: dealing with a non-conventional learning context, the challenge of designing an appropriate learning design and instructional architecture.

Section V: School Context

Section V examines a number of school-based contexts. These three chapters examine the development of a physical and health educators' community of practice, an online classroom simulation for pre-service and in-service teachers, and the design and development of an e-learning management system in Hong Kong.

In Chapter XVII, *Lori Lockyer, John Patterson, Gregg Rowland* and *Doug Hearne* explore the perspectives of an instructional design team that designed and developed an online environment to facilitate the Australian physical and health educators' community of practice. The objective of the multidisciplinary design team was to determine the activities and supporting technologies that would help invigorate senior members, and to initiate novice members to this well-established community. The chapter describes the community and the particular challenges it faces; details the design, development and implementation processes for the online environment and activities; identifies the issues addressed during the design and implementation process; and analyses the experiences of the initial implementation.

In Chapter XVIII, *Brian Ferry* and *Lisa Kervin* report on the research associated with the development and implementation of prototype versions of an online classroom simulation.

It examines how the simulation assisted in the development of a community of practice among pre-service teachers. In addition, this chapter examines how a team of researchers, an instructional designer, programmers and graphic artists worked within a community of practice as the simulation software was created.

In Chapter XIX, *Kar-Tin Lee* reports on a case study that examines the process of implementing an e-learning management system (ELMS) for learning science in secondary schools in Hong Kong. It describes the challenges, issues and problems associated with creating science content and then integrating it with both a diagnostic and an open-content marking tool. To achieve its purpose, a team of instructional designers worked closely with content and technology experts to digitise science content for online delivery. It is argued that when teachers are actively involved in an implementation of a technology rich environment, they begin to see the benefits of teaching science differently. Given the opportunity to use the online system, students also tend to take more responsibility for their own learning.

Acknowledgments

I would like to thank my colleagues within my own community of practice who assisted me to complete this project by reviewing chapters and providing extensive feedback to improve the quality of each chapter. Within the academic community this is a priceless contribution. I wish to thank the following reviewers: Barney Dalgarno, Ross Dewstow, Robert Fitzgerald, Kathleen Gray, Gordon Joughin, John Hedberg, Dale Holt, Tony Herrington, Patrick Kunz, Gerry Lefoe, Lori Lockyer, Joe Luca, Catherine McLoughlin, Mark McMahon, Carmel McNaught, Koren Mitchell, Rob Phillips, Mary Rice and Patty Stevenson. In particular I wish to thank Patty Stevenson and Koren Mitchell for their significant editorial contribution to the book.

I would also like to thank the staff at IGI Global, and extend a special note of thanks to our development editor, Kristin Roth.

I would also like to thank the many people I have worked with on educational projects. Each project provided insight into the many nuances of instructional design and academic development in diverse communities of practice throughout the world.

Section I

Professional Practice

Chapter I

Instructional Designers' Perceptions of Their Agency: Tales of Change and Community

Richard A. Schwier, University of Saskatchewan, Canada

Katy Campbell, University of Alberta, Canada

Richard F. Kenny, Athabasca University, Canada

Abstract

Instructional designers provide more than service in the design and development of instruction; they also act as social change agents. This chapter draws on the stories of instructional designers to develop a model of change agency that includes interpersonal, professional, institutional and societal dimensions. The model provides guidance for the development of new skills in instructional design, for serious reflection by instructional designers about their own influence as agents, and for graduate programs in instructional design to address agency.

Introduction

In addition to the important role instructional designers play in the design and development of instructional products and programs, they also act in communities of practice as agents in changing the way traditional colleges and universities implement their missions. Designers work directly with faculty and clients to help them think more critically about the needs of all learners, issues of access, social and cultural implications of information technologies, alternative learning environments (e.g., workplace learning), and related policy development. As such, through reflexive practice, interpersonal agency and critical practice, they are important participants in shaping interpersonal, institutional and societal agendas for change.

This chapter will draw on the stories of instructional designers in higher education to highlight their interpretations of their own agency in each context. In essence, this chapter deviates from the understanding of a case study as occurring in a single setting in that it draws on the experiences of several instructional designers in several contexts. Rather, we accept Yin's (2003, p. 13) definition of case study as a research strategy; that is, as an empirical inquiry that "investigates a contemporary phenomenon within its real-life context," and view our study in this regard as a multiple-case design with the instructional designer as the unit of analysis. Taken as a group, these designers tell a strong story of struggle and agency in higher education contexts, and it is a story that portrays designers as active, moral, political and influential in activating change. So from their rich descriptions of practice, we attempt in this chapter to weave a composite case study of an instructional designer's experience that is true to the collective narrative of the designers we have interviewed. Any single person's story of agency is by necessity narrow and contextually bound, and these are both the greatest strengths and limitations of individual cases. We hope that by viewing the stories of instructional designers through the macro lens of narrative, we can better illustrate the scope of agency and community that instructional designers practice each day.

Background

Conventional literature in instructional design concentrates very intensively on process—how instructional design is carried out, what strategies and approaches work in various contexts, and how designers should systematically practice their craft (e.g., Dick Carey, & Carey, 2005; Morrison, Ross, & Kemp, 2004; Seels & Glasgow, 1998; Shambaugh & Magliaro, 2005; Smith & Ragan, 2005). Models no doubt serve a useful purpose, one part of which is to help ground our identities as practitioners. Bichelmeyer, Smith & Hessig (2004) asked ID practitioners what instructional design and technology meant to them, and while the most frequent response was that it was broad and diffuse, the second most frequent response was the ADDIE (analyze, design, develop, implement, evaluate) model or systematic design of instruction. This may signal the possibility of developmental levels—stages of development or growth in an individual's agency. It seems overall that younger or less experienced designers tend to talk about tasks and technologies rather than larger implications of their work (Schwier, 2004, October). But the actual use to which ADDIE and similar systematic models of instructional design are put, and the worth of such models, has been called into question many times and for several reasons over the years (Gordon & Zemke, 2000; Molenda, 2003; Rowland, 1992; Tripp & Bichelmeyer, 1990). Systematic models of ID have been accused of not reflecting actual practice, of being cumbersome, ineffective, inefficient and costly to implement. So, what is the value? Elizabeth Boling offered a fresh interpretation: "I was so puzzled when I started in this field—the ADDIE model is just exactly like every other generic description of the design process in every other field that ever was. To me, this discussion is a little bit off the mark—it's not about whether ADDIE stays or goes, but whether or not ADDIE may be viewed appropriately—we're trying to make it serve as a roadmap—you can't use it effectively as a literal road map for ID—we're looking for something that doesn't exist—it's a quality of designer" (Bichelmeyer, 2004, pp. 4-5).

Recent research examining the actual practice of instructional designers suggests that designers do refer to conventional processes in instructional design, but practice varies significantly according to context (Cox, 2003; Cox & Osguthorpe, 2003, May/June; Kenny, Zhang, Schwier, & Campbell, 2005; Rowland, 1992; Visscher-Voerman & Gustafson, 2004). Other critics argue that the field lacks focus (Bichelmeyer, Smith, & Hessig, 2004), and still others argue that key aspects of instructional design have been overlooked in conventional literature. For example, Gibbons (2003, September/October) argues that we need to re-examine the assumptions and foundations of instructional design and align it more closely to other design sciences such as architecture and engineering, while Schwier (2004, October) calls for instructional designers to consider the larger purpose or vision that guides their practice. Wilson (2005) and Parish (2004) further suggest that craft and aesthetic issues, while important, haven't been included in our training or incorporated meaningfully into our practice. And Bichelmeyer, Boling, and Gibbons (2006) argue forcefully that the continuing focus in our field on ADDIE as a "model" of instructional design has a detrimental impact on both what we research and what we teach, and that the goal of faculty should be to develop instructional designers rather than to teach design models. We are sympathetic with these arguments, and in this chapter we join their voices: in our interviews with instructional designers we have heard many stories of transformation and courage that transcend the technical and systematic boundaries of conventional ID, even when instructional designers aren't necessarily aware of this transcendence.

We suggest that clients working with instructional designers in development projects are actually engaging, as learners, in a process of professional and personal transformation that has the potential to transform the institution. Rogoff (1990) argues that participation in learning hinges on communication between people in a group, in terms of shared understanding or shared thinking. Glaser (1991), Tergan (1997), Ewing, Dowling, & Coutts, (1998), and others (cf., Jonassen, Dyer, Peters, & Robinson, 1997; Gunawardena, Carabajal, & Lowe, 2001; Thomas, 2002) believe that learning is most effective if it is embedded in social experience, and if it is situated in authentic problem-solving contexts entailing cognitive demands relevant for coping with real life situations, and occurs through social intercourse. The instructional design process, in which faculty, designers, and others develop new ideas and understandings through conversation, may be a form of cultural learning or collaborative learning.

In essence, we are arguing here that clients (e.g., faculty, in our research), while having high status in the institution, are actually novices in the teaching-learning community and are being invited to engage in legitimate peripheral participation in this arena. IDers may never achieve full participation in the university communities because they never learned their skills there as novices (Keppell, 2004). But the converse may be true as well; faculty participating in a *design* community of practice may not achieve full participation in the instructional design community of practice because they did not learn instructional design skills as novice academics. There seem to be multiple reciprocating or overlapping communities of practices in the process of instructional design—the community of designers, the community of the client's academic discipline, and the teaching-learning community within which projects are embedded. In this chapter we acknowledge that multiple communities of practice exist, but we concentrate on the ID community of practice and how it expresses change agency.

This chapter, and our entire program of research, is embedded in two theoretical constructs: instructional design as a social construct and critical pedagogy, in which designers act as agents of social change. A cultural shift has been occurring over the past decade in education—a shift towards environments and approaches based on the ideas of social constructivism. In this worldview, learning is situated in rich contexts, and knowledge is constructed in communities of practice through social interactions. Cobb (1996) argues that knowledge is not held objectively, but is unique, wholly subjective, and passed on by establishing common ground between the knower and the learner. This common ground must embrace interests and personal values, which requires a sharing at both the socio-cultural and the cognitive levels. (Ewing, Dowling, & Coutts, 1998, p. 10). Constructivists are interested in prior experience, but prior experience that is shared, through conversation, negotiation, and construction of new knowledge products. In other words, an individual's (designer's) practice, to which self-reflection is critical, will reflect his or her values and belief structures, understandings, prior experiences, and construction of new knowledge through social interaction and negotiation.

Our team of researchers conducted a three-year program of research to investigate the roles of instructional designers as agents of social change and transformation in higher education. Very little of the extensive work describing the development of theoretical models of instructional design (e.g., Reigeluth, 1983, 1999) has been drawn from the lived practice of the instructional designer and, consequently, instructional design theory is not grounded in practice. Institutions of higher education increasingly seek the expertise of instructional designers to facilitate the strategic development of technology-based instructional programs, and the professional development of involved faculty who themselves become critically reflective designers of learning. Therefore it becomes important to examine the theoretical and experiential backgrounds of these agents of instructional technology, their personal understanding of and values related to learning with technology, and the relation of these to their practice and continuing professional development in the higher education setting.

This program of research investigated the nature and relation of instructional design practice to cultural change within higher education institutions, and implications for socio-cultural change leading to agency in the global knowledge economy. More specifically, can instructional designers be viewed as agents of social change and transformation, promoting the cultural shift "required" of emerging learning systems? As part of this larger program of research, we argue that the practice of instructional design is collaborative, and the effective practice of instructional design requires that instructional designers draw on current and emerging knowledge and experience. In this chapter we address how instructional designers describe their roles as agents of social change and transformation.

Research Design

Two different approaches were used for gathering data. Initially, instructional designers in higher education institutions were interviewed using a semi-structured interview protocol, and participants were asked to discuss their backgrounds, identities, practices, communities and concerns. Participants were also encouraged to tell stories of their practice. Transcripts were sent to participants for correction, clarification, elaboration, and approval. Post hoc analysis of transcripts was done using Atlas.ti software, and data were analyzed to identify shared themes and understandings. Two researchers reviewed each transcript and negotiated the units of meaning that were extracted from the data.

For most interviews, we used narrative inquiry and the storying of experience because they are socially and contextually situated interpretive practices, starting from the personal as "personal knowledge has a practical function, not in a technical sense, or as an instrument for previously determined outcomes, but leading back to Aristotle, as a source for deliberation, intuitive decisions, daily action and moral wisdom" (Conle, 2000, p. 51). Narrative inquiry is transformative, because as we critically examine ways to understand our own practice, the practice itself is examined and understood. In this way, thinking about and telling stories of practice requires a critical, reflective engagement leading to changed or transformed practice. Thus the methodological approach for the study mirrors a social constructivist framework for instructional design practice, which is one of social interaction and construction of meaning through conversation and within a community of practice.

Findings

The data, and especially the stories told by instructional designers, suggested that instructional designers think deeply about their practice, and their professional and personal identities are intertwined in a zone of moral coherence, although they are sometimes required to practice outside that zone. The importance of values and how they informed the practice of instructional design emerged as a resonant theme that ran through stories that instructional designers told.

The Importance of Moral Coherence

Instructional design is more than a technical or systematic process; we contend that it is a moral practice that embodies the "relationship between self-concept and cultural norms, between what we value and what others value, between how we are told to act and how we feel about ourselves when we do or do not do act that way" (Anderson & Jack, 1991, p. 18). Agency refers to doing and implies power (Hartman, 1991). Designer agency is at its most powerful when it is acted out from a foundation of moral coherence, where the designer's values are aligned with the values of the clients and their institutions.

Can instructional design be practiced in a morally incoherent environment? Yes, and it often is; instructional designers with whom we spoke often felt at odds with the value systems of clients, their presumptions about learning, and even the motivations of the sponsoring organizations. Sometimes instructional designers must deliver products they don't believe in, and in some cases they work on projects that offend their own value systems or challenge their identities as moral actors. Moral incoherence causes dissonance for instructional designers, particularly when they feel powerless to challenge the source of the dissonance, and it sometimes leads instructional designers to question whether they can stay in the profession. On the other hand, a strong sense of moral coherence among designers, clients, organizations, and ultimately learners contributes to a feeling of purpose and meaning, and probably leads to a high degree of contentment and commitment. Where instructional designers share similar interpretations of moral coherence, this probably contributes to shared identity and a more coherent community of practice. Our own sense of it is that instructional designers sometimes operate within a zone of moral coherence and sometimes don't, but the more they find themselves in a morally coherent environment, the more satisfied they are with the work they do.

The Multivariate Nature of Agency

It became clear to us from the stories we heard from designers that what we initially thought of as change agency was actually multivariate. There were several different types of agency in play, and individuals expressed their agency in quite different ways. We categorized the expressed types of agency as personal, professional, institutional and societal as a convenient way to discriminate among the stories of agency we were hearing.

Interpersonal agency is characterized by the moral commitment made by instructional designers to the other people involved in projects and it is, at least, bi-directional and directed to clients and to learners who will eventually experience the product directly. Collegial advocacy is often directed to subject matter experts, but it may include other team members on projects, for example, among participants on a small scale, project-level community of practice or a larger "improving teaching and learning at the university" community of practice. The emphasis in this type of personal agency is on collegial engagement and advocacy, and our interviews suggest that instructional designers have a strong sense of responsibility to their clients; their desire to do a good job is felt deeply and personally. In addition, they see themselves in a professional development role, often helping clients to view teaching and learning in new, transformative ways.

And I think that that's really important and not only because faculty then begin...this cross-fertilization, if you will, and a deeper understanding of what the issues are in teaching and learning within a multitude of disciplines.

I think the effect of that might be that people who maybe have never thought about what their process is to teaching and learning, or how it might be thought or how it might be improved, made it more positive. ...But what are the values ... that work together and [clients] get exposed to—I think this has an opportunity for transformation.

But interpersonal advocacy is more than just collegial; it is also expressed as a responsibility felt to learners—those whose learning will be influenced by the success of the instructional design project. This level of advocacy is deeply held, morally entrenched, and profoundly reflects the personal values and philosophy of the designer. One designer described his role this way:

I need to be the learner before there is one. I design for people who don't usually have a voice in what happens to them in their educational lives, and I have to be their voice until they can speak for themselves.

And in some cases, the agency takes on the flavour of advocacy:

I am working on a Palliative Care project. There's meaning in this... . I don't think I would have stayed as long as I did ... If I couldn't find meaning in the project ... if I didn't find meaning in the people; if I didn't find meaning in supporting their success.

So, we argue that at the personal level agency is a moral relationship with others. Essentially, we extend Christians' (2000) observations about qualitative research, and believe that instructional design practice is not primarily a rational process, but rather an intimate social process in which caring values are contextualized in webs of relationships.

Professional agency is characterized by a feeling of responsibility to the profession and the ID community of practice to do instructional design well and to be acting in a professionally competent manner. In many cases, this is expressed as pride taken in doing a good job through the "war stories" shared among colleagues. It is clear to us that the instructional designers with whom we spoke took their positions very seriously, and even if they were not formally trained to be instructional designers, they saw themselves as part of a larger community of practice. It was even expressed as a concern about "doing instructional design the right way." There was some discomfort about whether the models of instructional design that designers learned about in their formal training actually described the processes they employed in their work-a-day lives. They puzzled over whether ADDIE and similar models of instructional design were relevant to their work, yet worried that they weren't performing their roles as designers well if they augmented or ignored particular parts of the conventional ID process. The fact that instructional design practice is such an ill-structured problem domain (Jonassen, 2004) filled with conceptual and practical ambiguity, is also a source of stress and doubt for designers.

I needed to synthesize a wide range of experiences and educational considerations in order to make decisions. I often felt the need to vet these decisions with experienced designers; however, I also needed to prove that I was capable of being a designer in my own right. Finding an appropriate balance was a challenge.

The whole nature of instructional design with its military origins, and the connotations that it has of putting people in straight jackets so they'll sit right, I think has turned a lot of people off.

Institutional agency includes responsibility felt by instructional designers to advance the agenda of the host institution. If universities, for example, are promoting a teacher-scholar model, then instructional designers may emphasize activities that tie the research programs of faculty to their teaching, or help them see ways to include the scholarship of teaching (Boyer, 1990) as part of their research programs. If the institution emphasizes a cost-recovery model, instructional designers may see themselves as leaders in developing learning environments that the organization can market to a wide audience. In any case, this type of agency considers the way that instructional designers align their work with institutional goals, or with institutional needs and wants, and it may be expressed in tension they feel between organizational needs and personal values. For example, if instructional designers feel a moral/ethical responsibility to provide the best possible learning experiences for students, and they feel that an institutional emphasis on cost recovery is in conflict with that goal, the instructional designer may feel in conflict with the organization, what we have elsewhere called a lack of moral coherence (Campbell, Schwier, & Kenny, 2005). The designer's effectiveness is also related to the broader university community of practice, and the instructional designer's status in the institution.

I think every institution has an embedded culture. That culture thrives on shared values and shared perspectives of the world. An open learning perspective of the world carries with it a different set of assumptions than a traditional university carries.

There are some really huge issues that are moving forward in distance education, especially technology-enhanced learning issues. If the institutions -the academies- do not look at these issues very seriously, very soon, they're going to find themselves in policy nether land, where nothing works.

Societal agency is characterized by a need to see beyond the confines of immediate work, and to know that the work of instructional design is contributing to a larger, more significant societal influence. In many organizations, instructional designers are considered "instructional support" instead of "instructional leaders" and this translates into an important disconnect between their perceived responsibility and their perceived authority to influence change on a meaningful scale.

I see ... the same parallel in working on a project in instructional design as doing development work in emerging countries ... this comes from my studies in global and human rights education and critical theory ... this has been fundamental in shaping my own philosophy of design and education. Any time (an OECD country) went in and said, 'This is the way we think you should develop ... This is the right way, this is our way ... there has been no success...Social change requires that people change how they are in the world—their thinking—their feelings—their actions—and this is extremely personal.

Dr. B. could have come out of that (project) hating technology ... but the major change he experienced ... wasn't really his attitude towards technology, but rather his view towards instructional design—it was like, 'Wow, instructional design is an area of expertise that is necessary and important!'

But if someone said that's what you're going to be doing for the next ten years. Look, I'll do it for a year because I think there's a lot to learn, but then I think I'll move on. Because I do need that. I don't know if it's a kind of megalomania driving it—I want to have an impact on a lot of people, but it has to be on a topic I want to be working with.

It's one of those things where you feel—you know—you make a difference. You know you have an impact at times, and sometimes you come away feeling really good about it. But rarely do I feel like it's a consistent difference. Rarely do I feel like it's a widespread margin of difference to my liking. So, I'm more frustrated than I am satisfied with the level of difference I make. I'm always looking to have impact on a large scale.

This may be especially true of ethical stances and higher values, and how holding to them can have profound effects. Perhaps humility about our influence is reasonable and sufficient, even admirable. Instructional design may not be so important on a grand scale, but the contributions made can have wide and profound influence in the long run. For example, if we insist on gender-neutral language, we may in the long run, contribute to a new understanding of equality.

Interactions Among Types of Agency

We suggest that the different types of agency necessarily interact. Interpersonal, professional, institutional and societal categories of agency are not mutually exclusive; in fact, we speculate that they seldom work in isolation. As areas of agency interact, we use three levels to describe the types of interactions that take place: micro-level, meso-level, and macro-level interactions, and these interactions can be based on coherent, incoherent or conflicting expressions of the types of agency.

We classify micro-level interactions as those that stay within the personal or professional contexts of instructional design performance. This agency is typically local, intimate and concrete and often tied to particular projects, although the level of influence is bounded only by the size of the communities within which the practice occurs. Examples of micro-level interactions include instances where interpersonal dimensions conjoin professional dimensions. For instance, if a client advocates an instructional methodology that can interfere with learning, the instructional designer might draw on persuasion based on the trust within their relationship (interpersonal), but might also draw on the experiences of other instructional designers and the literature to recommend alternative approaches (professional). As agencies interact, so do the communities of practice that bound each type of agency.

... as developers and designers, we then went back and said, 'Ok, how can these learners feel valued? What can they bring to the learning that they feel is of value and how as a designer do you build on that?

At the macro-level of interaction, we see the interplay of societal and institutional agency. Examples of macro-level interactions are characterized by instances where institutional needs and goals interact with societal influence. For instance, if an institutional goal is to increase access to courses and programs, the societal influence might be the intention to increase the literacy and productivity of the population, and through that, effectively contribute to a robust economy. But in most cases in our research, macro-level interactions revealed a recognition that institutional and societal issues interacted to allow the instructional designer to have a wider range of influence than other educational positions allowed.

I found it hugely satisfying that I could write materials that would affect more people than just my class. And I found it most annoying as a teacher that I could do a good job in my own class, and Joe Blow next door could do a really shocking job, and you know, we were having about the same kind of impact on about 30 people each. So I found that once I got into doing resources that I didn't want to go back to teaching.

And meso-level interactions occur when interpersonal or professional agency engages institutional or societal agency. For example, if institutional goals are in conflict with individual goals, the effectiveness of any agency may be threatened. Interpersonal agency, for instance, might be based on advocacy for equitable treatment of French and English students, but institutional agency might emphasize marketing to one group to increase the cost-benefit to the organization. Or an interpersonal level of agency can give rise to a concern for a much larger issue, one that has institutional or societal implications.

In one conversation, a participant told a story about a campaign to get the central computing support group on his campus to make some changes in WebCT and student lab support to shift the orientation of the support group from emphasizing technology/security/software to emphasizing the faculty and students who use WebCT. The instructional designer spoke about "using the professors' voices" to make these changes because they were politically aligned with the issue and in a stronger strategic position to influence change. The end goal was better learning support, and it was the instructional designer who was the catalyst for change at the intersection of personal and institutional levels of agency.

Another instructional designer spoke of paying attention to language in products, and how careful language can contribute in small ways to much larger societal concerns.

So I do think we can have an impact. And certainly, in terms of when I'm working on (it might be a minor thing), but I'm working on something and I think the writers have used a whole new stereotype. They've referred to this person who was really difficult, and said "of course he was the union rep." And just by saying that's not a reasonable thing to do and changing it, I think, "I was lucky to have spotted that. It's going to go out to thousands of people. It's just a minor thing, but I just think it's good for us to be informed and to be aware of those types of issues around stereotyping and to talk about goals and what we want education to be like. We may get frustrated with one little unit, but a lot of students are going to have to engage with that unit for a long time.

In cases where there is agreement among agencies concerning the values, ethical and functional dimensions of agency, we suggest that the overall agency is operating in a zone of moral coherence. Where the agencies are incoherent or in conflict, we argue that the overall effect of agency at every level is tempered, and potentially negated. And instructional designers often find themselves navigating levels of agency that are in competition with each other, and the resolution of these interactions, if recognized at all, requires personal and moral courage.

These interactions illustrate that a great deal of agency is tied to a strong sense of responsibility—to colleagues, students, the profession, institutions, and society. It is not surprising that instructional designers sometimes feel conflicted about what they do. But we are reminded in our research that instructional designers feel responsibility for more things than they have authority to influence, and that they regularly find themselves in positions that require them to act beyond their authority, or in a vacuum of authority. A dramatic example of this was illustrated by an instructional designer who was on the verge of leaving her position after a series of deep staffing cuts were made in the organization. She was the only remaining instructional designer in the organization, and yet her commitment to her clients and responsibility to the organization was firm.

I have about three weeks to wind down our unit and complete two contracts for external clients. As of July 1, it's just me in [this organizational unit] (the sole survivor), so if I don't do it, it won't get done. I've basically dropped everything else in order to complete those contracts before I quit.

There are also a few projects we were working on for the college that someone will have to accept responsibility for, or the work will have been for nothing. But I know what to do about those. I am burning the projects onto CDs and requesting the deans or department heads sign a deliverable acceptance form. A couple of departments don't have a dean (actually 3 were fired) so the president will have to sign off on them. He feels so bad about our unit right now I think he might actually do it. Then at least someone will be thinking about what to do with those courses, and hopefully they'll assign an instructor to them in the fall.

Intentional and Operational Dimensions of Agency

When we considered the types of agency and the interactions among the various types, it became apparent that instructional designers make decisions that emphasize intentional dimensions and operational dimensions of their work. By intentional, we refer to those dimensions of instructional design that are related to the intentions, principles or values associated with actions—deciding which things are important and those things we mean to do. In this sense, intentional dimensions include personal judgments about what is significant, preferential, moral or ethical. By contrast, operational dimensions include the practical implications or the expression of particular intentions, principles or values. In other words, intentional dimensions deal with what we feel we should do, whereas operational dimensions deal with concrete actions or outcomes.

These are significant dimensions because instructional designers often find themselves under pressure to emphasize the operational aspects of their work—the tangible decisions that are made in projects. Intentional dimensions are often assumed, but unless both the intentional and operational dimensions of agentic decisions are considered explicitly, the instructional designer runs the risk of making design decisions that are inconsistent with the underlying intentions of the work. For any single intentional dimension, there can be several operational expressions that are consistent with it. For example, an intention of efficiency can spawn a host of efficient practices depending on the context of the decision, such as choosing inexpensive media for production, building a boilerplate for a development team, or using outlines in lieu of text wherever possible.

We suggest that the greater the propinquity of intentional and operational dimensions of agency, the greater the possibility that decisions will be made within a zone of moral coherence. In Table 1, we provide simple examples of how intentional and operational dimensions might be manifested in various types of agency. These are simple examples and aren't meant to be epitomes of the categories, but we hope they illustrate the relationship between intentional and operational dimensions of agentic actions.

As an example of the use of intentional and operational dimensions of agency by designers, one participant related her experiences working with marginalized groups early in her career, over time reflecting on the interaction between that background and her value system. When working in a university with health professionals, her background influenced her to write case studies/narratives with a social justice bent, working with faculty to get them to think about this in the institutional context. She used design projects as an opportunity to challenge an ethnocentric understanding of access, actually writing about digital divide issues. All the while she problematized her role/identity/agency as a designer in higher education, but she found a way to advocate for social issues through her work and relationships at the intentional and operational levels:

So I don't know if I do that in a meaningful way. I think the chance to write about it in this book chapter is important to me just because I think digital divide issues, the fact here's a person who is developing a book on technological and information literacy and had a list of chapters, calling for proposals for these and nothing on digital divide, nothing on it. So just keeping that at the table ... A lot of people don't want to look at it though. ...I think a lot of professors think everybody's got a computer, everybody's got high speed, everybody ... I think the university would love to close the institutional labs but you really can't. And there's an argument for that. Let's face [it that] a lot of students are using those computers for chat and things like that. I can see the other side of that too. I guess we just live in an era where education continues to be under funded for what it's expected to do. So as a result ... it's easy not to look at let's say groups who don't fit into your top 5 percent... .

Table 1. Discrete examples of intentional and operational dimensions for interpersonal, professional institutional and societal types of agency

	Intentional	Operational
Interpersonal	The learner's experience is central to how instruction should be designed, and is more important than measured learning outcomes. Clients should be treated respectfully and instructional designers should protect the interests of participants in the process.	Lucid, fluid and frequent communication with end-users and clients. Create a climate of trust and mutual respect among members of the design team.
Professional	Complete projects on time, on budget and beyond expectations. Treat clients fairly and never participate in deceptive activities or designs. Above all, do no harm.	Prepare project time lines and project blueprints that communicate tasks, assignments and deadlines. Employ usability tests and universal design strategies.
Institutional	Subjects of usability testing should be treated ethically. Instruction should be cost-effective and should promote the idea that the institution is progressive, dynamic and professional.	Usability test protocols should be subjected to review and approval by a research ethics committee of the institution. Designs should be minimalist, particularly in their use of media that are expensive to produce. Professional visual designer should be employed in all projects.
Societal	Pay attention to equitable treatment of end-users. Be sensitive to unfair or stereotypical treatments. Seek out projects that can make a positive social contribution beyond the confines of the immediate instructional experience.	When using pseudonyms or characters in projects, deliberately employ people of different ethnicities, and challenge gender stereotypes that find their way into instructional designs. Communicate with the media; write feature articles for the print media or participate in interviews with electronic media. Use websites, blogs and podcasts to discuss the societal importance and implications of projects.

A Tentative Model and Advice to the Designer

The stories we are hearing from instructional designers are leading us toward a model of change agency, and we offer a tentative picture of what the model is beginning to look like. We do not want to suggest that this model is complete; it is emerging as our investigations continue to alter and elaborate our understanding. But we propose it as a departure point for discussion and as a method of organizing our preliminary conclusions, many of which have been discussed in this chapter.

Yet, many questions remain. Do different types of agency share variance? Can you have societal agency without interpersonal agency? Can either institutional or professional agency exist on its own? Does professional agency or some other type of agency have to be in place before the designer can work on another? Does a matured level of agency lead to leadership in the profession? If we are each fully integrated does that allow us to be scholars of, and leaders in, ID?

If instructional design is intimately bound up with moral agency, what are the implications for practice? The answer to this question is also still emerging and may well lead to recommendations for the development of communication and team-building skills, at the very least. Based on our work so far, we can certainly say that instructional designers should at the very least engage in some serious reflection about these aspects of their practice, Perhaps more importantly, scholars, teachers and coaches of instructional designers should examine their own embodied practices and begin to challenge our dearly-held beliefs about the shape and sequence of graduate programs and early enculturation into the field. Here are some tentative principles to consider:

1. Designers should be aware that instructional design is a social practice and that designing is not simply the rote application of instructional models, but to engage in the process of change. Designers, both individually and in conversation with their peers, should reflect on what types and levels of agency—interpersonal, professional, institutional or societal—they engage in.
2. Designers should also be aware that change agency necessarily involves a moral relationship with others and that their actions are not value neutral. Rather, one always acts purposefully on the basis of one's personal values. Designers should, at a minimum, reflect on their own perspectives on the teaching—learning process and what these mean for their interactions with others in their practice.
3. Designers should keep in mind that there are intentional, as well as operational, dimensions of their practice and consider ways in which these may conflict. In essence, designers should reflect on the how to move into the zone of moral coherence.
4. Graduate curricula might include opportunities to engage pre-service designers early in identity work through approaches such as autobiographical writing, providing more situated experiences that are then deconstructed in group conversations, working with cases based on ethical dilemmas, developing international links and project teams that challenge cultural assumptions about learning, and internship placements that either align with or challenge the designer's developmental stage, experience and beliefs.
5. Re-examine the focus in many programs and courses on the mastery of tools.
6. Centers or units of faculty development and support should work closely with faculty and designers to align values and goals, or at least to acknowledge when values and goals are in conflict.
7. Given the growing acceptance of instructional designers in higher education and increased mobility, designers could seriously consider matching their own expectations to institutional values, mission and goals.

Figure 1. Emerging model of change agency in instructional design

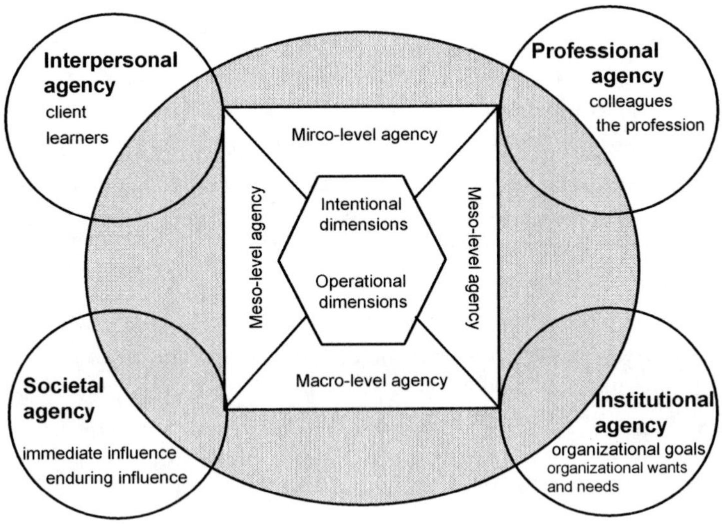

In our research, we have found that instructional designers recognize that they have a role to play in the sweeping changes currently underway in education, but less understanding of how to express that role forcefully and demonstrate leadership. We see that the agency focus of designers is interpersonal and institutional more than societal, but that they exhibit high standards of performance and care for the appropriate integration of technology into learning environments.

Designers know that they have a great deal to contribute, and that they make a significant difference in the quality of instruction they influence. But they work in a shadow profession, one that is not fully understood or appreciated by those in management. In order to be effective in promoting social change, instructional design needs to clarify the kinds of contributions it can make, and make other educators aware of those contributions. It isn't sufficient to work quietly and effectively in the shadows, and hope that the profession is understood and appreciated. The discussion of agency provides language for discussing the roles played by instructional design in the larger context of education and society.

Acknowledgments

This research is supported by a grant from the Social Sciences and Humanities Research Council of Canada.

References

Anderson, K., & Jack, D.C. (1991). Learning to listen: Interview techniques and analyses. In S.B. Gluck & D. Patai (Eds.), *Women's words: The feminist practice of oral history* (pp. 11-26). NY: Routledge.

Bichelmeyer, B. (2004). *The ADDIE model: A metaphor for the lack of clarity in the field of IDT*. Paper presented at the annual conference of the Association for Educational Communications and Technology, Chicago. Retrieved June 11, 2005, from http://www.indiana.edu/~idt/shortpapers/documents/IDTf_Bic.pdf

Bichelmeyer, B., Boling, E., & Gibbons, A. (2005). Instructional design and technology models: Their impact on research and teaching in IDT. In, M. Orey, J. McLendon, & R. Branch (Eds). *Educational media and technology yearbook 2006* (pp. 33-50). Westport, CT: Libraries Unilimited.

Bichelmeyer, B., Smith, K., & Hessig, J. (2004). *Graduate students' perceptions of the field of IDT.* Paper presented at the annual conference of the Association for Educational Communications and Technology, Chicago.

Boyer, E. (1990). *Scholarship reconsidered: Priorities of the professoriate.* The Carnegie Foundation for the Advancement of Teaching: Princeton University Press.

Campbell, K., Schwier, R.A., & Kenny, R. (2005). Agency of the instructional designer: Moral coherence and transformative social practice. *Australasian Journal of Educational Technology*, *21*(2), 242-262.

Christians, C.G. (2000). Ethics and politics in qualitative research. In N.K. Denzin & Y.S. Lincoln (Eds.), *Handbook of qualitative research* (2nd ed.) (pp. 133-155). London: Sage Publications.

Cobb, P. (1996). Where is the mind? A coordination of sociocultural and cognitive constructivist perspectives. In C.W. Fosnot (Ed.), *Constructivism: Theory, perspectives and practice*. New York: Teachers College Press.

Conle, C. (2000). Narrative inquiry: Research tool and medium for professional development. *European Journal of Teacher Education, 23*(1), 49-63.

Cox, S., & Osguthorpe, R.T. (2003, May/June). How do instructional design professionals spend their time? *TechTrends*, *47*(3), 45-47.

Cox, S. (2003). *Practices and academic preparation of instructional designers.* Unpublished master's thesis, Brigham Young University, Provo, UT.

Dick, W., Carey, L., & Carey, J.O. (2005). *The systematic design of instruction* (6th ed.). New York: Allyn & Bacon.

Ewing, J.M., Dowling, J.D., & Coutts, N. (1998). Learning using the World Wide Web: A collaborative learning event. *Journal of Educational Multimedia and Hypermedia*, *8*(1), 3-22.

Gibbons, A.S. (2003, September/October). What and how do designers design: A theory of design structure. *TechTrends*, *47*(5), 22-27.

Glaser, R. (1991). The maturing of the relationship between the science of learning and cognition and educational practice. *Learning and Instruction*, *1*(2), 129-144.

Gordon, J., & Zemke, R. (2000). The attack on ISD. *Training, 37*(4), 42-54.

Gunawardena, C., Carabajal, K., & Lowe, C. (April, 2001). *Critical analysis of models and methods used to evaluate online learning networks*. Paper presented at the annual conference of the American Educational Research Association, Seattle.

Hartman, J.E. (1991). Telling stories: The construction of women's agency. In J. Hartman & E. Messer-Davidow (Eds.), *(En)gendering knowledge: Feminists in academe* (pp. 11-31). Knoxville: University of Tennessee Press.

Jonassen, D.H. (2004). *Learning to solve problems: An instructional design guide*. San Francisco: Jossey-Bass.

Jonassen, D., Dyer, D., Peters, K., Robinson, T., Harvey, D., King, M., & Loughner, P. (1997). Cognitive flexibility hypertexts on the Web: Engaging learners in making meaning. In B.H. Khan (Ed.), *Web-based instruction* (pp. 119-133). Englewood Cliffs, NJ: Educational Technology Publications.

Kenny, R.F., Zhang, Z., Schwier, R.A., & Campbell, K. (2005). A review of what instructional designers do: Questions answered and questions not asked. *Canadian Journal of Learning and Technology, 31*(1), 9-16.

Keppell, M. (2004). Legitimate participation? *Instructional designer-subject matter expert interactions in communities of practice. World Conference on Educational Multimedia, Hypermedia and Telecommunications, 2004*(1), 3611-3618.

Molenda, M. (2003). In search of the elusive ADDIE model. *Performance Improvement, 42*(5), 34-36.

Morrison, G.R., Ross, S.M., & Kemp, J.E. (2004). *Designing effective instruction*. Hoboken, NJ: John Wiley & Sons.

Parish, P. (2004). Embracing the aesthetics of instructional design. *Educational Technology, 45*(2), 16-24.

Reigeluth, C.M. (1983). *Instructional design theories and models* (Vol. I). Mahwah, NJ: Lawrence Erlbaum.

Reigeluth, C.M. (1999). *Instructional design theories and models* (Vol. II). Mahwah, NJ: Lawrence Erlbaum.

Rogoff, B. (1990). *Apprenticeship in thinking*. New York: Oxford University Press.

Rowland, G. (1992). What do instructional designers actually do? An initial investigation of expert practice. *Performance Improvement Quarterly, 5*(2), 65-86.

Schwier, R. (2004, October). *A grand purpose for instructional design*. Paper presented at the annual conference of the Association for Educational Communications and Technology, Chicago. Retrieved June 11, 2005, from http://www.indiana.edu/~idt/shortpapers/documents/IDTf_Schwier.pdf

Seels, B., & Glasgow, Z. (1998). *Making instructional design decisions* (2nd ed.). Upper Saddle River, NJ: Merrill Prentice Hall.

Shambaugh, N., & Magliaro, S.G. (2005). *Instructional design: A systematic approach for reflective practice*. Boston: Allyn & Bacon.

Smith, P.L., & Ragan, T.J. (2005). *Instructional design* (3rd ed.). Hoboken, NJ: John Wiley

& Sons.

Tergan, S.O. (1997). Misleading theoretical assumptions in hypertext/hypermedia research. *Journal of Educational Multimedia and Hypermedia*, *6*(3/4), 257-283.

Thomas, M. (2002). Learning within incoherent structures: The space of online discussion forums. *Journal of Computer Assisted Learning*, *18*, 351-366.

Tripp, S., & Bichelmeyer, B. (1990). Rapid prototyping: An alternative instructional design strategy. *Educational Technology Research & Development*, *38*(1), 31-44.

Visscher-Voerman, I., & Gustafson, K.L. (2004). Paradigms in the theory and practice of education and training design. *Educational Technology Research and Development*, *52*(2), 69-89.

Wilson, B. (2005). Broadening our foundation for instructional design: Four pillars of practice. *Educational Technology*, *45*(2), 10-15.

Yin, R.K. (2003). *Case study research: Design and methods* (3rd ed.). Thousand Oaks, CA: Sage Publications.

Chapter II

Exploring the Tensions in Educational and Instructional Design in Australian Universities

Jenny Bird, Southern Cross University, Australia

Chris Morgan, Southern Cross University, Australia

Meg O'Reilly, Southern Cross University, Australia

Abstract

Recent trends in higher education have led to notable impacts upon the profession of educational or instructional design. This chapter presents some of the major challenges faced by the profession and explores the tensions arising when current practices are pushed by the momentum of a quality assurance agenda, technology and flexible learning imperatives, an increasing diversity within our student demographics and the emerging models of educational design practice across national contexts. The chapter also discusses the current status of the profession itself, debates and trends towards professionalisation and accreditation, and the manner in which designers and developers operate as a community of practice.

Introduction

The changing practices of educational designers in higher education have evolved in response to continuing changes in the broad contexts within which they find themselves. However, these changes to the profession have not occurred without tension.

The list of pressures which have had an enormous impact on higher education in the UK, Australia and New Zealand since the 1980s is now familiar: massification, globalisation, technology, economic rationalism, transdisciplinarity and new forms of knowledge. To varying degrees, some or all of these pressures are evident in higher education sectors in the U.S., Europe, Asia, India and Africa. Responses to these pressures vary enormously from country to country, influenced by government policy, funding, GNP, national technology infrastructures, geography, culture, and political and economic alliances between developed and developing countries' education sectors. For individual higher education institutions, responses will depend on a number of factors: the size of the institution, its location (metropolitan or regional), its history and age, the nature and extent of its research quantum, its delivery culture (traditional face-to-face, distance education, dual mode, online), its student population (school leavers, mature-aged, international, offshore), its wealth, and its strategic priorities.

Designers have responded to these pressures by adapting their role, learning new skills, and embracing technology. However, new pressures, not yet fully articulated or debated, are bearing in on the profession. What, for example, is the impact upon designers of the recent trend in the UK, Australia and New Zealand towards institutional performance-based funding, based on identified performance indicators for teaching and learning; and standards frameworks for academic teachers. This broad policy and funding framework, driven by quality assurance and accountability imperatives places the "institutional spotlight" squarely on both meeting and proving certain measurable standards for teaching and learning. Just where designers sit in this picture, both from their own professional perspective and from the perspectives of their institutions, remains to be seen.

For educational designers, questions of how we engage with standards of practice for teaching and learning, and how we find them explicated within our own institutions, are key. Our capacity to reconcile the institutional requirements for both quality enhancement and quality assurance affects our day-to-day focus as well as our professional identity. Do we invest our effort at the macro level of curriculum development and ensure that questions of design are informed at the program level or do we find ourselves concerned with the entire process of learning materials development and multiple modes of delivery?

In this current climate of the "government's managerialist agenda" (Parry & Debowski, 2004, p. 13) in which we see explicit concern with quality, accountability and their associated rewards, how do educational design theories inform current practices? Where data on student satisfaction with teaching, learning and the curriculum is a criterion for government funding, how do the changing profiles of university learners and their increasingly diverse backgrounds impact upon the decisions negotiated with the subject matter expert through the educational design process?

As the sector examines how to create efficiencies and measure and reward improvements in teaching and learning, the approaches to educational design can also be reconsidered. What are the implications of a move away from a systems model of design to a staff development model? With the increase in staff development commonly evident in the role played by educational designers, can educational design professionals leverage further by bringing academic staff together for effective cross-fertilisation of ideas from outside traditional disciplinary boundaries?

This chapter will focus the spotlight on a few of these key concerns. While its focus sits primarily within the Australian higher education sector, links are made to the literature from other countries.

Background to Educational Design in Australia

Educational design, or instructional design, as it was more commonly referred to, began life in Australia mostly in regional universities during the 1980s, as distance education underwent a rapid expansion. No doubt there were earlier manifestations, but the profession gained its first significant foothold in universities due to the complex challenges of designing, writing, producing and supporting the delivery of large quantities of print-based teaching and learning materials. Instructional designers came from a variety of professional backgrounds: some were media professionals, some teachers, others writers, editors and print production specialists.

As distance education continued to flourish in the 1990s and moved into the mainstream of higher education, so too did the instructional designer. However, the profession's most significant boost was the advent and rapid uptake of online learning and delivery in the late 1990s. Suddenly, distance teaching and dual mode universities were seeking instructional design expertise, as well as the large on-campus teaching universities around Australia who were keen to explore this new medium. Within the broad framework of flexible learning, which took purchase in the Australian higher education sector during the 1990s, all but a few universities employed designers to assist academic staff to rethink their teaching and their learning materials for flexible learning.

Today instructional and educational designers belong to a larger group of professional staff employed in Australian universities who are engaged in various ways in the design, development and production of educational programs and materials across a range of media. They work within professional and institutional contexts that are highly varied. It is difficult to estimate the number of people working in this field in higher education institutions in Australia, but the figure is in the vicinity of 200-250 (Bird, 2004).

Bird (2004), in a national survey of "flexible learning professionals" conducted in 2002 across 35 Australian universities found that this group of staff are employed under a wide range of titles including instructional designer, educational designer, educational developer, multimedia/online/e-learning designers/developers and lecturers with additional specialist descriptors (e.g., lecturer: educational designer). The most common job title is educational designer. Comparing these findings with those of Allen (1996) it is clear that the title instructional designer has lost currency in the Australian higher education sector over the last 10 years. The majority of designers work in central units within their organizations. The units have a variety of names reflecting the particular institution's strategic and organisational priorities, for example, flexible learning centres and teaching and learning units.

Designers are employed under both academic and administrative awards. With the exception of Web/online/multimedia designers who were all employed under administrative awards, all other titles were represented under both. They do not share a common qualification nor a common professional development pathway. This finding is consistent with both previous Australian research (see Allen, 1996; Fraser, 2003) and recent Canadian research (see Schwier, Campbell, & Kenny, 2004). This bifurcation between academic and administrative staff may create difficulties for the professionalisation movement, and potential tensions within the profession itself. Whilst staff in both groups may engage in similar duties, institutional expectations, status in the academic community and promotion processes can all differ markedly.

The four most frequent activities in which flexible learning designers/developers engaged were: designing teaching and learning activities; staff development in online teaching and learning; designing for online; and staff development in the development of flexible learning materials. Clearly evident here is a shift away from print-based editing and layout (Allen, 1996) to online design and development and staff development.

Clearly the identity and practices of designers working in Australian universities is dynamic and highly contextual. The diversity of title, award, qualifications and roles and responsibilities of this group of staff is closely linked to the manner in which individual institutions respond to the pressures common in higher education in Australia, New Zealand, the UK, the U.S. and Canada today.

Given the increasing level of investment in design by universities over the past five years in Australian higher education, it is interesting to speculate on the perceptions of employers. What is it, in the eyes of university management, which the designer will be able to deliver to the institution? Is it simply about assuring quality, or hosting the introduction of new teaching technologies? Or is it, as Campbell, Schwier, and Kenny (2005) suggest, a more complex change agency role? The "grand narratives" of instructional design, they suggest, which involve the systematic and rational, have collapsed in favour of a new, more fluid role in which we inspire, through conversation, new understandings at individual and institutional levels about teaching, learning and the curriculum. There is no doubt that perceptions of employers, and the way they seek to host and provide legitimacy for the role, will be critical to the evolution of educational design and its ability to effect meaningful change.

Tensions Relating to Professional Identity

A vein of debate about professionalisation and professional identity (see Parer, 1989, 1993; Andresen, 1991; Murphy, 1994) in the educational designer literature of the last 25 years demonstrates a consistent, yet unresolved desire to define and describe what it is that constitutes the body of knowledge and the body of professional practices of designers/developers. Researchers in this field share common difficulties in establishing the boundaries of this professional group (see for example, Inglis, 1996; Allen, 1996). Similar difficulties are reported by Canadian researchers Schwier, Campbell, and Kenny (2004). Parer's (1989) edited collection of contributions from instructional designers contains an entire section exploring the identity crisis of the role, with a series of self-portraits of idiosyncratic and highly contextual manifestations of the designers' role. At that time it was evident that the designer's role resided largely in the margins of higher education, with difficulties experienced in explaining itself beyond broad descriptors such as "distance education specialist."

Despite the apparent entry of design into the mainstream of most universities in Australia, largely through the advent of online learning, and also the quality assurance agenda, more recent empirical studies (Inglis, 1996; Allen, 1996; Bird, 2004) have confirmed a continuing absence of a shared role, professional identity, professional career path, or theoretical underpinnings. Designers' identities are continuing to be defined and shaped by individual institutional contexts and needs, and are still plagued by difficulties of explanation. Perceptions of educational designers abound that their role is misunderstood and the scope and complexity of the role overlooked by academic staff (Inglis, 1992; Roberts, Jackson, Osborne, & Somers Vine, 1994; Allen, 1996).

Issues about roles are but one of the issues facing current moves to professionalise educational designers. The "professionalisation push" must be viewed within the broader context of debate and pressure from higher education funding bodies to professionalise university teachers; in particular to formalise university teaching qualifications and accreditation procedures, which will develop agreed upon capabilities and standards. Whilst the movement towards establishing minimum standards of practice and formalising accreditation of academic teachers is inevitably difficult and contentious, academic teachers, in contrast to designers, enjoy the advantage of being easily identified as a group, with consistent job titles and clear boundaries. They are employed under defined awards with broadly similar duty statements, remuneration and promotion criteria across the sector.

By comparison, the professionalisation of designers in higher education poses much greater challenges. The traditional markers of a profession (see for example, Locke, 2001) are difficult to apply to designers for the following reasons:

> *Depending on the structure, size, history, culture, aims and goals of each university these people are variously employed as instructional or educational designers, educational developers, e-learning or online developers /designers and lecturers with associated specialist titles. The range of titles itself reflects a variety of orientations, approaches and theoretical frameworks. Some of these groups are employed as academics, others as administrative staff. Some of them work within schools or faculties; others work in central facilities like Teaching and Learning Centres or Flexible Learning Centres. Differences between the roles and responsibilities of each group are ambiguous, unstable, contextual and subsequently difficult to map. These groups are not represented by any one professional body or association, share neither a common statement of duties nor a code of practice, have no accreditation or registration requirements, come from diverse professional, theoretical and educational backgrounds and have no obvious career path.* (Bird, 2004, p. 123)

More recently Wenger's idea of "communities of practice" has been applied to the higher education sector, offering "an alternative analytical framework to the somewhat older and much used notions of career, culture, discipline and profession" (Tight, 2004). Wenger (2000) identifies three elements which, when combined, define the competence of members of a community of practice:

> *First, members are bound together by their collectively developed understanding of what their community is about and they hold each other accountable to this sense of joint enterprise. To be competent is to understand the enterprise well enough to contribute to it. Second, members build their community through mutual engagement. They interact with one another, establishing norms and relationships of mutuality that reflect these interactions. To be competent is to be able to engage with the community and be trusted as a partner in these interactions. Third, communities of practice have produced a shared repertoire of communal resources—language, routines, sensibilities, artefacts, tools, stories, styles, etc. To be competent is to have access to this repertoire and be able to use it appropriately.* (Wenger, 2000, p. 229)

Campbell, Schwier, and Kenny (2004) have applied Wenger's notion of "community of practice" in their research with Canadian instructional designers. They conclude that:

> *We see a profession that knows itself, but is struggling for identity and acceptance in the larger educational community. We find that instructional designers invent and participate in communities of practice in ways that challenge our understanding of models of communities. We learned that there isn't a single or global community of ID practice, but rather, hundreds of small, local, effervescent and convenient communities of practice. We see instructional designers struggling to identify their own tacit knowledge, and without systematic avenues for sharing their tacit knowledge with other designers... We see that the focus of designers is institutional more than societal, but that they exhibit high standards of performance and care for the appropriate integration of technology into learning environments.* (Campbell, Schwier, & Kenny, 2005, pp. 96-97)

These findings from Canada resonate with the professional status of designers in Australia [see for example, Bird's (2004) research findings]. The professional development needs of Australian designers are met by a variety of professional organizations, national and regional networks, and formal and informal professional relationships. Historically designers working in print-based distance education were represented by ODLAA (the Open and Distance Learning Association of Australia). However more recent affiliations with ASCILITE (the Australasian Society for Computers in Learning in Tertiary Education) and HERDSA (the Higher Education Research and Development Society of Australia), along with ODLAA's recent focus on ICT, reflect the twin impacts of technology and staff development on the professional development needs of designers. Regional forums are also scattered across the country: for example, the new "Learning Designers Association" (previously known as the "Instructional Design Forum"), which serves designers in southeast Queensland and northern NSW.

Despite these challenges, efforts are being made towards professionalisation in some domains of professional activity within the more broad community of practice described here. In the

UK, the Association for Learning Technology launched its Certified Membership Scheme in 2005, having gained support from its members for "a simple, economical, voluntary, peer-based structure to accredit individual members as learning technologists, in collaboration with HE [Higher Education], FE [Further Education], and Industry Bodies." The seeds of similar developments are currently being sown in Australia and New Zealand. For example, in Australia there is now a national database of designers working in higher education, a Learning Designers Association, and regional networks and forums have become more formalised. National representative bodies such as ACODE (the Australasian Council for Distance and E-Learning) are funding research into professionalisation issues. It is anticipated that these developments will continue, contributing to the overall jigsaw of a community of practice with stronger professional links than in the past, a more clear description of their professional practice, and perhaps the articulation of professional standards and values.

Tensions Relating to Quality Assurance

Traditionally many designers in Australia have worked within a quality enhancement model, that is, working developmentally with academic staff to enhance the quality of distance and open learning materials and the experience of distance learners. Commonly, this has taken the form of a "partnership" or "team approach," where the designer has collaborated with academic and other technical and production staff to bring about the best possible result in terms of quality (for example, Jackling, 1989; Meacham, 1989). The academic staff member, who is usually also the person who delivers, assesses and evaluates the course, has been ultimately responsible for its quality, while the designer offers suggestions and support where appropriate, and develops an ongoing rapport and relationship of trust with the staff member. Although this model has enhanced the quality of materials and distance learning experiences over time, it provides no guarantee to the university that a minimum standard has been met at any one time.

By contrast, other designers have operated more as project managers overseeing a prescribed process of development of learning materials. In some instances the designer imposes a pre-ordained pedagogical model as the blueprint for development, and oversees the development from its inception to a quality-controlled end product. While criticised in Australia over the past twenty years (Nunan, 1983; Meacham, 1989; Evans & Nation, 1989, 1993) the project manager role of instructional design has fulfilled the institutional need that a "product" meeting minimum standards is produced and delivered on time to students.

With the advent of the Australian Universities Quality Agency, and the subsequent quality audits occurring over the past three years, universities have been under increasing pressure to provide evidence that quality standards are being achieved, rather than just being sought. In addition, the newly established Federal Learning and Teaching Performance Fund and the Carrick Institute for Learning and Teaching in Higher Education are, in differing ways, addressing the issue of quality and standards in Australian higher education, in moves that mirror the quality assurance agenda over the past decade in the UK and U.S.

The designer, familiar with a formative role, is under increasing pressure to be the summative judge of whether nominated standards for teaching and learning have been achieved.

This may take the form of reporting mechanisms that require the designer to be "whistle-blower" if developments are not, in their view, shaping up to required standards. While it is not unreasonable that educational managers should require accountability in relation to the quality of practices in their domain, it does pose particular problems for the designer in terms of allegiances and relationships. When operating in a formative role, the tendency for the designer is to adopt a longitudinal view about the achievement of standards, and the kind of encouragement and practical support required in these circumstances is easily eroded by systems of quality assurance and the ambiguity associated with the designer simultaneously adopting both formative and summative roles.

A concurrent pressure is felt, in the currently constrained funding climate, for designers to provide evidence of their value. What can the university reasonably expect for its investment? Moreover, how can designers actually demonstrate their worth? Traditionally, we have been able to point to the number of resources developed, combined with satisfaction surveys of academic staff with whom we have collaborated. Yet in the corporatised enterprise university, these kinds of indicators may not be sufficiently direct or tailored to university mission statements, or to the requirements of external funding sources such as the Learning and Teaching Performance Fund. Can designers show that they are contributing to student satisfaction or the retention rates of the university? How do we contribute to the efficacy of student learning? Although these are difficult links to make in any circumstances, they are particularly so for those designers whose role is focussed on quality enhancement rather than quality assurance.

Tensions Relating to Theory and Practice

A further tension relates to the question of which theory base informs designers' work with academics, and how do they articulate it and apply it? Attempts to map this complex field are problematic, and tend to result in long lists of groupings of theories, models, authors and processes under idiosyncratic and debatable headings. Models build on multiple theories, authors move between theories and models, and processes are not differentiated from theories. Ryder (2006) for example lists forty "instructional design models" and sixteen broad "theoretical sources" on his Web site at the University of Colorado, while Kearsley (1994-2001) lists 52 "theories" on his Web site. Joughin and Johnston (1994) suggest that: "The instructional design and course development processes can potentially draw on an almost unlimited source of educational theory" (p. 8).

Academic teachers are faced with a similar, and overlapping, array of theory from which to inform and describe their teaching practice. Meacham (1989) refers to models of teaching as "a morass of unsubstantiated theory and ideology, with little empirical evidence of effectiveness, particularly in relation to distance education" (p. 68).

In broad terms, academic teaching and instructional/educational design is informed by learning theory, a field of study within the discipline of psychology. Gros, Elen, Kerres, van Merriënboer, and Spector (1997) suggest that instructional design models aim to provide a link between learning theories and instructional systems; that in fact they inhabit the space between theory and practice. Histories of instructional design (see, for example, Leigh, 2006) are often framed as a chronological development, linked closely to developments in learning theory, from early behaviourist approaches, to cognitivist approaches, to constructivist approaches.

In 1997 an entire issue of the journal *Educational Technology* was dedicated to theory in instructional design, with many authors calling for new models based on constructivist approaches to learning. Traditional positivist approaches were criticised on a number of grounds. Gros, Elen, Kerres, van Merriënboer, and Spector (1997) summarised the major criticisms of a number of authors, and argued that traditional models have been linear and inflexible, and need to become iterative. They pointed to the argument put forward by Reigeluth [1996, in Gros, Elen, Kerres, van Merriënboer, & Spector (1997)] that as society has moved from Industrial to Information Age thinking, instructional design must move from standardised teacher centred models to customised learner centred models. Winn [1997, in Gros, Elen, Kerres, van Merriënboer, & Spector (1997)] argued that traditional models incorrectly assume that human behaviour is predictable, and argued that instructional design decisions should be made "on the fly." Jonassen et al. [1997, in Gros, Elen, Kerres, van Merriënboer, & Spector (1997)] offered an alternative approach to design based on Hermeneutics, Fuzzy Logic and Chaos Theory.

Willis (1995) suggested a new model of instructional design based on constructivist learning theory that challenged the "old" behaviourist models, and in doing so, offered an alternative to the systems-based models so prevalent in the U.S. and in Australia up to the 1980s. Willis's model was characterised by the following (Willis, 1995, p. 12):

1. The instructional design process is recursive, non-linear and sometimes chaotic;
2. Planning is organic, developmental, reflective and collaborative;
3. Objectives emerge from design and development work;
4. General instructional design experts don't exist;
5. Instruction emphasises learning in meaningful contexts;
6. Formative evaluation is critical; and
7. Subjective data may be the most valuable.

How important is it then for designers/developers to articulate their particular theoretical framework(s)? Candy (1993) states that, "the process of adopting, adjusting or developing a theoretical perspective is a vital one. It can be implicit or explicit; it can be homespun or informed by research; it can be eclectic or pure; but some view about learning is essential" (p. 105). Boud (1993) suggests:

Each one of us has our own theories and conceptual frameworks which influence and inform what we do and how we do it; these apply as much to teaching and learning as to other aspects of our lives. However, these theories are usually unarticulated, quite private and perhaps difficult to explain or to justify. They seldom take the abstract form that we expect of formal theories. (p. 33)

How then do designers/developers best apply their theoretical knowledge, however well articulated, in their work with academic staff? To what degree should designers/developers bring their own theoretical perspectives to bear on their work with academic staff? Is the task, as Parer (1989) states: *"to change their [academics'] perspective to teaching and learning and so help them to think differently about student learning and become critical of their own teaching?"* (p. 11). Or is it the case, as Meacham (1989) argues, that the relationship between designers and academics will be least successful if designers *"attempt to legitimise their control of the situation by an appeal to theory divorced from practice?"* (pp. 62-63).

In their study of 10 academics "going online," Torrisi-Steele and Davis (2000) characterise the relationship between the academics and the educational designers as taking place *"in a context characterised by interplay among traditional academic teaching culture, personal philosophies of teaching and learning, and principles of teaching and learning which underpin student centred approaches to online learning"* (p. 290).

In this way academics and designers can engage in rich and fruitful conversation about their respective philosophies and practices of teaching and learning. Their continuing reflections on practice result not only in being able to evolve theory from practice but furthermore fit very well with the thrust of the Learning and Teaching Performance Fund which has espoused a scholarship of teaching and learning as one of the models for enhancing quality in the sector.

Tensions Relating to the Changing Identities of Learners

The number of students participating in the higher education sector in the UK and Australia since the 1980s has grown exponentially. Government funding has not supported this growth in either country, with students now responsible for major costs of their own higher education. Academic teachers face the dual challenge of offering their courses not only to more students, but also to students with more diverse learning needs, and with different expectations about what a university education will offer them. While academic teachers scramble to adjust their curricula, their teaching styles, their learning materials, their delivery methods and their expectations to best meet the needs of their students, designers face similar challenges. How exactly does one assist an academic to design a program of study for a student cohort who might display some or all of the following diverse characteristics: school leavers, mature-aged, full-time, part-time, working, partnered, with children, located on and off campus, possibly in another country, with English as a second language, international studying abroad, with individual learning styles, with highly varying degrees of technological capabilities, educational backgrounds, literacy, and numeracy? While the design and teaching and learning literature is rich in case studies showcasing individual efforts to meet the diversity challenge, most focus on one or two of the variables described above (for example focussing on school leavers versus mature-aged, focusing on cultural diversity, on technology needs, on learning styles and so on), leaving designers and academic staff with the task of fitting together various best practices to meet their own complex needs.

Students have become discriminating consumers of higher education. Universities have been driven by government policy and funding to shape and deliver their curricula to suit market demand. As students pay more for their education, and expect to graduate in debt, they choose their courses carefully. Henkel (2000) describes a shift in student expectations from being an educational experience to being a credentialing one. Evidence of this trend appears in diminishing interest in the humanities and "pure" disciplines such as physics and history (Becher & Parry, 2005). Barnett and Coate (2005) describe the situation thus:

Courses are designed to offer the kinds of skills and knowledge that attracts students who anticipate having to compete in the labour market. Modularization has become a key signifier of consumption, as programmes are repackaged and even rebranded for students to choose amongst. (p. 37)

Designers clearly must be apprised of the competing pressures, demands and expectations on the curriculum, and what students expect to "get" from their university experience. This comes into sharp focus when considering the current practice in Australian universities to develop and design graduate attributes for all courses of study. If designers are involved in graduate attribute projects, or the design of student assessment tasks, it is important to understand the changing nature of what motivates students to learn.

Another significant and related issue for higher education students in Australia is the need to work during study. Long and Hayden (2001) conducted a national survey of undergraduate students' finances and found that students' financial circumstances influenced their choice of course, university, and mode of study. They found that over the last two decades the proportion of full-time students in paid employment during semester had increased from 5 out of 10 to 7 out of 10. They also found that those students who are working during semester are working longer hours—from an average of 5 hours per week in 1984 to an average of 14.4 hours a week (about two days per week) in 2000. The survey found that 2 out of 10 working students said that the work adversely affected their study "a great deal" (iii). Small proportions of students also reported adverse study effects of childcare costs and availability and travel costs. The findings of this survey provide very important information to designers and academic staff considering how best to offer courses to students. Design issues arising from the Long and Hayden (2001) survey include choices about flexible and/or multiple modes of delivery; academics' expectations about attendance, independent study time, and online participation; the timing of assessment and teaching and learning activities, the structure and amount of content and the nature and timing of student support.

Students' use of technology is another significant issue for designers and academic staff. In the introductory chapter of their edited work, Oblinger and Oblinger (2005) paint a picture of the different technology needs of university students according to their age or the generation. For example, the current Net generation (born after 1982) have never known a world without the Internet and cannot imagine life without constant connection to others—their friends, family and sources of instant information. By contrast, most academic staff are from generations where the pace of access to networks of information and communication was slower and technology was introduced as an additional network to other primary forms such as libraries and social gatherings.

The most surprising implication of these differences is that the Net generation, so familiar and fluent with technology, see its use as simply a means to an end. When it comes to learning, the Net generation students value face-to-face involvement with academic staff and other students. Furthermore Oblinger and Oblinger (2005) describe these (usually) younger learners as having a preference for:

- Working in teams: A peer-to-peer approach is valued highly
- Structure rather than ambiguity: A focus on achieving their goals quickly
- Interactive engagement to allow for discovery and inductive reasoning
- Image-rich environments
- Applying their effort to "things that matter" in real-world exercises, such as addressing environmental or community concerns

When designing courses to make best use of technology, academic staff need to understand the Net generation's preferences. In describing this dissonance, Oblinger and Oblinger (2005, p. 214) quote Fletcher (2003):

Digital natives accustomed to the twitch-speed, multitasking, random-access, graphics-first, active, connected, fun, fantasy, quick-payoff world of their video games, MTV and Internet are bored by most of today's education, well-meaning as it may be. But worse, the many skills that new technology [has] actually enhanced (for example, parallel processing, graphics awareness, and random access)—which have profound implications for their learning—are almost totally ignored by educators.

At the same time as the Net generation enters higher education, mature-aged adults are also entering higher education to complete tertiary programs as a means to achieving their own goals. Though less *au fait* with technology, these mature-aged students are much more likely to be satisfied with an online course than the younger students. For them it is not the social contact associated with learning but time that is of premium consideration. How best can designers embrace the diversity of student experience and preferences for technology in education?

One response involves the design of "flexible learning" courses, where there is an emerging trend to design courses of study in multiple modes in an attempt to maximise the likelihood of meeting most student needs. New converged, or hybrid models, offer students considerable choice in the manner in which they access the content and the interactive elements of a course. Lecture materials are also available online for those who miss lectures, online discussions offer alternatives to tutorials and content is delivered via multimedia to accommodate different learning styles.

Tensions Relating to Disciplinarity

In Australian universities, educational designers, with only a few exceptions, work as "generalist" consultants located in centralised units or centres serving the whole university community, or sections thereof (Bird, 2004). The centralised location of designers within institutions can be explained in a number of ways. Firstly, from the institution's perspective it is less expensive. Bird (2004) found that of the 38 universities in Australia only two had School/Faculty-based designers (with 24 and 30 designers employed respectively). Centralised designer positions in institutions of comparable size employ five or six designers to work across the University. Secondly, the central location of designers in some Australian institutions can be traced historically to the existence of the old "DECs" (distance education centres) where designers, desktop publishers and proofreaders worked centrally on the design and production of print-based distance education materials. Thirdly, authors such as Willis (1995), criticise the centralised "expert" model as a characteristic of older systems models of instructional design with theoretical roots in behaviourist learning theory.

Should educational designers be centrally located "generalists" who work across the whole curricula, bringing to their work with academic staff "expert" knowledge, or should they be immersed within disciplines, becoming specialists in particular disciplinary cultures, pedagogies and systems? Borrowing Becher's (1989) conception of disciplines as "tribes," should designers visit tribes or belong to them?

On the one hand, to extend the tribal metaphor, Giacomi, Mosher, and Swenton-Wall (1993) argue that designers should take an ethnographic approach to their work, which: "with its emphasis on 'natives' point-of-view,' holism, and natural settings, provides a unique perspective to bring to bear on understanding users' work activities" (p. 123). Similarly Willis (1995) argues:

> *...general ID specialists, who can work with subject matter experts from any discipline, are a myth. You must understand the 'game' being played before you can help develop instruction. If specialists are used, they should be immersed in the environment of use before assisting with design.* (p. 12)

On the other hand, it has been argued that designers/developers do have specialist knowledge that can be considered unashamedly "generic" which does not necessarily align with outmoded behaviourist models of learning and systems models of design. Perhaps, for example, it is possible to take an ethnographic approach to design work from a central location within an institution by establishing stable and trustworthy relationships over time with particular disciplines. A "trusted friend" model has a number of advantages:

1. It prevents designers becoming "siloed" within one discipline, allowing for not only a more rich professional life for the designers themselves, but for the cross-pollenation of ideas and practices by designers across disciplines;
2. It mitigates against the current pressures to embed designers as quality assurance "police" and locates them as "advisors" and quality enhancers;

3. It allows for a model of design which can be characterised by what Klein (2004, p. 517) describes as "complexity, hybridity, non-linearity, reflexivity, heterogeneity and transdisciplinarity."

Becher and Parry (2005) describe the broad epistemological landscape of higher education where the traditional disciplines, that is, Becher's (1989) "tribes," are no longer the sole producers of knowledge. The shift towards Mode 2 knowledge production (described by Gibbons, Limoges, Nowotny, Schwartzman, Scott, & Trow, 1994) as knowledge which is generated in applied settings, drawing on more than one traditional discipline, and valued for its usefulness) and the application to higher education of Wenger's (1998) "communities of practice" concept have contributed to a "relative downgrading" of the traditional disciplines, particularly in the social aspects of knowledge production (Becher & Parry, 2005, p. 142). In this landscape, where boundaries between disciplines have blurred and applied fields of study continue to emerge, new models of transdisciplinary design work are being successfully explored. Transdisciplinary design involves small groups of subject matter experts from across a range of fields of study who team up with technical and library staff and educational designers in the process of designing, developing, implementing and evaluating pedagogically sound teaching, learning and assessment designs (O'Reilly, 2004).

Transdisciplinary design processes involve the application of discipline-based theories and methods from one discipline across other disciplines in order to test their usefulness and contestability. This works particularly well when designing assessment (O'Reilly & Ellis, 2005). While assessment is a mandatory component of all accredited courses of study, assessment design can sometimes become a torpid process characterised by tasks that have a sameness and expediency from the students' point of view. Transdisciplinary educational design is now being explored as a means of breaking through this torpor to facilitate a creative design approach by academic teaching staff.

Just as seen in development teams in the early adoption of technology in teaching (McDonald & Postle, 1999; Thiagarajan, 1999), collaborative educational design approaches that now work across disciplines often result in more realistic and more authentic learning designs, because teaching staff are prompted by the critical questioning of colleagues in a development context which stands outside the boundaries of complexity associated with their single discipline or field. In this context, the exploration of particular learning theories and teaching approaches within and across disciplines can readily be facilitated by educational designers in order to begin building the bonds and the bridges needed in this age of diversity and dynamic change.

Conclusion

In the context of constant change, this chapter has explored several historical and contemporary tensions in the professional practice of educational design arising within the higher education sector. From an organisational, professional and practice level, educational designers in Australia, UK, Canada and New Zealand can be seen as continuing to adjust their practice to the environment in which they work. Emerging national quality assurance and funding agendas combine with individual institutional contexts, the shifting needs of academic staff, and a new generation of students to provide the profession with ongoing opportunities to reflect upon its identity and the contribution it makes to building strong foundations of quality in learning and teaching. Reflectivity and flexibility are the key to educational designers' maintaining relevance in a higher education sector where the "rules of engagement" are rapidly changing.

References

Allen, M. (1996). A profile of instructional designers in Australia. *Distance Education, 17*(1), 7-32.

Andresen, L. (1991). Educational developers: What do they know? *HERDSA News, 13*(1), 5-7.

Becher, T. (1989). *Academic tribes and territories, intellectual enquiry and the culture of disciplines*. Buckingham: The Society for Research into Higher Education & Open University Press.

Becher, T., & Parry, S. (2005). The endurance of the disciplines. In I. Bleiklie & M. Henkel (Eds.), *Governing knowledge, A study of continuity and change in higher education: A Festschrift in honour of Maurice Kogan* (pp. 133-144). The Netherlands: Springer.

Barnett, R., & Coate, K. (2005). *Engaging the curriculum in higher education.* Buckingham: The Society for Research into Higher Education & Open University Press.

Bird, J. (2004). Professional navel gazing: Flexible learning professionals into the future. In R. Atkinson, C. McBeath, D. Jonas-Dwyer, & R. Phillips (Eds.), *Beyond the Comfort Zone: Proceedings of the 21st ASCILITE Conference,* Perth, Australia, December 5-8, 2005 (pp. 123-133). Retrieved May, 20, 2006, from http://www.ascilite.org.au/conferences/perth04/procs/bird.html

Boud, D. (1993). Experience as the base for learning. *Higher Education Research and Development, 12*(1), 33-44.

Campbell, K., Schwier, R., & Kenny, R. (2005). Agency of the instructional designer: Moral coherence and transformative social practice. *Australasian Journal of Educational Technology, 21*(2), 242-262.

Candy, P.C. (1993). Learning theories in higher education: Reflections on the keynote day. HERDSA 1992. *Higher Education Research and Development, 12*(1), 99-106.

Evans, T., & Nation, D. (1989). Dialogue in practice, research and theory in distance education. *Open Learning, 14*(2), 37-43.

Evans, T., & Nation, D. (1993). *Reforming open and distance education* (Ch.12). London: Kogan Page.

Fletcher, D. (2003). *Higher education leaders symposium: Unlocking the potential of gaming technology*. Redmond, WA: Microsoft Corporation.

Fraser, K. (2003). *Academic developers: Career paths, qualifications and personal professional development.* Retrieved February 10, 2003, from http://www2.auckland.ac.nz/cpd/HERDSA/HTML/StaffDev/fraser.HTM.

Giacomi, J., Mosher, A., & Swenton-Wall, P. (1993). Ethnographic field methods and their relation to design. In D. Schuler & A. Namioka (Eds.), *Participatory design: Principles and practices* (pp.123-155). Hillsdale, NJ: Lawrence Erlbaum.

Gibbons, M., Limoges, C., Nowotny, H., Schwartzman, S., Scott, P., & Trow, M. (1994). *The new production of knowledge.* London: SAGE.

Gros, B., Elen, J., Kerres, M., van Merriënboer, J., & Spector, M. (1997). Instructional design and the authoring of multimedia and hypermedia systems: Does a marriage make sense? *Educational Technology, 37*(1), 48-56.

Henkel, M. (2000). *Academic identities and policy change in higher education.* London: Jessica Kingsley.

Inglis, A. (1992). Two viewing points, one viewer. In B. Scriven, R. Lundin, & Y. Ryan (Eds), *Distance Education for the Twenty-First Century, Selected Papers from the ICDE 16th World Conference, ICDE & QUT* (pp. 73-76).

Inglis, A. (1996). Teaching-learning specialists'conceptions of their role in the design of distance learning packages. *Distance Education, 17*(2), 267-288.

Jackling, N (1989). Weaving my own design. In M.S. Parer, (Ed.). *Design, development and distance education.* Churchill: Monash Centre for Distance Learning.

Joughin, G., & Johnston, S. (1994). The experience of collaboration: Writing and instructional design in distance education. *Distance Education, 15*(1), 6-22.

Klein, J.T. (2004). Prospects for transdisciplinarity. *Futures, 36*, 515-526.

Leigh, D. (2006). *A brief history of instructional design.* Retrieved January 13, 2006, from http://www.pignc-ispi.com/articles/education/brief%20history.htm

Locke, T. (2001). Questions of professionalism. *Change: Transformations in Education, 4*(2), 30-50.

Long. M., & Hayden, M. (2001) *Paying their way: A survey of Australian undergraduate student finances, 2000.* Report to the Australian Vice-Chancellor's Committee. Retrieved October 6, 2005, from http://www.avcc.edu.au/policies_activities/teaching_learning/students/

McDonald, J., & Postle, G. (1999). Teaching online: Challenge to a reinterpretation of traditional instructional models. Paper presented at The Web After a Decade. In *Proceedings of AusWeb99, the 5th Australian World Wide Web Conference* (pp. 570-579). Ballina.

Meacham, D. (1989). The role of designers and developers in distance education. In M. Parer (Ed.), *Development, Design and Distance Education* (pp. 57-76). Victoria: Centre for Distance Learning Monash University.

Murphy, D. (1994). Pathways to a profession: What profession? In M. Parer (Ed). *Unlocking open learning* (pp. 145-159). Melbourne: Monash University.

Nunan, T. (1983). *Countering educational design.* London: Croom Helm.

O'Reilly, M. (2004). Educational design as transdisciplinary partnership: Supporting assessment design for online. In R. Atkinson, C. McBeath, D. Jonas-Dwyer, & R. Phillips (Eds.), *Proceedings of the 21st acilite Conference* (pp. 724-733). Perth, Western Australia.

O'Reilly, M., & Ellis, A. (2005). Transdisciplinary educational design: Creating a structured space for critical reflection on e-learning assessment practices. In *Proceedings of Ed-Media 2005, World Conference on Educational Multimedia, Hypermedia and Telecommunications* (pp. 4924-4931). Montréal, Canada.

Oblinger, D., & Oblinger, J. (2005). *Educating the net generation.* Retrieved July 22, 2005, from http://www.educause.edu/educatingthenetgen

Parer, M. (Ed.). (1989). *Development, design and distance education.* Victoria: Centre for Distance Learning, Monash University.

Parer, M. (1993). The educational developer's role: Past and future. In T. Nunan (Ed.), *Distance education futures* (pp. 413-426). Adelaide: Australian and South Pacific External Studies Association, University of Adelaide.

Parry, S., & Debowski, S. (2004). The evaluative state. *HERDSA News, 26*(3), 12-13.

Roberts, D.W., Jackson, K., Osborne, J., & Somers Vine, A. (1994). Attitudes and perceptions of academic authors to the preparation of distance education materials at the University of Tasmania. *Distance Education, 15*(1), 70-93.

Ryder, M. (2006). *Instructional design models.* Retrieved May 27, 2006, from http://carbon.cudenver.edu/~mryder/itc_data/idmodels.html.

Schwier, R., Campbell, K., & Kenny, R. (2004). Instructional designers' observations about identity, communities of practice and change agency. *Australasian Journal of Educational Technology, 20*(1), 69-100.

Thiagarajan, S. (1999). *Rapid instructional design.* Retrieved April 19, 2004, from http://www.thiagi.com/article-rid.html

Tight, M. (2004). Research into higher education: An a-theoretical community of practice? *Higher Education Research & Development, 23*(4), 395-411.

Torrisi-Steele, G., & Davis, G. (2000). "A website for my subject": The experiences of some academics' engagement with educational designers in a team based approach to developing online learning materials. *Australian Journal of Educational Technology, 16*(3), 283-301.

Wenger, E. (1998). *Communities of practice: learning, meaning, and identity.* Cambridge: Cambridge University Press.

Wenger, E. (2000). Communities of practice and social learning systems. *Organisation, 7*, 225-246.

Willis, J. (1995). A recursive, reflective instructional design model based on constructivist-interpretivist theory. *Educational Technology*, 5-23.

Chapter III

Strategies and Heuristics for Novice Instructional Designers as They Work with Faculty Content Experts in a University Setting

Min Liu, University of Texas at Austin, USA

Coco Kishi, University of Texas at Austin, USA

Suzanne Rhodes, University of Texas at Austin, USA

Abstract

Universities increasingly expect faculty to integrate technology in their teaching and deliver instructional materials in innovative ways. The responsibility for creating technology-enhanced instruction typically falls on faculty who want to deliver instruction more effectively and efficiently and on students who are hired or assigned to assist them. In creating an instructional technology product, faculty members usually serve as content experts and students often serve as technology developers. In this chapter, we describe the development process we have used in training and working with student developers and faculty-student project development teams. We outline critical issues instructional designers face when working with faculty content experts, and provide suggestions for becoming effective designers and overcoming the obstacles in this academic setting. We hope the strategies and heuristics discussed will assist novice instructional designers to become better prepared, avoid pitfalls, and find the design experience to be both challenging and rewarding.

Introduction

Using technology to enhance teaching and learning has become an emphasis in higher education in the United States. Universities increasingly expect faculty to integrate technology in their teaching and deliver instructional materials in innovative ways. Relying on professional instructional designers to create these materials is often not possible due to budget constraints most universities face. The responsibility for creating technology-enhanced instruction, therefore, typically falls primarily on the faculty who want to deliver instruction more effectively and efficiently and on students who are hired or assigned to help them. In creating a technology product (e.g., a Web-based course, a Web site for a grant funded project, or a CD/DVD-based simulation), faculty members usually serve as content experts and students often serve as technology developers. While many students are often technology savvy, they may lack training in instructional design (ID) or have learned ID models only through coursework, without real-world experience in applying what they have learned.

Imagine these two scenarios: (1) A student with strong programming skills is assigned to assist a faculty member in developing an interactive simulation to aid learning of a difficult concept the faculty is teaching. The faculty member and student focus on the mechanics of the simulation, and the student starts building the simulation without considering the learning goals, audience, and appropriate instructional strategies to implement. (2) An instructional technology major is assigned to assist a faculty member in creating a Web site that will assist students to easily access course resources. After providing lecture notes, PowerPoint slides, and some videotapes, the faculty member becomes too busy to engage with the student on a regular basis and, being new to the technology development process, does not understand what specifically is expected of him/her as a participating client. The student is at a loss and, not knowing how to proceed, consults textbooks on ID but does not find the strategies and heuristics needed to complete the project.

Such situations are not uncommon when students are assigned to work on technology projects for faculty on university campuses. Faculty and students work together with loosely defined and flexible roles where faculty often rely on students to take on the main responsibility of project design and development. The role of the instructional designer can be shared by both faculty and students or taken on by either, depending on circumstances.

Instructional designers have their own community of practice. However, as Keppell (2004) argues, instructional designers almost always work outside their community of practice. The job of an instructional designer is to work with subject matter experts to translate "their needs and desires into the design specifications that will yield a successful product" (Cennamo & Kalk, 2005, p. 2), often for a topic foreign to them. This means instructional designers must not only have solid knowledge of instructional design, but also understand how other communities function. They must have a good understanding of other disciplines' practices, language, procedures, and processes (Keppell, 2004). This is very challenging, especially for novice designers. Developing skills to work effectively and gain legitimate participation takes time and practice.

As we have supervised student developers who worked on technology projects in diverse subject areas—from engineering to science, from language learning to education—and taught courses to prepare instructional designers, we have found that few textbooks cover real-world design scenarios. Novice designers, whether they are faculty or students, lack the knowledge of what is actually involved in creating technology products and how to deal with various problems.

In this chapter, we share our experiences and observations from training and working with student developers and guiding faculty-student project development teams. Our goal is to discuss the development process used in an academic setting—outlining critical issues instructional designers face when working with faculty content experts in creating technology-enhanced instructional materials—and provide suggestions for becoming effective designers and overcoming the difficulties in this environment. The audience for this chapter includes (1) students who are assigned to work on a technology development project, (2) instructional technology majors who are trained to be instructional designers and intend to pursue a career in instructional technology, (3) faculty who teach instructional technology courses or who work with student technologists, and (4) professional staff members who manage instructional technology development projects and programs. We hope the strategies and heuristics discussed in this chapter will assist novice instructional designers and other audiences to become better prepared, avoid pitfalls, and find the design experience to be both challenging and rewarding.

Background

Instructional design refers to "the systematic and reflective process of translating principles of learning and instruction into plans for instructional materials, activities, information resources, and evaluation" (Smith & Ragan, 2005, p. 4). In its 60-year history, the discipline of instructional design (ID) has seen many models—some behaviorist, others cognitive- or constructivist-based. Gustafson and Branch (2002) provided a good overview of major ID models, offering a taxonomy to classify models depending upon when they should best be applied.

According to their taxonomy, certain models are clearly intended for classroom instruction, such as those by Heinich, Molenda, Russell, and Smaldino (1999) and by Morrison, Ross, and Kemp (2001). The backward design process by Wiggins and McTighe (2000) also belongs to this category. Some models are most suitable for developing products for implementation by users other than the developers, such as those by Bergman and Moore (1990) and Seels and Glasgow (1998). Systems-oriented models such as Dick and Carey's (2001) and Smith and Regan's (2005), on the other hand, are more appropriate for larger and more complex instructional systems directed at a problem on a large scale.

These ID models, many of them prescriptive, offer useful conceptual frameworks for developing instructional and training materials and are widely taught in instructional technology programs at universities. However, as pointed out by Kenny, Zhang, Schwier, and Campbell (2005), practicing instructional designers who use these models in the field rarely follow them rigidly.

The field of instructional design is heavily influenced by advancements in learning theories, communication theories, and computer technology (Reiser, 2001) and is changing rapidly as we gain understanding of how people learn and communicate; and of how technology can enhance learning and communication. What is often not covered in traditional ID textbooks is how designers apply ID models in practice, what procedures are useful to them, how they face challenges, what strategies they have developed, what tips they can provide, and how they address the complexity and ever-changing nature of their jobs. Such practical information would be especially valuable for beginners who are about to enter the practice of designing instruction with technology.

Students often lack competence in professional practice that requires practical knowledge and insight gained through practice (Gentry, 1994; Quinn, 1994). Realizing this need, Liu and her colleagues conducted two studies with ID practitioners. In the first study (Liu, Jones, & Hemstreet, 1998), they used extensive interviews with selected, experienced developers of multimedia educational materials to report in detail (1) how the multimedia production process works, (2) what the roles and responsibilities of team members were, (3) what factors contributed to successful multimedia development, (4) what tips and techniques in multimedia development were offered by practitioners, and (5) what popular hardware and software were used. In the second study (Liu, Gibby, Quiros, & Demps, 2002), they focused on the roles of an instructional designer, looking again to practitioners in the field to find out how their roles were defined and changed, how they handled their job challenges, and how they adapted to frequent changes in technology and market demands.

In an attempt to integrate academic knowledge and practical experience, Cennamo and Kalk (2005), in addition to discussing key design elements, described important tasks a designer is likely to perform. For example, they shared their experiences of how to write a project proposal, how to write a design document, what a kick-off meeting is like, and how to prepare a budget. They also offered tips and templates for carrying out various tasks. Such a real world perspective is valuable to novice designers.

Regardless of whether an ID model is grounded in behavioral, cognitive, or constructive learning theories, some activities are common among ID models. Five considerations underlying many ID models are analysis, design, development, implementation, and evaluation (ADDIE) (Gustafson & Branch, 2002; Reiser, 2001), though the application of an instructional design model is often context sensitive (Yang, Moore, & Burton, 1995). Depending on the context of a given project, one or more ID models should be selected (Gustafson & Branch, 2002). The community of practice in which instructional designers work often exerts considerable influences on the design approaches and strategies they select (Keppell, 2004). In the following, we present the development process that we have used in our practice and have found most suitable for the context we described in this chapter: developing small scale technology-enhanced instructional materials in an academic setting with limited budgets. The process is based upon various ID models mentioned by Gustafson and Branch (2002) with strong emphasis on its practical and iterative nature for short-term projects.

Case Description

We are situated in a large research university in the U.S., where services for the development of instructional resources, tools, and products are somewhat decentralized and unevenly distributed. Although some colleges and departments employ teams of professional developers who serve the instructional needs of faculty, not all colleges and departments have such resources, leaving most faculty to seek limited university-level support or help from student assistants. It is a growing practice to involve students in working on faculty projects through academic internship or job programs. Students in the instructional technology program are also regularly assigned to work with faculty clients as part of class projects. In central or college-level instructional technology service units, students are recruited from various disciplines such as education, communications, and computer sciences and hired to work on projects under the supervision of professional developers who also train and mentor these student developers. Outside of these organized programs, faculty who obtain their own funding or desire to create technology products also hire students to work on various instructional projects. Students are often eager for the experience and the wages associated with the jobs. Also, in a large university, students benefit from the opportunity to experience a working relationship with a faculty member, and faculty in turn benefit from the enthusiastic, relatively inexpensive and diverse talent of student workers.

Project development undertaken by faculty and their student developers follows phases very similar to those in a business environment. Nevertheless, developing technology projects within an academic setting poses unique challenges for all members of a project development team, especially novice instructional designers.

The university follows a cycle that is tied to the school year, resulting in regular turnover in project personnel that affects the project development time frame. Because faculty and students arrive for classes in fall and spring (such as in our case), and because in summer students often take a break or graduate while faculty often leave to pursue their research, projects are typically developed within the time-frame of a 15-week semester. The roles of client, subject matter expert, and developer are also loosely defined and transitory, because these roles are filled by faculty and students who have different skills and competing priorities calling on their time.

Faculty members formulate and initiate the project, but they usually serve as clients as well as subject matter experts and content developers. While faculty can be accomplished teachers in their areas of expertise, most have had no formal training in instructional design and have had little experience with the technology development process.

Although faculty members seek and enthusiastically welcome assistance on instructional technology projects, they are often too busy to manage a project and its developers consistently and effectively. Faculty members' multiple responsibilities for teaching, research, and service often call them away from a project, sometimes for weeks. Faculty members preparing for tenure promotion are especially subject to the pressures of competing priorities. And because faculty members are also interested in obtaining grants, they often think of technology projects on a larger scale. Thus, many projects must be sequenced to begin on a small scale (one semester or two) as a pilot or seed for a multi-year, grant-funded effort.

Students provide a technically diverse and transient work force, subject to high turnover due to competing priorities such as schoolwork, social activities, and graduation. Because the amount and pace of work that students can do vary depending on whether there is an upcoming exam or a break, not all students can work steadily throughout the project development period. A student's work pattern does not always correspond to that of faculty or other members of the development team.

In addition, a student often takes on multiple roles, such as an instructional designer, programmer, project manager, animator, and video- or audio-specialist. "Different titles will require different mixes of skills at different stages in each project to achieve effective implementation" (Hudson, 1995, p. 46). When student developers tackle various aspects of production, the pace of development can vary depending on the students' skill and experience. As novice designers, students are usually not proficient in all necessary technical skills when joining the project; in fact, it is often the case that student developers are motivated to work on a project in order to gain experience. They often lack the type of experience and technical expertise possessed by their professional counterparts to efficiently complete the task. They must, therefore, learn how to assess the needs of the project and factor in the time required to acquire the skills needed to complete it.

Finally, because budgets follow an annual cycle, the timing of available funds for project development can be affected. Budgets for technology development projects by our university are reviewed in winter and spring and are implemented or renewed in the fall. Recruiting of student developers and purchase of equipment and upgrades must be timed to this budget cycle, which often does not correspond to the release of software and equipment upgrades by vendors. Budgets are usually tight, limiting development projects to a short time frame or a small development team.

In short, the project development cycle in a university setting is often short-term and episodic, constrained by high turnover of student developers, busy schedules of faculty and students, the academic calendar, and limited funding. However, while the cyclical and academic nature of the university creates a unique work setting with many challenges, the academic setting fosters an environment of on-the-job learning, exploration, and experimentation that characterizes many project development efforts. The dynamic nature of the development process brought by the energy and creativity of the faculty and students guided by a professional manager or ID instructor at a central level creates an opportunity for the end-products to reflect the most current theories and research findings in teaching and learning. These products often serve as the basis for larger and better-funded projects later on.

While working in such an academic setting, what ID models should be used, what ID strategies are most useful, and what process should be followed? In our work, we have learned that a flexible and practical model works more effectively in our setting and should be seamlessly integrated into the project development process.

A Development Model in the University Setting

Technology-enhanced instructional materials developed at a university can range from online resources for classroom or individual study (collections of digital assets, simulations,

Figure 1. Project development model used in an academic setting

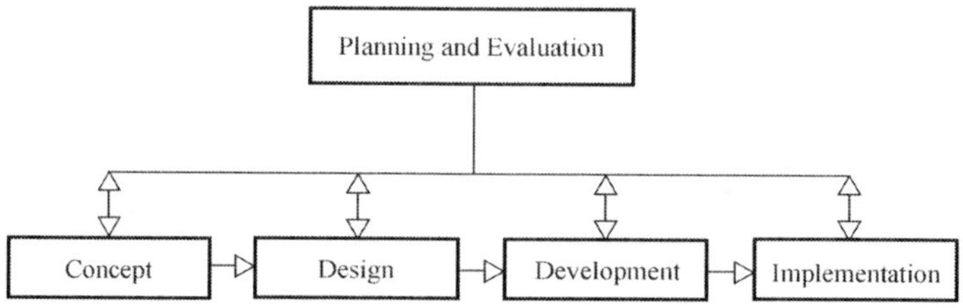

tutorials) to integrated learning management systems. We have seen growing sophistication in the use of technology and the types of projects being developed, led by faculty innovators who are excited by technology and motivated to incorporate it in their teaching. Regardless of whether a project aims to develop a simple animation or the curriculum for an online course, the most successful projects follow a development process that can accommodate the academic environment.

Here we describe a four-phased, iterative development model that we have learned from practitioners in the field and used in our own projects, effective for technology development projects in a university setting (see Figure 1). The four phases are concept, design, development, and implementation, with the tasks of planning and evaluation integral to each phase and performed iteratively.

Concept Phase

During the *concept phase*, the goals, objectives, and desired outcomes of a project become clearly articulated. In an academic setting, the faculty client usually comes up with the concept and the student developer assists in detailing the concept. The requirements and scope of the project are established, assessed, evaluated, and revised; together, the project team moves from amorphous ideas to carefully articulated statements. It is critical to establish a clear sense of direction and vision at this early stage to ensure that subsequent phases proceed smoothly and efficiently and satisfy expectations. The client should provide information about the audience, additional collaborators and stakeholders, content, and the delivery system. *Client input document* as provided in Appendix A can be used as a template to gather such information. Some key ID tasks during the concept phase include:

- Determining the needs of the client and learner: for example, addressing the teaching and learning problem;
- Determining main learning goals and outcomes,
- Researching and analyzing what has already been done on the topic by others,
- Creating and planning the high-level instructional approach based on sound teaching and learning theory as well as best practices,

- Performing a content audit to determine gaps and needs,
- Writing the ID plan for the next phases.

The deliverable for this phase is typically a project concept document and sometimes a proposal in response to a request for proposal (RFP).

Design Phase

During the *design phase*, the team (primarily faculty and student) articulates everything they can about the learning product to be produced, how it works, what it will look like, what it will say, how it will behave, and how it will evolve based on the budget and timetable. The best possible designs are produced when communication is clear. The team details how they are going to produce and implement the project and what the learner will experience. That is, the client's vision is translated into a carefully laid out design plan that specifies presentation style, delivery platform, and the overall approach to be used. Details are worked out, such as the design of key screens, the type of navigation to be used, and the interactive characteristics of the interface. Flowcharts and storyboards are often used to layout these specifications. In consultation with the client, detailed timelines and major milestones should be established for the critical phases of the project. Making sure all the details are worked out *before* the development occurs provides the team with a blueprint for an efficient, cost-effective, and easier development experience. Some key ID tasks for the design phase include:

- Writing the learning objectives,
- Consulting with subject-matter experts,
- Determining the assessment approach and assessment strategies as well as writing the assessment plan,
- Communicating the detailed ID approach, possibly using flowcharts, storyboards, scripts, workbooks, guidebooks, outlines, and so on,
- Developing the plan for content acquisition and development,
- Coordinating and leading focus groups with product prototypes,
- Evaluating and reporting data.

The deliverable for this phase is usually a design document.

Development Phase

During the *development phase*, all the pieces of a project are organized and built according to the design plan. Successful products depend on the active involvement of all team members as they implement and fine-tune the ideas formalized in the design phase. Each team member (client and student developer) must be committed to ensuring the quality of every piece he or she creates and must actively participate in the review of the final product. Quality management systems, whether technological or pedagogical (the latter especially pertinent to an instructional designer), should be in place throughout the process, and particularly in the development phase. Key ID tasks for the development phase include:

- Writing or supervising writers; creating content or supervising content developers; designing the storyline and direction; writing scripts, user guides, and instructional text,
- Developing and writing assessment materials,
- Coordinating and leading focus groups with alpha and beta product versions; evaluating and reporting the findings.

Web Development Design Specification Document in Appendix B is an example tool to facilitate various tasks in the design and development phases and can be adapted for use.

Implementation Phase

It is important to see a product used in action to determine whether the instructional and learning goals have been met. The *implementation phase* gives the client and the development team an opportunity to test the assumptions upon which the product was built. It is vital to receive feedback from the project team and audience, because feedback on learning, usability, and technology drives revisions and is a source of lessons learned for the current project and any future development. The main ID task for the implementation phase is to observe how the audience uses the product and to evaluate and report the findings.

Planning, Evaluation, and Revision

Unlike tasks during the other more discrete phases, the tasks of planning, evaluation, and revision are ongoing and should occur at each phase throughout the development process. At each milestone during the process, members of the team reflect on the project progress to date, assess and evaluate the process and outcomes, and make revisions and new plans based on the results. This shared process among client and developers objectively identifies what is working and what is not working. From this information the team will come up with a plan to improve the entire project. These "lessons learned" also become part of the shared knowledge base applied to future projects. As a critical part of the process, the ongoing planning, evaluation, and revision tasks allow a team to proactively recognize obstacles and make necessary just-in-time modifications.

Professionals stressed the importance of having such continuous evaluation as a key tool for ensuring the quality of the product (Liu et al., 1998). In an academic setting, the close working relationship between faculty and students in a smaller development team makes it easier to implement such an ID process. The iterative and flexible nature of this development process is reflected by the practice of professional instructional designers (Liu et al.,

1998) and is consistent with emerging tends in instructional design (Schoenfeld & Berge, 2004/2005). Some recent versions of traditional ID models also begin to incorporate the importance of ongoing planning, evaluation, and revision in their process (Gustafson & Branch, 2002).

Defining Roles and Responsibilities: Strategies and Tips

Many people contribute to the success of a product, fulfilling a number of roles and responsibilities (Cennamo & Kalk, 2005; Liu et al., 1998). In general, instructional designers assist in a project by determining how theories and practices of learning, communication, and pedagogy combine to affect the learning process as well as reinforcing the validity of an instructional approach. Instructional designers strengthen the development process by entering the process at key points (for example, at kick-off meetings or design reviews) or working on the project throughout its lifecycle.

For a large project, instructional designers often have to work on multiple projects that have multiple team members and clients, playing a critical role in the design process, so their ability to communicate effectively with multiple stakeholders is essential for project success. For smaller scale academic projects, instructional designers often take on more than one role in addition to their primary responsibility as a designer. In fact, taking on other roles is common for designers in the field (Kenny, Zhang, Schwier, & Campbell, 2005; Liu et al., 1998; Liu et al., 2002). Three roles that an instructional designer works closely with and is likely to play sometimes are that of a client, project manager, and subject matter expert (SME).

Whether an instructional designer takes on one responsibility or several, having a good understanding of what each role entails and its associated responsibilities will help prevent misunderstanding and ensure successful project implementation. In the following, we describe these three roles, their associated responsibilities, and their expectations for designers. We also include tips on how an instructional designer can best work with persons assuming the roles.

Clients

Roles and Responsibilities

Clients drive a project, determining its goals, direction, and success criteria. Faculty clients tend to be more involved in day-to-day project activities, with responsibilities that include:

- Providing the project vision, concept, requirements, and success criteria
- Approving deliverables

- Providing timely feedback on work
- Providing content (usually written)—as well as examples of materials that have style and direction similar to the content to be developed—and editing all written content.

Expectations

Clients expect an instructional designer to be accurate and articulate, to interpret their requirements, and to work the client's input into the process and the product. An instructional designer should expect his or her client to provide timely, constructive, and specific feedback on work.

Tips for Instructional Designers for Working Successfully with Clients

Instructional designers should:

- Be good listeners
- Ask questions
- Understand that clients sometimes know what they don't want, but don't know exactly what they do want
- Realize that clients probably will change their mind
- Explain the thought process behind decisions
- Offer an alternative solution if a client's request cannot be met
- Fix things that are "broken" immediately, especially during implementation, and
- Pamper clients, always keeping in mind that this project is very important to the clients.

Project Managers

Roles and Responsibilities

Project managers guide the design and development process, relying on strong verbal and visual communications skills that allow them to serve as the main point-of-contact between the project team and the client. Project managers champion the project, building shared vision and consensus among stakeholders. They help set and maintain project direction, expectations, requirements, and scope, while charged with responsibility for finishing the project on time and on budget. Project managers' responsibilities include:

- Overseeing all aspects of the process
- Coordinating the efforts of all other roles

- Consolidating documentation
- Acting as the primary client contact
- Assuring that project requirements are met
- Managing the budget
- Staffing the project
- Tracking and managing progress and status
- Resolving conflicts
- Evaluating work
- Generating tools to facilitate development.

Expectations

Project managers expect instructional designers to provide the theoretical support for a quality project, to provide regular reports of progress, status, and number of hours worked, and to deliver expected work on time. Instructional designers should expect project managers to:

- Coordinate meetings that have goals and an agenda,
- Support all ID decisions,
- Set reasonable expectations and timelines, and
- Integrate ID input into the project plan and any other project documentation.

Tips for Instructional Designers on How to Work with the Project Manager

Instructional designers should:

- Communicate often.
- Meet deadlines, letting the project manager know immediately if the project falls behind schedule, giving reasons without excuses, giving an estimated time of delivery, reporting what is needed to get the work completed, and remembering that missed deadlines may affect others on the team.
- Show proof of work done.
- Keep in mind that project managers like to feel that they are in control of the project and process—they do not like surprises.

Subject Matter Expert (SME)

Roles and Responsibilities

SMEs exhibit the highest level of expertise in performing a specialized task or possessing knowledge for the project. SMEs offer a wealth of experience and ideas from domains specific to the project. SMEs do not drive the process but inform it and are usually hired by the client. For small-scale projects in an academic setting, faculty members are SMEs, whose responsibilities include:

- Consulting with the instructional designer during the concept and design phases,
- Providing materials on the subject matter,
- Evaluating content for accuracy, integrity, and validity.

Expectations

SMEs expect an instructional designer to learn the subject adequately and to interpret and work the SME's input into the process and the product. On the other hand, an instructional designer should expect SMEs to have a broad and deep subject expertise and to provide instruction on the subject.

Tips for Instructional Designers on How to Work With SMEs

When working with SMEs, instructional designers should listen carefully, ask questions, and trust that the SME is providing accurate information.

Attributes of an Effective Instructional Designer

Liu, Gibby, Quiros, and Demps (2002) found that good practicing instructional designers in the new media field were (1) quick studies who were willing to learn new things, (2) team players, (3) attentive to details, and (4) good oral and written communicators. We have found the following key characteristics in effective designers:

- good listener
- flexible
- detail-oriented
- willing to learn
- open to new ideas

- having strong oral and written communication skills
- able to work and be creative under constraints in time, resources, or budget
- able to work with and respect people performing different roles.

What Role am I Playing and What Do I Do?

In the business world, a project team is usually comprised of many specialists (e.g., project manager, assistant project manager, programmer(s), 3D artist(s), 2D artist(s), instructional designer, quality assurance tester(s), etc.) who are paid to work full-time and usually work on several projects at a time (with the possible exception of the project manager). In a university setting, having a dedicated team of developers to support each faculty member is beyond most budgets. Thus, we have found it is more efficient and effective to employ a model of fewer team members who assume multiple roles to work on a single project, especially if it is short-term. Because of limited funding, a relatively small audience base, and a more tightly focused instructional goal, the scope of projects for a faculty client in academia is usually quite small (typically 100-500 person hours) as compared to a larger-scale university project or projects done in the business world. There are many students with media and technical skills that are self-taught or acquired through formal classes as part of their academic program. However, only a small number of students also have the project management, instructional design, subject matter expertise, or experience required for a typical project with a faculty client. While an experienced and credentialed ID instructor or staff project facilitator is always available to provide training, direction, and guidance during key points of the development process, the student developer and faculty client must shoulder a large percentage of the actual work and share roles in a way that leverages the knowledge and expertise of each.

In a typical one-student one-faculty member project, the faculty member is clearly the client and subject matter expert, while the student is clearly the main developer to build project. But during certain phases or for certain tasks, faculty clients and student developers should each assume project manager and instructional designer responsibilities for maximized efficiency (if the student developer has not already assumed all ID responsibilities as a novice instructional designer). Sharing roles can and often does increase the complexity of the project process. It is essential that the responsibilities are discussed at the beginning of the project and confirmed by both team members throughout the project process through good communication to ensure an efficient process and a successful project. Given the two types of roles—instructional designer and project manager—to be shared by one faculty member and one student during a project cycle, the question is who is performing what role and when? The following decouples the shared responsibilities for five key, yet possibly ambiguous, project tasks.

Instructional Design

Faculty member: The faculty member assumes an instructional designer role primarily during the concept and implementation phases, determining the teaching and learning problem, writing the learning goals and objectives, and determining the high-level instructional and assessment approach. The faculty member researches and analyzes what has already been done on the topic by others, interprets data gathered from user testing, and revises project requirements based on the results.

Student developer: The student assumes an instructional designer role primarily during the design and development phases, translating faculty client requirements to create the overall project architecture and design, starting with flowcharts and storyboards. The student supervises production of any written content created by the faculty member, interprets data gathered from user testing, and revises requirements and makes recommendations for improvements in project features and functionality.

Project Management

Faculty member: Especially during the concept, design, and implementation phases, the faculty member oversees all aspects of the project, coordinating the efforts of the student developer, assuring that project requirements are met, evaluating work, and tracking work progress and status.

Student developer: The student documents all project processes, primarily oversees the development phase, acting as project manager for the faculty client for written content. The student developer builds the product, consolidates documentation, provides status and progress reports, and generates tools to facilitate current and future development.

Content Development

Faculty member: The faculty member executes the content audit, provides all written content, locates and acquires accurate subject matter-specific content and media, and obtains copyright permissions.

Student developer: The student develops content audit tools to assist the faculty client in identifying available materials as well as gaps where content must be acquired or developed. For a content audit tool, using a spreadsheet and listing each page or module on the rows and content types on the columns works well. The student creates all content that does not require subject matter expertise and modifies and prepares content supplied by the faculty client into the format required for the project. If the student developer has ID experience, he or she advises on the type of content and media that will best fit the subject matter, delivery mode, design, and instructional approach.

Asset Management

Faculty member: The faculty member organizes all original content assets and project materials based on the content audit, keeps a record of all original materials handed off to the student developer, and updates asset requirements during development.

Student developer: The student develops the asset management plan for digital content and media to identify required assets, recommends file structure and file naming conventions, and creates an asset management schedule for tracking and organizing assets. The student instructs the faculty client on the use of the conventions for new asset creation or modifies existing assets to fit the new rules. The student is responsible for implementing the asset management plan and keeps a record of all original materials received from the faculty client, checks that the rules are being followed, and updates asset status according to requirements on the spreadsheet.

Testing

Faculty member: The faculty member provides feedback for the quality assurance plan, reviews the accuracy of all information throughout the project, tests functionality during the development phase, organizes any user testing sessions, and thoroughly reviews and tests all parts of the project when it nears completion. The faculty member administers project assessments and documents the results and any problems found by users during implementation.

Student developer: The student develops the quality assurance plan and tests the features and functionality of each piece of work before handing it off to the faculty client for review, documenting problems found by himself or herself, the clients, and other users. While the student is not responsible for editing or proofreading text, he or she is responsible for making text-based changes within the project. If the student developer has ID experience he or she assists the faculty member in creating instruments to assess the impact and success of the project during implementation.

Dealing with Difficult Situations

Even with the best of intentions, enthusiasm, and stated commitment from all parties, circumstances can arise that lead to difficulties during project development. The most common problems we have seen are delays or lack of progress, going over budget, and projects growing beyond their scope. Such problems are usually the result of some combination of the following difficulties between faculty client and student developer:

- Poor or miscommunication, leading to confusion
- Lack of consistent or regular communication, follow-up, or feedback
- Lack of organization
- Missed deadlines
- Lack of assertiveness or action to address any of the above.

Because students and faculty play multiple roles, critical to project progress are clear communication, understanding of each person's responsibilities, and commitment. It is also important to remember that ID drives the use of technology, not the other way around. Both faculty and students can get carried away with technical innovation and lose perspective on the original instructional goals. Sufficient time must be spent communicating clearly during the concept and design phases so that project goals, responsibilities, schedules, and deadlines are carefully considered and confirmed, without vagueness or misunderstanding. Faculty content experts and student developers should be careful to speak in a language that both sides understand, avoiding subject matter and technical jargon. Students as well as faculty should not be afraid to ask many questions, document all communication and decisions, and then share them.

In an academic setting, it is important for students to feel a strong sense of collaboration and partnership on the project, especially when projects are short-term and students can come and go. Too often, students—as well as faculty—believe the project belongs to the faculty client and that students are just workers-for-hire. Faculty should recognize and credit their student developers once they realize the significance of students' roles. Students should become comfortable asserting themselves, reminding faculty members of the instructional goals or their responsibility as content providers. Students should also overcome timidity about actively and even aggressively seeking faculty for feedback, even when they are behind schedule. Students as well as faculty must also remember to conduct themselves as professionally as possible and meet their deadlines.

During the early stage of a project, students can be too eager to please their clients, be overconfident about their abilities, and underestimate their workload, agreeing to deadlines or use of technology that they cannot deliver. Faculty members, likewise, often underestimate the amount of time it takes to organize and deliver content, overestimating their available time. It is important to carefully plan ahead, review project progress, and consider all competing commitments (classes, exams, conferences, breaks, etc.), revising the development schedule as needed. As indicated above for the development process, implementing planning, evaluation, and revision at each of the four phases is critical.

Meetings are an opportunity for client and student to communicate face-to-face and report on project progress and exchange feedback. Because both faculty and student are pressed for time, it is important to prepare for all meetings and be well organized. Meetings do not have to be long to be efficient. Each meeting should have a purpose—a desired outcome or goal—and follow an agenda. Each meeting should also serve to make progress toward the greater goal of project completion. We recommend having a short progress review meeting every other week during initial stages and having regular meetings about every three weeks throughout the projects.

Before a project begins, we highly recommend that the faculty client and student developer establish an agreement or informal contract outlining what steps to follow if a difficult situation arises. Below is a sample of challenging situations that we have seen, the likely causes, and some recommended solutions for dealing with them.

- *The faculty client needs "just one more thing" (to be added to the project).*

  Cause: unbounded enthusiasm

  Solution: Stand firm on the original goals, objectives, and production schedule. Remind the client that additions will cause the project to go over budget and be delayed. Suggest that additions be considered in the next version.

- *The faculty client is not providing needed materials or information to the student.*

  Cause: The client does not understand the development process due to inexperience, or competing priorities are taking their toll.

  Solution: Persist in initiating communication, and educate the client about the development process and what is needed by the student to move the project forward. Because the client must understand the primary goal, be sensitive to the client's lack of technical knowledge by avoiding technical language or ID jargon. The client may be too embarrassed to admit lack of understanding, so when the project stalls, both faculty and student become frustrated. In our experience dealing with such a situation, we have sometimes had the client fill out a *Client Input Document* (see the Appendix A) to help articulate the developer's needs.

- *The student developer does not have a clear picture of exactly what the client wants, and the client does not know how to communicate it.*

  Cause: lack of clear communication and lack of common language

  Solution: Continue to ask for clarification; reiterate what you think you understand. Having the client fill out the *Client Input Document* (see Appendix A) may help to articulate project objectives.

- *An overly demanding faculty client does not take* no *for an answer and expects miracles with unrealistic deadlines.*

  Cause: The client lacks a good understanding of the development process or has an unprofessional attitude toward student developers.

  Solution: Continue presenting alternatives to the client. It is important to try to educate the client and to work on the relationship to move the project forward. However, it is also important to know, in an extreme situation, when to walk away before the relationship—as well as the project—fails.

- *The project is stalling, especially near the end of the development period.*

  Cause: The priorities of the client or student developer change, or the client considers the project to be never-ending, or the semester is ending and the faculty client or student developer moves on.

  Solution: Spend the necessary time at the initial meeting determining what exactly is to be built and stick to that decision as much as possible. Go with the flow up to a point (where it feels uncomfortable or unrealistic for you to continue); take the initiative to postpone or cancel the project if it is in the best interests of everyone. Remember when a project is cancelled, it is not the end of the world—the relationship built may be more important than the project because of the potential for future projects.

- *Missing files*

  Cause: disorganization and lack of proper content management

  Solution: Follow a content management scheme that includes conventions for file naming, locations for storing files, and version control (see Appendix B for a template).

- *Meetings feel arbitrary and like a waste of time.*

  Cause: lack of organization, lack of purpose for the meeting, meeting too long, no next steps, meeting not even needed, or wrong people invited

  Solution: Involve only stakeholders or decision makers; keep meetings efficient and short; have an agenda and follow it; make sure everyone leaves with action items or things they are responsible for getting done even if they do not need to do them themselves; foster ownership and accountability.

At our university, technology project development often occurs under the auspices of an instructional technology services unit or a program manager at the university level. Working in a team situation can be challenging, so both clients and student developers are encouraged to stay proactive and seek early guidance from these third party mentors before difficult situations lead to project failure.

Conclusion

In our case description, we discussed an increasingly common scenario that in a university setting, technology-enhanced instructional materials are typically created by student developers working with faculty content experts. During project development, students take on multiple roles, including that of instructional designer. Although many students are technically proficient, they lack project development and management experience or training in ID. Traditional courses and textbooks on ID models do not adequately cover strategies or solutions to the challenges encountered by novice designers working in a real-world situation.

We shared a flexible and iterative development process that we have found useful for carrying out technology development projects in an academic setting. Although some of the tasks and phases bear similarities with many other ID models, the process is highly situated in the academic context we described here. Using this development process will help address situations like that in the first scenario introduced at the beginning of the chapter, so both faculty members and students will realize the importance of ID and perform ID tasks at appropriate times.

We also described the challenges novice designers are likely to face in an academic context, suggested various roles and responsibilities a student or faculty member are likely to perform competently during the development process, and some heuristics for dealing with difficult situations. Such discussions can help the project team develop a clear understanding of the expectations of each member before the project begins and can help avoid situations like that in the second scenario at the beginning of the chapter. We hope the strategies and heuristics provided here will help faculty and students maximize chances for project completion and success and prepare students to be effective instructional designers beyond the academic environment.

References

Bergman, R., & Moore, T. (1990). *Managing interactive video/multimedia projects*. Englewood Cliffs, NJ: Educational Technology Publications.

Cennamo, K., & Kalk, D. (2005). *Real world instructional design*. Belmont, CA: Thomson Wadsworth.

Dick, W., Carey, L., & Carey, J. (2001). *The systematic design of instruction* (5th ed.). New York: Longman.

Gentry, C.G. (1994). *Introduction to instructional development: Process and technique*. Belmont, CA: Wadsworth.

Heinich, R., Molenda, M., Russell, J., & Smaldino, S. (1999). *Instructional media and technologies for learning* (6th ed.). Upper Saddle River, NJ: Merrill, Prentice Hall.

Hudson, B. (1995, July). The art and science: A matter of principles. *CD-ROM Professional, 8*(7), 44-54.

Gustafson, K.L., & Branch, R. (2002). *Survey of instructional development models* (4th ed). ERIC Document Reproduction Service No. ED477517.

Kenny, R.F., Zhang, Z., Schwier, R.A., & Campbell, K. (2005, Winter), A review of what instructional designers do: Questions answered and questions not asked. *Canadian Journal of Learning and Technology, 31*(1). Retrieved August 5, 2005, from http://www.cjlt.ca/content/vol31.1/kenny.html

Keppell, M. (2004). Legitimate Participation? Instructional designer-subject matter expert interactions in communities of practice. In *Proceedings of World Conference on Educational Multimedia, Hypermedia and Telecommunications* (Vol. 1, pp. 3611-3618).

Liu, M., Jones, C., & Hemstreet, S. (1998). A study of the multimedia design and production process by the practitioners. *Journal of Research on Computing in Education, 30*(3), 254-280.

Liu, M., Gibby, S., Quiros, O., & Demps, E. (2002). Challenges of being an instructional designer for new media development: A view from the practitioners. *Journal of Educational Hypermedia and Multimedia, 11*(3), 195-219.

Morrison, G., Ross, S., & Kemp, J. (2001). *Designing effective instruction* (3rd ed.). New York: John Wiley & Sons.

Quinn, J. (1994). Connecting education and practice in an instructional design graduate program. *Educational Technology Research & Development, 42*(3), 71-82.

Reiser, R. (2001). A history of instructional design and technology. Part II: A history of instructional design. *Educational Technology Research and Development*, *49*(2), 57-67.

Schoenfeld, J., & Berge, Z.L. (2004/2005). Emerging ISD models for distance training programs. *Journal of Educational Technology Systems*, *33*(1), 29-37.

Seels, B., & Glasgow, Z. (1998). *Making instructional design decisions* (2nd ed.). Upper Saddle River, NJ: Merrill, Prentice Hall.

Smith, P., & Ragan, T. (2005). *Instructional design* (3rd ed.). New York: John Wiley & Sons.

Yang, C.S., Moore, D.M., & Burton, J.K. (1995). Managing courseware production: An instructional model with a software engineering approach. *Educational Technology Research and Development*, *43*(4), 60-70.

Wiggins, G., & McTighe, J. (2000). *Understanding by design* (2nd ed.). Upper Saddle River, NJ: Prentice Hall.

Appendix A
Client Input Document

Project Title:

(Please limit to 75 characters or less)

Proposal Abstract:

(Please summarize your project in 100 words or less)

Audience:

What do we know about the audience that will help us for design and development? What is their general personality type?

What is their need? What do they want from your product that will address this need?

What do they currently know or do?

What would you like them to know or do?

Where will your audience be using the materials? Please select all that apply.

- ❐ Class
- ❐ Home
- ❐ Lab
- ❐ Other:

Content Requirements:

What types of digital content should the final product include? Please select all that apply.

- ❐ Video
- ❐ Audio
- ❐ Graphics 2D
- ❐ Graphics 3D
- ❐ Photographic images
- ❐ Text
- ❐ Animation 2D
- ❐ Animation 3D

- ❒ Other: field
- ❒ N/A

Describe the total amount of content you require for each content type you selected. If content not applicable, please enter N/A.

Is your content in a format that is organized and ready to hand off for development?

- ❒ Yes
- ❒ No
- ❒ N/A

If you answered "No" to the above question, what date will all the content be acquired or created and what percentage is already ready to hand off for development?

In what format will your content be at project kick-off?
If content not applicable, please enter N/A.

Describe any content that will need to be developed from scratch:
If content not applicable, please enter N/A.

If you plan on using copyrighted content, have you secured permission to use these materials?

- ❒ Yes
- ❒ No
- ❒ Some
- ❒ Not sure
- ❒ N/A

Technology Requirements:

What is the main platform your audience will be using? Please select all that apply.

- ❒ Windows
- ❒ Macintosh
- ❒ Both
- ❒ Other:

What is the delivery system for your project? Please select all that apply.

- ❐ Web
- ❐ CD
- ❐ DVD
- ❐ Other:

What is your target browser? Please select only one.

- ❐ Internet Explorer
- ❐ Netscape
- ❐ Firefox
- ❐ Mozilla
- ❐ Safari
- ❐ Other:
- ❐ N/A

Please select the minimum connection speed required for access:

- ❐ Dial-up (56K modem)
- ❐ DSL
- ❐ Cable
- ❐ T-1
- ❐ N/A

Are there specific technologies (Flash, DHTML, JavaScript, Real Audio, etc.) that you already use or would like to use in the project? If so, how will they enhance the learner experience or the development process?

Development Information:

What will be the name of the final product (For example, the title of your Web site or DVD)?

If you are proposing a Web-based project, what is your intended URL, or what server will host your site?

What assistance and resources are you planning to provide for your project?

When should this project be completed? Are there any outside considerations that might affect the schedule (i.e., book launch, conference, annual report)?

Who will be responsible for updating and maintenance after the project is complete?

Project Goals:

What teaching or learning problem(s) are you trying to solve with this project?

What is the primary goal of the project?

What are the secondary goals of the project?

What are the long-term goals?

Project Description:

Describe your vision for what the final product will look like as if it were already built.

Describe how a single member of your audience will use the final product.

- What is the primary "action" your audience should take when using the final product (For example, attain a competency, communicate information, locate resources)?
- What are the typical tasks your audience might perform while using the final product? (For example, log on, search for information, fill out a survey, take a test, read a book chapter, watch a video.)

List and describe examples of other projects that are similar to what you are proposing. Please provide URLs if possible.

Product Assessment:

Describe your plan for assessing the impact of your project on teaching and learning. Please list the criteria you will use to measure impact.

Other Support:

Please provide names of any additional project collaborator(s):

If you have received or are currently receiving support from another avenue for this project, please describe that support:

Additional notes, comments

Appendix B
Web Development Design Specification Document

I. Major Design Decisions and Layout

Main Structure to Present Information:

Flash file

HTML file

PDF file

Dynamic Pages (and database related features)

META Tag

Home Page:

What content will be placed?

What media will be used? (e.g., Flash movie or just a simple graphic)

Screen/Layout:

Size of screen (W x H in Pixels)

Size of header of each screen (title of site and logo)

Size of navigation areas (W x H in Pixels)

Size of content area (W x H in Pixels)

Scroll screens

Color scheme for Main page/Section Pages/Subtopic Pages

Navigation titles

Site Contents or Index based site map

Font:

Navigation

Menus

Main Navigation Headings

Sub-Headings

Content

Font Size:

Navigation

Menus

Main Navigation Headings

Sub-Headings

Content

Font Color:

Navigation

Menus

Main Navigation Headings

Sub-Headings

Content

Color for the Links:

External link

Internal link

Spacing:

Text space for the content

Space between navigation bars on the side(s) and body

Main Navigation Headings

Sub-Heading

Content

Text in field

Next button

Back button

META Tag:

Keywords

Description

Your index.htm page should contain appropriate Meta tags

Dynamic Pages:

Which database and server will be used? (e.g., Access or SQL; php or cfm)

Where will each be located? Provide Department that hosts them and contact person's name, email & phone #

How will dynamic pages be related and interact with other pages?

II. Media Types & Related Info

Graphics:

Size of graphics (W x H in Pixels)
File size
Compression steps and color
Naming Alt tags
Types of graphic files

Audio:

Length of audio (time)
Maximum file size (MB)
Types of audio clip
Compression
Audio display (will audio be in htm full page or window?)
Looping

Video:

Length (time)
Maximum file size (MB)
Types of movie clip
Window size
Frame rate for the movie
Compression
Video display (will video be in htm full page or window?)
Looping
Opening and ending screens

Flash Movies:

Maximum file size of Flash (MB)

Window size of Flash movie

Color scheme of Flash movies

Provide the explanation for the waiting time.

Write-up on what people will miss if they do not see your Flash site

Skip Flash movie option

PDF File:

Graphics in PDF

Color or black and white

Page size

III. Testing Guideline and What to Consider

Platform Consideration:

Mac and PC

Browser Consideration:

Browser versions

Testing in Browsers:

Test without graphics

Test on different platforms

Test with different major browsers

Test in different monitor/screen settings

Test with different color choices (True 32 bit to 256)

Test buttons and links

Test audio, video, movies

Test download and performance speed with different modems

Flash Tests:

Test downloading Flash movies on PC/Mac platforms

Test Flash movies on major browsers

Test linking from one Flash movie to another Flash movie.

IV. File Organization

Web Files:

Create and name a folder where all files such as HTML, graphics, and media (audio, video, animation) files will reside when they are uploaded to the Web server. Use simple and meaningful word(s).

Create second level folders for graphics, media, and each section within the first level folder and name each folder.

Example:

images

videos

section1

section2

Title the home page and put it in the first level folder

Example:

index.htm

Title the main or home page for each section and place it in the second level folder you have created above.

Example:

section1.htm

section2.htm

Database Files:

Name the file using simple and meaningful word(s). Upload the file to the appropriate location on the Web server.

File Naming:

Label all files with the appropriate suffix

Example:

.htm .cfm .doc .gif .jpg

.mov .php .avi .mpg .wav .swf

Give file names meaningful titles. The title of the pages is usually the best file name. The purpose of the graphic is the best file name. For filenames it is a good idea to limit the filename to 8 characters, use all lowercase, and use underscore in place of spacing.

Example:

funding.htm

cognitive.htm

backgrnd.gif

techhmpc.jpg

For pages with the same title that may be part of a sequence, give the title a number.

Example:

funding.htm

funding2.htm

funding3.htm

Final Versions vs. In-Progress Versions:

When developing graphics and video, it is important to maintain a clear record of revisions. Many times you or someone else must go back and modify a graphic after it has been placed on the Web. It is recommended to clearly label the original files. Name your files in the same manner as you would for finished material but with the program suffix (.psd, .fla, .png).

For graphics and movie files, be sure to save the original un-flattened files as well as the .gif or .jpg file, or .mov files.

In-Progress Files:

You may be working on a particular file over a period of time. For files that have a few simple changes done to them, just save them under the current file name. When major modifications occur, give the file a version number.

Example:

techhmpc.psd

techhmpcV1.psd

techhmpcV2.psd

It is a good idea to keep all versions of your files and store them in appropriate places (e.g., a portable backup device or hard-drive) for future reference.

Final Versions:

Upload all final versions of the files to the designated space on a server.

If you are creating movies, make a folder for that movie and place all files used to compile your final movie, including raw footage and graphics files, within that folder and name the folder appropriately.

It is a good idea to archive these final versions of files.

Files Not Used:

Some of your work may not be used at all. You may place them on a storage device to be archived with all the other files at the end of the project for future reference.

Chapter IV

Instructional Designers on the Borderline: Brokering Across Communities of Practice

Michael J. Keppell, Hong Kong Institute of Education, Hong Kong

Abstract

This chapter examines the unique role of instructional designers within the university setting, particularly when their knowledge is combined with leadership positions to broker across communities of practice. In their role as brokers, they coordinate multi-disciplinary projects and collaborations that foster connections across communities of practice, acting effectively as language translators. The instructional designer has an influential position in an organisation when they can utilise their multi-disciplinary perspective to create new possibilities for innovative design and professional development. This borderline position needs to be carefully managed as it is a precarious balance between being accepted as a change agent, and being ineffective. This chapter will outline a case study that examines the role of an instructional designer in influencing institutional change through the introduction of blended learning.

Introduction

Instructional designers have a unique professional role as they apply their knowledge and skills to the improvement of teaching and learning in many different disciplines. Within the university context these disciplines may include medicine, nursing, dentistry, law and education. Instructional designers may be involved in a range of activities, from focusing on individual projects through to leading major faculty-wide and institution-wide initiatives. For instance, Mitchell, Keppell, and Johnston (2005) designed a multimedia module to advance the practice of preparing children and families for hospitalisation. At a higher level, Keppell (2002) discussed the development of multimedia programs that were used to complement a problem-based learning curriculum in a health sciences faculty. This chapter will focus on an institution-wide initiative that introduces blended learning in a university context.

Instructional designers have enormous potential to influence the policy and practices of university institutions, because they have a unique position within the institution. This unique position may include institution-wide roles such as professional developers and centre directors who focus on enhancing teaching and learning, or enhancing the capability of academic staff. These concepts of change-management and agency of change are also reflected in the research literature. For instance, there has been a recent trend to focus on the change-agent role of the instructional designer within organizations, as opposed to specific instructional design models (Schwier, Campbell, & Kenny, 2004). Schwier, Campbell, and Kenny (2004) also suggest that instructional designers have the potential to transform the institution in which they work through their professional practice. The ability to transform professional practice has implications for both the current and future roles of instructional designers. This chapter examines how instructional designers can influence organizational change, particularly when they hold leadership positions within an institution. As the director of three educational technology centres over the last 12 years, the author has been at the forefront of instigating change across and within institutions.

The author will document how instructional designers act as change agents in the university through the process of *brokering* (Wenger, 1998). Instructional designers may be able to broker across faculty and departmental communities to develop innovative practice in professional settings. By acting as brokers, instructional designers translate between different communities of practice—in a way similar to a language translator—and coordinate multi-disciplinary projects that foster connections across and within communities of practice. As a "border dweller," the instructional designer has a unique vantage point that may allow new possibilities for innovative design and professional development, and allow for the transformation of practice within the institution. This chapter examines the concept of the instructional designer as a broker, and the implementation of blended learning as an institute-wide initiative within a traditional university in Hong Kong.

Communities of Practice

A community of practice can be defined as "groups of people who share a concern, a set of problems, or a passion about a topic, and who deepen their knowledge and expertise in this area by interacting on an ongoing basis" (Wenger, McDermott, & Snyder, 2002, p. 4). University departments are a typical example of a community of practice. Roth (1998) suggested that communities "are identified by the common tasks members engage in and the associated practices and resources, unquestioned background assumptions, common sense, and mundane reason they share" (Barab & Duffy, 2000, p. 10). For instance, an instructional designer working with a Chinese department in Hong Kong, versus an English department, may need to utilise different approaches, as each department is likely to have different practices, assumptions and departmental customs. Barab and Duffy (2000) also suggest a number of characteristics of communities of practice. Firstly, they have common cultural and historical heritages with shared goals, belief systems and collective stories. Learners need to access and inherit this heritage to become enculturated into the community of practice. This assures the continuity of the community through the acceptance of new members. Secondly, within a community, the individual transforms and maintains the community by learning the practice. At the same time the community transforms and maintains the individual by allowing them to become gradually enculturated. Thirdly, communities also have a reproduction cycle, which allows newcomers to move from peripheral to core membership through a process of enculturation. Legitimate peripheral participation appears to be a "primary motivation for learning and involves participating in authentic activities and creating an identity that moves an individual toward becoming more centripetal to a community of practice" (Barab & Duffy, 2000, p. 39).

Core Professional Membership

Learners study a field of knowledge within the university setting for a significant period of time. For example, medical students gradually learn what is expected of them within their field of practice through the process of enculturation. In studying a problem-based learning curriculum, they learn the process of how to make a diagnosis and work with patients. "Problem-based learning is an example of one approach to creating practice fields" as students "are presented with real historical patients to diagnose" (Barab & Duffy, 2000, p. 30). The medical students have the status of legitimate peripheral participation when they begin their degree program and work towards attaining full participation within the medical profession. They may also specialise and enter other communities of practice and work towards attaining full participation as a radiologist, dermatologist, psychiatrist, pediatrician, and so forth. In this case, learners will need to master knowledge and skills and "move towards full participation in the socio-cultural practices of the community" (Lave & Wenger, 1991, p. 29). Through this process, newcomers become part of the community of practice, and eventually attain the status of core members with full participation in the professional community of practice. This process is similar whether one is a lawyer, doctor, engineer, or accountant, and it appears to be the goal of most professionals.

Peripheral Access to Communities of Practice

Although instructional designers attain core membership in their own field of instructional design, there is one major difference from many other professions. Instructional designers specifically apply their skills in other communities of practice as a core function of their role. Instructional designers and academic staff-developers may work across several departments in an institution-wide role, which means they may not be core members of a faculty or department. For this reason, instructional designers may never attain core membership in any of the faculty or departmental communities of practice in which they work. This is because they have never progressed from peripheral membership to core membership of the specific community. Instructional designers must therefore address this unique factor as they work in institution-wide roles. However, although this could be considered to be a disadvantage, the peripheral membership of the instructional designer within university faculties and departments can provide a unique perspective for influencing institutional change (Keppell, 2004).

Wenger (1998) suggested that, "peripherality is an ambiguous position" (p. 118). It is ambiguous because it can be a welcoming experience at some times, while at other times it can be confronting. It can be both an open door and a closed door at the same time, varying between a welcoming experience as if you are a full member, to, at times, feeling excluded or being an intruder. Wenger (1998) also suggested that there is "a degree of permeability" between peripheral membership and core membership (p. 117). This permeability represents an important concept for instructional designers, as it enables them to interact on a casual but legitimate basis with different communities of practice.

By undertaking their role on the boundary of other professional communities, instructional designers have opportunities to understand organisations in different ways. It may be that "understanding is something one does best when one is on the borderline" (Hoeg, 1994, p. 37). Wenger (1998) took a similar view and suggested that, "understanding is always straddling the known and unknown in a subtle dance of itself" (p. 41). Increased understanding may be the key aspect of being a peripheral member of multiple communities of practice in a university. Instructional designers may therefore have a unique perspective and understanding of the institution in which they work, which can be beneficial when instigating institutional change. This cross-disciplinary understanding of the institution, and the concept of change agent, may foster innovative professional practice within the university. Unlike new professionals who work towards core membership and full acceptance in a community of practice, the instructional designer must obtain a high degree of legitimacy in order to be successful through their peripheral membership.

Legitimate Participation of the Instructional Designer

Instructional designers tend to be process-oriented individuals, in order to apply design principles to a wide range of unfamiliar content areas to enhance learning in face-to-face, blended learning, distance education and technology-enhanced environments. Designers assist in the learning design of content by utilising principles from cognitive, constructivist and social-constructivist theories. The designer has a generic "design model," which can assist in developing learning interactions, activities and learning spaces to engage learners. This design model includes the designer's beliefs about teaching and learning (behaviourist, cognitive, constructivist and social constructivist) and a repertoire of learning designs such as project-based learning, problem-based learning, case-based learning, authentic learning interactions, online communities and technology-enhanced learning environments. This approach is process-oriented and focuses on utilising principles, as opposed to procedures, to design learning interactions. Willis (2000) likewise calls for constructivist instructional design and suggested three principles of recursion, reflection and participation. Recursion suggests that design is not linear, but is recursive and iterative like a spiral. It also allows for collaborative input from the design team. Reflective design suggests that an experienced designer approaches an instructional design problem using a heuristic, as opposed to a procedure. Participatory design involves the user in the design process as an active contributor.

In addition, instructional designers are often confronted with ill-structured problems to solve at many levels, from individual projects through to an institution-wide level. These ill-structured problems may include issues such as integration, staff capacity, and acceptance of new forms of teaching and learning, such as blended learning. Design is an ambiguous activity by nature (Keppell, 2003). Instructional designers also face ambiguous milieu by being only peripheral members of the communities of practice with which they work. However, the concept of ambiguity can be used to advantage by the instructional designers as they work with different departments and faculties. As suggested by Wenger (1998), "ambiguity is not simply an obstacle to overcome; it is an inherent condition to be put to work" (p. 84). In other words, if we begin with ambiguity as a context, we can then determine strategies to utilise ambiguity as an opportunity for negotiation. Negotiation provides an opportunity for designers to open dialogue with academic colleagues, which has the potential to explore the advantages of new initiatives like blended learning.

Instructional Designers as Brokers

This chapter focuses on the application of brokering by an instructional designer involved in introducing blended learning to a university. Brokering is defined as "connections provided by people who can introduce elements of one practice into another" (Wenger, 1998, p. 105). Because the instructional designer is able to liaise with different departments and faculties, there will be different implementations of a new initiative, such as blended learning, due to the different departmental contexts. Instructional designers need to creatively account for the different departmental context as they discuss the relevance of blended learning in other contexts. Brown and Duguid (2001) suggested that, "the greater challenge lies in brokering knowledge across the borders that lie between practice" (p. 59). In addition, Wenger (1998) also suggested that, "brokering…involves processes of translation, coordination, and alignment between perspectives. It requires enough legitimacy to influence the development of the practice, mobilize attention, and address conflicting interests. It also requires the ability to link practices by facilitating transactions between them, and to cause learning, by introducing into a practice, elements of another" (p. 109). It is essential to understand that in any organisation, each community of practice overlaps with other communities of practice. If it is possible to deconstruct the various aspects of this definition, characteristics of brokering can be identified that are useful for instructional design.

Brokering Involves Translation

Instructional designers must act in a similar way to a language translator. They must interpret a departmental context, understand its uniqueness, and then translate principles relevant to the academic practitioners in the department into terms they can understand. By a process of negotiation and creative design, instructional designers should be able to provide a basis for the adoption of a new initiative such as blended learning. They are able to link practices, and potentially influence learning by another department. To be able to translate effectively, the instructional designer needs to have a "broad understanding of all the communities involved" (Brown & Duguid, 2001, p. 59). Good translators rely on trust and are "extremely valuable, extremely powerful and, equally, extremely difficult to find" (p. 60).

Brokering Involves Alignment Between Perspectives

This is similar to Biggs's (1999) model of "constructive alignment" which suggests synergy between the curriculum, teaching methods, assessment procedures, interactions with students, and institutional climate. In this case, constructive alignment occurred between the strategic plan, teaching and learning development plan, departmental approach to teaching and learning and academic teaching and learning strategies. In this case, the instructional designer explicitly linked macro and micro perspectives across the institution.

Brokering Requires Legitimacy to Influence the Development of Practice

Academic staff-developers and instructional designers focus on enhancing teaching and learning, and need to carefully manage their own credibility to be able to influence practice. For this reason, as an initial step, instructional designers need to hold academic staff appointments in order to have sufficient credibility to influence practice. Wenger (1998) suggested that, "newcomers must be granted enough legitimacy to be treated as potential new members" (p. 101). Instructional designers need to have some common memberships with academic staff that allows informal communication channels between communities.

Brokering Relies on the Individual to Have Diverse Identities

We all participate in multiple communities of practice in our daily and professional lives. Instructional designers working as change agents must foster multi-membership as a principle of their work within the university setting. For instance, as the head of a centre and associate professor, the author has the following diverse identities: academic staff member, teacher, lecturer, middle manager, instructional designer, educational technologist, researcher, administrator, department head, multi-committee representative, as well as holding international memberships in professional associations, and so forth. Although it is sometimes difficult to juggle multi-memberships, it is essential that the instructional designer fosters, enhances and maintains these memberships as a means of assisting in the introduction of university-wide initiatives. Without an awareness of concerns and issues at multiple levels of an organisation, the instructional designer may be ineffective. To be successful, the instructional designer must manage membership and non-membership by "yielding enough distance to bring a different perspective, but also enough legitimacy to be listened to" (Wenger, 1998, p. 110).

This principle is probably the most difficult to choreograph, as the communities of practice are constantly evolving and changing.

Brokering may be Best Suited to Certain Individuals

Brokers by nature may tend to thrive on challenging, ill-structured situations, which require a high degree of evaluation, synthesis and reconceptualising of professional practice. Good brokers enjoy being able to create connections across different communities of practice. They also prefer being on the boundary of professional practices as opposed to being a core member of one professional practice in a university setting. The predominant motivation may be creativity, as they are able to open new possibilities for meaning, and design creative and innovative approaches to ill-structured problems (Wenger, 1998).

Case Description

The following case examines the implementation of blended learning across an institution in Hong Kong by the author, who utilises brokering as an integral part of his work. This case will examine the approaches and challenges involved in this major organisational change. Blended learning, which involves a combination of face-to-face teaching and online learning, may represent "the single greatest unrecognized trend in higher education today" (Young, 2002, p. 33). This simple definition of blended learning does not focus on instructional modalities or blended instructional methods, as these definitions can encompass all forms of learning (Graham, 2006). As head of the Centre for Learning, Teaching and Technology (LTTC), instructional designer and professional developer, the author will outline the context, challenges, strategies, recommendations and principles of the case study.

Context

Institutional Context

The Hong Kong Institute of Education (HKIEd) is a dedicated teacher-education university, and one of eight universities within Hong Kong. Within the Institute, there are two faculties and eight departments. The Faculty of Languages, Arts and Sciences oversees the Departments of Chinese; English; Creative Arts and Physical Education; and Mathematics, Science, Social Sciences and Technology. The Faculty of Professional and Early Childhood Education oversees the Departments of Curriculum and Instruction; Early Childhood Education; Educational Policy and Administration; and Educational Psychology, Counseling and Learning Needs. Although each of these departments is part of a single Institute of Education, they each have a distinctive culture, academic tribe and academic ideas. In this context, culture refers to "sets of taken-for-granted values, attitudes and ways of behaving, which are articulated through, and reinforced by, recurrent practices among a group of people in a given context" (Becher & Trowler, 2001, p. 23). There are approximately 350 academic staff and 700 non-academic staff on campus. Approximately 70% of modules are taught in Cantonese and 30% in English. There are approximately 8,000 full-time and part-time students. All modules are traditionally taught in a face-to-face mode.

The institute has a relatively short history in the use of blended learning. In September 2003, the institute adopted the Blackboard multi-lingual learning management system (LMS) to enable teaching online in both English and Chinese. The Centre for Learning, Teaching and Technology (LTTC) is responsible for the coordination of the professional development activities and pedagogical aspects of the Blackboard LMS. The interactive aspects of the Blackboard LMS are emphasised throughout all professional development activities of the LTTC. The LTTC works in conjunction with Information Technology and Services (ITS), who provide infrastructure for the LMS. As an indication of the usage of online learning, the following details are provided for a typical semester of teaching. In Semester 2 of 2004/05, 53% (176) of academic staff utilised the online learning platform for teaching and learning. There were 367 modules that utilised the Blackboard LMS in academic departments. *Table 1* outlines the percentage of academic staff in the eight academic departments who utilise the Blackboard LMS for teaching and learning.

Centre Context

The Centre for Learning, Teaching and Technology has a primary role in fostering the use of blended learning across the Institute. It is an Institute-level centre that has the dual role within the Institute of fostering appropriate integration of information and communication technology (ICT) and enhancing professional development of academic staff in teaching and learning. In particular, the LTTC:

Table 1. Percentage of academic staff utilising the Blackboard LMS in one semester in the 2004/05 academic year

Department	Percentage of Academic Staff in Each Department who use the Blackboard LMS
Creative Arts and Physical Education	30%
Chinese	73%*
English	59%
Mathematics, Science, Social Science and Technology	46%
Curriculum and Instruction	82%
Early Childhood Education	29%
Educational Policy and Administration	71%
Educational Psychology, Counselling and Learning Needs	52%

**Chapter XIV discusses the implementation of blended learning in the Chinese department at the Institute of Education (HKIEd)*

- is proactive in monitoring and promoting best practice in teaching, learning and educational technology in higher education;
- works collaboratively and at multiple levels—with faculties, departments, individual staff, and students;
- supports innovations in teaching, learning and educational technology that enrich the students' experience of learning;
- promotes blended learning, learner autonomy, learning-oriented assessment, peer learning, and project-based and problem-based learning; and
- initiates and conducts research into teaching, learning, assessment and educational technology in higher education.

Figure 1 conceptualises the functioning of the centre in relation to blended learning by combining the levels of engagement (institute, faculties, departments, individual academic staff, students) and the specific themes of peer learning, learner autonomy, learning-oriented assessment, inquiry-based learning (problem-based and project-based learning), educational technology and research.

In addition, the explicit management approach to the Centre focuses on the concept of a learning organization (Senge, 1990). Integral to this approach are aspects of building shared vision (goals, values and missions that are understood); accounting for mental models (deeply ingrained assumptions of how we understand the world); team learning (thinking together, achieving something that cannot be achieved alone); and personal mastery (continually learning and improving) (Senge, 1990). A learning organisation continually evolves by building learning into all day-to-day practice.

Individual Context

This chapter suggests that instructional designers broker across communities of practice to foster institutional change, so it is important to examine the individual role of the instructional designer within this context. This section has been quoted from the position description of the Centre Head (the author). "The Centre Head will be expected to foster excellence in research, learning enhancement, teaching, professional development activities and policy development in relation to the application of information and communications technologies (ICT) and professional development activities for teaching and learning by academic staff."

In particular, the following responsibilities are relevant to this chapter:

- Development and promotion of institutional teaching and learning strategies that exploit the potential of ICT (information and communications technologies) in interactive and innovative methods of teaching, learning and assessment;
- The development of institutional plans for ICT, online learning, and professional development which account for future strategic directions of the institute;
- Leadership in the design, development, delivery, evaluation and research of online learning;

Figure 1. Strategic focus of the LTTC in relation to blended learning

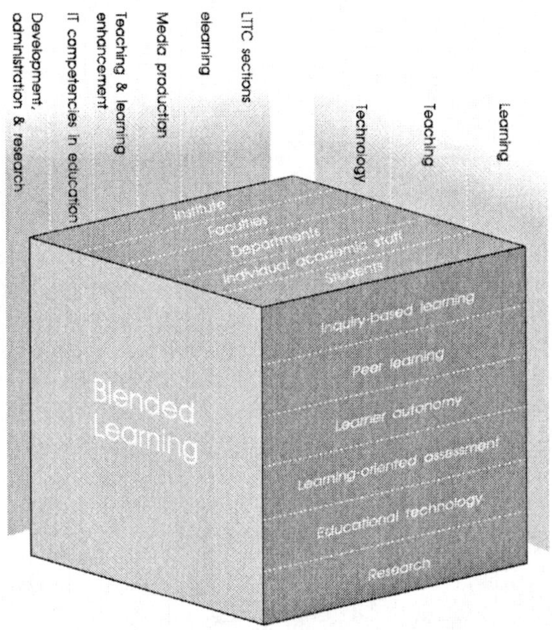

- Overall management of the online learning management system (e.g., Blackboard) to complement the Institute's strategic teaching and learning developments;
- Developing policy and providing leadership within the institute.

Multi-membership is an essential factor in achieving these goals, and it has been essential for the Centre Head to be involved in a range of strategic initiatives. He was a member of the Institute Strategic Planning Committee that developed the Institute's strategic directions for 2006-2012. In addition, the author assisted in the development of the Institute Teaching and Learning Development Plan, and is a member of several middle management and other decision-making committees. It is essential that an instructional designer makes new connections through these multi-memberships, and begins to examine new possibilities for meaning by brokering across each departmental community of practice. It is also important to examine the challenges to an institutional change such as blended learning, as major undertakings like this are met with both enthusiasm and resistance.

Challenges

There are a number of challenges to the introduction of blended learning across an institution with diverse departmental perspectives. One major challenge involved the constructive alignment of blended learning with the Institute Strategic Plan, the Teaching and Learning Development Plan and the Strategic Plan of the LTTC. In addition there needed to be constructive alignment between the approaches of the instructional designer and the strategies utilised by the academic staff. *The overall goal was to develop academic staff capacity to use blended learning as an integral part of ALL modules within the Institute.* Table 2 outlines the explicit constructive alignment of blended learning from the Institute Strategic Plan, Teaching and Learning Development Plan and the Strategic Plan of the LTTC.

Strategies

Academic development/professional development is defined as the "provision of pedagogically sound and discipline relevant development for academic staff across the broad spectrum of disciplines present within a university so as to impact effectively on student learning" (Hicks, 1999, p. 12). Stefani (2003) suggested that the educational development offers opportunities for staff to develop their full potential and the following professional development approach focuses on enhancing innovative teaching and learning through blended learning at the institutional level. The approach articulates the need to work in different ways. It is necessary to work vertically across the Institute by working with senior management, deans and heads of department. It is also necessary to work horizontally across the Institute with academic staff and other departments and centres (Macdonald, 2003).

Firstly, initial approaches to the discussion of blended learning with academic staff (one-to-one consultations, seminars, workshops, projects, etc.) have focused on defining blended learning. For instance, what are the distinguishing features of the approach? Discussion has revolved around differentiating supplemental applications of online learning with blended learning approaches. Supplemental applications retain the same in-class time and tasks, and add online learning to teach a course. The disadvantage of this approach is that the online component creates additional work for both the academic staff member and the students. A preferred approach is to blend off-line and online work in an appropriate way to enhance teaching and learning (Littlejohn, 2005). Blended learning combines face-to-face teaching approaches with online learning to best achieve learning outcomes. The emphasis is on enhanced learning and teaching by using the unique affordances of the medium. An expanded range of learning spaces can be created for students and teachers. Fully online modules focus on using the affordances of the learning management system to teach the entire course. The use of fully online modules may be a future initiative of the Institute in certain areas of the curriculum. This discussion involves the instructional designer explaining the approaches through exemplars used across the campus. This provides concrete ideas for other colleagues to adopt.

Blended learning emphasises the creation of *alternative learning spaces*. This approach emphasises both the pedagogical dimensions and affordances of the technology in a synergistic relationship. *Alternative* suggests that there are different ways of teaching and learning that are undertaken by any good teacher. Academic teachers make choices as to which approach is more appropriate for the learner. Educators often attempt to provide multiple ways of approaching teaching to optimise the learning of students. *Learning spaces* refer to both real and virtual learning spaces that can be utilised for teaching and learning. For instance, in a face-to-face class, small group discussion can be undertaken on the topic of Web design. A student may be asked to facilitate the discussion by making sure all students have some input into the discussion topic. This learning space allows students to see and hear about the

Table 2. Constructive alignment of blended learning within the institute

Goal: To develop academic staff capacity to use **blended learning** as an integral part of ALL modules within the institute.
Institute Strategic Plan The strategic objectives and strategies relevant to this strategic objective include: • To provide more learning opportunities and educational experiences for our students through a flexible curriculum that will prepare them as education professionals who adapt easily and effectively to different work settings. • To promote teaching that will stimulate students to become independent, analytical, critical and creative thinkers who can readily apply their knowledge. • To continue to develop a supportive campus environment that will help students take responsibility for their learning, facilitate their social and intellectual engagement and prepare them as educated and responsible local and global citizens. • To encourage students to make better use of the institute's rich learning environment, e.g., the library, IT and language facilities (Institute Strategic Plan 2006-2012).
Institute Development Plan – Goals for Teaching and Learning • Students working collaboratively in face-to-face and online learning settings • The use of educational technology integrated into teaching and learning • The use of online learning in modules, as appropriate, to create alternative learning spaces (Teaching and Learning Development Plan)

LTTC Strategic Plan
Strategy 1: To **support** academic staff in the use of the Blackboard learning management system (LMS)
• Provide user support for staff and students
• Assist staff and students to use the affordances of the Blackboard LMS
• Create new modules for academic staff
• Compile reports in relation to support on a bi-annual basis
 	
Strategy 2: To encourage staff to utilize **blended learning** in their teaching and learning through both proactive and reactive strategies such as: 1-1 consultations, in-class demonstrations, projects, workshops, seminars, guest speakers, self-directed learning modules.
• 10% annual increase in staff utilizing blended learning
• Fully develop online learning workshops and **self-instructional resources** on:
    ■ Building your First Online Module
    ■ Blended Learning Design
    ■ Moderating Online Communication
    ■ Online Problem-based and Project-based Learning
    ■ Online Assessment
 	
Strategy 3: To support each department receiving **IT Development Grants**
• Provide 100 hours of in-kind support for each department
• Complete departmental workshops for each department
• Work in conjunction with departments to develop their ITDG
• Organise and develop lunch-time seminars for reporting on each ITDG project
• Complete video-interviews with each team and archive material on the LTTC Web site for other staff at the institute
• Further develop the dissemination of ITDG outcomes through the LTTC Web site

Table 3. Alternative learning spaces and their affordance within the Blackboard learning management system

Blackboard Learning Space	Affordance
Announcements	• regular one-way communication with students e.g., welcome message for each class • overview/advance organizer for each class
Course information	• posting general documentation about module • allows the attachment of word documents, e.g., module outline, schedule, assessment outlines
Staff information	• contact details • office location, consultation times, etc. • personal background and pedagogical approach of lecturer
Course material	• posting of presentation files and handouts for each class • creation of separate folders • lecture notes provided to students as a scaffold for note-taking in the face-to-face class
Assignments	• intermittent quizzes or surveys • weekly revision quiz • assessment items
Books	• list of recommended books or chapter readings
Communication	• e-mail to individual students, groups or entire class • list of students in module with their homepages
Discussion board	• whole class discussion forums (asynchronous) • writing activities • critical thinking activities (e.g., evaluation, synthesis, multiple perspectives, etc.) • summaries of readings and peer feedback • class presentations via PowerPoint and debates • use of external websites, images, photos, video and audio to initiate and enhance student discussion • non-course related discussion – area for general discussion to foster the development of a community atmosphere • peer support network discussion forum allows students to provide feedback to each other (24/7) • student and tutor facilitation of discussion
Groups	• small group clustering for group projects and activities • synchronous class discussion < 10 students • 1-person groups – reflective journals, field experience reflective journals and lecturer reflective journals • partner activities • area allows discussion within group, file exchange within group, e-mail within group and synchronous communication within group
External links	• links to Web sites • online resources
Students tools	• assignment submission to lecturer • creating a homepage
Assessment	• development of quizzes and surveys that can be tracked by the lecturer

multiple perspectives of other students in relation to Web design. The learning space is both physical (students seated around a table in a circle) and cognitive. The learning space in this instance *affords* listening to other students' ideas about Web design. This should reinforce their own design principles if they constantly evaluate and synthesise other students' ideas in relation to their own. However, an alternative learning space for this activity could use a virtual learning space. In an online environment, students could discuss the same topic on Web design with the same group of students and student facilitator. In this instance, instead of listening to other students' perspectives, the technology *affords* the use of writing about their perspective, so that other students can read their ideas. The same activity has used a similar pedagogical approach that has considered the affordances of the specific learning space. Figure 2 attempts to detail the affordances of the learning management system utilised at the Institute for professional development purposes. The concept of alternative learning spaces provides an important instructional design approach in encouraging academic colleagues to utilise blended learning for sound pedagogical reasons.

Secondly, a number of critical decisions about the approach to blended learning need to be considered. Littlejohn (2005) suggested that there are at least three main design considerations: development of learner activities, integration of online and off-line tasks and the affordances of the technology. Herrington and Oliver (2001) suggested that it is useful to differentiate the different forms of blended learning. *Information access* conveys information alone to the learner and may be useful for delivering the module, assessment, presentation and task outlines to the students. However this is not blended learning. *Interactive learning* increases the level of engagement with the resources. Examples include asking students to search and review documents, search a database, view a Web site and examine a multimedia module. *Networked learning* provides communication between students and teachers. Examples include discussion forums, group tasks, online debates and real-time chats. *Materials development* emphasizes learner autonomy and peer learning, and asks students to develop and present products and artifacts. Examples include the development of digital stories, reflective journals, reports, presentations, videos, portfolios and projects. Learning design will focus on designing a module using problem-based learning, project-based learning and authentic learning cases. It is essential that we differentiate these different forms of blended learning, as "universities and other educational institutions have failed to perceive the difference between educating learners and simply providing them with information and content" (Herrington, Reeves, & Oliver, 2005, p. 365).

A third strategy used a variety of approaches for enhancing staff capacity with blended learning. These ranged from one-to-one consultations, workshops, seminars, whole department approaches, development-based research approaches and the invitation of international speakers on blended learning. McCartan, Watson, Lewins, & Hodgson (2000) suggest that these types of initiatives are "enabling mechanisms … to ensure the effective use of learning technology" (p. 70). Most institutions utilise a variety of approaches for achieving their objectives in relation to professional development (O'Reilly, Ellis, & Newton, 2000; Weaver, 2006); however, the approach outlined below has two unique strategies: departmental grants and development-based research projects.

At the department level, the author managed and facilitated an internal grant allocation scheme in 2004/05 and 2005/06. Each department was allocated an internal Institute grant for developing online learning involving several staff members within each department. The amount of the grant was sufficient to hire a research assistant for 12 months. Most departments sought advice from the author before applying for the grant, which allowed the shaping of the grant to enhance its impact on teaching and learning at the Institute. This process of reviewing and making recommendations on grants in the initial stages of their development is a good example of brokering. As suggested previously, instructional design brokers open new possibilities for meaning and may enable creative design. Because the instructional designer was on the boundary of the departments, he could provide guidance from a unique perspective. The value of this early input into grants and projects from an instructional design perspective cannot be overestimated.

In addition, it was a requirement of the grant to include the head of department as the principal investigator. This approach was advocated by senior management and proved to be a highly strategic decision. This meant that each department head became a change agent for teaching and learning within their own department. The inclusion of the head of the department also assured a significant degree of impact for each grant. A departmental workshop was offered by the LTTC to provide ideas and enhance staff skills in the use of the Blackboard LMS. This workshop was carefully designed so that blended learning was used to enhance the teaching and learning of each department's specific content area. Around one-third of the departments arranged these workshops with the LTTC: Music, Visual Arts, Chinese, and Curriculum & Instruction. (In 2005, the existing 12 departments were restructured and renamed to form eight departments.)

Each department was required to report on their project through a presentation to Institute colleagues. This seminar provided an excellent means of encouraging members of each grant to reflect on their redesign of teaching modules and the benefits of blended learning. They needed to address the following questions in their seminar: What was the aim of your project? How did you modify your teaching practices using online learning? How did you evaluate your project? How did students respond to online learning in your department? The seminar also allowed each department to report on their progress to an audience of colleagues, which provided a sharing of ideas and advice to other academic staff who were implementing blended learning for the first time. To further enhance the sharing of ideas, the author interviewed each of the academics about their experiences in implementing blended learning in their teaching. These video interviews provided another means of sharing ideas within the Institute. As a means of disseminating these ideas to Institute staff, the video of the seminars and interviews with the staff were made available on the LTTC Web site. The streaming video summarises the key points used by each department in five-minute vignettes (see LTTC Web site, http://www.ied.edu.hk/lttc/).

Another approach utilised by the author in fostering institutional change was the use of development-based research projects in collaboration with Institute academic staff. Development-based research is defined as "research focused on the dual objectives of developing creative approaches to solving human teaching, learning, and performance problems while at the same time constructing a body of design principles that can guide future development efforts" (Reeves, 2000, p. 7) (see Figure 2). These teaching development grants and internal research grants focused on key aspects of blended learning including authentic assessment, peer learning, teacher-educator perceptions of online learning, problem-based learning, project-based learning, and learning design. The grants were obtained with the explicit purpose of completing innovative projects that would encourage the use of blended learning by academic staff, as well as create a critical mass of champions who would become ambassadors for encouraging change in teaching and learning at the institute. Jennings and

Figure 2. Development-based research process as outlined by Reeves (2000, p. 9)

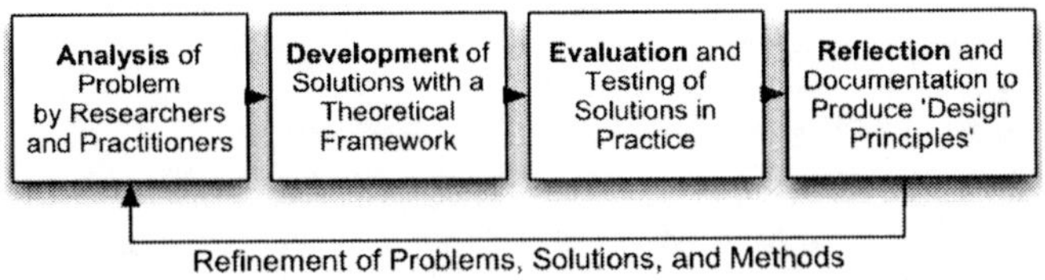

Dirksen (1997) support this approach, and suggest that when the change agent fosters a champion, they assist the diffusion process of the technology. More than 20 academic staff participated in these projects over the last three years. Some projects involved two years of analysis, design, evaluation and reflection about the use of blended learning, while others focused on integrating assessment activities. An additional aim of these projects was to form a collaborative environment for redesigning teaching and learning modules that would encourage innovation in blended learning. An incentive for each member of the team was an explicit agenda from the beginning of the project to develop a number of joint publications in relation to each project (see Keppell, Au, & Ma, 2005; Keppell, Au, Ma, & Chan, 2005, 2006).

One project examined teacher perceptions of online learning, and found that their perceptions of technology appeared to be key factors in the successful adoption of learning technologies (Keppell, Cote, Chen, Leung, Jones, & Richards, 2004). In addition, when learning technologies were considered to be part of the teaching approach, they were seen to be more readily integrated. For instance, one lecturer focused on the benefits of students learning from each other:

I saw an amazing opportunity for students to learn from one another, so the main purpose of this online part of the module [was] to get students to share their opinions; and interact; and learn from each other.

The reason why I think this is amazing is to encourage...my students to learn better and comprehend issues; and learn from one another; and also learn to respect other people's point of view.

Another lecturer also emphasised students learning from each other:

I think I would like to say...the student stands on other people's shoulders and...can see much farther than just by themselves...so they actually use other people's opinion, other people's contribution and...not only learn by themselves. I think this is the main advantage.

As the facilitator of each development-based research project, the author had three explicit professional development goals. These goals comprised the production of personal knowledge, local knowledge, and public knowledge (Ashwin & Trigwell, 2004). The investigation into learning-oriented assessment, peer learning, authentic assessment and blended learning focused on the production of personal knowledge. Personal knowledge development occurred throughout each of the development-based research projects, in the examination of individual beliefs about learning, teaching, technology and assessment, and the redesign of modules. Secondly, the participants in each of the projects produced local knowledge to inform departmental practices through the development of exemplars, which could be shown to other colleagues. Local knowledge was also exchanged through a number of presentations within the Institute setting. Thirdly, the projects produced public knowledge to inform a wider audience, including international academics, through publications and conference presentations. By focusing on the development of public knowledge, the team members also developed new personal knowledge. Ashwin and Trigwell (2004) suggested that most professional developers tend to focus on the development of personal knowledge, while often neglecting the development of public knowledge. A unique characteristic of this professional development approach within each project was the simultaneous focus on the production of personal, local and public knowledge.

Recommendations and Principles

Enhancing staff capacity in blended learning has been approached from an instructional design perspective throughout the implementation. In the initial stages it was important to examine whether blended learning was a needs-based priority. Prioritising focused on importance and feasibility (Sork, 1995). For instance, how many individuals would be affected by this need? In this instance the use of blended learning affected most staff and students within the institute. Academic staff, pre-service and in-service teachers learned about the advantages of blended learning for creating alternative learning spaces. These principles could then be used for their own teaching of kindergarten, primary and secondary school students. The feasibility of the initiative focused on how blended learning contributed to organisational goals. As outlined previously, blended learning was aligned with both the Institute Strategic Plan and the Institute Teaching and Learning Development Plan. The next question that needed to be asked focused on the willingness of the Institute to change (Sork, 1995). This was (and still is) the most difficult aspect of institutional change, and the following principles provide suggestions on achieving this goal.

Firstly, *systems-thinking* is essential when undertaking the development of blended learning at an institutional level. Systems-thinking is a conceptual framework that examines the interrelationships between management, teaching, learning, technology, students, academic staff and institutional goals. By brokering across communities of practice, the instructional designer is in an ideal position to manage these complex issues.

Secondly, as blended learning has gathered momentum, the *non-adopters* of an initiative often become the minority group. For instance, it was found that the "implementation of innovations required awareness on the part of and strong support from administrators...

and a climate that makes nonadopters feel as though they are 'out of it' unless they begin to adopt or move forward" (Altschuld & Witkin, 2000, p. 182).

Thirdly, it was important that all participants developed a *sense of ownership* with blended learning. In addition to developing a sense of ownership, it is necessary to allow staff sufficient time to adjust to the initiative. In any context "change and stability will always be in a subtle tug-of-war" (Altschuld & Witkin, 2000, p. 181), which needs to be carefully managed by the instructional design change agent. In addition, the implementation requires an ability to adapt blended learning so that it is useful to academic staff. This initiative needed to be fine-tuned and adapted throughout the last three years, and this process will probably continue for the next three years. Altschuld and Witkin (2000) also suggest that academic staff will need to "feel its texture" (p. 185) before they implement it. In other words, strategies that immerse staff in blended learning will be most effective. As soon as they see its relevance, the process of adoption is more acceptable. It is important to create a vision that has some significance for their teaching and learning (Sydanmaanlakka, 2002).

Fourthly, it is essential that we provide *evidence* that a new initiative like blended learning is effective in enhancing teaching and learning. Within the LTTC, the author focussed the role of one research assistant on analysing the usage of the Blackboard LMS for each semester. These statistics focused on analysing the usage of interactive features such as discussion groups and small group activities that would suggest more constructivist approaches to blended learning.

Fifthly, these reports were often explained to heads of departments and to senior management within the Institute. The introduction of blended learning is becoming a key change-agent which may influence teaching and learning at the Institute. It is a planned and strategic initiative that needs to become a mainstream approach of educational development centres, as opposed to responding to one-off teaching and learning initiatives. As suggested, it is essential that a centre like LTTC works closely with senior management by not only providing evidence for initiatives, but also "preparing people for likely futures before these arrive" (Percival & Tucker, 2004, p. 20). Blended learning is one attempt to do this at the Hong Kong Institute of Education. If there is ownership from senior management, deans, heads of departments and professional development centres, there is a strong possibility that initiatives like blended learning can be successful.

Conclusion

A key factor in this discussion has been the role of the instructional designer in institutional change. Instructional designers who are able to broker across communities of practice must be able to successfully *translate* principles from one department to another context. Because they are focusing on the institutional level, the instructional designer is able to assist in the *alignment* of perspectives in relation to an initiative such as blended learning. The designer must carefully manage their own *credibility,* and must model good practice in blended learning. Being able to juggle *diverse identities* and multi-membership is critical to being able to understand the real issues and concerns. Successful brokering across different communities of practice requires legitimate participation. By acting as brokers, instructional designers translate between different communities of practice, and coordinate multi-disciplinary projects and collaborations that foster connections across and within communities of practice.

The above discussion has examined the role of the instructional designer as broker within a higher education setting. It has examined the explicit strategic and operational factors used by the author in the implementation of blended learning at a university-level institute in Hong Kong. Although the initiative has been largely successful, there is still a long journey to progress the use of blended learning and alternative learning spaces across the Institute. The next step in the process is the development of an Institute policy on the use of blended learning. This policy should assist to further consolidate the importance of blended learning within the Institute, and should provide further opportunities for negotiation.

References

Altschuld, J.W., & Witkin, B.R. (2000). *From needs assessment to action: Transforming needs into solution strategies.* Thousand Oaks, CA: Sage Publications.

Ashwin, P., & Trigwell, K. (2004). Investigating staff and educational development. In D. Baume & P. Kahn (Eds.), *Enhancing staff and educational development* (pp. 117-131). London: Routledge Falmer.

Barab, S.A., & Duffy, T.M. (2000). From practice fields to communities of practice. In D.H. Jonassen & S.M. Land (Eds.), *Theoretical foundations of learning environments.* (pp. 25-55). Mahwah, NJ: Lawrence Erlbaum Associates.

Becher, T., & Trowler, P.R. (2001). *Academic tribes and territories* (2nd ed.). Suffolk, UK: The Society for Research into Higher Education & Open University Press.

Biggs, J. (1999). *Teaching for quality learning at university.* Suffolk, UK: Society for Research into Higher Education & Open University Press.

Brown, J.S., & Duguid, P. (2001). Structure and spontaneity: Knowledge and organization. In I. Nonaka & D.J. Teece (Eds.), *Managing industrial knowledge: Creation, transfer and utilisation.* (pp. 44-67). London: Sage Publications.

Graham, C.R. (2006). Blended learning systems: Definition, current trends, and future directions. In C.J. Bonk & C.R. Graham (Eds.), *The handbook of blended learning: Global perspectives, local designs* (pp. 3-21). San Francisco: Pfeiffer.

Herrington, J., Reeves, T.C., & Oliver, R. (2005). Online learning as information delivery: Digital myopia. *Journal of Interactive Learning Research, 16*(4), 353-367.

Hoeg, P. (1993). *Borderliners.* New York: Delta Trade Paperbacks.

Jennings, M.M., & Dirkson, D.J. (1997). Facilitating change: A process for adoption of web-based instruction. In B.H. Khan (Ed.), *Web-based instruction* (pp. 111-116). Englewood Cliffs, NJ: Educational Technology Publications.

Keppell, M. (2002). Creating quality multimedia and online learning: Blending management, design, development, evaluation and training. In H. Hansson (Ed.), *Eight contributions on quality and flexible learning* (Report 1:2002) (pp. 69-89). Distum: Swedish Agency for Distance Education. Nybrogatan.

Keppell, M. (2003). Making explicit our theories of teaching and learning: Designs that motivate our work as instructional designers. In G. Crisp, D. Thiele, I. Scholten, S. Barker, & J. Baron (Eds.), *Interact, Integrate, Impact: Proceedings of the 20th Annual Conference of the Australasian Society for Computers in Tertiary Education* (Vol. 2, pp. 633-637). Adelaide, Australia.

Keppell, M. (2004, June 21-26). Legitimate participation? Instructional designer-subject matter expert interactions in communities of practice. In L. Cantoni & C. McLoughlin (Eds.), *Proceedings of ED-MEDIA 2004 World Conference on Educational Multimedia, Hypermedia and Telecommunication* (pp. 3611-3618). Lugano, Switzerland.

Keppell, M., Au, E., & Ma, A. (2005). Authentic online assessment: Three case studies in teacher education. In S.L. Howell & M. Hricko (Eds.), *Online assessment and measurement: Case studies from higher education, K-12 and corporate* (pp. 42-61). Hershey, PA: Information Science Publishing.

Keppell, M., Au, E., Ma, A., & Chan, C. (2005). Curriculum development in technology-enhanced environments. In C. Howard, P. Rogers, J.V. Boettcher, G.A. Berg, L. Justice, & K. Schenk (Eds.), *Encyclopedia of distance learning* (Volumes I-IV, (pp. 492-504). Hershey, PA: Idea Group Reference.

Keppell, M., Au, E., Ma, A., & Chan, C. (2006). Peer learning and learning-oriented assessment in technology-enhanced environments. *Assessment and Evaluation in Higher Education, 31*(4), 453-464.

Keppell, M., Cote, P., Chen, S., Leung, P., Jones, J., & Richards, C. (2004). Staff perceptions of online learning: Five cases from a teacher-education setting in Hong Kong. In R. Atkinson, C. McBeath, D.J. Dwyer, & R. Phillips (Eds.), *Proceedings of the 21st Annual Conference of the Australasian Society for Computers in Tertiary Education,* Perth, Australia. Retrieved June 3, 2006, from: http://www.ascilite.org.au/conferences/perth04/procs/pdf/keppell.pdf

Lave, J., & Wenger, E. (1991). *Situated learning: Legitimate peripheral participation.* Cambridge University Press.

Littlejohn, A. (2005). *Planning for blended learning.* Institute for Learning Technology, University of Dundee, Scotland, UK. Paper presented at Hong Kong Institute of Education, Hong Kong, China.

LTTC. (2006). *Centre for Learning, Teaching and Technology.* Hong Kong Institute of Education. Retrieved May 5, 2006, from: http://www.ied.edu.hk/lttc/

Macdonald, R. (2003). Developing a scholarship of academic development: Setting the context. In H. Eggins & R. Macdonald (Eds.), *The scholarship of academic development.* Suffolk, UK: The Society for Research into Higher Education & Open University Press.

McCartan, A., Watson, B., Lewins, J., & Hodgson, M. (2000). Enabling learning through technology: Some institutional imperatives. In D. Squires, G. Conole, & G. Jacobs (Eds.), *The changing face of learning technology* (pp. 70-76). Cardiff: University of Wales Press.

Mitchell, M., Keppell, M., & Johnston, L. (2005). Using educational technology to advance the practice of preparing children and families for hospitalisation. In H. Goss (Ed.), *Balance, Fidelity, Mobility: Maintaining the Momentum? Proceedings of the 22nd Annual Conference of the Australasian Society for Computers in Tertiary Education* (pp. 483-492). Brisbane: Teaching and Learning Support Services, Queensland University of Technology.

O'Reilly, M., Ellis, A., & Newton, D. (2000). *The role of university Web pages in staff development: Supporting teaching and learning online*. AusWeb 2000. Retrieved December 2004, from http://ausweb.scu.edu.au/aw2k/papers/o_reilly/?paper.html

Oliver, R., & Herrington, J. (2001). *Teaching and learning online: A beginner's guide to e-learning and e-teaching in higher education.* Centre for Research in Information Technology and Communications. Edith Cowan University, Western Australia.

Percieval, F., & Tucker, G. (2004). Developing institutional policy and strategy for academic development: How can senior management and educational development units work productively together? In D. Baume & P. Kahn (Eds.), *Enhancing staff and educational development* (pp. 18-35). London: Routledge Falmer.

Reeves T.C. (2000). *Enhancing the worth of instructional technology research through "design experiments" and other development research strategies*. Paper presented on April 27, 2000, at session 41.29. International Perspectives on Instructional Technology Research for the 21st Century a Symposium sponsored by SIG/Instructional Technology at the Annual Meeting of the American Educational Research Association, New Orleans, LA, U.S. Retrieved November 1, 2005, from http://it.coe.uga.edu/~treeves/

Roth, W-M. (1998). *Designing communities*. Dordrecht, Germany: Kluwer Academic Publishers.

Schwier, R.A., Campbell, K., & Kenny, R. (2004). Instructional designers' observations about identity, communities of practice and change agency. *Australasian Journal of Educational Technology*, *20*(1) 69-100.

Senge, P.M. (1996). *The fifth discipline: The art and practice of the learning organization.* London: Currency and Doubleday.

Sork, T.J. (1995). *Needs assessment in adult education*. Workshop followed by Faculty of Extension, University of Alberta, Edmonton, Alberta, Canada.

Stefani, L. (2003). What is staff and educational development? In P. Kahn & D. Baume (Eds.), *A guide to staff & educational development* (pp. 9-23). London: Kogan Page.

Sydanmaanlakka, P. (2002). *An intelligent organization: Integrating performance, competence and knowledge management.* Oxford: Capstone.

The Hong Kong Institute of Education. (2006). *Strategic plan 2006-2012.* Hong Kong.

The Hong Kong Institute of Education. (2006, March). *Institute development plan for teaching and learning for 2006-2009 triennium.* Hong Kong.

Weaver, D. (2006). The challenges facing staff development in promoting quality online teaching. *International Journal on E-Learning*, *5*(2), 275-286.

Wenger, E. (1998). *Communities of practice: Learning, meaning and identity.* Cambridge University Press.

Wenger, E., McDermott, R., & Snyder, W.M. (2002). *Cultivating communities of practice.* Boston: Harvard Business School Press.

Young, J.R. (2002). Hybrid: Teaching seeks to end the divide between traditional and online instruction. *Chronicle of Higher Education*, 33.

Section II

Cross-Cultural Context

Chapter V

A Great Wall of Difference: Musings on Instructional Design in Contemporary China

Susan Crichton, University of Calgary, Canada

Abstract

Instructional design is typically viewed as a process for identifying and solving instructional problems. However, for designers who work on international development projects, the "western" assumptions of instructional design may pose particular challenges as project participants work together to find solutions to teaching and learning problems. The challenge is to find culturally sensitive ways to create resources and provide training for individuals who have different cultural backgrounds. After almost three years of work on the project shared in this article, there are still a number of questions. For example, why has there not been the development of a community of practice around instructional design with the project members? In addition, why has the Canadian project team been unable to encourage our Chinese colleagues to value the instructional design process? This paper offers a number of musings and insights about the field of instructional design within the Chinese context.

Introduction

Instructional design (ID), as a field of study and a growing profession, is typically viewed as a "...process for examining human performance problems and identifying solutions" (Rothwell & Kazanas, 2001, p. 5). However, for designers who work on international development projects, the "western" assumptions of instructional design may pose particular challenges as project participants work together to find solutions to teaching and learning problems. The challenge is to find culturally sensitive ways to create resources and provide training for individuals who have different cultural backgrounds. A further complexity occurs when the project also attempts to build the capacity of novice instructional designers. In 2003, I became involved in a Canadian International Development Agency (CIDA) project, which aims to reduce poverty in Western China through enhanced teacher training systems using distance education. It is a five-year, $12 million project conducted in partnership with the Chinese government. Within the project, Canada provides expertise in student-centred instruction (SCI) and distance delivery and China provides context expertise and an understanding of the reform curriculum. Distance delivery is critical because of the number of teachers requiring training and the large geographic area of Western China. Distance delivery necessitates thoughtful design and production of resources and this project also focussed on the design, implementation and long-term sustainability of a teacher education system that relies on learning support centres.

After almost three years of work there are a number of questions in relation to the project. For example, why has there not been the development of a community of practice around instructional design with the project members? In addition, why has the Canadian project team been unable to encourage our Chinese colleagues to see the value of the instructional design process? This paper reports on this international project and attempts to raise questions that might be of value to other groups considering international partnerships. This chapter offers some musings and speculations about the field of instructional design within the Chinese context. The Chinese project partners in this project include professionals drawn from the National Centre of Educational Technology (NCET) and their counterparts (PCETS) in each of the project's three provinces (Sichuan, Ningxia, and Xinjiang). On the Canadian side, consultants from the Athabasca University, University of Calgary, University of Alberta, and Alberta Education participated in the project. In addition, Agriteam Canada provided the project management.

Background

As early as 1960, China implemented a distance education system through the development of an educational broadcasting network to promote continuing education and lifelong learning. China became the first country to design and implement a strategy for the use of radio and television to provide higher education and professional development opportunities (Yuhui, 1988). Since the early 1980s, China has expanded universal basic education (learning opportunities for all children—rural and urban—in grades 1-9) across the country by using *minban*, community-paid teachers who have limited amounts of formal education

(Robinson & Latchem, 2003, p. 7). Typically, *minban* teachers may have only completed grade 10, and often they have received little or no training in teaching strategies. The national government is now trying to phase out the education system's reliance on *minban* as it begins to shift from simply offering access to basic education to all its students in grades 1-9 to improving learning opportunities for rural and ethnic minority citizens. This is a daunting task in a country with the geographic size and population of China. In order to reach this goal, "some (minban) have achieved qualifications through distance education and joined the government paid (gongban) teaching force" (p. 7).

Consistent with the commitment to quality universal education, is the government mandated professional development (PD) for teachers and the development of a new, reform curriculum. "In China the amount of continuing professional development is legislated by the central government and every teacher is required to undertake a fixed number of hours (currently seventy-two) of professional development a year" (Robinson & Latchem, 2003, p. 16). PD has typically taken the form of self-study using content delivered by television broadcasts. In terms of the New Curriculum initiative, boxes of print materials, CD-ROMs, and texts were distributed to the local county boards of education (CBEs) with the anticipation that CBE staff would disseminate the materials and offer training opportunities. Regional universities also offer PD during the teachers' summer vacations. This PD is often paid for by the teacher.

China requires distance education to be both scalable and sustainable. Scalability refers to the ability of a program to provide PD activities to the millions of teachers across the country—both rural and urban. Sustainability reflects the need that programs within the distance education system can be duplicated and re-purposed for other content, thereby creating a pattern of learning easily used at the CBE and school levels. These two factors have shaped the direction and scope of the CIDA project described in this chapter. When the initial project design group developed the five-year project plan, they placed emphasis on (1) content development for professional development and (2) system development for the distribution of content via distance delivery. Therefore, all the activities conducted within the five years of the project needed to support these two areas. Hon-Chan and Mukherjee (2003) suggest that China uses a complementary top-down and bottom-up approach to professional development. Top-down refers to the impact that far-sighted, progressive ministries, donor agencies, teacher training providers, and/or professional organizations have on the design, development and implementation of PD initiatives. Bottom-up approaches rely on far-sighted schools, departments and groups of teachers to implement, support, and sustain PD. The majority of schools within the project received PD via a one-way IP satellite system. This is a receive-only system that requires schools to download content on their computer hard drives and print or save content locally on CD-ROMs. Because many schools have only one computer, educators form study groups and share ideas. Content sharing among the teachers is a challenge as many schools have only one computer, and electricity costs are a concern for the school budget, further restricting teachers' access. However, it is the blend of distance delivery and site-based facilitation that constitutes the blended model of PD envisioned by the project.

As the donor agencies (e.g., CIDA in this case study) interact with the other players in China's top-down/bottom-up approach to distance education, three aspects identified by Wang, Wang, Fang, and Tuzlocova (2003) impact the process. These are: learning, technology, and culture. If learning is the goal and technology is one of the means of accomplishing this goal, then it must be recognized that culture will directly impact the facilitation of the learning and the engagement of the students. Culture is multifaceted and consists of three types—national, organizational, and the educational/learning system culture. Within this project, national factors are reflected in the homogenous, urban culture, typically Mandarin-speaking Han Chinese. Organizational factors are reflected in the national education system, which directs the provincial level agencies. Educational/learning culture factors are reflected at the county/school level where rural issues as well minority languages and ethnic diversity exist.

Luger (2005) supports the notion of cultural impact on system development by suggesting that the "...traditional Chinese approach promotes less interactive learning and...a reliance/preference for instructor-centred learning" (p. 2). Craig and Perraton (2003) echo this point and found that Chinese teachers enrolled in professional development activities preferred modes of delivery that put them closest to an actual teacher. Further, they found that "any formal accreditation for DE courses needs to have parity of esteem with that given to traditional face-to-face programs" (p. 108). They suggest that new approaches (distance education and self-study) should retain some traditional features to be successful. These new approaches must also be perceived to have the same value as traditional learning opportunities such as face-to-face training. In addition, while diversity tends to be a "...policy objective that most systems...pursue although to different degrees" in the west, it has only been recently that China has considered this issue. For example, "North American colleges and universities...are among the most diverse in the world. In the East, Chinese universities have until recently tended to be highly homogeneous" (Lang & Zha, 2004, p. 1).

The impact of culture and diversity also affect the application of instructional design. The development of Internet-based learning to support teacher development requires the collaborative development of content. In this project, international experts in instructional design needed to work together with Chinese experts with different views of teaching and learning. This was a significant challenge in this project as illustrated by Figure 1. Lin (2001) elaborates on the factors that impact the development and use of content, development processes, and instructional methods on a global scale. These factors include political systems, perceived economic benefit, cultural exclusion, and protection of intellectual property.

Within this project there did appear to be a number of cultural differences that influenced our approach. Firstly, our Canadian project team assumed a partnership that emphasised teamwork, indicative of Canadian work practices, whereas traditional Chinese culture traditionally focuses on the status of individuals. For example, our Chinese colleagues were unaccustomed to questioning the work or process of those individuals who were considered

Figure 1. Factors impacting content development and distribution in donor-funded international projects

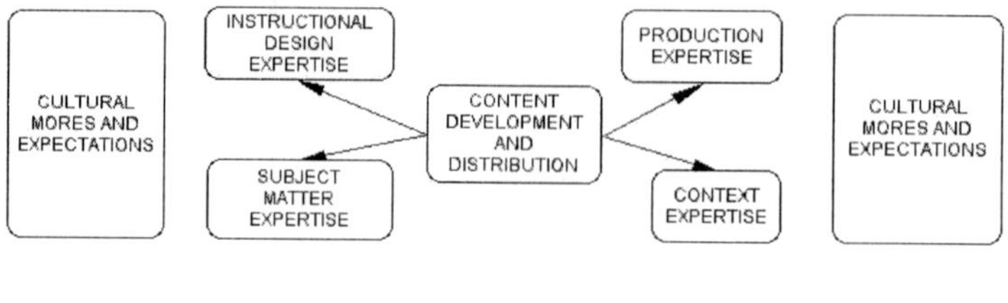

higher in status to them. They preferred to be responsible for a specific task and not to engage in work beyond their specific task. Secondly, our desire to question everything on the project was inconsistent with the "...basic tenet of Asian management: 'If you don't have the position, don't question the policy'" (p. 217). In particular, the following quote captures our understanding of the situation: "Act like a guest, realizing that you are different and not equal, and that you must work to learn the traditions of your hosts" (Helmreich & Merritt, 1998, p. 219). Specifically, it may be that traditional instructional design strategies, such as the customary needs assessment, may be difficult to implement as it questions all aspects of the situation which was not a usual approach of our Chinese colleagues. Consequently, it is the premise of this chapter that the Western basis of the instructional design process is potentially in opposition to some core principles held by our Chinese colleagues, which may explain some of the difficulties we experienced on our project. Therefore, the perceived failures and frustrations of the case presented here may have more to do with *culture* than project design.

Smith and Ragan (2005) suggest that instructional design is about problem solving, applied decision-making, and finding solutions to ill-structured problems. It is a complex process, although "novices sometimes have the impression that doing design work is a 'cut and dried' activity" (p. 7). Our approach in this project focused on the development of Chinese instructional designers through a series of introductory workshops and content development opportunities that made sense to our project team. However, fundamental to the Western view is that instructional design is a learning process, not a learned process. Another question, pointed out by the editor, may be even more fundamental—if a process, such as instructional design, has limited or no cultural currency, should one project partner make the other do it?

Therefore, it appears that before international development projects can attempt to introduce instructional design in their project goals, they may need to convince their colleagues that:

- Considering production before design is ineffective in many contexts, especially those that are diverse or ill-structured.
- Ill-structured design problems exist and can be solved.
- Content development should support and encourage diversity (ethnic, gender, language, learning skills, modes of delivery, outcomes, etc.).
- The need to refine, modify, adapt and revise material is not due to a lack of expertise or weakness, but rather part of the learning process required to develop a quality product.
- Process and product are related and, to be efficient, one should not choose the production of products over a design process that guides the production phase.
- While costly, changes in the content development process are required to support new teaching approaches.

It is important to note that coping with ill-structured problems is not something unique to this project. What appears to be unique was the expectation that foreign experts would come with the problem conceptualized, structured and solved before taking account of the local context. This was not the case, and in working through the ill-structured problem, the Canadian instructional designers felt they were modelling good practice by sharing the process. However, it appears that our Chinese partners viewed this process as uncertainty and a lack of expertise as opposed to the sharing of ideas.

Within the case study presented here, the Canadian instructional designers have begun to build a community of practice among themselves. At this point the community of practice consists of the five Canadian consultants hired by the project. Members of this group have shared their professional knowledge and best practices and discussed problem-solving techniques that have worked within this project context. This instructional design group is becoming a community of practice as described by Wenger (2004). Members of this community are working professionals with vast and varied instructional design experiences. They are "... people who share a concern or a passion for something they do and learn how to do it better as they interact regularly" (Wenger, 2004).

Case Description

Context and Organization

While it must be noted that China has made progress in poverty reduction, currently 17% of the world's poor live in China. Peter Morgan, the former Strengthening Capacity for Basic Education in Western China (SCBEWC) project manager in China, states that there are four significant challenges for basic education in Western China, each of which impacts the project partners in significant ways. The challenges include:

- The need for large, scalable solutions that have not been attempted before. For example there are 10 million teachers in China, over one million schools and hundreds of millions of students.
- The need to increase the effectiveness of schools by making the school environment more appealing to learners and their parents, and making the benefits of higher education accessible to the graduates.
- The relatively low level of existing educational achievement of teachers, the need for further academic upgrading, and the lack of access to required academic and professional development training.
- Financial arrangements that make it difficult to offer cost-free basic education for students, and that make professional development unaffordable for teachers, schools and the County Bureaus of Education.

Three provinces in Western China (Sichuan, Xinjiang, and Ningxia) were selected for the SCBEWC project based on need, culture and language. Six counties (two in each of the provinces) functioned as the project hub within each province. The languages and cultures reflected in the three counties include Tibetan, Kazak, Uygher, and Mongol, and Hui in addition to Han (Mandarin language). By the end of the project, all materials will be translated and delivered in these languages.

The two major project partners (CIDA project partners and the Chinese Ministry of Education) assigned specific tasks (project management, content development, and implementation) to individual agencies and organizations in their respective counties (see Figure 2).

In the case of CIDA, direct responsibility for project management was awarded to Agriteam Canada, a Canadian consulting company specializing in international development. The Chinese Ministry of Education (MoE) involved its National Centre for Educational Technology (NCET). Agriteam and its partners (three Canadian universities and one provincial ministry of education) worked with their Chinese counterparts (the Chinese MoE, NCET and three provincial centres for educational technology – PCET), to share Canadian expertise in teacher education and distance education. The goal of this collaboration was to develop a systematic approach to improving basic education, and to build Chinese capacity in a manner that is respectful of the various cultures and minority groups in Western China. Further, the partners agree that it is important that this approach is sustainable beyond the project and Canadian involvement.

The dual goals of the project (improved teaching and capacity building) require project managers to focus on issues related to content development, delivery, and implementation.

Figure 2. SCBEWC project participants

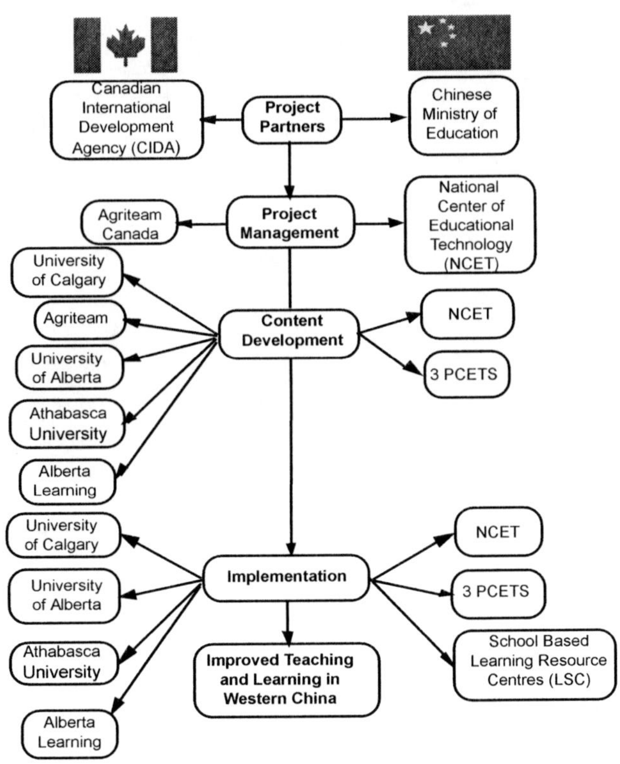

Scalability and sustainability are critical concerns. To achieve the project goals, distance education via existing satellite delivery is the most reasonable option. While the initial professional development content was developed for face-to-face training, ultimately all subsequent content was designed for distance delivery utilizing a blended learning approach. Further, because the Chinese government had recently embarked on a reformed curriculum for basic education (grades 1-9), the instructional strategy underpinning content development is student-centred instruction and inquiry-based learning.

In order to accomplish project goals, project management contracted the services of subject matter experts, instructional designers, media developers, distance education experts, classroom teachers, government officials of various levels, and ministry of education personnel at various levels (national, provincial, and county) from both Canada and China. Figure 3 illustrates the areas of expertise within the SCBEWC project and the roles and responsibilities required to achieve project goals.

As one might expect, linking the various levels of experience and expertise has been challenging. Also, as this is a five-year project with multiple partners as reflected in Figure 2, there has been a turnover of consultants and experts in the project. Figure 4 shows the composition of the design teams for the resource projects as of November 2005.

From Figure 4 one can see that communication across project components and partners was going to be challenging because each course/resource was under the jurisdiction of a specific institution. Because the NCET and PCET leaders wanted to widely use the foreign expertise,

Figure 3. Roles, responsibilities, and expertise within the SCBEWC Project

Roles and Responsibilities		
Subject matter expertise (SME)	Yes – especially content for courses and resources	Yes – especially context and specific content areas
Instructional design	Yes	No
Media development	Yes – especially as related to content and process of instructional design	Yes – especially as related to TV production. Excellent skills with HTML, Flash and digital video
Distance education	Yes – especially as related to interaction and multimedia content design	Yes – especially as related to TV broadcasts
Classroom context	Yes – but limited to western context	Yes – but limited because NCET and PCET personnel typically not educators and have limited classroom or pedagogical experience
Government officials of various levels	No	Yes – many levels represented
Ministry of education at various levels (national / provincial)	Yes – but only in terms of policy	Yes – especially at provincial and county levels

Figure 4. Members of design projects within the SCBEWC Project challenges

Project		
1. SCI Course One	University of Calgary – 3 writers / SME	3 SME 2 Distance Education Experts 1 Ministry of Education person
2. SCI Course One – Distance	1 SME from University of Calgary (different from #1) 1 from Athabasca University – Distance Education expertise 1 Beijing Project Office member	2 Classroom context experts – teachers from project schools 1 Distance Education Expert (from Team #1) 1 Distance Education Expert (new) 1 Media Development expert
3. Science Resource	2 SME experts – one from University of Alberta & one consultant 1 Instructional Designer from University of Alberta 1 Beijing Project Office member	2 SME 5 Media Development experts 1 Distance Education Expert (from #2 team) 2 Classroom context experts – teachers
4. ICT in the Classroom – Course 3	1 SME from University of Calgary (from Team #2) 1 Instructional Designer from University of Calgary 1 Beijing Project Office member	4 Classroom context experts – teachers 1 SME 5 Media Development experts
5. ESL Resource	1 SME from University of Calgary 1 Instructional Designer – consultant 1 Beijing Project Office member (from Team #3)	4 Classroom context experts – teachers 1 SME 5 Media Development experts (one from Team #4)
6. Leadership – Course 4	1 SME from University of Alberta 1 Instructional Designer – consultant 1 Beijing Project Office member	4 Classroom context experts – teachers 1 SME 5 Media Development experts (one from Team #5)

different participants were assigned to each resource project. In hindsight, the development of an online forum or a face-to-face meeting with all participants might have connected each of the six resource projects and allowed for the development of a community. During the development of a set of guidelines for the SCBEWC project, the instructional designers have collected guidelines, templates, suggestions, and general content from each of the six individual projects. An outcome from this informal collaboration is the development of a course for Chinese instructional designers, so that the knowledge, skills and abilities required to develop distance education materials are shared in a more formal manner. The project plans to develop a certificate for those completing the course. This is an important step toward capacity building and the development of a community of practice that may extend beyond the conclusion of the project.

It appears that the development of a community of practice among our Chinese colleagues has not occurred for a variety of reasons. Without a forum, such as an online conference or a face-to-face meeting, the Chinese participants did not have a mechanism to continue communication and once the specific project was completed each of the participants resumed their regular work. We intend to offer an online discussion environment (to be launched Spring 2006) to encourage participants to discuss their experience. This forum devoted to instructional design issues could help to support the adoption of the instructional design process and encourage its use by Chinese content developers.

The SCBEWC project has adopted the following instructional design model (see Figure 5) for the development of its materials.

All steps within Figure 5 contain supporting templates provided in the project distance education guidelines to inform the process. The development of the guidelines document is a critical step in the SCBEWC project, as it anchors a process for content development that can be generalized across future project activities, thereby helping to achieve the primary project goal of improved access to quality professional development. Further, it was felt that an understanding of the instructional design process would help to achieve the second project goal—sustainability of a robust system for subsequent content development within the Chinese context.

The project involved two approaches to training our Chinese instructional designers. The first approach consisted of two formal workshops designed to introduce the instructional

Figure 5. Instructional design model for SCBEWC course and resources (items in parentheses refer to specific appendices and templates within the DE Guidelines)

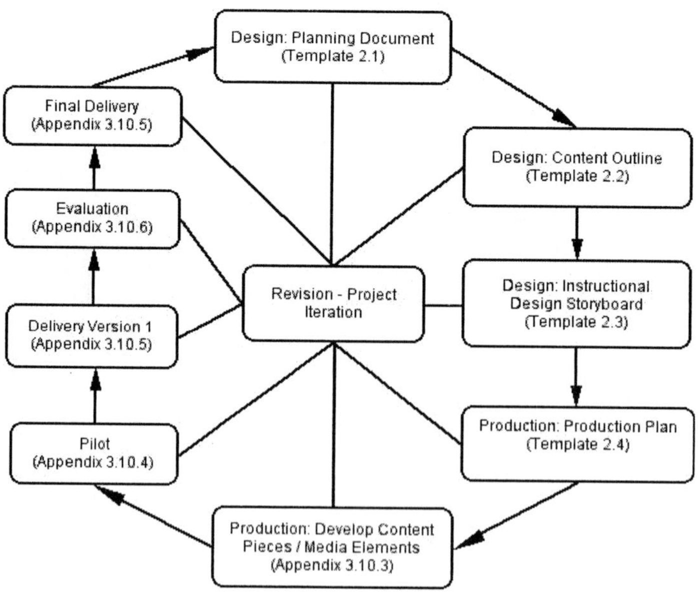

design process. The first was held in China after the face-to-face training using the content development in Project One (see Figure 4). The training workshop (Norman, 2003, July 28) was designed to offer a general overview of the instructional design process (background, link to learning strategies, and process steps). While the Chengdu workshop did not specifically work with project content (e.g., content from SCI Course One, which eventually was converted to distance delivery), a second workshop held at the British Columbia Institute of Technology (BCIT) in Canada did. The BCIT workshop presented instructional design templates that would be used for Project Two (see Figure 4). This workshop was designed to be a hands-on opportunity where participants were guided through all aspects of the instructional design process (Beers, 2005 March).

There seemed to be two factors that affected the success of the workshops. Firstly, the same participants from the Chengdu workshop did not attend the Vancouver workshop. It was assumed that a core group of Chinese colleagues would complete both workshops and then work on the project, whereas there was a need by our Chinese colleagues to include as many people as possible in all the workshop opportunities. The Canadian team had assumed that the two conferences could be offered as an introduction with a follow-up application workshop. Secondly, Chinese colleagues found the workshops concerning production issues to be too basic, and the content of the instructional design process did not connect with the actual workflow of the production. There appeared to be a mismatch between expectations and planning. Based on communications with Chinese colleagues over the past few years, it appears that the instructional design process is seen as an exercise that is not essential in the everyday production of content. Our Chinese partners typically produce content by repurposing existing materials, so the complete ID process, as described in Figure 5 is rarely, if ever, employed. The actual design of the project itself (the number of project partners and the lack of continuity of participation) has created enormous challenges in terms of communication, continuity, and communications.

Strategies and Solutions

It is clear that cultural differences have had an impact on communication and the development of a community of practice among project partners. It is hoped that the completion and distribution of the Distance Education Guidelines will be an important first step in the development of our community of practice. The guidelines will form the common understandings necessary to unite the various participants/partners in the project. Further, the Canadian instructional designers are beginning to consider the development of a certification process for Chinese instructional designers, opening the conversation among project partners about the importance of instructional design within the Chinese system. The Canadian instructional designers will now form a team and identify Chinese colleagues who will be invited to collaborate on a basic certification process. For this team to be successful, it must work from the Distance Education Guidelines to create a structured learning opportunity for project partners interested in instructional design. This online course will result in a Level One certification that would allow for the development of a professional community of practice. This will be a first step towards establishing a community of practicing instructional designers in China.

Experience with the SCBEWC project suggests that open and honest communication about actual successes and failures are most effective. While the Canadian team typically preferred to couch criticism in positive language, this was unclear to our Chinese colleagues who preferred open, clear statements that state the problem and offer a solution. It is obvious that the project team, at times, has confused its Chinese colleagues. The challenge for our team is to embrace this more direct approach and to tackle the present challenges with direct, constructive criticism.

Additionally, the Canadian team tended to present the *big picture*, then the individual, specific tasks. It was assumed that this was a logical way to examine the project. However, our Chinese colleagues preferred to be presented with a specific activity or approach and then, after it has been clearly explained, the presenter(s) can elaborate on how it connects to the larger project. Upon reflection, the Canadian partners noted how this difference in view-point has impacted participant understanding of the course and resource development.

As the project draws to a close in March 2007, the project management will need to focus on lessons learned concerning the use of a side-by-side approach to content development. For example, there is approximately an eight-month development cycle for the production and initial testing of courses and resources. Therefore, management will need to be strategic as to which tasks to complete. Further, the project must improve on its original attempts to build the capacity of its Chinese partners if there is to be a lasting system of DE content development to promote improved teaching and learning in the project schools, thereby accomplishing both the project goals. At this point it would seem logical that the next steps for the project should correspond to the following principles.

Principles

Project managers need to recognize the degree to which the context impacts the instructional design process. It appears that a number of factors will need to be addressed in order for the project goals to be reached. These factors include:

- A difference in dealing with content design,
- The impact that different cultural contexts have on compartmentalizing work flow, thereby potentially limiting access to and understanding of various levels within the hierarchy, and
- The importance of the development of a community of practice for instructional designers to ensure clear communications, sharing of best practices and lessons learned, and
- Supporting the sustainability of the effective processes developed once the project is completed.

However, the development of conditions that would favour the development of a community of practice is something that the Canadian project management can address. As stated throughout this chapter, attempts are being made by both the Chinese and Canadian partners to address this situation. These attempts include:

- Development of clear guidelines that place the instructional design process within the context of the SCBEWC project,
- Design of a resume format that allows partners to clearly understand the skills required for specific tasks and the qualifications of those wanting to do the work,
- Development of an online platform to support discussions and content sharing, and
- Development of an online learning activity that would begin to train potential instructional designers and allow them to practice their new skills within a supportive community of practice.

The community envisioned for the project will be built on three specific principles (Wenger, 2004). "Communities of practice are formed by people who engage in a process of collective learning in a shared domain of human endeavor" (p. 1). Further, "communities of practice are groups of people who share a concern or a passion for something they do and learn how to do it better as they interact regularly" (p. 2).

The three key principles crucial for communities described by Wenger include (1) domain, (2) community, and (3) practice.

Domain refers to subject area or field which unites the potential community members. In terms of this case, it is the discipline and theory that underpins instructional design. Initially, the SCBEWC project felt that exposure to the instructional design process through workshops and side-by-side mentoring could address domain issues. The project managers now recognize that this was not the case. Therefore, it is hoped that exposure to the content through the guidelines and a workshop will assist the process. *Community* is not simply the collection of people. While existing members will form the initial community, it is hoped that it will continue to evolve and include individuals who complete the proposed instructional design workshop and begin to work together on future resource and course development in the remaining months of the SCBEWC project. The development of this community holds the greatest potential for the sustainability of the entire SCBEWC project. While this community goal may not happen during the life of this project, this goal will hopefully be achieved through the CIDA project. *Practice* refers to the fact that members of the SCBWEC instructional designers' community are actual practitioners in Canada. By working together to develop resources and courses in this last phase of the project, members of this community will begin to "...develop a shared repertoire of resources: experiences, stories, tools, ways of addressing recurring problems" (p. 6). By working together to solve design problems, the members should begin to value instructional design in the production of content. The opportunity to work together and build professional relationships should be consistent with the Chinese notion of *guan xi*—relationships (Helmreich & Merritt, 1998).

Conclusion

It appears that the SCBEWC project must re-consider two core aspects: (1) the way in which it has presented the instructional design process and, (2) the assumption that a side-by-side mentoring process would support the development of a Canadian/Chinese community of practice.

Firstly, the project must reduce the perceived ambiguity of the process, and emphasise why design must precede production. For example, the project has experienced instances of Chinese colleagues storyboarding content after it has been produced. The project also has experienced situations in which Chinese content developed in urban centres was used in tiny rural schools without knowing the context in which the content was being used. These inconsistencies in practice and process are a reality of the existing project design workflow.

Secondly, because respect for gender, minority, and language issues are at the heart of the SCBEWC project design, it appears that project management must continue to build an appreciation amongst Chinese colleagues for a needs assessment as part of the production process. As Chinese colleagues begin to consider content development for a less homogeneous audience (rural, minority teachers), the project must build understanding of how a needs and task assessment will assure that content is of value to the end users. A recently completed evaluation of Course 1, DE (see Figure 4) should help to strengthen this aspect as the project now has tangible examples of each step in the instructional design process (Figure 5) to illustrate their practical application.

Thirdly, the project management team must recognize that all participants of a design team (see Figure 4) do not have access to the same information. There is not a tradition of questioning the work and practices that are perceived to be above or below one's position within the organization. In Canada, questioning all aspects of practice and product is inherent in the instructional design process. Being able to question is core to initial parts of the needs assessment and the context analysis phase of the work. Determining how best to proceed with the development of content and building of capacity will be a challenge for the project in the future.

As the Chinese National education system shifts from its traditional practices, and moves toward full scale adoption of its new national curriculum, shifts will need to be made in the design of content for both training materials and classroom resources. This need may create the climate for a Chinese version of instructional design that may be more appropriate to the local setting. Because the new curriculum is based on inquiry-based learning, collaboration, and self-study, project partners are beginning to see that the current practices of centralized production and the re-purposing of existing content will not work. By recognizing these factors, further consideration of the instructional design process within the Chinese context appears to be timely.

References

Beers, M. (2005). The multimedia development process: Beijing to Vancouver. *Sidebars*. Retrieved October 15, 2005, from http://online.bcit.ca/sidebars/05march/inside-out-1.htm

Craig, H., & Perraton, H. (2003). Open and distance education for teachers' continuing professional development. In B. Robinson & C. Latchem (Eds.), *Teacher education through open and distance learning* (pp. 91-111). New York: Routledge Falmer.

Helmreich, R., & Merritt, A. (1998). *Culture at work in aviation and medicine: National, organizational and professional influences*. Brookfield: Ashgate.

Hon-Chan, C., & Mukherjee, H. (2003). Policy, planning and management of distance education for teacher education. In B. Robinson & C. Latchem (Eds.), *Teacher education through open and distance learning* (pp. 48-71). New York: Routledge -Falmer.

Lang, D., & Zha, Q. (2004). Comparing universities: A case study between Canada and China. *Higher Education Policy, 17*, 339-354. International Association of Universities. Retrieved October 15, 2005, from http://www.palgrave-journals.com/hep/journal/v17/n4/pdf/8300061a.pdf#search='comparing%20universities'

Lin, F. (2001). A critique of Stephen Downes' article, "Learning Objects": A Chinese perspective. *International Review of Research in Open and Distance Learning, 2*(1).

Luger, T. (2005). *The role of instructional design and technology in the education and practice of TCM.* Retrieved October 20, 2005, from http://www.chineseherbacademy.org/articles/idt_tcm.shtml

Norman, S. (2003). *Instructional design: Tips and techniques.* Retrieved May 26, 2006, from http://72.14.203.104/search?q=cache:LmYjfDMaRX4J:www.ncet.edu.cn/cida/en/download/de_m/ID%2520Tips%2520and% 2520Techniques%2520ver%25203.pdf+%22Tips+and+Techniques+ ver+3%22&hl=zh-TW&gl=hk&ct=clnk&cd=1

Robinson, B., & Latchem, C. (Eds.). (2003). *Teacher education through open and distance learning.* New York: Routledge Falmer.

Rothwell, W., & Kazanas, H.C. (2001). *Instructional design.* Hoboken, NJ: Jossey-Bass Inc.

Smith, P., & Ragan, T. (2005). *Instructional design* (3rd ed). Hoboken, NJ: John Wiley & Sons.

Wang, G., Wang, P., Fang, M., & Tuzlocova, V. (2003-2004) Internet-based learning in China, Russia, and the U.S.: A cross-cultural comparison. Retrieved October 15, 2005, from www.irex.org/programs/starr/research/04/wang.pdf

Wenger, E. (2004). *Communities of practice: A brief introduction.* Retrieved July 26, 2005, from http://www.ewenger.com/theory/

Yuhui, Z. (1988). China: Its distance higher-education system. *Prospects, 18*(2), 217-228. Retrieved December 2005, from http://www1.worldbank.org/disted/Technology/broadcast/tv-02.html

Chapter VI

An Emerging Model of Community Collaboration During the Construction of E-Learning Resources: Implications for Papua New Guinea

Lalen Simeon, Pacific Adventist University, Papua New Guinea

Gwyn Brickell, University of Wollongong, Australia

Brian Ferry, University of Wollongong, Australia

Abstract

For many lecturers within the academic community, the increasing emphasis on the use of ICT for research and teaching can be threatening, but these fears can be eased if professional development is supportive and ongoing, and provided in flexible, appropriate and adaptable ways. This is particularly relevant in institutions in developing countries where the increasing availability of e-learning technologies poses a challenge to ICT experts and trainers in assisting and supporting lecturers in adapting to the use of these technologies in the teaching/learning environment. This chapter focuses on the results of two case studies and describes the roles that the two instructional designers (IDs) played in facilitating the professional development of lecturers that were constructing e-learning environments. The findings suggest that the lecturers needed ongoing support, advice and technical assistance for an extended period of time. This study has enabled the researchers to develop a team collaboration model for planning and designing e-learning resources that would be piloted in tertiary institutions in Papua New Guinea. The findings also contribute to the research literature about the design processes needed to improve the quality of learning resources.

Introduction

The Papua New Guinea (PNG) government plans to develop a network system for education and research aimed at linking the five universities and other tertiary institutions. In addition to this development, AusAid has funded information and communication technology (ICT) and multimedia centres in five teacher colleges (AusAID is the Australian Government agency responsible for managing Australia's overseas aid program). It is claimed that the long-term sustainability of these centres depends on the ability of selected lecturers to become technical assistants and instructional designers (IDs) to provide basic ICT support to both academics and non-academics within these institutions. AusAid recognises the important role that IDs play and has commenced training programs that instruct selected lecturers to effectively use ICT for teaching and learning purposes. However, the availability of new technologies at these institutions, such as Pacific Adventist University (PAU), poses a challenge for these newly trained "experts," as they are still developing their own expertise as they support other lecturers to develop suitable online courses for their students. Traditionally IDs focus on the effective design of instruction in order to meet the agreed learning outcomes, but they achieve this within a human context. Therefore, effective IDs have to be capable of effectively harnessing the human potential at their disposal. This relies on their ability to form viable communities of practice (Wenger, 2002). In the context of PAU the ID is a work colleague who is developing their ID expertise. This person has to develop his/her credibility as an ID and to develop a viable community of practice among colleagues who are novices in the use of ICT to support learning.

This chapter describes how two IDs worked with lecturers (who were novices in the use of ICT for instruction) to prepare e-learning resources. It describes the issues facing the implementation of the technology and the implications for continued development and use of computer-based technologies within PNG. The chapter concludes with the presentation of a training model that emerged from this study, and discusses how this model could be applied in the PNG context.

Background

Universities in the 21st century are exposed to different types of technology and lecturers are expected to become equipped with the skills needed to apply ICTs to support and enhance teaching and learning within their subjects. However, many lecturers find the increased emphasis on the use of ICT for research and teaching to be threatening (Alexander & McKenzie, 1998). These fears can be eased if professional development is supportive and ongoing, and is provided in flexible, appropriate and adaptable ways (Holt & Thompson, 1998).

Supporting lecturers in achieving this skill-development has traditionally been one of the roles of the instructional designer. In this role the instructional designer provides advice in the design and development of instructional material in consultation with the lecturer(s). Such a process of social learning may be regarded as a community of practice (Lave & Wenger, 1991). A community of practice is where participating members, with a common interest in subject development, collaborate to share ideas, find solutions, and build innovation into instructional material to enhance student learning.

This study was motivated by the need to find ways of assisting, training and supporting lecturers in the development of quality e-learning resources that enhance student learning. The study focused on the collaboration strategies employed by four lecturers and two IDs as they worked within a community of practice to develop online learning environments and learning resources. It focuses on two case studies and describes the roles that the two IDs played in facilitating the professional development of lecturers who were constructing e-learning environments. As team members share and learn from each other's experiences and expertise, they create authentic and student-centered learning environments. Observation of interactions within these communities of practice has led to a proposed team collaboration model for planning and designing e-learning resources that will be piloted in tertiary institutions in PNG.

PAU is a senior tertiary institution operated by the Seventh-Day Adventist Church in PNG. PAU is located about 17 kilometres from Port Moresby, the capital city of PNG. The university commenced operation as Pacific Adventist College in 1983, and obtained university status in 1997.

The university provides tertiary education from all over the Pacific Islands to an increasing number of students in the fields of business, education (secondary & primary), arts and humanities, office administration, nursing, theology, science and technology. Just like any other modern university, PAU is committed to ensuring that the staff and students have access to the latest computer-based technologies. However, the availability of the Internet and other ICTs does not guarantee that lecturers will be comfortable to use such resources in their teaching. They are inexperienced in the use and application of e-learning resources and still require basic ICT training and support to give them confidence to use ICT for teaching.

Jonassen, Peck, and Wilson (1999) argued that technology is more than hardware: "Technology consists of the designs and the environments that engage learners to facilitate ideas and construct knowledge" (p. 2). In order for the lecturers to use ICT to support learning, they require assistance and technical support from instructional designers during the process of planning and designing their online subjects. King, Frizler, and Vigallon (2000) pointed out that every educational institution needs an instructional designer to provide technical advice and support to academics. The process of designing online environments requires a collaborative approach since both groups (lecturers and IDs) are experts in their own fields and have a lot of experience to share with each other (King et al., 2000).

A survey conducted by Vaa (2002), funded by UNESCO, resulted in a report about the current level of ICT access and use in PNG. It noted that the PNG government recognises the importance of ICT and its benefit to the country, and has allocated a centralised ICT budget with an aim to "…develop and launch an ICT policy in the country" (Vaa, 2002, p. 204). Unfortunately, since the establishment of such budgets, all attempts at encouraging the use of ICT have been unsuccessful for a number of reasons, including the installation of incompatible appliances and applications and different approaches to the use of ICT by many users. As a result, organisations and educational institutions have developed their own policies on the use of ICT for their institutions. The report stated that:

- PNG does not really have an ICT infrastructure.
- There needs to be a blueprint for ICT development so that change is uniform.
- PNG needs as much assistance as possible otherwise it will fail to realise its plans.

The introduction of ICT at PAU challenges ICT support staff and IDs to provide support for lecturers who will be expected to use these technologies to support their teaching. Traditional face-to-face teaching has been, and still is, the main method of instruction used in PAU. Students attending PAU come from different developing countries around the South Pacific and most of these students have very little knowledge of how to use computers. To help address this situation all students are required to complete a compulsory subject known as *Introduction to Computer Studies*. However, the experience of lecturers is slightly different. Lecturers at PAU are computer-literate, as most of them are quite familiar with the Internet and use a range of software products in their work, but they are novices in the application of ICT to support their teaching. It is important to have training and development processes in place that enable them to collaborate with IDs in designing ways of using ICT to support their subjects.

PAU has the available ICT resources but needs to initiate a professional development program for lecturers. The next step is to use the available ICT resources to provide further learning experiences for students. This is a new and challenging experience for lecturers who need to develop greater competencies in using ICT, and to develop the confidence to take risks and try new teaching practices.

A number of researchers (Collis, 1996; McNaught, 2001; Oliver, 1998) have reported on instructional models that were used to assist and support faculty members who were novice online users in their institutions. An emerging theme from these reports indicates that lecturers who attempt to use online learning environments require a great deal of support and advice. The reports also claim that assistance from instructional designers/learning designers; IT technicians, graphic designers, and other academics who are experienced in the use of ICT are needed to support novice lecturers throughout the design process. According to Fisher and Nygren (1999), introducing technology in the classroom helps to provide a catalyst for embedding concepts such interdisciplinary studies, team teaching and different student learning styles into practice. This enables students and teachers to collaborate as partners in the learning process.

Jonassen, Peck, and Wilson (1999) also suggest that when teachers (lecturers) become comfortable in using ICT, they are more likely to adjust their approach to teaching and learning from teacher-centred to learner-centred, from individual tasks to collaborative tasks, and from passive learning to active learning. He also suggests that technologies are tools for learners to construct their own knowledge. Therefore teachers (lecturers) need assistance from IDs to help them learn the skills and knowledge they need to effectively use ICT to enhance learning.

Challenges Faced by Instructional Designers

IDs are focused on best teaching practice and their aim is to help lecturers "…meet students' needs using the most appropriate and effective tools, resources and strategies available…" (King et al., 2000, p. 2). Ideally they have the experience and expertise to assist lecturers in developing online courses, which they believe will promote quality learning outcomes (Keppell, 2000) and to provide "…support and advice in the design, development and use of electronic and print media used for teaching and learning" (Torrisi-Steele & Davis, 2000, p. 5).

In meeting the requirements of this role, the ID faces challenges from academics, who bring to the discussion their individual beliefs on what they would like their students to experience in their online subjects. Such challenges require the ID to understand these different perspectives and alternate pedagogical approaches, and relate these to the values and knowledge expected within the subject. Lecturers know what they want students to learn in their online environments, but the challenge for the instructional designer is to develop a good working relationship. The relationship should allow free communication and the development of a mutual understanding of their roles and expectations. The development team works as a community of practice during the design process (Wenger, 2002). Team collaboration is paramount in creating effective, better quality and engaging e-learning environments. This develops as a result of the inputs that members make to their community of practice.

The Study

This study was motivated by the need to develop effective ways to support lecturers in developing countries (such as PNG) to produce ICT-supported online learning environments. Lecturers in both developed and developing countries, who may be experts in their subject areas, cannot be expected to automatically transfer their subject matter skills and knowledge and their pedagogical expertise into an ICT-supported learning environment. They may not have the experience in developing and using such learning environments. To facilitate effective transfer, lecturers require support from instructional designers, who are experienced in designing educational resources for online learning environments. The role of the ID is to encourage and facilitate the development of plans and learning designs to make effective use of ICT in supporting student learning. This requires lecturers and IDs to collaborate as a community of practice. At times the ID may lead this community, but at other times the lecturer or the programmer or graphic artist may also lead. If the ID leads the process, then their role is more than the analysis of learning needs and systematic development of instruction. It may also involve the organisation and facilitation of meetings, so that all members of the design team are empowered to contribute to the community's understanding of the learning needs of the users.

A successful working team is one where members have a strong relationship among themselves (Price & Schlag, 2002). Oliver (1998) stated that proper planning, organisational support and technological team support is needed by the development team as they collaborate to designing e-learning environments. Keppell (2000) expresses a similar view, but emphasises the need for lecturers to have access to ongoing support, as this enables them to use the full potential of ICT for student learning. Collis (1996) and McNaught (2001) agree with Keppell, and report that lecturers who receive ongoing support and training gain the skills and knowledge needed to utilise the potential of ICT.

The purpose of this study was to describe the roles and facilitation strategies that two IDs employed as they each supported lecturers in the development of a suite of ICT-supported subjects in two graduate courses. The study was based on two cases. The first involved three lecturers and one instructional designer who created an online subject Web site with supporting resources in the form of a handbook and CD-ROM. The second case consisted of one lecturer and one ID as they collaborated to plan and design an e-learning environment for a complete course. This would be used by a variety of lecturers who taught different subjects within the course. This Web site was designed to evolve with time and to have provision for user input. The study was conducted at a tertiary institution in Australia and adopted the seven-stage model of team development outlined in Johnson and Johnson (1997). The main question underpinning the research was:

What professional development processes and strategies do IDs and lecturers use as they collaborate to design e-learning environments?

Data Analysis

The various data gathering methods employed in this study, such as interviews, observations, lecturers' written work on lecturers' views, ideas and plans, group discussions, meeting reports, e-mail conversations, artefacts and professional training program plans provided enough information for the researcher to cross-check the accuracy of data that was vital to the study. A member check was completed on the data where individual participants were asked to confirm the accuracy of information in the record. Table 1 indicates the data sources, techniques and analysis methods for each of the research questions

Themes and categories were identified and listed from the data right at the preliminary stage. The categories were revisited, renamed, linked and organised to form patterns to give meaning to the data when new information was gathered. The list below shows the main categories that formed the basis of the study. These categories will be discussed in detail in Table 2.

- Roles
- Strategies
- Technical requirements and support
- Professional training
- Collaboration
- Concerns

The lecturers and IDs in the study were qualified professionals but collaborated as a community with an aim to create e-learning environments.

Roles

The ID outlined the lecturers' roles during the first group meeting and agreed on the due date for each assigned task.

We were to produce a study guide for the ID to see and comment on (L1).

I began writing my study guide soon after the first meeting...which is to become Web-supported and it will be put on the Web. I thought it was appropriate to begin this way then initiate a meeting with the ID to see my work (L2).

Table 1. Data sources, techniques and methods used in analysing the data

Focus Question	Research Questions	Data Sources	Techniques	Analysis Method
What professional development processes and strategies do IDs and lecturers use as they collaborate to design e-learning environments?	• What strategies did the IDs and lecturers employ as they worked in teams to develop e-learning environments? • How did the IDs and lecturers use these strategies (in meetings, communication and design) in the design process?	• Verbalisation of reflections or meaning of the results of an action or interaction • Verbalisation of a reason or intention for acting in the environment. • Verbalisation of decision making process. • Verbalisation of strategies for taking action.	• Think aloud protocols. • Interviews. • Individual written work. • Analysis of history of recorded solutions.	• Identification and categorisation of approaches used by IDs. • Comparison of themes and patterns. • Analysis of themes and patterns into categories. • Participant verification of categories.

The IDs were prepared to assist individual lecturers as the need arises. They expressed their role as:

Part of my role is almost like doing a psychological assessment of where the lecturer is at, work collaboratively with him or her in designing what they want on their Web sites and see how far I could move them forward technically. I see my role as a coordinator, technical advisor, guide and supporter (ID1).

I see myself acting ... to some extent as a mediator, a collaborator. I don't see myself as taking over the design, I see myself as merely working with them in what they want to do. I also see my role as technical advisor and trainer (ID2).

Strategies

Through on-going collaboration and discussion, lecturers relied on the IDs to advise and guide them in each stage of the planning and design process.

I was quite worried ... during the first meeting. I did not know what to expect. However, ID1 was very helpful and the proposed plan she had for us seemed quite easy for a beginner like me to follow (L1).

The ID was great; she always goes through my work, ideas, plans and objectives before we decide on what I should do (L2).

Within the community, lecturers were given ample time to plan the materials for their e-learning environments and spent time discussing their ideas with the ID.

The planning process was a slow process for me, I started off planning something very simple but after several meetings with the ID I finally decided to take a step further and that is to include a chat session (L2).

However, one lecturer did not spend enough time with the ID due to additional work commitments and this was reflected in later discussions.

I wish the activities in my subject were designed differently, but I could not do anything better than what I had on my subject Web site because I did not spend enough time with ID1 (L3).

Lecturers expected the IDs to explain the basic steps of the planning process before they could carry out their roles.

Technical Requirements and Support

Although computer literate lecturers participated in the study, they had limited technical skills in applying their knowledge to the online environment. Their initial remarks in the early stages of collaboration reflected their expectations of the role of the ID.

ID will provide technical advice, training and support (L1).

ID has the technical skills to support me in this project (L2).

ID will suggest better ways of teaching the subject online (L3).

ID will design more technical aspects of the website (L4).

Experienced IDs know how to guide and work with their clients. For example:

When I first meet with a group, I always try to understand their background before showing them sample Web sites ... I then assign tasks for the lecturers to do while assuring them that I will be providing technical and pedagogical assistance throughout the design process (ID1).

The continuous support from the ID enabled the lecturers to change their negative ideas towards using technology in the learning environment. For example:

The ID was always available to answer my queries and questions. I was able to carry out my plans and I had no doubt that she would help me out (L2).

Professional Training

Lecturers struggled during the design process because they lacked basic ICT technical skills. IDs were also busy with other commitments so they designed some parts of the Web sites but delegated more advanced technical design to other ICT technicians and graphics designers.

I have worked on the basic navigation ... Bill (the programmer) is going a level down by working on the actual Web page and some of the things like the pin board (ID2).

For successful collaboration within a community, lecturers should receive additional training and development before engaging them in the design process.

Collaboration

Lecturers admitted that they needed the IDs' assistance throughout the design process. For example:

You cannot do it alone, you need support from experts who have experience in technology and online learning (L1).

I think it was ... very important teamwork. It is a teamwork that has its boundary ... The production of the materials and the production of the readers in my judgement is the ambit of the academic. However the advice in instructional design should come from IDs (L4).

ID2 shared my aspirations and understands the problems I've been experiencing ... someone who shares your ideas is just great (L2).

Both IDs suggested that lecturers collaborated within the community to share ideas and build innovation into the instructional material.

For me, the exciting thing about lecturer 1 coming on board was having the person to bounce pedagogical ideas with (ID2).

In addition, cooperation among team members brings positive results.

Concerns

Lecturers were mainly concerned about receiving basic ICT training before working with IDs. They were also able to see different opportunities of using ICT in the learning environment.

This experience has helped me to see the potential of technology and has helped me to assess my IT skills and needs (L3).

Some lecturers were concerned about the extra workload. For example:

The more assignments students put in, the more work I have to do (L2).

Development of the online environments challenged lecturers to think about designing more creative assignments, as working within a community of practice allows lecturers to provide students with opportunities to produce high-quality work. From the data collected, it was apparent that lecturers enjoyed the design process despite lacking the basic ICT skills.

Discussion of Findings

The development of e-learning resources is a new experience for many lecturers, and it is one that demands careful preparation. It presents challenges to academics who are already busy with lectures, research and administrative duties. In each of the cases in this study the lecturers needed the ongoing support, advice and technical assistance from the community leader (the instructional designer) for extended periods of time. During this process the skills of the lecturers gradually improved from a very basic level to using more advanced techniques as they gained confidence in the use of ICT. The results are consistent with previous research which emphasised the need for community members to collaborate and share their ideas, knowledge, expertise and skills in order to plan and design effective and meaningful e-learning environments (Bennet, Priest, & Macpherson, 1999; Oliver, 1998; Torrisi-Steele & Davis, 2000).

Meeting Strategies

At the commencement of the study both IDs initiated group meetings where members of each community met and outlined their individual expertise and plans for their specific online subject. Each ID took the opportunity to assess the level of ICT knowledge and skills of the lecturers and responded to their questions, requests and foreseeable difficulties each of them may experience during the design process. Further group meetings throughout the development process provided an opportunity for the ID in each case study to address and reflect on the different perspectives, problems and issues as experienced by the lecturers. The results of this study suggest that an effective strategy for instructional designers to follow should encompass the following ideas:

- Explain the meeting agenda to assist lecturers in understanding what will be discussed;
- Select appropriate examples according to the subjects taught;
- Encourage questions during the meeting(s) and generate discussion;
- Allow lecturers to express ideas and opinions;
- Involve other IDs/ICT experts in the design process;
- Encourage reflection on the process.

Communication Strategies

In any community of practice, open communication is a necessity for achieving successful outcomes. Communication flows smoothly when members demonstrate commitment to the task in hand, show they understand their roles and those of others in the team, and share common goals such as the creation of an effective and quality e-learning environment (Price & Schlag, 2002). Participants in each of the cases were willing to listen and openly communicate with their team members during group and individual meetings. The open communication in the meetings reinforced the understanding each team member had developed in their roles and tasks, which led to closer collaboration in the process and sharing of ideas. To save time for each team, design plans that required additional programming were directed to other ICT experts to complete. This expertise was readily available within the campus community.

In both cases communication flowed smoothly and effectively after both IDs assured lecturers that they would support and guide them throughout the design process. The IDs must spend ample time to understand the lecturers' needs to guide them to develop online subjects that complimented their own individual styles of teaching. Aside from the regular team meetings, communication took place via e-mail, telephone, and one-to-one meetings with individual members as required. In the cases under examination effective communication between participants occurred when the following factors were present:

- Positive and constructive feedback from the ID;
- Prompt responses by the ID to all requests and queries from lecturers;
- Regular sharing of individual design plans and problems among team members; and
- Acceptance and willingness to experiment with new ideas presented by peers.

Planning Strategies

The planning process was similar in both cases. Teams began using charts and diagrams to illustrate their ideas. These are convenient instruments for use in the planning process. The IDs prepared suitable examples for the lecturers, as initially they were likely to follow the ideas and structures presented by the IDs. The design experience was quite a challenge for all lecturers in the study. The findings also indicated that lecturers, whether novices or experienced users of ICT, required assistance from an ID to advise and guide them during the design process.

The lecturers had many initial concerns. For instance, they were concerned that their students may not really use their individual Web sites and other learning resources (handbook & CD-ROM for Team One users) they designed. The lecturers who were novices were pleased that the ID gave them the opportunity to plan the content and resources for their own subjects, as there was a concern among some that the ID would "take over." The constraining challenge for participants was the limited time allocated to complete the subject Web sites. They also felt that the planning process was demanding, because they had to learn basic ICT skills. It did not take them long to realise that prior attendance at the basic ICT skills courses provided by the institution would have helped to prepare them with the necessary technology skills needed to begin developing their individual Web sites. A further challenge for novices was to critically reflect on their current pedagogical methods and modify these in ways that suited the e-learning environments. During this study, this was not an easy step to take, as long-established ideas were open to challenge. However, assistance from the ID provided the motivation for lecturers to complete the share of work expected of them. Thus the ID was a support, a coach and a guide at each stage of the design process.

The IDs empowered the lecturers early in the development process to take full responsibility for the planning and designing of appropriate learning resources for their students. After a few weeks of consulting with the IDs, the lecturers realised they needed to learn basic ICT skills in order to implement their paper-based plans. After they planned their work on paper, they invited the ID to comment on their plans. Once there was agreement on the design, they were then shown by ICT experts how to use the software to implement their plans. This method provided an opportunity for IDs and ICT experts to discuss and fully explore the different design options available to meet the plans of the lecturers. At this stage the amount of ID assistance depended on the type of design strategies that the lecturers were using.

Producing effective and high-quality learning resources takes time and effort (Collis, 1996; Torrisi-Steele & Davis, 2000). Many e-learning environments have merely duplicated lecture notes from a traditional classroom situation that have been posted online for learners (Sims, Dobb, & Hand, 2002), but the trend and quality of using ICT for education purposes has improved. Many studies (Sherry et al., 2001; Salpeter, 2003) illustrate that online learning is more effective when the learner is empowered to be in control of their learning. As demonstrated in this study, most lecturers were coached, supported, and guided throughout the design process. Both IDs were committed to assist lecturers to learn the basic ICT skills. This would enable them to create simple but challenging and effective activities for the learners. Table 2 summarises the development process used by the community members in constructing their online learning environments.

Team collaboration within a community of practice opens up opportunities for members to share ideas, knowledge and expertise from a wide range of experiences that will enable them to peer-assess their work and develop a greater understanding of individual needs. This study supports the findings of previous research (Bennett et al., 1999; Torrissi-Steele & Davis, 2000; Phelps et al., 2000). These researchers reported that shifting from traditional teaching to e-learning necessitates a change in the staff development culture. The process of developing e-learning resources requires a collaborative team-based approach between lecturers and IDs that can be facilitated through a community of practice. In this study, collaboration developed through the various interactions that occurred through formal group meetings, and informal meetings between individuals which assisted to develop clear communication, planning and design strategies. Lecturers in both case studies emphasised that the continuous support they received from the IDs encouraged them to organise, plan and develop the learning resources for their specific subjects, further developing their confidence in using ICT in their teaching.

Table 2. Developmental processes of the online resources in the study

Community	Development process
Strategies	▪ Community discussions to generate ideas ▪ Use of charts and diagrams to generate and refine ideas ▪ Use of established web site models to generate ideas ▪ Took advice from technical experts ▪ Incorporated individual ideas from community members ▪ Resource collection and sorting ▪ Assessment strategies required ▪ Discussions on interface design ▪ Ongoing communication (e-mail, telephone, face-to-face) through group meetings and individual contact. ▪ Save back-up copies of development regularly
Roles	▪ ID took leadership role to facilitate site development. Each had good communication skills and experience in small-scale project management. ▪ Lecturers provided content expertise and individual requirements for Web site ▪ Community collaboration developing website
Learning	▪ Improvement in technical skills and knowledge (more confident working with distance education students) ▪ Greater confidence in utilising ICT for learning (more confident in developing a wider range of resources) ▪ Improved ability in editing Web site ▪ Greater confidence in working in community of practice
Concerns	▪ Extra workload (concern alleviated through individual training) ▪ Lack of ICT skills (addressed through individual training) ▪ Website management ▪ (concern alleviated through individual training and use of technical experts) ▪ Different individual requirements for assessment strategies (community discussion and agreement reached)

Implications for PNG

This study demonstrates that introducing e-learning programs requires team members (lecturers and IDs) to form an effective community of practice. This allows them to discuss the design plans and development issues collaboratively throughout the resource development process. Involving lecturers from the beginning of the process provides a sense of ownership in their subject development. It encourages them to express their concerns and fears about using ICT to the IDs who provide the support and guidance throughout the design process. Tertiary institutions in PNG, especially PAU, should begin the design process by analysing the ICT needs and requirements of lecturers, so that appropriate training and support can be given ahead of time. This will help to prepare them to integrate ICT into the learning environment. Welsh (2002) expressed the view that:

> *...new technologies offer designers many options for mixing and matching instructional contexts. Monolithic concepts of instructor-led workshops, computer-based training and classroom instruction give way to hybrid course designs that include a combination of technology-mediated events.* (p. 1)

According to Dede (1996), IDs and ICT experts have to be prepared to face the challenge of working with a wide variety of clients to design quality and effective learning resources that will supplement and/or replace face-to-face learning. Lecturers should be prepared to create learning activities that require students to:

- Use their initiative
- Work in teams on authentic, real world tasks
- Select the best method of carrying out the task from a diversity of learning methods
- Utilize the powerful features of advanced technologies
- Engage in activities that will challenge their cognitive abilities

In furthering this development, they should also be trained to access and analyse the tremendous amounts of information that is available on the World Wide Web. Tertiary institutions in PNG have different equipment, so training programs should be planned according to the needs and resources available in these workplaces. The multimedia centres provided by AusAid for the teacher colleges in PNG have confirmed that providing basic training and continuous support encourages lecturers to consider different ways of teaching through the use of ICT as a learning tool (Shaw, 2002). Shaw further stated that under this AusAid funded program:

> *... the centres will provide opportunities for different, improved and more efficient ways of teaching and learning. To make best use of this potential will require some changes in teaching approaches and methods.* (p. 3)

This study provides suggestions in relation to the approaches and methods that may be undertaken. For example, IDs and educational trainers should conduct basic ICT training workshops on how to use and design learning activities using ICT. Technology itself does not guarantee learning (Jonassen & Land, 2000), therefore it is important to prepare lecturers to use technology, while realising that they will have to change their teaching approaches and methods. Lecturers need the skills to communicate, reflect and revise their students' work, while at the same time they should assist learners to engage in e-learning. They need to develop engaging online lectures and learning activities.

Felton and Evans (2001) reported that staff training in using ICT for learning was successful when it was based on the individual lecturer's needs, before actually engaging them in designing their online subjects. Lecturers who are comfortable in using ICT in the learning environment would begin planning more advanced work for the learners. It was seen throughout the design process in this study that many of the participants would verify their ideas with the ID before including these in their e-learning environments. This supports findings from other studies (Ellis & Phelps, 2000; King et al., 2000), which emphasised the need of having IDs and ICT experts in academic institutions to provide the support and the assistance lecturers/educators would require. Tertiary institutions in developing countries such as PNG should have ID staff or an ICT expert to assist in developing e-learning environments.

PAU, where the first author works, is also planning to offer distance-learning programs in the near future. This is where training would be required for lecturers who would be involved in the program. PAU does have enough technological resources and facilities to use e-learning, but the main problem at this stage is to prepare lecturers who would be involved in distance education by offering basic training programs. Lecturers at PAU are computer-literate but they would still require training and support to use ICT in learning and teaching. Being familiar with the use of technology is not enough because teachers need to think about designing learning that will be student-centred. It is essential to prepare lecturers well in advance to master technology that will give them the confidence to plan and design effective learning resources with assistance from IDs or ICT experts. Lecturers and ICT experts may successfully collaborate when there is mutual understanding between them on the purpose of the project and the reasons why they are encouraged to use and integrate ICT learning environments. The collaboration process will be effective when lecturers know that the head of the faculty, the course coordinator and the ID/ICT expert fully support their plan to use ICT in learning.

Tertiary institutions in PNG, especially PAU, should begin the design process by analysing the ICT needs and requirements of lecturers so that appropriate training and support would be given to help prepare them to integrate ICT into the learning environment.

Although participants in this study were experienced lecturers, they nevertheless had difficulties in selecting suitable e-learning teaching methods for their individual subjects. They mostly used the teaching ideas and techniques supplied by the ID. Designing specific training lessons for busy lecturers, as demonstrated by Team Two in this study, will only work when training and mentoring is provided to address each individual's need. Team collaboration requires regular communication among team members and leads to a good working relationship. The lecturers in this study had good rapport with each ID, and had confidence that the ID would be able to assist them to create effective learning resources for their subjects. Cross fertilization of ideas will only work well when team members communicate well, and respect each other's expertise. The consensus from participating lecturers was that setting appropriate activities in the online learning environment was a great challenge, and they were grateful to the ID for supporting and directing them throughout each stage of the design.

This study has discussed that:

- Lecturers who are novices in using ICT in the learning environment can become discouraged if they do not receive sufficient support and assistance from an ID/ICT expert.
- Basic ICT training programs should be specifically designed to meet the needs of participants. Individual training should be undertaken as required.
- Ongoing support should be provided to lecturers throughout the design process.

- Lecturers will lose interest in the initiative if appropriate technological resources are not provided to them.
- It is necessary that IDs and ICT experts respond in a timely fashion to the lecturers' questions, concerns and problems. This motivates lecturers to continue working more effectively.

The authors have used the findings of this study to inform the development of a model that would assist the ID, ICT experts and lecturers to plan an appropriate ICT training program for lecturers at PAU, but it would also apply to other institutions. The proposed training model is shown in Figure 1 and is supported by the findings of the study and the lead author's experience in this university.

This model presents a five-step process designed to support the development of lecturers who are novices in the design of e-learning environments.

The steps may be summarised as follows.

- **Step 1:** The ID will analyse lecturers' ICT needs and create a policy that will guide both lecturers and the ICT technical team.
- **Step 2:** Lecturers will be given basic ICT skills training before involving them in the project.
- **Step 3:** ID and ICT experts work closely with the PAU administration and lecturers.

Figure 1. A basic ICT training model for PNG

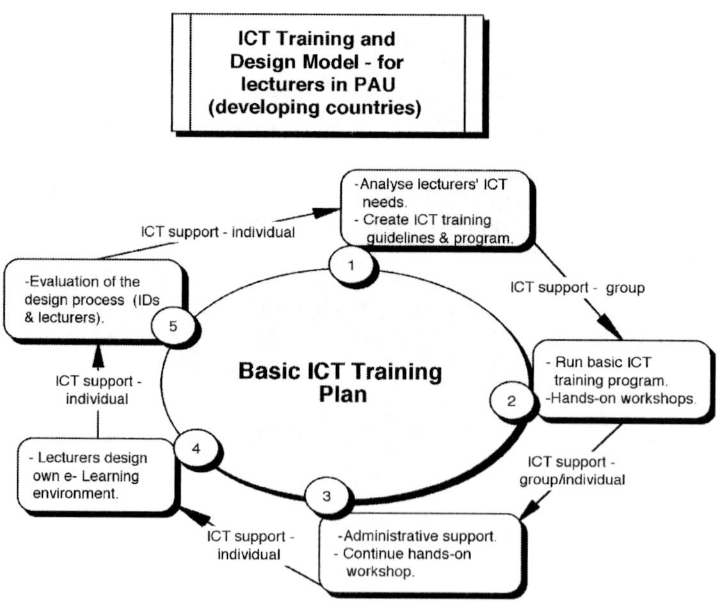

- **Step 4:** Lecturers apply the new skills acquired in their own e-learning environments. ID will provide on-going support and guidance.
- **Step 5:** Participants will evaluate their work. This cycle begins again but at a higher level.

Conclusion

Communities of practice have existed in a general sense since humans formed groups to share knowledge about performances (such as hunting and gathering of food, health) that were important for the well-being of their community. Lave and Wenger (1991) have formalised our understanding of this concept by associating it with knowledge management. As such it is used to describe the ways that people share existing knowledge, and cultivate or nurture new knowledge within an organised community.

Joint collaboration between members of a community of practice presents opportunities to share ideas, knowledge and expertise through mutual cooperation. However one of the lecturers in the larger team, who was overseas for part of the time, could not be fully involved in the project. Even though she used e-mail in a valiant attempt to keep in contact with her peers, she admitted that she was more like a legitimate peripheral participant, and her learning and personal contribution to the community of practice was at the periphery. Such situations will always occur with busy academics, and it is better to acknowledge this and accept that this creates unavoidable limitations on the outcomes of projects. The others in her group were able to meet regularly, and the processes of discussion helped them to enhance and refine the Web sites that they were developing.

The authors believe that the findings from this study suggest that the role of the ID changes from context to context. But in general, regular group meetings that focus on the development of a viable community of practice are essential for a successful design process. In the interim period, between meetings, the ID needs to find ways of ensuring that the lecturers have access to individual ICT support and training, and access to advice from the ID. In addition, the ID needs to subtly motivate the lecturers to complete the tasks that are required for the success of the next meeting. It is essential that the ID develop a good rapport with all members of the design team. This will help to decrease members' concerns and motivate all members of the community to fully participate. The context of PAU in PNG is different from the context of this study, but we believe that the key general principles apply.

First it will be important to develop viable and sustainable communities of practice that have a long-term view of their role, as there are many pedagogical, cultural and infrastructure issues to address. The role of the ID in this process cannot be overlooked. IDs are highly skilled professionals who will play a critical role in forming and sustaining these emerging communities of practice. Financial resources will need to be invested into the recruitment and professional development of IDs. We argue that this is a vital first step in the process as too often there is a temptation to purchase hardware and software because it is visible and tangible. This ignores the fact that lecturers and students need to be able to effectively use ICT to support and enhance learning. Placing a person in front of a computer does not guarantee learning any more than placing a person in front of a book.

Second, there is a need to provide lecturers and students access to the suitable technologies, but money also needs to be invested into their professional development. This will ensure that the lecturers develop the skills necessary to integrate the new technologies within their subjects, to extend the learning potential of their students.

These suggestions have the potential to create a social setting that encourages dialogue among members of the community. Under ideal conditions, this dialogue becomes a process of reflecting, interpreting, and negotiating meaning among members of a community of practice that has a focus on effective online learning. An essential member of this community of practice is the ID and the authors believe that the expanded view of the role of the ID is essential for the formation of viable communities of practice within a range of contexts that include the PNG setting.

References

Alexander, S., & McKenzie, J. (1998). *An evaluation of information technology projects for university learning*. Canberra. Department of Employment, Education, Training and Youth Affairs. Retrieved February 26, 2003, from http://www.dest.gov.au/archive/cutsd/publications/exsummary.html.

Bennett, S., Priest, A., & Macpherson, C. (1999). Learning about online learning: An approach to staff development for university teachers. *Australian Journal of Educational Technology*, *15*(3), 207-221.

Collis, B. (1996). Does more technology mean more choice for the learner? Experiences from the TeleScopia Project." *European Vocational Training Journal*, *7*(1), 13-21.

Dede, C. (1996). Distance learning-distributed learning: Making the transformation. *Learning and Leading with Technology*, *23*(7), 25-30.

Ellis, A., & Phelps, R. (2000). Staff development for online delivery: A collaboration, team based action learning model. *Australian Journal of Educational Technology*, *16*(1), 26-44.

Felton, E., & Evans, P. (2001, December 9-12). *Collaborative staff development across a diverse organization.* Proceedings from the 18th Annual Conference for Australian Society in Learning in Tertiary Education, University of Melbourne. Retrieved June 23, 2003, from http://www.ascilite.org.au/conferences/melbourne01/

Fisher, S., & Nygren, T. (1999). *Experiments in the cost-effective uses of technology in teaching: Lessons from the Mellon program so far*. Englewood Cliffs, NJ.

Holt, D.M., & Thompson, D.J. (1998). Managing information technology in open and distance higher education. *Distance Education, 19*(2), 197-216.

Johnson, D., & Johnson, P. (1997). *Joining together, group theory and group skills* (6th ed.). Boston: Allyn and Bacon.

Jonassen, D.H., Peck, K.L., & Wilson, B.G. (1999). *Learning with technology: A constructivist perspective*. Upper Saddle River, NJ: Merrill.

Jonassen, D.H., & Land, M. (Eds.). (2000). *Theoretical foundations of learning environments*. Mahwah, NJ: Lawrence Erlbaum.

Keppell, M. (2000, December 9-14). *Principles at the heart of an instructional designer: Subject matter expert interaction.* Proceedings from the 17th Annual Conference for Australian Society in Learning in Tertiary Education, Southern Cross University, Coffs Harbour. Retrieved September 19, 2003, from http://www.ascilite.org.au/conferences/coffs00/

King, H., Frizler, K., & Vigallon, S. (2000, November 15-18). *Why every college needs an instructional designer to support faculty innovation.* Conference Innovation in the Community College Conference on Information Technology, Anaheim, CA.

Lave, J., & Wenger, E. (1991). *Situated learning: Legitimate peripheral participation.* Cambridge: Cambridge University Press.

McNaught, C. (2001, December 9-12). *Quality assurance for online courses from policy to process to improvement?* Proceedings of the 18th Annual Conference of the Australian Society for Computers in Learning in Tertiary Education, University of Melbourne. Retrieved May 28, 2004, from http://www.ascilite.org.au/conferences/melbourne01/pdf/papers/

Oliver, R. (1998). Exploring strategies for online teaching and learning. *Journal of Distance Education, 20*(2), 240-254.

Phelps, R., Ledgerwood, T., & Barlett, L. (2000, December 9-14). *Managing the transition to online teaching: Role of project management methodology in the learning organization.* Proceedings of the 17th Annual Conference of the Australian Society for Computers in Learning in Tertiary Education, Southern Cross University, Coffs Habour. Retrieved May 28, 2004, from http://www.ascilite.org.au/conferences/coffs00/

Price, D., & Schlag, P. (2002). *Bringing classroom curriculum up to e-speed.* American Society for Training and Development. Retrieved February 12, 2004, from http://www.learningcircuits.org/2001/sep2001/price.html

Salpeter, J. (2003). 21st century skills: Will our students be prepared? *Technology and Learning, 24*(3), 17-26.

Shaw, G. (2002). *Computer literacy and the curriculum in Papua New Guinea.* Retrieved June 22, 2004, from, http://www.pngteachereducation.com/pastep/shaw.php

Sherry, L., Billig, S., Jesse, D., & Watson-Acosta, D. (2001). Assessing the impact of instructional technology on student achievement. *T.H.E. Journal, 28*(7), 40-43.

Sims, R., Dobb, G., & Hand, T. (2002). Enhancing quality in online learning: Scaffolding planning and design through proactive evaluation. *Distance Education, 2*(23), 135-48.

Torrisi-Steele, G., & Davis, G. (2000). A website for my subject: The experience of some academics' engagement with educational designers in a team based approach to developing online learning materials. *Australian Journal of Educational Technology, 16*(3), 283-301.

Vaa, R. (2002). *Papua New Guinea ICT use in education: UNESCO report in education.* Retrieved July 27, 2004, from http://www.unescobbkk.org/education/ict

Welsh, T. (2002). *Implications of distributed learning for instructional designers: How will the future affect the practice*? Retrieved March 15, 2004, from http://www.saskschools.ca/-parkland/implications.htm

Wenger, E. (2002). *Cultivating communities of practice*. Harvard Business School Press.

Chapter VII

Instructional Design, Development, and Context Expertise: A Model for "Cross Cultural" Collaboration

Cathy Gunn, University of Auckland, New Zealand

Beth Cavallari, University of Queensland, Australia

Abstract

The work of instructional designers in the current higher educational context is part of a complex process that traverses a range of professional relationships and communities of practice. The requisite professional skills include the ability to operate and communicate effectively across these different professional cultures. The term "culture" is used in a novel way to reflect the "academic tribes" concept described in the literature, and to highlight the complexity of working relationships in teams that are often transitory. This chapter presents a model that situates the instructional designers' role within the process of educational design and development. The model is derived from many years experience of managing development teams of different size and composition. Representative case studies provide evidence of its effectiveness across a range of projects and situations.

Introduction

This chapter presents an experientially derived process model that situates the work of university sector instructional designers within teams of discipline-based content experts and materials production personnel. The basis of this model in experience may assist practitioners in the field to fully understand the current demands of the role. The authors acknowledge that in many tertiary institutions, the process of curriculum or educational materials development is fragmented within the overall structure of the organization, and that this can impede progress towards implementation of teaching and learning enhancement strategies. In many cases, efficient systems, structures and channels of communication to facilitate this implementation process have yet to be fully established. It is particularly common in the case of e-learning, where many of the roles involved have been only recently established and the remainder are still evolving. Opinions vary on the ideal constitution of roles, location of services and means to formalize functional relationships between existing organizational units. One common approach is for a central unit to employ instructional design specialists to serve an entire institution, and subject matter experts to join transitory teams that are set up to work on specific development projects. While this centralized model is efficient in terms of resource use, the advantage may be offset by high demand for a range of management services. An emergent and increasingly common alternative is a networked model that creates opportunities for cross-functional synergies of the type that sustained working relationships allow to flourish. While a degree of replication may occur when this model is applied, the discipline-based instructional design specialist may offer a greater range of benefits. The current set-up in many tertiary institutions reflects a combination of these two models, with the optimum structure and network of relationships yet to be fully established. Our aim in this chapter is to provide an experience-based model to guide effective navigation of the terrain of the practicing instructional designer. While the model was developed in a university setting, the principles of good practice could equally be applied in commercial training development contexts. Instructional designers in commercial contexts may be working in institutions and professional cultures that are completely unfamiliar to them. They must therefore be able to apply principles and practices that allow them to operate effectively from day one.

Background: The "Cultural Landscape" of Instructional Design

Use of the term "culture" in the title and throughout this chapter requires a brief explanation, as it does not conform to the most common understanding of the word. Here, it refers to the professional culture that exists within organizations and established communities of practice rather than to world cultures. So the "cultural landscape" relates to the range of academic and/or professional contexts that instructional designers work in. Related to this definition, the term "context expertise" is used to refer to experience of working within the range and type of professional environments that instructional designers must operate within.

A recent trend towards team-based educational development in industry and tertiary institutions has brought many changes to existing roles, as well as the establishment of new ones. It is noted in the literature that established instructional design models do not reflect the reality of the role, nor fully describe the range of activities that instructional designers may engage in (Kenny, Zhang, Schwier, & Campbell, 2005). The traditional roles of individual training designer and educational developer are rapidly disappearing as the range of specialist contributions and the complexity of e-learning systems increases. While some development projects remain relatively small, others may involve as many as 20 team members. A typical list of roles involved in development teams might now include:

- Instructional designer
- Academic/professional development specialist
- Content specialist/provider
- Multimedia consultant/developer
- Subject librarian
- Project manager
- Researcher
- Programmer
- Independent evaluator
- Administrator
- Graphic designer
- Desktop publisher
- Video/sound producer
- Scriptwriter

These functional roles are not necessarily assigned to separate individuals, and the variety of activities attached to each one can be considerable. While communities of practice (Wenger, 1998) often exist within functional areas, "cross-cultural" communities are less common, so early identification of areas of common interest is critical to timely and successful outcomes. The common features of communities of practice include:

- Mutual engagement with common problems
- Joint enterprise
- Shared repertoire

Academic disciplines represent the communities of practice of content providers. These cultures are known to be distinctive and difficult for outsiders to penetrate. Becher and Trowler (2001, p. 21) describe "academic tribes and territories" as sets of taken for granted values, attitudes and ways of behaving." Within these cultures, there exists a complex web of inter-dependent relationships between disciplinary knowledge and the social interaction of individuals and groups. Much of the knowledge is implicit and the social behaviour is conditioned by long-term involvement. It is therefore a challenge for individuals from outside these cultures to enter and operate effectively within them. Less has been written about communities of practice that exist within the other functional areas involved in educational development, for example, graphic design, programming and multimedia development. Some literature addresses the often uneasy relationship between technical and academic roles (Burbules & Callister, 2000, chapter 1), and it may reasonably be assumed that other professional communities are equally complex and distinctive. The challenge of successful teamwork is further increased by the typically transient nature of development teams, even where a networked model is applied. A common process is for personnel to be allocated to teams, which are dissolved on completion of a project. The first challenge is to define a shared language and knowledge base to facilitate working relationships within a limited time frame. Another key task is to establish communication channels that allow continuity to be maintained when the various team members may not meet on a regular basis to follow-up issues and gain feedback on their respective contributions. The success of the production and completion phases depends heavily on the relationships and trust that are established in these initial phases. The experience-based model presented in this chapter was developed to define and facilitate the process of educational resource development within the context of a large traditional Australian university. It draws on the two underlying principles of heuristics and participative design to address these challenges and to promote effective "cross-cultural" working relationships.

A Heuristic Approach to Instructional Development

A heuristic approach to instructional development conforms to the definition offered by the Chambers Science and Technology Dictionary (Walker 1999, p. 557), that is, "an approach based on common sense rules and trial and error rather than on comprehensive theory." For instructional development, this involves exploratory problem-solving techniques followed by attempts to improve performance based on results of previous actions. The common method is gathering and evaluating feedback as the basis for improving performance. In the context of educational materials development, this approach maps onto the key concepts of design-based research (The Design Based Research Cooperative, 2003), an emerging paradigm for educational enquiry, and a methodology that both underpins and reflects the work described in this chapter. The principal aim of design-based research is to develop and improve educational artefacts through systematic evaluation and to improve purposively designed, or, to use Barab and Squire's (2004) term, "engineered" learning environments. Within this broad aim, a number of complementary objectives are served, that is, to:

- **Capture and reflect contextual complexity:** It has long been recognized that contextual factors are important to the extent of potentially making the difference between success and failure of an educational initiative regardless of the quality of pedagogy and resources. It is therefore important to recognize the complex interaction of contextual factors that impact on educational environments, for example, institutional culture, student characteristics and technology support systems.

- **Use empirical evidence as the basis for purposive design of learning environments:** Assumptions about the efficacy of any educational environment should be based on theoretical concepts that relate to the discipline, to accepted pedagogical principles and methods as well as to the needs of specific target users (Reeves, 2000). With the design-based research approach, practice is driven by evidence-based theory and the usefulness of theory is determined by its relevance to practice across a range of situations. This represents a systematic approach to design and implementation that addresses concerns within the educational community that innovation has emerged on an ad hoc basis that does little to illuminate anything beyond the specific development context (Liberty & Millar, 2003 chapter 1).
- **Evaluate and continually enhance educational design:** This process also addresses concerns about the lack of rigour applied to educational design and evaluation (Moran, 2004, pp. 3-7). Responsive evaluation methods that are capable of identifying all influential factors and acknowledging their impact are key drivers of continuous improvement. This type of evaluation reflects the quality assurance process that many teachers engage in as an integral part of their teaching role. However, the methods are often implicit aspects of professional practice that go largely unreported. When educational development is scaled up to team-based projects involving a range of specialist skills, more explicit methods and formal reporting procedures become necessary.
- **Move research beyond simple observation and "one-off" case studies:** A persistent challenge to e-learning development and evaluation, particularly noted by those outside the discipline, is that studies are too context-specific to contribute to a growing body of educational design knowledge. The need to begin with specific cases is justified by the unique aspects of each situation under study. However, once the unique aspects are recognized, ways are needed to move towards more generally applicable educational design principles and methods (Beetham, 2005). Recent experience has shown that quantitative methods alone are inadequate as a means of assessing the impact of educational innovations, and that qualitative and responsive methodologies are also required (Gunn, 2000). A heuristic approach is both the conceptual basis of design-based research and a suitable means through which to develop and refine an appropriate research methodology.
- **Facilitate learning from collective experience:** The shared experience of many educational design practitioners is a key element of the emergent knowledge base of the contemporary academic community (Beetham, 2005). The principle of shared experience in educational innovation finds a parallel in the open source software movement where individuals and groups base their own work on the experience of others. They then contribute new knowledge and developments back to the community for further reflection and development. Grounding in a common disciplinary culture within a community of practice needs to be encouraged for experience-sharing of this nature to occur.

Instructional design that reflects the heuristic, design-based research approach drives incremental development of educational concepts, content and activities in a way that supports mutual learning throughout the process within a multidisciplinary team. It also serves to promote organizational learning over the longer term. This is a critical contribution where educational development is part of a strategic initiative and investment.

The Role of Participative Design

Hurley (1992) proposed a simple model of the acceptance of new technology within organizations. This model, along with other more recent evidence, such as that presented by Light (2005) shows that full user participation in the educational design process is beneficial for a number of reasons:

- To ensure that system design reflects the specific needs of the target groups
- To ease acceptance of the resultant system by teachers through a real sense of ownership that is established during the development phase
- To support development of operational fluency through conceptual understanding and full participation in design, development and testing phases (Gunn, Woodgate, & O'Grady, 2005).

However, Mumford (1991) notes that participation across functional boundaries is often not part of an organizational culture. This is generally true for technology/pedagogy relationships within the e-learning context, whether those boundaries are between faculties or central units such as e-learning/educational development, IT and library services. Cross-functional collaboration brings together expertise in education, design, development, production and implementation. Two key challenges are:

- To find a shared language and knowledge base to support a meaningful level of participation.
- To facilitate productive working relationships across the different cultures of the individuals, groups and communities of practice involved.

Responsibility for fostering this collaboration may rest with the instructional designer or elsewhere in the team. However, understanding that this is the nature of the landscape of professional practice is a key success factor, regardless of where this responsibility lies.

Mapping the Process Terrain

A process model that has evolved to support the development of educational projects in an established Australian university is presented in Figure 1. The model has been applied and refined over a number of years, and the aims and principles that underpin the project development process are described below.

The model was first developed as an attempt to resolve an internal issue in a team that contained both instructional designers (IDs – employed as general staff), whose main role was to design educational resources, and educational developers (EDs – employed as academic staff), whose main role was to support curriculum development. Unsurprisingly, both the roles of these team members and the scope of their work tended to overlap. Although the two groups of staff worked within the same central unit, they also usually worked on different campuses, and had little time or opportunity for face-to-face interaction. The main issues that needed to be resolved related to open, effective communication and a clearer definition of the different roles. It was also important to identify the entire project development process in order to determine who took responsibility for particular elements.

The process illustrated in Figure 1 was initially developed and tested over a period of several months, starting with mapping of the complete process and the roles involved. All relevant staff participated in the analysis process, and this activity in itself helped to build trust and respect within the team. It led to a better understanding of the each person's role and activities within those roles, increased awareness of the external (and internal) forces generating barriers or constraints on the process, and facilitated the development of a cohesive, shared view of the process. This development of mutual understanding was subsequently recognized as a critical success factor, both for development of the process model itself, and for development of productive working relationships within project teams. It is also important for the model to be developed by those who participate in the process rather than being presented as part of a top-down, management defined structure. As a consequence, the entire group developed a sense of ownership that facilitated acceptance and implementation, as Hurley's (1992) acceptance model suggests it would. They also felt that they each had an equal say in its continued use or modification and the ongoing implementation of the model quickly became part of the culture of the group. Although the model is designed to show that overlap exists, it clearly identifies who is the main person responsible for each aspect of the development work. However, it is also designed to be flexible, so that a team of ID/ED staff working on any course or subject can make their own decisions about who should undertake aspects of the work. Decisions regarding specific roles and means of communication within the team are made prior to meeting with the content experts or teaching staff for whom the team is working, thus presenting an established team structure at the start of the project.

Following this initial development phase, the model was applied to a number of centrally funded projects, and was found to work well, particularly as it was employed in a flexible manner. Following this success, the funding centre chose to stipulate that access to funds for the development or redevelopment of curricula and associated resources depended on the teaching staff working with the ID and ED staff from the central unit. This approach is clearly seen to provide a comprehensive service that achieves professional outcomes.

Guiding Principles for the Design Process

The ED and ID staff involved in the development of the model agreed on the following guiding principles. These are the core principles that they would try to adhere to during implementation.

Client-Centred

The "client" is usually an academic content expert or team of academic content experts. In order to streamline processes and focus on the client's experience, points of contact (with many team members) are minimised. A corollary of this is that comprehensive notes must be taken so that the client does not need to repeat their requirements to various people in the team. This is achieved through additional processes requiring project staff to complete a "scope document" that outlines the client's requirements, and to enter additional notes, changes and other details into a project tracking system. The system notifies team members when an update to information has been entered. This forms part of the overall team communication strategy.

Project-Focused

As the client views all components of a "project" as one entity, the course-developers attempt to do the same. Previous practice had been to treat curriculum design and resource development as separate projects; and in fact, to treat the development of more than one resource for a course as a separate project. Each resource may have had a different instructional designer allocated to it. The curriculum development would have had an educational developer, and these people may never have discussed the project together. The obvious disconnectedness of this practice, which could easily lead to confusion on the part of the client and a disparity of educational approach on the part of the staff, obliged the group to recognize the need for a team-driven process and a whole project focus.

Team-Driven

All staff are full members of the development team, and work within the team for the life of the project. They have equal responsibility for maintaining open and informative communication. Project management is seen as an administrative function, and is carried out by a single individual who oversees all projects. The main roles of other staff involved, particularly in the development of resources, are reasonably self-explanatory, and on the whole more self-contained than the roles of the ID and ED. However, at any point, team members might request meetings or e-mail the entire team with issues or suggestions and involve the team in their development responsibilities. This is considered an essential aspect of communication, and to facilitate it, team e-mail lists are set up for each project. At the commencement of each project the project manager allocates the necessary staff; however, the team may be built-up over a period of time, with new members being assigned as the project brief is developed and requirements become clearer. This reinforces the necessity to document progress, so that staff who are new to the project have access to all prior information through the project tracking system. An example of the fluid nature of the model where team members are brought in as necessary is in the area of identification and design of learning experiences. This is shown as a shared responsibility of the ED and ID. While the ED and ID share overall responsibility, they also seek input from the subject librarian and the multimedia developers (for example, programmers, graphic designers and desktop publishers).

Case Description

Figure 1 identifies the stages of the process, and the team members who are involved at each stage. Initial descriptions of the phases were developed with the model and reworked following initial implementation.

Phase One: Initial Consultancy

In this phase the client meets with designated members of the development team—usually the instructional designer and the educational developer. The aim is to determine the "point of entry," that is, to identify where the client is located in relation to the overall process, and the type of support required.

The outcomes of this phase include:

- A shared understanding of the client's beginning location on the continuum and the next step.
- Definition of the parameters of the project, clarification of the expectations and identification of roles. This includes roles such as who will take notes, write-up and distribute notes, and to whom they will be distributed; how the team will communicate with each other and the client; who will arrange meetings and agendas; and who will attend meetings.

Figure 1. Educational and instructional design process model

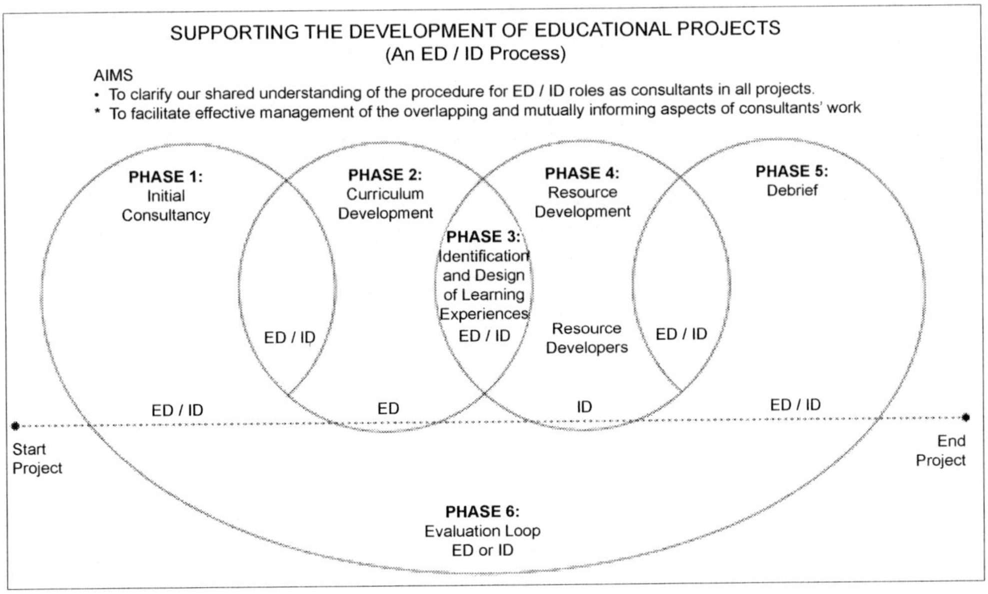

Phase Two: Curriculum Development

This phase focuses on curriculum development, including learning objectives, graduate attributes, assessment and approaches to teaching and learning. It will predominantly involve the educational developer in consultation with the client.

The outcomes of this phase include:

- Completion of relevant details for the course profile, and a proportion of the content development for the course.
- An update of the project's development to the whole project team.

During this phase a project briefing or scope document is generated to provide a record of the project's evolution, particularly of specific project meetings or developments that involve key project participants. This continues into Phase Three. Information and notes that do not seem to fit within the template or purpose of a project brief or scope are kept in the project tracking system.

Phase Three: Identification and Design of the Learning Experiences

The majority of the content is prepared prior to commencement of this phase, in continued consultation with the educational designer as required. This phase involves members of the development team and the client in discussion and design of learning activities and the overall learning environment. It includes the design of face-to-face activities, student directed activities, and activities for inclusion in a resource that might be developed or acquired. This phase draws upon the professional expertise and experience each member brings to the team, with the aim of designing an effective learning experience for students, and an overarching concern for the quality of educational outcome(s).

Outcomes from this phase include:

- Detailed notes of specific resources to be developed or sourced for this project.
- Consolidation of the curriculum development phase of the project.
- A completed project brief providing key information to assist in the handover of the project to different members of the teams; for example, members responsible for instructional design, materials development and production.

Project briefs differ according to the respective combination of personalities, approaches and contexts involved. However, a brief might typically address:

- Project rationale as described by project participants,
- The project development context,
- Proposed project timelines,
- Available funding and other resources committed to the undertaking,
- Specific concerns or difficulties likely to impact on the project, such as the availability of key participants,
- Plans for evaluation of the general quality and educational usefulness of the resource.

There is no prescribed format for the document, however it is essential for the brief to locate the development of specific educational resources in the wider context of the educational change/development that is being supported. In this way, the brief serves as a record of the support and resources committed to the initial development of the project, and will aid internal processes to document the various activities.

Phase Four: Development of Resources

This phase represents the major commitment of the instructional designer and the resource development team—including desktop publishers, graphic designers, multimedia producers, and/or programmers. Sign-off of the scope document is the first part, and completion of resources is the last part of this phase. Sign-offs for milestones and other intermediate steps, such as graphic style/interface sign-offs, are also a key feature.

Outcomes from this phase include:

- A fully detailed scope or specification document describing all the learning resources required.
- Written acceptance of the document by the client.
- Development, testing and delivery of all resource materials.

This phase generally involves client meetings to check materials, drafts of materials, client's acceptance of drafts, and/or editing of drafts. At the end of this phase, resources are complete and distributed, and client satisfaction is achieved.

Phase Five: Project Debrief

This phase involves appropriate members of the development team and the client reviewing the outcomes and effectiveness of the project and the process. This may be done as separate processes, as a team debrief does not usually include the client, whose feedback is sought independently.

Outcomes of this phase include an opportunity for all involved to view the final resources. This should also include decisions about the evaluation of the finished project, and of the development process. Implementation of the course may run concurrently with this phase, creating opportunities to review the work in the context of use, and to invite student, tutor and teacher feedback.

Phase Six: Evaluation

Ideally, project evaluation follows the design-based research approach, which aims to capture the contextual complexity of situations and to build on collective experience to enhance educational design on an ongoing basis. Evaluation of the performance of completed projects is not the starting point for evaluation in the sense that educational and instructional design is informed by evidence-based educational theory. The integration of professional wisdom with empirical evidence informs instructional development decisions. To this end, as an early milestone of a project, it is good practice to develop a prototype of a product for evaluation by staff and students. Evaluation of the finished product aims to confirm the relevance of these decisions, and the fact that they work in practice within the context of application.

Evaluation methods may include any qualitative and/or quantitative techniques that are available and accessible within a case study framework—techniques such as student behaviour and performance analysis, observation, surveys, interviews and system log data. In reality, this phase often falls short of the ideal, as time and funding for evaluation may be limited. In effect, responsibility for evaluation beyond the sign-off stage passes from the development teams to the lecturers using the resources. The lecturers may conduct formal or informal evaluations, and may exercise their professional judgment about improvements, enhancements or other revisions that the experience of use in context may suggest. The formal process of teaching evaluation allows the lecturer to request a set of questions relating to their use of technology, or to invent their own questions. Unfortunately the development teams rarely have access to that data to know what impact their work has on the target groups of students.

Principles: A Flexible Model

Following several months of implementation of the model, areas were identified where the processes needed to be sufficiently flexible to meet the needs of clients and to fulfil the educational philosophy within which the teams were working. It was acknowledged, in particular, that this process would not run in a linear fashion from start to finish, and many interruptions and reiterations might be expected to occur within any project. Provided it is accepted that this will occur, and that communication channels are operating well, they need not affect the integrity of the process or the quality of the outcomes. Some of the more commonly occurring adjustments follow.

The client may:

- Enter the process at any point
- Have already completed work in any of the phases, not necessarily involving what an educationalist would consider to be essential groundwork
- Not wish go over any ground they have already completed
- Not wish to avail themselves of all services available to them
- Choose to use instructional or educational design support, but complete resource development independently, or vice-versa
- Only require minor work that does not need full development team participation

The process may differ if the client is redeveloping or updating previous curricula and/or resources, and projects may include work done by other groups or organizations. The process depends on a good collaboration within the development team, as well as with the client. The efficiency and effectiveness of the development process will vary according to how well this is achieved.

The model has been applied to a wide variety of projects, from small Web site developments, to large faculty-wide projects involving the development of many resources for different subjects and courses. As the model is flexible and iterative, it has proved to be equally useful across all projects, providing a scalable, reusable and versatile strategy.

This completes a comprehensive description of the educational resource development process that is reflected by the model in its current form. The following section will now illustrate the initial development, application and refinement of the process model through case studies. Points where good practice has been facilitated by key knowledge and strategies on the part of the instructional designer will be identified.

Case Studies in Complex Domains

The process described in the model has proved to be effective across a range of different cases, therefore confirming its value as a theoretical approach. However, the nature of a model means that it provides a map of the process in a context-free manner. As such, it does not reflect the reality of application in different cases, as the nature of each situation is different, and a range of context specific variable factors comes into play. The nature of challenging content areas adds a common dimension of complexity to development projects. The instructional design and production staff may know little about these content areas. Three cases are elaborated as examples that describe the heuristic development process of the model itself. The first is a typical case from before the model was developed. The second case shows the progression of practice that led to development of the model, and the third describes a case in which the application and value of the model can be clearly seen. The case studies highlight some of the possible variable factors that may be encountered during the development process. They also provide the basis for compiling a list of such factors, and suggested ways in which these might be addressed.

For the instructional designer to be able to understand the context to make rational suggestions about learning and resource design, there must be a high level of communication and understanding with content experts. Pedagogical content knowledge (Barnett & Hodson, 2001), appreciation of the culture of the discipline, and what is readily acceptable to practitioners in that field needs to be communicated to the instructional designer. The designer requires the skills to be able to elicit such information, identify it from the bulk of information they will be given, and then to communicate it back to the content expert to ensure mutual understanding has been achieved. The same process needs to work in reverse, as decisions made by the instructional designer need to be communicated to the content expert so that they can recognize their relevance to the objectives and the context in which they are working. In essence, this is individual, situation-specific academic development. Given the depth of the shared understanding that defines academic and professional communities, finding a common language that spans all these different groups may indeed be considered a cross-cultural communication issue. The heuristic approach described in the opening sections of this chapter offers a practical way to facilitate this communication, to support development of mutual understanding and to implement an incremental development process. The three cases presented include:

1. A CD-ROM developed eight years ago. This, to some extent, initiated a series of project management processes and served as a catalyst for the consideration of interweaving curriculum design into the planning phase of the development of an educational resource.
2. Development of a Web site that followed a lengthy process of curriculum design and demonstrated the wisdom of having curriculum design specialists on development teams. This case also laid the foundation for the development of the current model.
3. A whole of faculty initiative which aimed to enhance the educational quality of specified teaching programs and resources for both distance and on-campus delivery, through curriculum design and improved integration of learning resources into faculty teaching practices (Steel, 2004).

Case Study One: Oxidative Phosphorylation

This project commenced before the development and implementation of the model, and before the development and implementation of a wide range of project management processes. The development process took more than 12 months, and the CD-ROM was then revised following a period of use and both formal and informal evaluation. The formal evaluation took place as part of the university's teaching evaluation processes. The results were sufficiently significant to warrant the project's continued development, and in addition, specific informal student and colleague feedback was sought and improvements were made accordingly in the subsequent phases of the project. The final version was made available three years after the project began.

Oxidative Phosphorylation (oxphos) is a process taught in the field of metabolic biochemistry. Students tend to have considerable difficulty mastering the concepts involved, which originate from the three disciplines of chemistry, physics and biology (Holzl & Reilly, 2000). The initial brief from the client was to create a CD-ROM to help students understand the concepts involved in the oxphos process.

Working almost entirely in isolation from other instructional designers and educational developers, the instructional designer in this case worked closely with the lecturer to first identify why the students had such difficulty with the concepts. It became clear that there had been no supported curriculum development for many of the courses teaching the oxphos process. There was no formal collaboration between the lecturers of all these courses, and a number of (erroneous) assumptions had been made about the level and substance of the prior knowledge of the students.

Other information not made explicit initially included course objectives, such as how the oxphos concepts fitted into the courses being taught, how those courses fitted into programs of study, and how the students' understanding of the concepts was to be assessed. An additional challenge was that research in this area was current. Throughout the life of the project, the lecturer found additional information, which required, at the very least, changes to the content and sometimes to the structure of the software that was being developed.

The instructional designer felt that these issues needed clarification before designing a piece of software that would effectively support students' learning. He followed a number of procedures to achieve this:

- Set-up and attended meetings with the client to discuss curriculum development issues
- Attended some of the lectures. This allowed him to not only come to grips with the difficult concepts, but also to see how they related to the rest of the content of the course, and how they fitted in with the overall program of study. The instructional designer was also able to identify teaching strategies currently in use, and have first hand observation of the student experience.
- Discovered as much as possible about the courses teaching the concepts—reading the course profiles and objectives, and meeting with the various lecturers
- Investigated the students' background and previous study

Before the involvement of this instructional designer, the normal practice would have been to develop the resource as described by the lecturer, with little or no inquiry into any curriculum design aspects. There would still have been close collaboration with the client, and the resource would have been developed in line with the best educational principles of resource-based teaching. The process would have followed the second half of the model, starting midway through Phase 3, where the client had already decided the appropriateness of the learning resource (in this case a CD-ROM).

The resource was designed and development started following several months of investigation by the instructional designer. It became clear during development that the team needed to learn the best ways to communicate with each other and with the client to make the process efficient. The client's initial preference was to sit with each team member as they developed specific parts of the resource. This proved to be very inefficient and frustrating for both the client and team members, as these meetings were disruptive and sometimes became acrimonious. A decision to limit the frequency and improve the structure of meetings helped to gain the necessary client feedback in a proficient manner. Such decisions should have been agreed much earlier in the process, and in consultation with the instructional designer and the client.

The iterative manner in which this project progressed facilitated identification of necessary internal processes such as writing clear scope documents, developing sign-off documents for various milestones and discrete project elements, dealing with content changes mid-stream and the introduction of new "great ideas," and formalising a debrief process.

Following debrief sessions, it became clear that improvements to the process should be established if such projects were to be embarked upon and carried out efficiently and agreeably. The debrief sessions provided specific (albeit anecdotal) evidence which informed the development and implementation of these processes. The main outcomes of this project, in terms of the model and processes were:

- Recognition of the importance of integrating curriculum development early in the resource development cycle.
- Development of clear processes, particularly within phases four and five of the model, which ensure consistency and clarity for all staff involved in development.
- Recognition that there was a three-way "battle" of disciplines between the content expert, the development team and the instructional designer. It was felt that there were also nuances between the development team, including the instructional designer (all general staff) and the client, as an academic staff member. This led to the development of better communication processes.
- Identification of some negative perceptions of team members: some felt that their opinions were undervalued; the client at first felt that the development team—as non-scientists—would not be able to offer anything useful. This prompted a process for identifying and clarifying everyone's roles at the commencement of a project. It also identified the need for a much higher level of team collaboration and trust.
- Acknowledgment that not having efficient processes caused much frustration, too much iteration and significant delays in the development cycle.
- Acknowledgment that there was frequently no common goal or level of understanding within the development team. This prompted clarity of goals, roles and the necessity of open communication and clear and accessible documentation.
- Recognition that due to the nature of academic work, the client was sometimes hard to contact and could not always provide content within the time expected by the development team. This led to the development of more efficient and better-negotiated time-line processes, as well as an understanding on the part of the development team that delays are sometimes unavoidable. It also led to the understanding that undertaking multiple projects is likely to result in less development team downtime than working on one large project at a time.

The Oxidative Phosphorylation CD was conceptualised by Dr. Paul Reilly, formerly of the University of Queensland's Department of Biochemistry, and developed by the Teaching and Educational Development Institute (TEDI). The project won an internal award for excellence in educational multimedia in 1998, and was short-listed in *The Australian* Awards for Excellence in Educational Publishing in 1999.

Case Study Two: Thermodynamics

Thermodynamics—The Virtual Power Plant Web site—was designed to help undergraduate mechanical engineering students understand thermodynamic principles through their exploration and manipulation of power plant operations in a virtual learning environment. The usual teaching methods involved textbook representations, descriptions of plant operations and a visit to a coal-fired power plant. The lecturer found that the students had difficulty in relating their abstract, theoretical understanding of thermodynamics to the plant operations they encountered on their field trip, and then to the diagrammatic and text-based content (Kelly, 2002).

The process used to develop this Web site was much more closely related to the model in both organisation and implementation. This project went through a lengthy and thorough planning period, which followed an action learning cycle. This action learning cycle occurred in place of phases one, two and three of the model, and although curriculum development was not the main focus, it was certainly an essential part of this process.

The development, debrief and evaluation phases of this project also followed the principles of action learning, including reflection and review cycles which created an iterative and comprehensive sequence of events.

Following the planning phase, a prototype was developed and tested by members of the target audience. Although the final version of this project was published nearly four years after the planning commenced, the Web site was in continual use by students from the development of the prototype. Both formal and informal feedback was sought from the students at key points in the project's development; the feedback regarding the usefulness of the site in meeting the educational objectives was always positive. The lecturers involved also felt that by using the site the students showed a significantly better understanding of the relationship between the theoretical and practical sides of the subject and that this was borne out in their assignments and results.

The action learning team consisted of educators with various roles and backgrounds, a librarian, and the course lecturer. The team practices of the action learning process provided flexibility, full group consultation, considered action and creativity. The recurrent cycle of action informed by group reflection was facilitated by a mentor, and allowed team members with different areas of expertise to have input at the design phase. For example, the initial concept of building a three-dimensional "walk-through" environment was superseded by the development of a multi-layered two-dimensional interface, which connects to external software packages running in parallel in separate windows (Kelly, 2002).

Compared to the project described in the first case study, this project progressed more smoothly and was a more enjoyable process for the client and the team. Following debrief discussions with the team, the outcomes of this project, in terms of the model and the project management processes were:

- The instructional designer was able to work much more effectively as she was not isolated from others with educational input, or from the development and client teams. The instructional design role was fully integrated into a "whole team" approach.
- This project followed the new project management processes. There was very little re-development required during the first phase, which produced a functioning prototype.
- It was agreed that the successful progress of this project was an outcome of the considerable amount of initial groundwork and the application of good project management practices, therefore underlining the importance of good planning processes to project success.
- The communication methods employed during the life of this project were discussed at the commencement of the project, and adhered to by all members of the project team, including the client. The client was considered as an integral member of the project team, which engendered a collegial spirit and built a high level of trust and cooperation within the team, from the beginning of the project. This reflects the benefits of participative design and a "whole team" approach.
- Following the development of the initial prototype, the action learning team was disbanded, leaving the client and the development team as the only participants in the ongoing design. The instructional designer felt that the continued development of the project would have been more successful if an ED could have been involved at key points along the way.

The Virtual Power Plant Web site was conceptualised by Dr. Srdjan Nesic, formerly of the University of Queensland School of Mechanical Engineering, and developed by the Teaching and Educational Development Institute (TEDI). In 2002, it won Best Tertiary Web site at *The Australian* Publications Association (APA) Awards for Excellence in Educational Publishing; Best Web Project in the 2002 ASCILITE (Australasian Society for Computers in Learning in Tertiary Education) Awards, and was short-listed in the E-learning category in the 2002 Asia Pacific ITC Awards (for details see www.tedi.uq.edu.au/virtualpowerplant).

Case Study Three: Distance Learning Enhancement Plan

The third case study—the Distance Learning Enhancement Plan (DLEP)—is one that encompasses the curriculum review and development of a large number of courses, many with accompanying print and multimedia resources. This project was funded at the school level from central sources. Based on experience of the need for systematic and thorough educational design support, the funding included a position for a full-time educational developer and a full-time instructional designer for the duration of the project.

The major aim of the project was to improve the quality and flexibility of both targeted distance and on-campus education programs and resources. It was proposed that this could be achieved through curriculum design and improved integration of innovative educational technologies into faculty teaching practices. Schools within the faculty were requested to put forward courses they considered of key importance within their programmes, and thus to facilitate a programmatic approach to enhancement (Steel, 2004, p. 866).

The processes and principles used to achieve these aims were aligned with the phases of the model, with the initial work of curriculum design being instigated at the outset of each project, encompassing collaboration with the instructional designers and lecturing staff, as well as resource coordination personnel (for example, from the library and the distance education unit). The subsequent design and development work was organised and achieved, again with appropriate levels of consultation, using the iterative and reflective process that the model requires.

The funding provided was sufficient for a variety of print, Web site and CD-ROM resources to be created by a development team which included programmers, graphic designers, Web developers, animators, additional instructional designers and a project manager. Over 70 courses were involved in curriculum design review and support, with major resources finally being developed for about half of these.

The timeframe for this project was three years, commencing in 2002. With specific educational and instructional design staff dedicated to the project, considerable progress was achievable in that time period. There was an added advantage that the education staff were situated on the same campus as the lecturing staff involved. As the campus is comparatively small in terms of staff and internal students, there were many more opportunities for direct contact, productive collaboration and community building.

To ensure a process that was consistent, dynamic and effective, the educational developer also performed overall project management tasks, and set up her own project management structures. She recognised the need to instil and maintain momentum on the project. Again, this was achievable due to the proximity and dedication (both in the sense of "single focus on" and "commitment to" the project) of the education support staff involved.

The outcomes of this project in terms of the model and our project management processes were significant compared to other experiences of similarly large and reasonably well-funded projects. Success in this case is measured by the number of successful multimedia and curriculum design projects being developed and the continued enthusiasm and commitment of the lecturing staff and the development teams involved. The outcomes included:

- Recognition of the necessity for academic staff development in relation to curriculum review and design and resource development, to be an integral part of the process during the initial consultancy phase. This was undertaken as individual work-based staff development by the educational support staff. Managing the curriculum and resource design process in a similar way was seen as the most appropriate method. "Traditional workshop approaches to academic staff development (ASD), while still valuable for various staff development situations, may only play a minor role. To some extent workshops disaggregate innovation into less integrated aspects of development (e.g., technical skills, teaching approaches, assessment etc). A number of researchers have concluded that many academics are now resistant to workshops and do not have time to attend sustained staff development courses" (Steel, 2004, p. 865).

- The quality of each individual curriculum development and resource development project is thought to be very high, this appraisal being based on informal client and student feedback, as well as feedback from the development teams who have compared the achievements with other projects. Formal feedback via the university's teaching evaluation processes is yet to be compiled. An evaluation of the entire project is in-progress.
- The majority of the involved teaching staff reported a high level of satisfaction with both the process and outcomes.
- From discussions with the participants in this project, it appears that its acknowledged success was consistent with the application of the model. Key success factors were a) insistence on following consistent and efficient project management processes and b) the availability, enthusiasm and perseverance of the education support staff who were not only involved in the project, but essentially managed it from start to finish.

The majority of the educational resources stemming from this project are undergoing a process of formal evaluation. One example, which has completed every phase of the development process, is the "Hang in There" distance learner support kit. This is a resource kit designed to support first year, undergraduate distance learners. It comprises a print resource and a comprehensive Web site that can be viewed at (http://www.uq.edu.au/hanginthere)

Full implementation and evaluation of this kit by distance students took place in 2004 with significantly positive results. The development team received a commendation at the University of Queensland Excellence in Teaching Awards for the category "Enhancement of Student Learning."

Common Factors Encountered

Common factors that may arise during different phases of the project development process can be anticipated reasonably well based on the experience recorded to date. While the model is constantly under review in terms of revision and further enhancement, the list of factors noted so far is detailed below.

Effective Communication

Communication is such a key factor that conscious effort and strategies to develop good channels, common language and shared understanding within teams are necessary items in the instructional designers' toolkit. Experience shows that benefits are gained from sustained working relationships that are characteristic of the networked model.

The Life Span of Content Material

One of the case studies showed that strategies to accommodate mid-stream changes to content material might be necessary in disciplines that are particularly dynamic. Such strategies may include choice of technology, frequent revisiting of specifications, or other communicative elements.

Overall Coherence of Courses and Programs

The first case study revealed what may be recognized as a common situation in many disciplines and institutions. Where curriculum review has not taken place for some time, courses are not well coordinated into a coherent whole. In this case, the role of the instructional designer extended far beyond focus on design and development of content specific materials. The value of employing heuristic and responsive design-based research methods is illustrated by the context-specific nature and scope of the initial problem the designer had to solve.

Ability to Conceptualize the Problem or Challenge to Learners

In one respect, instructional designers may have an advantage over content experts. As relative novices in the subject, they may come from a perspective closer to that of the learner than most experts who have long since moved on from the novice/learner position. There is also a skill in relating specific learning challenges to "bigger picture" scenarios that helps to lead to good solutions. Part of the communication process between the instructional designer and content experts is focused on accurate conceptualization of the problem that then drives development.

Recognizing Phases of the Model that Relate and Those That Don't

Strict adherence to a model is not appropriate in every case, and instructional designers should be able to recognize when this is the case. Flexibility means being aware and able to respond to the needs of specific clients and situations.

Levels of Commitment and Capability of Staff

These dimensions can vary widely, and different levels of overall success and integrated professional development will apply. Recognizing these aspects and how to address them can be a complex process due to the variable reactions of people to change within organizations. The nature of the disciplinary culture of expertise may be challenged by the introduction of new technology and educational strategies.

Effectiveness of Community Building

This also depends on a number of factors that may be more or less within the scope of influence of the instructional designer. Obvious factors such as proximity and personality, and the less apparent cultural and personal issues, may all come into play.

The skill required to identify and manage variations related to these factors generally comes with experience, though reference to the model and records of previous experience are a good starting point.

Conclusion

The methodological approach to development of the instructional/educational design model described in this chapter has resulted in improved service to the institution, and enhanced performance by development teams. Being experientially based, it offers useful guidelines and a workable process model for use beyond its development context. This assertion is borne out by two factors. One factor is the many common situational characteristics shared with other institutions in the current context. The other factor is that significant successes have resulted from repeated application and refinement of the model within a fairly typical institutional context. Kenny et al. (2005) note that:

While instructional designers apparently do make use of the techniques delineated by traditional, process-based models, it is clear that they do not spend the majority of their time working with them nor do they follow them in a rigid fashion ... They also engage in a wide variety of other tasks that are not reflected in ID models.

A model that is derived from experience may partially address this problem. The design-based research approach underpinning the development of the model has proved useful as a methodology—both for refinement of a model that can be applied in a wide range of situations, and as a basis for project work with clients. To conclude this chapter, some general principles derived from the three case studies and from additional experience of the authors follow.

- The heuristic approach supported by principles of design-based research ensures that specific contexts are well-served and best educational practice results.
- The instructional designer should be aware of all aspects of the design process, including systematic evaluation methods. While they may not be individually responsible for all functions, they need to be familiar with the processes as their contribution both affects, and is affected by all others. It is therefore critical that they understand the role and inter-dependence of all other contributions.

- Development of the process model reflects the heuristic and participative design principles recommended for instructional design work within teams, and therefore demonstrates by example the successful application of those principles.
- Generation of the project brief is a key aspect of the communication and mutual learning process within projects. This phase of the process clarifies the roles and responsibilities of all team members. It also facilitates development of the shared language and communication channels that are essential to successful projects.

The instructional/educational design process model will continue to evolve over time as a guide to effective team-based development in the rapidly advancing field of educational technology and e-learning design.

Acknowledgments

The following group of staff at TEDI contributed to development of the original model of ID and ED interaction throughout the lifespan of a project:

Trish Andrews, Beth Cavallari, Wendy Chalmers, Paul Fenn, Clair Hughes, Greta Kelly, Chris Newman, Mia O'Brien, Lara Ross, Emma Somogyi

References

Barab, S., & Squire, K. (2004). Design-based research: Putting a stake in the ground. *Journal of the Instructional Sciences, 13*(1), 1-14.

Barnett, J., & Hodson, D. (2001). Pedagogical content knowledge: Toward a fuller understanding of what good science teachers know. *Science Education, 85*(4), 426-453.

Becher, T., & Trowler, P.R. (2001). *Academic tribes and territories* (2nd ed.). The Society for Research into Higher Education & Open University Press.

Beetham, H. (2005). E-Learning research: Emerging issues. *ALT-J, Research in Learning Technology, 13*(1), 81-89.

Burbules, N., & Callister, T. (2000). *Watch IT: The risks and promises of information technologies for education*. Boulder, CO: Westview Press.

Gunn, C. (2000). CAL evaluation: Future directions. In G. Jacobs, D. Squires & G. Conole (Eds.), *The Changing Face of Learning Technology* (pp. 59-67). Cardiff: University of Wales Press.

Gunn, C., Woodgate, S., & O'Grady, W. (2005). Repurposing learning objects: An alternative to reuse*? ALT-J, 13*(2), 189-200.

Holzl, A. & Reilly, P. (2000, November). *The application of a strategic curriculum design model to the teaching of biochemistry*. Paper presented to The Effective Teaching and Learning at University Conference, University of Queensland, Brisbane. Retrieved May 22, 2006, from http://www.tedi.ug.edu.au/conferences/teachconference00/papers/holzl-reilly.html

Hurley, J. (1992). Towards an organizational psychology model for the acceptance and utilisation of new technology in organizations. *The Irish Journal of Psychology, 13*(1), 17-31.

Kelly, G. (2002). A powerful virtual learning environment. In A. Williamson, C. Gunn, A. Young, & T. Clear (Eds.), *Winds of Change in a Sea of Learning: Proceedings of the 19th Annual Conference of The Australasian Society for Computers in Learning in Tertiary Education* (pp. 827-831). Auckland, New Zealand: Unitec Institute of Technology.

Kenny, R.F., Zhang, Z., Schwier, R.A. & Campbell, K. (2005). A review of what instructional designers do: Questions answered and questions not asked (Electronic version). *Canadian Journal of Learning and Technology, 31*(1). Retrieved January 16, 2006, from http://www.cjlt.ca/content/vol31.1/kenny.html

Liberty, K., & Millar, J. (2003). *Research as a resource for evidence based practice*. Palmerston North: Dunmore Press.

Light, A. (2005). The principle of genuine user participation, usability news. In K. Bødker, F. Kensing, & J. Simonsen (Eds.), *Participatory IT design: Designing for business and workplace realities*. MIT Press. Retrieved January 16, 2006, from http://www.usabilitynews.com/news/article2170.asp

Moran, D. (2004). *Evidence-based educational methods*. Elsevier Inc.

Mumford, E. (1991). Participation in systems design: What can it offer? In B. Shakel & S.J. Richardson (Eds.), *Human factors for information usability* (267-290). Cambridge University Press.

Reeves, T.C. (2000). *Enhancing the worth of instructional technology research through "design experiments" and other development research strategies.* Paper presented at a Symposium on International Perspectives on Instructional Technology Research for the 21st Century at the AERA Annual Meeting, New Orleans. Retrieved July 12, 2006, from http://www.coe.uga.edu/~treeves/AERA2000Reeves.pdf

Steel, C. (2004). Establishing a zone where technology innovation is supported. In R. Atkinson, C. McBeath, D. Jonas-Dwyer, & R. Phillips (Eds.), *Beyond the Comfort Zone: Proceedings of the 21st Annual Conference of The Australasian Society for Computers in Learning in Tertiary Education* (pp. 865-874). WA: Perth, Australia.

The Design Based Research Collective. (2003). Design-based research: An emerging paradigm for educational inquiry. *Educational Researcher, 32*(1), 5-8. Retrieved May, 22, 2006, from http://www.aera.net/pubs/er/pdf/vol32_01/AERA320104.pdf

The University of Queensland. (n.d.). *Hang in there: The distance learning support kit.* Retrieved May 29, 2006, from http://www.uq.edu.au/hanginthere.

The University of Queensland. (2002). *The virtual power plant.* Teaching and Educational Development Institute. The University of Queensland. Retrieved May 29, 2006, from http://www.tedi.uq.edu.au/virtualpowerplant

Wenger, E. (1998). *Communities of practice: Learning, meaning, and identity.* Cambridge University Press.

Section III

University-Wide Context

Chapter VIII

Educational Design at Southern Cross University Australia: A Case Study

Chris Morgan, Southern Cross University, Australia

Jenny Bird, Southern Cross University, Australia

Meg O'Reilly, Southern Cross University, Australia

Abstract

This case study provides an overview of educational design practice in a relatively small regional Australian university with a unique profile of highly distributed, mature-aged learners, and a particular mandate regarding its students and the region in which it is located. In its 15-year history at Southern Cross University, educational design practice has been significantly shaped by its context, and has evolved continuously to meet the changing needs of the university and its student profile. This case study charts educational design evolution over the 15 years, the impact of online learning upon roles and practice, the current institutional "footprint" of the educational designers, the convergence of roles with academic staff development, and its current research agendas. Chapter II should be read as the companion to this chapter for a more extensive exploration of the issues and dilemmas of educational design practice.

Introduction

Southern Cross University is one of Australia's 37 publicly funded universities, located in the growing regional area of northern New South Wales. It is relatively small in size, but has three campuses and covers a large regional catchment extending 500 kilometres along the eastern-Australian seaboard. It has approximately 12,000 students, a little under half of whom are studying in distance mode. It is one of Australia's newer universities and was quick to embrace flexible learning methodologies in order to serve the needs of its widely dispersed community, as well as to attract students from across Australia to its innovative programs. In contrast to many other universities in the sector, Southern Cross has a high level of mature-aged students, often returning to study after long absences, and with a relatively low average socio-economic status. School leavers occupy only approximately one quarter of the total student intake each year. In line with its open learning philosophy, the university has liberal admission procedures, various alternative entry schemes and a strong emphasis on student support and learning assistance to enable students to gain the confidence to succeed in their tertiary studies (Morgan & Hayden, 2002).

In this context, the practice of educational design has always been mindful of the critical importance of a well-planned and developmental first year student experience that accounts for the needs of tentative, inexperienced learners. Units and courses have also required considerable flexibility and a realistic workload to enable the many mature-aged, part-time students to successfully manage competing commitments. With its heavy reliance on distance education, a further key focus of educational design practice is to foster interactive communities of learners, to bridge isolation with the intelligent use of accessible communication technologies. These issues are further explored in this case study and discussed in the context of the rapidly changing Australian higher education scene, along with other technological and pedagogical advances in the sector.

Instructional Design at Southern Cross University: A 15-Year History

Early Days

Instructional designers were first engaged in 1988 as the university moved seriously into distance learning. It was recognised at that time that faculty could no longer deal individually with the increasingly complex task of teaching in dual mode (internal and distance education), and that expertise was required to guide teaching staff through the processes involved in the development and delivery of distance learning materials. Expertise was particularly sought in issues such as how to write and structure distance learning materials, how to assess student learning at a distance, and support was also required in the production processes that enabled quality controlled, user-friendly resources in a variety of media to be provided to students in a timely manner for commencement of their studies each semester.

The instructional designer was primarily, at this time, a project manager who had oversight of the process from initial conception of the subject through to delivery of materials—more or less consistent with Allen's (1996) profile of instructional designers in Australia. It was a collaborative, team process that included the subject writer, the instructional designer, an academic reviewer, and production workers that usually included the desktop publisher, proofreader and any other specialist media developers as required. Distance learning packages usually took the form of a print-based study guide and book of readings, combined with supplementary media options such as video or audio. Usual phases in development included initial team meeting, development of a subject blueprint, first draft, final draft, and then production and materials assembly. The instructional designer retained oversight of the various phases and was responsible for the overall quality and pedagogical soundness of the materials.

At this time, instructional designers were a relatively new kind of higher education worker. Most academic staff were unfamiliar with the role, responsibilities, authority, and place within the academic structure of the university. In some quarters, suspicion existed about the rigour of the theory underpinning their practice, and concerns were expressed that these new "educational technocrats" were eroding the natural domain of the teacher. Yet to the degree that instructional designers were able to provide practical and timely advice and support to faculty, and shaped their support intelligently to meet individual personalities and needs, the role was widely embraced (Allen, 1996; Inglis, 1996). By the mid- to late-1990s, approximately half of the university's total student enrolment was studying at a distance. The instructional designer, by this time, was built into the fabric of the university.

An Open Learning, Adult Education Focus

It became apparent that, as the new distance programs gathered pace at Southern Cross, the overwhelming student profile was the part-time, mature-aged student, often returning to study after long absences (Bird & Morgan, 2003). Sometimes study was undertaken for recreational purposes, but the greater majority were interested in upgrading qualifications or retraining with a new career path in mind. Many had substantial work and family commitments, and study necessarily occupied a third priority. Students commonly welcomed the flexibility that distance study afforded them, but often lamented the isolation inherent in distance learning. Their work and family commitments meant that study was usually undertaken in spurts, as time permitted, and that they did not follow the usual, regular study patterns of internal students. They needed clear direction regarding university expectations and timely support in order to work efficiently in the scarce time available to them.

The profile of distance learners at Southern Cross provided a very clear mandate to instructional designers regarding the design of materials. The philosophy of open learning, along with adult education principles (see for example, Rowntree, 1990, 1992) were infused throughout study materials to offer as much support to learners in pacing themselves through the materials and preparing for formal assessment tasks. Common strategies included advance organisers, a first person teaching narrative representing a "tutorial-in-print," in-text activities with feedback, commentary on readings, assignment choices, flexible study periods, academic skills development, designated teleconferences to discuss issues and toll-free connection to the university. Instructional designers were instrumental in introducing these strategies in recognition of the hurdles that distance learners face, borne out by the consistently high attrition rates.

By the mid-1990s, instructional designers at Southern Cross had eschewed the title instructional design—indeed "instruction" was the antithesis of pedagogical underpinnings of adult learning and open learning theory. The title "educational designer" was substituted and remains to this day.

Moving Online: Beyond Dual Mode

By the late 1990s, online learning had moved from the margins of early adopters into the mainstream of the university, with the institutional licensing of an online learning management system. At this time the educational designers supported the exploration of a number of models of online delivery to distance learners, from fully online to various forms of usage supplementary to existing print-based resources. Fully online models of delivery proved unpopular with students, who neither wanted to read on screen, nor bear the cost of printing large digital documents. However supplementary online interactions, in concert with print-based study material, proved to be enormously popular with distance students who could now freely interact with fellow students and their tutors and lecturers. This gave rise to far more dynamic teaching and learning designs and assessment opportunities that educational designers were keen to explore and evaluate.

However, for teachers who had coped with the complexities of supporting both internal and external cohorts of students in the one subject, a new, third mode of delivery had the potential to over-burden staff with duplicated effort. Educational design staff, supported by a new flexible learning policy, were keen to develop hybrid models of delivery that integrated the best components of face-to-face, print-based and online learning, and can be made available to all students whether studying locally or remotely. Progress has been slow on this front, largely due to an entrenched academic culture regarding teaching practices, administrative difficulties, and conservative expectations of students regarding what constitutes a university education.

Convergence of Educational Design and Academic Staff Development

In recognition of the commonality between educational design staff and the academic development staff, the two combined forces in 1997 to form the Teaching & Learning Centre at Southern Cross University. This convergence of educational design with academic staff development acknowledged the common theoretical foundations in student learning theory, and the very practical orientation of both towards developing and skilling academic staff to be better teachers. It also recognises that flexible delivery requires a more flexible deployment of expertise.

Since 1997 there has been considerable further convergence between the two roles, to the degree that today they are barely distinguishable—all are involved with a variety of one-on-one sessions with individual staff, small group workshops, policy development, teaching in the Graduate Certificate in Higher Education (an accredited academic staff development program) and a variety of other tasks as represented below:

Current Role of Educational Designers

Educational designers at Southern Cross are classified as academic staff and are no longer project managers of the development of course materials. Project management and quality assurance of course materials occurs in the academic faculties who retain a high level of ownership of these processes. Educational designers now consult, when requested, on all aspects of the teaching and learning process, whether in face-to-face settings or in distance mode. In some universities educational design staff may be classified as academic or professional staff or even a mixture of the two within the same team. The tensions arising in these circumstances are further explored in Chapter II.

The following model has been developed at the Teaching and Learning Centre at Southern Cross to represent the flexible learning cycle and the various points in which educational designers can offer their expertise. It is a model that extends most conventional curriculum models by the inclusion of student support and the development of learning resources, reflecting an integrated flexible delivery philosophy.

Educational designers provide support at all points in the quality cycle (also known as *Pathways to Good Practice*) in the following ways:

1. **Designing and re-designing units:** Educational designers continue to provide support to academic staff in all aspects of the design of units, with a particular focus on the constructive alignment of the curriculum (Biggs, 1999), the appropriate use of technology, and sound assessment practices which support meaningful learning.
2. **Developing and producing resources:** Educational designers consult with course authors about best practice in writing and developing educational resources. They provide support about structure, style, use of media, and best use of communication

Figure 1. Intersection of roles between academic developers and educational designers

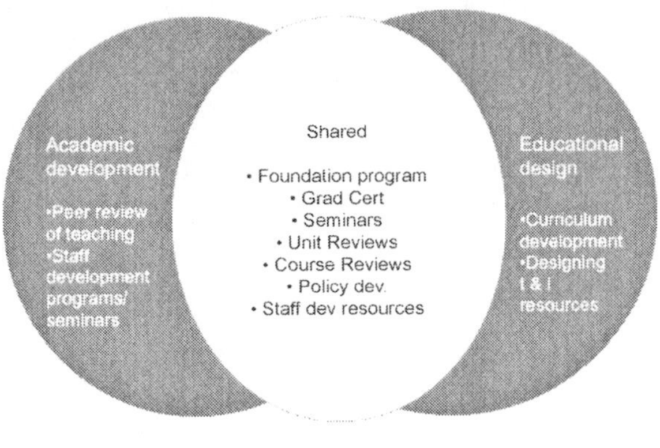

Figure 2. Flexible learning quality cycle at Southern Cross University (http://www.scu.edu.au/services/tl/pathways)

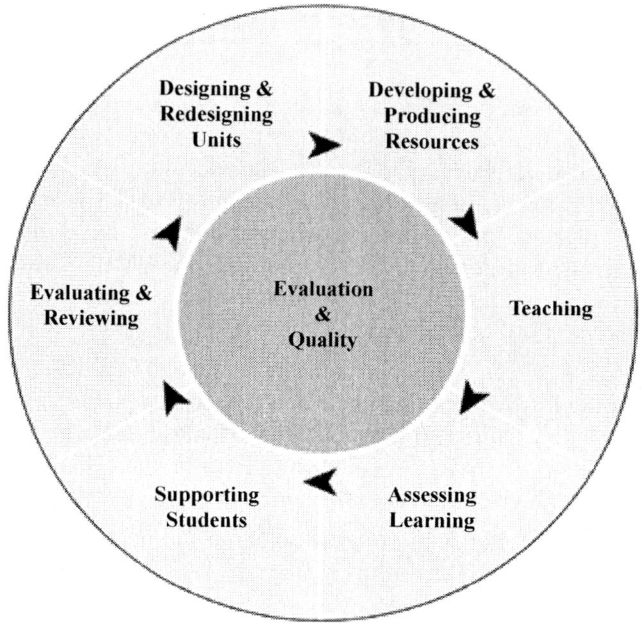

technologies. Feedback is often provided on drafts of work for inexperienced writers.

3. **Teaching:** Individual staff often consult educational designers about appropriate teaching practices, particularly in the context of distance education. This includes establishing and facilitating distributed communities of learners and fostering interaction at a distance.
4. **Assessing learning:** Apart from the design of assessment tasks, educational designers consult on the process of quality assessment including developing good marking criteria, communicating and supporting assessment tasks, marking and grading, academic integrity and plagiarism, and authenticating student work.
5. **Supporting students:** Educational design staff have developed particular expertise in the support of distance learners, and offer advice on possibilities such as the appropriate use of technology, residential schools, travelling workshops and distance mentoring schemes (Morgan & Smit, 2001).
6. **Evaluating and reviewing:** Educational designers provide advice on all feedback mechanisms for unit and course reviews, and provide input to the review process. Support is also offered to enable staff to gather and interpret evaluation data and ways in which units and courses can be improved.

The Institutional Footprint of the Educational Designer

In response to a range of internal and external forces, educational designers now provide input into many levels within the institution. Forces that have enabled educational designers to take a much wider role within the institution include:

- Increased numbers of courses and units being externalised and offered flexibly, making unsustainable the project management model of individual unit development.
- The development of the converged educational design/academic staff development model with associated enhancements in staff development, course and unit review, and evaluation opportunities typically more closely associated with academic development.
- Institutional responses to quality assurance audits requiring policy development in areas associated with teaching and learning, and the development and implementation of associated systems for monitoring and reviewing teaching and learning associated activities within the university.
- Developments in the national higher education arena towards quality assurance and teaching and learning performance-based funding models.

School (Faculty) Level

The educational designers each carry a portfolio of five or six schools across a variety of fields of study. This portfolio approach encourages longitudinal relationship building with academic teaching staff, academic managers, teaching and learning representatives, and production staff. This approach also encourages transdisciplinary educational design practices, as designers see opportunities for sharing knowledge and best practice across and between fields of study. Creating stable relationships with schools not only engenders professional networks and trustworthy relationships, but enables educational designers to become deeply familiar with the particularities of various disciplinary/pedagogic cultures, the needs of different student cohorts, variations in curriculum delivery, requirements of outside accreditation bodies, staff development needs, management styles, structures and processes, workload issues, and so on.

Within their portfolio of schools, educational designers typically engage in traditional unit design and development activities, but with more of a focus on making decisions about the curriculum and its delivery than on project management and production. Educational designers might spend anywhere between one and ten hours with an experienced academic designing assessment tasks, aligning objectives, discussing issues associated with the delivery of teaching and learning activities and content across on-campus, print and online delivery environments. In these instances educational designers rarely engage with production issues or staff, except to refer academics to appropriate production staff for specialist support and/or professional development.

New staff or off-campus experts contracted to develop flexible learning materials demand a more intense commitment, as educational designers induct new staff into the Pathways model of curriculum design, introduce appropriate support from other sections of the university (e.g., online support, printery, copyright officer), and provide feedback at key milestones throughout the materials development process.

Educational designers also engage with staff at the school level for group staff development sessions on teaching and learning related topics identified from within the schools. Designers might co-present with an academic developer, an e-learning trainer, or a visiting expert from within the field of study or from teaching and learning in higher education.

Increasingly educational designers are, alongside their unit development, working at the program level. Opportunities to engage with the design and development of whole curricula are afforded particularly by the university's Graduate Attributes Project. This project requires each program to develop a set of program-specific graduate attributes that cohere with those of the university, map assessment across the whole program, and redesign the curriculum so that it aligns with the stated attributes for that program. Similarly, opportunities arise through the Student Retention Project to work closely with teams of first-year teachers to redesign the first-year curriculum so that it supports students in the development of foundation skills relevant to the field of study, and creates communities of learners.

Divisional Level

Southern Cross University is divided organisationally, and loosely by field of study, into three divisions: arts, business, and health and applied science. Each educational designer attends one divisional board meeting. Divisional board meetings are opportunities for Schools within a Division to share information and discuss Division-based projects, new policy developments, and other university-wide initiatives. More importantly for educational designers, divisional boards are sub-committees of the university's academic governing body, the academic board. As such they play an important role in the vetting of course change submissions, new course submissions, changes to units, course review reports and other curriculum-related documentation on its way to academic board. It is here that educational designers can feel the tension between quality enhancement and quality assurance, as educational designers are expected to make summative judgements about the quality of curriculum documentation (with which they may not have been involved) weaving its way to academic board.

University-Wide Level

Over the last five years, educational designers have been deployed on university-wide projects at an unprecedented level. It is perhaps in this domain more than any other that the full impact of the converged Teaching and Learning Centre model has been felt. Under the old project management model of educational design, where designers worked on unit materials for external delivery, designers were commonly perceived as "editors" rather than as equal members of the academic community. Under the new converged model, educational designers are fully engaged in the academic processes of the university:

- as academic teachers and unit developers in the Centre's Graduate Certificate in Higher Education (Learning and Teaching);
- as professional developers of staff new to the teaching profession at the university through the Centre's Foundations in Teaching program;
- as professional developers involved in the selection and running of the Centre's research seminar series;
- as policy developers in learning and teaching related policies such as the Academic Integrity Policy, the Flexible Learning Policy;
- on working parties and committees related to learning and teaching: Learning and Teaching Advisory Committee, student retention, graduate attributes, assessment;
- as reviewers and evaluators of courses and units through the university's formal review processes, including peer review and student feedback mechanisms;
- developing resources relating to learning and teaching in higher education for the academic community, for example Pathways to Good Practice.

The first two of these processes are currently being considered in discussions in several Australian universities arising from the new Learning and Teaching Performance Fund. Questions being debated concern the relative benefits and drawbacks of making a teaching qualification compulsory for all academic staff, and how such a mandatory requirement might be built into probation and promotion procedures.

National Level

In response to the broader national context of teaching and learning in higher education in Australia, educational designers at Southern Cross are becoming involved in:

- the selection, design and development of projects worthy of becoming applications for various national learning and teaching awards;
- strategic support for university initiatives aimed at meeting indicators for performance-based Federal Government funding;
- national and regional professional organisations and networks of designers/developers such as the Australasian Council on Open, Distance and E-Learning (ACODE), the Australasian Society for Computers in Learning in Tertiary Education (ascilite), the Higher Education Research and Development Society of Australasia (HERDSA), National Foundation of University Teaching Colloquia, and Instructional Design Forum.

All Australian universities are now gathering, interpreting and representing to the federal government, according to national criteria, their institutional data on the quality of teaching and learning in their institutions. As this new mechanism for federal funding becomes apparent, the role that educational designers and academic developers play in the enhancement of teaching and learning will come into sharp focus. Should educational designers be advising, enhancing and developing staff and the curriculum in a voluntary capacity or should their work be systematised and structured into their institution's summative quality assurance processes? To what degree should educational design priorities be driven by the institution's strategic priorities? How can a balance be maintained between a problem-driven responsive development process aimed at improving the quality of teaching and learning on the one hand, versus a systematic approach to sound curriculum development on the other hand? These questions are more fully explored in Chapter II.

Educational Designer as University Teacher

In 2004 the Teaching and Learning Centre enrolled its first cohort of staff into the Graduate Certificate in Higher Education (Learning and Teaching). Within the merged Teaching and Learning Centre model (see Figure 1) educational designers and academic developers developed the overall curriculum as a team, with each staff member taking carriage of the full development and delivery of one of the four units of study offered. For the first time at this university, educational designers became academic teachers with all associated development, design, teaching, marking, grading, and administrative responsibilities.

The curriculum has been very carefully designed to model best practice in a number of key curriculum areas:

- The individual units are designed and delivered for flexible learning with varying combinations of print, online and face-to-face delivery methods.
- The assessment tasks are negotiated workplace projects offering participants opportunities to enhance their teaching practice.
- Participants are required to progressively develop a teaching portfolio throughout the program for the purposes of professional development, promotion and national teaching award applications.
- Participants are also required to engage in one project that adds to their scholarship of teaching activities. This might be a refereed journal article or conference paper, a learning and teaching related research grant application, staff development activities within their faculty, other faculty-focused learning and teaching projects or activities.

The outcomes from the Graduate Certificate can perhaps best be measured against that domain of higher education research referred to as "the scholarship of teaching."

Given the new focus in Australian higher education on quality teaching and performance-based funding, the imperatives for engagement in the activities comprising the scholarship of teaching are clear. These can include:

- Scholarly discourse,
- Scholarly peer review,
- Funding submissions,
- Presentations and publications,
- Teaching portfolios. (From Trigwell, Martin, Benjamin, & Prosser, 2000, pp. 166-167)

Participants in this graduate program become attuned to the imperatives arising from the national agendas in the Australian higher education sector, and through systematic and sustained attention to their own teaching, learning, curriculum and assessment practices are guided to accomplish their own scholarship of teaching outcomes and develop a reflective portfolio of evidence.

The development of a growing number of academic staff who are aware of the broad context of teaching and learning in higher education, are engaged in reflection and inquiry into learning and teaching, and are committed to communicating their scholarly outcomes to their peers through staff development, research and publications is a welcome outcome for educational designers. Not only are educational designers rewarded for their teaching efforts with participants in the program, but are enjoying the benefits of working within an academic community where a growing critical mass of academic staff have a new enthusiasm and commitment to learning and teaching in higher education.

The Educational Design Research Agenda

Educational Designers at Southern Cross are active researchers. Their individual and shared research agendas are driven by the need to explore research questions which arise from their practice, coupled with the need to explore research questions of value to the institution and its students. In this way research findings fulfil a number of functions. They:

- Inform the professional practice of educational designers
- Enhance the quality of teaching and learning
- Provide the wider university community with valuable data which informs both the administrative and academic functions of the university
- Inform policy development.

The following areas of focused research activity demonstrate the close relationship between research, educational design practice, enhancement of teaching and learning, and institutional policy development.

Student Assessment

The significance of assessment as a driver of student learning is well described in the literature (see for example, Brown & Knight, 1994; Ramsden, 1992; Rowntree, 1987) The Teaching and Learning Centre has been engaged in research about student assessment since 1998, when it embarked on a comprehensive evaluation of assessment, marking and grading practices across the whole institution. One key institutional outcome from this research was the decision by the university's Academic Board to change the rules relating to assessment from norm referenced marking and grading to criterion referenced, standards-based marking and grading. Several further research and scholarly initiatives on assessment practices have occurred over the ensuing years, including the publication of two books on assessment, the first focusing on assessment in open and distance learning (Morgan & O'Reilly, 1999) and the second a handbook on assessment written for a broad academic audience and structured around the development of Nightingale, Wiata, Toohey, Ryan, Hughes, and Magin's (1996) eight generic skills (Morgan, Dunn, Parry, & O'Reilly, 2004). This substantial research focus on assessment has informed the development of the university's Assessment Principles and Assessment Policy, the university's Graduate Attributes Project, professional development seminars and workshops, and the educational design of individual units of study. Unusually, and as a direct result of this research focus on student assessment, the university's Graduate Attribute Project is explicitly mapping assessment tasks across whole courses with the aim of developing horizontal and vertical alignment in assessment and teaching.

Technology

The Internet has become a feature of higher education world-wide, with access and usage increasing consistently throughout the western world (Gallagher, 2001; GlobalReach, 2004). Australian university students have an even higher usage than for the general population in Australia, with one survey finding that over 95% of students reported making regular use of Internet technology (Gallagher, 2001).

At Southern Cross, where the student demographic encompasses both on-campus and off-campus learners in almost equal measure, all units of study are supported in some way through the online environment. Academic staff must make informed decisions about appropriate pedagogical approaches for their units. Designs for online teaching, learning and assessment must be informed by rigorous research. Research into the pedagogy of online learning is evident through a long list of publications such as Ellis and O'Reilly (2001), O'Reilly and Newton (2002), O'Reilly, Gibson, Gordon, and Rimmington, (2003), Morgan and O'Reilly (2006), O'Reilly & Hayden (in press). In this research, educational designers have focused on online assessment, how technology can enhance student learning, how technology can be used to provide student support and pastoral care to students studying at a distance, and the professional development needs of academic staff, not educated at a time when the Internet was ubiquitous, learning to use technology to enhance their teaching practice.

Flexible Learning

Mention has already been made of the early and rapid adoption by Southern Cross of flexible learning in the 1990s. Schools, and individual staff, made decisions at the unit of study level about various delivery modes (print/face-to-face/online), made decisions at the course level about flexible course structures, entry schemes, pathways through programs and exit schemes, all informed to varying degrees by the philosophies of open learning, student-centred learning, lifelong learning and flexible learning.

However, the burgeoning literature on flexible learning provided little empirical evidence upon which institutions could rely when planning for flexible learning. The literature also points to various definitions of flexible learning, suggesting that institutional context plays a large part in the negotiation of meanings about flexible learning. It became clear that Southern Cross needed to reach an agreed, cross-institutional understanding of what flexible learning meant within its own organisational context, that a policy needed to be developed which would offer shape and guidance to schools, and that, in the first instance, institutional data should be collected about current flexible learning practices.

Educational designers at the Teaching and Learning Centre were commissioned by the university to conduct a survey to map, across all units of study for one teaching period, the manner in which the curriculum was delivered (how, when and where), the extent and nature of online teaching, and the degrees of student choice offered (Bird, 2003). The survey has provided the university with an empirical snapshot of its flexible learning activities, and as such has assisted the university in the planning, resourcing and delivering of flexible learning opportunities, as well as informing the development of the university's Flexible Learning Policy.

Southern Cross's Student Profile

As already described, students at Southern Cross are a highly diverse cohort, geographically dispersed across the university's regional catchment area, nationally and internationally; migrating between internal, external and multimodal enrolment categories; predominantly mature-aged, working, with families; and of relatively low socio-economic status. Educational designers have made students another focus of their research activities. In 2002 a research project (Bird & Morgan, 2003) was conducted into the mature-aged student experience at Southern Cross: what decisions propel adults to return to study? How do they prepare for a return to study? How do they manage their first student experiences? How do they juggle work, family and study? Where do they go for support? From this research, educational designers produced a film and booklet targeting adults contemplating a return to study, encouraging them to prepare, plan for lifestyle changes, and make informed choices about study options. The film is used by the student support services of the university, by Schools and Faculty during orientation week, the Learning Assistance Centre in their preparation programs, and Marketing.

Another current initiative is focussed on the first year experience whereby several factors for enhancing successful learning and teaching are integrated into a research-led development activity and guided through input from Teaching and Learning Centre staff. Accounting for the changing identities of learners in these kinds of projects is discussed in detail in Chapter II.

Educational Designers' Practice

The educational designers at Southern Cross are also active researchers into their own professional community of practice. Bird (2004) conducted a national survey of flexible learning professionals in order to profile the profession as it stands. The survey collected data on job title, award classification, qualifications, perceived changes in roles and responsibilities and frequency of core activities. The findings pointed to significant changes in all these areas since the early and mid-1990s. Across Australia, the title "instructional designer" has all but disappeared, replaced with a plethora of other titles, of which the most common is "educational designer." Staff are employed in about equal proportions on academic and administrative awards. A growing number of people are entering the field with multimedia and technology-related qualifications (not evident in Allen's 1996 study of instructional designers). Significant changes in core activities were evident when compared to Allen's 1996 study, especially in the areas of increased staff development and increased design work for online learning and teaching environments. The shift away from editing and layout activities related to print materials is clear. The findings from this research has provided invaluable benchmarking opportunities for the educational designers at Southern Cross, and has provided a springboard for further research commenced in 2005 (see also Chapter II).

Research exploring the staff development qualities of educational design practice is also being conducted by educational designers within the TLC. The fundamental tenets of this research are that academic staff from diverse disciplines rarely have the opportunity to share ideas about teaching, learning and assessment. Staff development is either tailored for discipline-specific issues or conversely explores questions of general interest for a broad audience. The four-year research exploration now being completed in this area shows that an educational design model that brings together staff from a range of disciplines to collectively focus on their assessment strategies can lead to creative assessment design as well as providing an opportunity for effective benchmarking across disciplines. This has been shown to be particularly effective when considering design for online assessment (O'Reilly, 2003; O'Reilly, 2004; O'Reilly & Brown, 2001; O'Reilly & Ellis, 2002; O'Reilly, 2002).

Retention and Attrition Issues

As a big distance education provider, and with a high mature-aged, part-time student profile, issues of retention and attrition are always the subject of scrutiny and research at Southern Cross. The situation is magnified by the rising costs of tuition and the low average socio-economic status of students. Regular studies in attrition rates at the university, which are amongst the highest in the Australian sector, indicate that work commitments (47% of discontinuing students) and family commitments (41% of discontinuing students) were the highest factors. However, among other contributing factors were institutional ones, including insufficient contact with tutors (20%) and lack of contact with other students (27%) (Parr, 1996).

Educational design research has taken two distinct directions:

- A focus on first year curricula and the teaching and assessment expectations of staff and students. Mapping of the first year experience is underway in a number of schools, looking particularly at course structures, investment in student support, the emphasis on developmental, formative-style assessment, and flexibility issues.
- A focus on preparedness of mature-aged students who are returning to study after a long absence. A series of focus groups were conducted which identified the particular issues, themes and concerns of mature aged students entering the university, resulting in recommendations regarding more flexible preparatory programs and pre-entry counselling. A video resource was also developed to support mature-aged students to make more realistic and informed decisions about entry into higher education (Bird & Morgan, 2003).

Conclusion

Educational design at Southern Cross University is shaped by its context, most notably the university's size and student demographics. Its history and evolution is closely connected to the evolution of the university as a regional Australian distance education provider. Taken together, these issues have impacted significantly on the focus of educational design, including its central location, diverse role within the university, and its research agenda.

One of the more distinctive elements of educational design at Southern Cross, when compared with other universities in the Australian sector, is the convergence of roles with academic staff development. This merger has been a thoroughly successful one because of the shared theoretical foundations espoused by staff in the two roles, as well as the very practical staff development approach that has always been adopted by the educational designers. This merger is one that has been embraced by all, as it has offered greater diversity of tasks, greater job satisfaction and the ability to be deployed more flexibly according to the university's needs.

The pathways model with its merged approach is now achieving recognition in the sector more widely through being showcased on the Australian Universities Quality Agency "Good Practice Database" (Southern Cross University, 2004) and thereby stimulating an interest from within Australia and abroad. As a small, innovative university, the flexible capacity of its educational design staff is seen as important if it is to meet its teaching and learning ambitions over the next 10 years and maintain respect within the higher education sector.

References

Allen, M. (1996). A profile of instructional designers in Australia. *Distance Education, 17*(1), 7-32.

Biggs, J. (1999). *Teaching for quality learning at university*. Buckingham: Society for Higher Education Research, Open University Press.

Bird, J. (2003). *Unit mapping survey report*. Unpublished manuscript, Southern Cross University at Lismore.

Bird, J. (2004). Professional navel gazing: Flexible learning professionals into the future. In R. Atkinson, C. McBeath, D. Jonas-Dwyer, & R. Phillips (Eds.), *Beyond the Comfort Zone: Proceedings of the 21st Annual Conference of The Australasian Society for Computers in Learning in Tertiary Education* (pp. 123-133). Perth, Australia.

Bird, J., & Morgan, C. (2003). Adults contemplating university study at a distance: Issues, themes and concerns. *International Review of Research in Open and Distance Learning, 4*(1). Retrieved May 29, 2006, from http://www.irrodl.org/index.php/irrodl/article/viewArticle/130/210

Brown, S., & Knight, P. (1994). *Assessing learners in higher education*. London: Kogan Page.

Ellis, A., & O'Reilly, M. (2001). E-Learning at Southern Cross University: Past, present and future. In *Proceedings of WebNET Conference* (pp. 349-354). Orlando, FL. Norfolk, VA: Association for the Advancement of Computing in Education.

Gallagher, M. (2001). *E-learning in Australia: Universities and the new distance education*. Tokyo: Centre for Educational Research and Innovation OECD.

GlobalReach. (2004). *Global internet statistics*. Retrieved July 14, 2005, from http://global-reach.biz/globstats/index.php3

Inglis, A. (1996). Teaching-learning specialists' conceptions of their role in the design of distance learning packages. *Distance Education, 17*(2), 267-288.

Morgan, C., Dunn, L., Parry, S., & O'Reilly, M. (2004). *The student assessment handbook: New directions in traditional and online assessment*. London: Routledge Falmer.

Morgan, C., & Hayden, M. (2002). Case studies of dual mode universities: Southern Cross University. In V. Reddy & S. Manjulika (Eds.), *Towards virtualization*. India: Kogan Page.

Morgan, C., & O'Reilly, M. (1999). *Assessing open and distance learners*. London: Kogan Page.

Morgan, C., & O'Reilly, M. (2006). 10 key qualities of assessment online. In M. Hricko & S. Howell (Eds.), *Online assessment and measurement: Foundations and challenges* (pp. 86-101). Hershey, PA: Information Science Publishing.

Morgan, C., & Smit, A. (2001). Mentoring in open and distance learning. In F. Lockwood & A. Gooley (Eds.), *Innovations in open and distance Learning* (pp. 160-171). London: Kogan Page.

Nightingale, P., Te Wiata, I., Toohey, S., Ryan, G., Hughes, C., & Magin, D. (1996). *Assessing learning in universities*. Sydney: University of New South Wales Press.

O'Reilly, M. (2003). Using cross-disciplinary action learning sets when designing online assessment. In G. Crisp, D. Thiele, I. Scholten, S. Barker, & J. Baron (Eds.), *Interact, Integrate, Impact. Proceedings of Australasian Society for Computers in Learning in Tertiary Education* (pp. 375-385). Adelaide, Australia.

O'Reilly, M. (2004). Educational design as transdisciplinary partnership: Supporting assessment design for online. In R. Atkinson, C. McBeath, D. Jonas-Dwyer, & R. Phillips (Eds.), *Beyond the Comfort Zone: Proceedings of the 21st Annual Conference of The Australasian Society for Computers in Learning in Tertiary Education* (pp. 724-733). Perth, Australia.

O'Reilly, M., & Brown, J. (2001). Staff development by immersion in interactive learning online. In *AusWeb2001 Conference* (pp. 259-268). Coffs Harbour, April 21-25. Retrieved July 10, 2006, from http://ausweb.scu.edu.au/aw01/papers/refereed/o_reilly/paper.html

O'Reilly, M. (2002). In at the deep end: Swapping roles through staff development online. In A. Williamson, C. Gunn, A. Young, & T. Clear (Eds.), *Australasian Society for Computers in Learning in Tertiary Education* (pp. 485-494). Auckland: UNITEC Institute of Technology.

O'Reilly, M., Gibson, K.L., Gordon, D., & Rimmington, G.M. (2003, June 23-28). Assessment strategies for global learning: II Case Studies. In *Proceedings of Ed-Media 2003 World Conference on Educational Multimedia, Hypermedia & Telecommunications* (pp. 2491-2494). Association for the Advancement of Computing in Education. Honolulu.

O'Reilly, M., & Hayden, M. (in press). *Hallmarks of excellence in online assessment.* Paper presented at the First International Conference on Enhancing Teaching and Learning through Assessment, Hong Kong.

O'Reilly, M., & Newton, D. (2002). Interaction online: Above and beyond the requirements of assessment. *Australian Journal of Educational Technology, 18*(1), 57-70.

O'Reilly, M. (2002). A breath of fresh air: Reflecting on the changing practices of assessment online. In Kinshuk, R. Lewis, K. Akahori, R. Kemp, T. Okamoto, L. Henderson, & C.H. Lee (Eds.), *International Conference for Computers in Education* (pp. 1030-1034). Auckland New Zealand, Los Alamitos, CA: IEEE Computer Society.

Parr, E. (1996). *Dropping in and dropping out: An alternative view of attrition.* Lismore: Southern Cross University

Ramsden, P. (1992). *Learning to teach in higher education.* London: Routledge.

Rowntree, D. (1987). *Assessing students: How shall we know them?* (revised ed.). London: Kogan Page.

Rowntree, D. (1990). *Teaching through self-instruction* (revised ed.). London: Kogan Page.

Rowntree, D. (1992). *Exploring open and distance learning.* London: Kogan Page.

Southern Cross University. (2004). *Educational design and development for quality learning.* Retrieved January 13, 2006, from http://www.auqa.edu.au/gp/search/detail.php?gp_id=1036

Southern Cross University. (n.d.). *Pathways to good practice: A guide to flexible teaching for quality learning.* Retrieved May 29, 2006, from http://www.scu.edu.au/services/tl/pathways

Trigwell, K., Martin, E., Benjamin, J., & Prosser, M. (2000). Scholarship of teaching: A model. *Higher Education Research and Development, 19*(2), 156-168.

Chapter IX

The Changing Role of an Instructional Designer in the Implementation of Blended Learning at an Australian University

Jacqueliné McDonald, University of Southern Queensland, Australia

Terry Mayes, Glasgow Caledonian University, Scotland

Abstract

This chapter presents a case study that reflects on the changing approach of an instructional designer at an Australian university. The designer moved from one-to-one interactions with subject matter experts in the design of traditional print-based distance learning courses to adopting a pedagogical framework that guides the use of technology in hybrid course design and encourages the subject matter experts to design their courses in a way that emphasises what Wenger (2005) has called the "horizontalisation" of learning. The subject experts were encouraged to experience some of the benefits of a community of practice (CoP) approach for themselves. The study contrasts the traditional approach to design with the framework used here, in which social constructivist principles of learning were offered to the subject matter experts in a way that was immediately engaging and usable for them. The chapter presents the subject experts' evaluation of the effectiveness of the approach described.

Background Influences of Changing Pedagogy and the Application of Technology to Instructional Design Practice

The development of mass higher education and the increasing access to technology has presented institutions of higher education with a variety of learners requiring greater flexibility in the way they access programmes and services (Laurillard, 2002). Until recently, distance education was largely structured on a rigid "delivery" model, organised around teaching and assessment rather than learning. The impetus for hybrid or blended learning depends partly on a growing application of social constructivist pedagogy that focuses on learner-centred, rather than teacher-centred design, and partly on the need to develop enhanced efficiency in the provision of teaching. These two pressures work in opposite directions and the sector is currently in the process of coming to terms with what these shifts imply in practice. Interactive education, which focuses on connection, interaction, exploration and discovery, rather than the transmission of information, moves the teacher away from the centre of the instructional activity and focuses on active student learning. These pressures also impact on the traditional instructional systems design (ISD) approach described as the "reflective process of translating principles of learning and instruction into plans for instructional materials, activities information resources and evaluation" (Smith & Ragan, 2005, p. 4).

Initially, most higher education institutions viewed investment in the application of information and communication technology as a way of delivering their educational provision to new kinds of students, typically off-campus. However, the idea that advanced learning technology could provide both more effective pedagogy and lower costs has been largely dispelled through the last few years in which e-learning has been conceptualised as the delivery of a product. It is now quite widely accepted that a sound pedagogical underpinning has been largely missing in these developments. A course does not become "learner-centred" by going online; in some respects it becomes less so. Perhaps the most striking example of the gap between e-learning rhetoric and the reality of implementation has been provided by the expensive failure of the UK e-University (House of Commons Education and Skills Committee Report, 2003). In their study of the failed uptake of e-learning in America, Zemsky and Massy (2004) suggest that, "the hard fact is that e-learning took off before people really knew how to use it" (p. iii). While many institutions of higher education are adopting technology, Ikenberry (1999) suggests that in most instances "the revolution proceeds without any clear vision or master plan" (p. 58). Now, with the concept of blended/hybrid learning, we see a more measured approach, acknowledging that learning technology has a role in achieving the learning-centred approach, but only when used in a way that enhances tutor-student dialogue. Young (2002) suggests that there has been a marked shift in the vision for online education, moving from the idea of fully online courses, with no face-to-face meetings, to hybrid courses that offer the best of both worlds. Instructional designers (IDs) have an important role to play in working with academic staff and management to design learning and teaching strategies that are learner-focused and cost effective, while still meeting the needs of external stakeholders, be they community, government or employers. Instructional designers may be work-based trainers, teachers involved in designing new instruction or designers working with subject matter experts designing learning environments using a range of media. As increasing numbers of academics (subject matter experts) consider the inclusion of information and communication technology in their courses, IDs are challenged to support these initiatives with new approaches to course design.

Blended/Hybrid Learning: The Application of Emerging Pedagogy and Technology

Australian distance education is moving into the blended/hybrid learning environment from an educational tradition based on an independent learner model. A small population spread over large geographic distances means that traditional distance education experiences have been historically based on self-contained and predominantly print-based learning packages. Tertiary distance education courses were traditionally designed as a "stand-alone" learning package, based on the presumption that remote learners would be unable to access other resources or have easy contact with peers or course leaders. In the independent learner model, students worked independently through course materials that were designed on the idea of "student/content," interactive approach. They submitted assessment items and received feedback and grades, with minimum interaction with course leaders and fellow students, unless an on-campus residential school was scheduled as part of the program. This differs from the Open University (United Kingdom) model, where distance learning materials are supported by local tutors, and some American distance programmes, where real-time video links beam lectures to students located at a distant campus. For this paper, "hybrid" education will be defined as the convergence of distance education and on-campus education (Waddoups & Howell, 2001). The hybrid initiative, which provides the context for this chapter, was specifically titled "hybrid," while the literature, particularly from America, tends to use the term "blended." Hybrid or blended learning means a combination of on-campus and media-enhanced or Web-based learning. In this paper, hybrid and blended are used as interchangeable terms.

In Australia there is a growing trend towards blended learning that incorporates the use of information and communication technology in the instructional process to augment, rather than replace, on-campus delivery (Eklund, Kay, & Lynch, 2003). A case study of Brigham Young University (Waddoups & Howell, 2001) reports how the process of convergence of on- and off-campus teaching and learning was at the core of the hybrid approach. They suggest that this process of convergence has been observed globally among open and distance learning institutions. Research at the University of Wisconsin-Milwaukee (Aycock,

Garnham, & Kaleta, 2002) found that both faculty and students were positive about the hybrid experience—with 100% of faculty participants recommending the approach to others and planning to teach again using the hybrid model. The main reason they believed it was valuable for student learning was that "student interactivity increased, performance improved, and faculty could accomplish course goals that hadn't been possible in their traditional course" (Aycock, Garnham, & Kaleta, 2002, p. 6). There is a general belief that a media-rich environment will improve student satisfaction and learning, as it will cater for different learning styles, however this belief requires further research. In the meantime the actual adoption of the innovation process and the role IDs play in the application of technology for both on and off-campus learning and teaching is still evolving. With the implementation of the hybrid initiative in this case study the challenge for subject matter experts and IDs was to use the hybrid initiative to move away from existing approaches to course design and delivery, and create learning environments informed by constructivism and supported by technology. This chapter presents a case study showing how this challenge was addressed at an Australian university within a community of practice. The following review of evolving instructional design theory and practice provides a background for the instructional design approach used in the case study.

Instructional Design Theory and Practice

Underpinning traditional ID is a broad theoretical stance on learning called associationism. In this approach, knowledge is an organised accumulation of associations and skill components and learning is the process of connecting the elementary mental or behavioural units, through sequences of activity. Associationist theory requires subject matter to be analysed as specific associations, expressed as objectives. This kind of analysis was developed by Gagne (1985) into an elaborate instructional task analysis of discriminations, classifications and response sequences. Learning tasks are arranged in sequences based on their relative complexity, with simpler components as pre-requisites for more complex tasks. Thus, sequences of instruction are designed for students to be able to learn in small and logically ordered steps. This assumption—that knowledge and skill needs to be taught from the bottom-up—has been the subject of long controversy (Resnick & Resnick, 1991), but still underpins much ID. The basic principle is that competence in advanced and complex tasks is built step-by-step from simpler units of knowledge or skill, finally adding coordination to the whole structure. Gagne (1985) argued that successful instruction depends on placing constraints on the amount of new structure that must be added at any one stage.

A widely used ID methodology for developing education and training programs is instructional systems design (ISD). There are more than a hundred different ISD models, but almost all are based on the generic ISD "ADDIE" model. This model uses a linear process, where each step—analysis, design, development, implementation, and evaluation—is dealt with one step at time and is based on the previous step. Essentially ISD requires an analysis of the subject or skill domain into a hierarchy of small units, and a sequencing of these so that a combination of units is not taught until its component units are grasped individually. Then, an instructional design for each unit in the sequence is required. Traditional ISD consists of guidelines and procedures for the decomposition of complex tasks into learning hierarchies and detailed prescriptions for the design of instructional programs based on such hierarchies. A theme in this work was the use of taxonomies representing different levels of complexity in learning outcomes. Different levels of intellectual skill were identified, such as discriminations, concepts, rules and higher order rules.

Traditional ISD assumes that successively higher-level skills are more readily learned when their subordinate skills are mastered first. However, since the 1980s, a growing body of empirical evidence has favoured a top-down superordinate learning model over Gagne's bottom-up cumulative model. This led Gagne (1985) to conclude that learning hierarchies can be fully applied only to a particular class of learning outcome—intellectual skills. Gagne eventually wrote about classes of learning outcomes to which cumulative learning did not apply: motor skills, attitudes, and higher order thinking skills.

The adequacy of the ISD model was questioned as early as the late 1980s by, for example, Merrill, Li, and Jones (1990), who identified shortcomings in what they termed *first generation instructional design (ID1)*. One shortcoming was that the first generation instructional design was based on behavioural outcomes rather than the mental processes of the learner. They also argued that the approach focused on what instructors do, thus limiting the learners to a passive rather than active role. Their *second generation instructional design (ID2)* was founded on cognitive rather than behavioural learning theory. With the emergence of constructivism in the mid-1990s, the ISD approach has come under further attack (Gordon & Zemke, 2000; Zemke & Rossett, 2002). The constructivist approach focuses on the active construction of knowledge by the learners, based on their existing knowledge. The use of technology also changes the way learning is conducted. One of the strengths of the Mayes pedagogical framework (Mayes & Fowler, 1999; Mayes, 2002) is that it focuses the design process and the application of technology onto activities which make the learner think, thus targeting the main focus of the educational process.

Gayeski (1998) argues that the traditional step-wise, linear models for instructional design (ADDIE) are no longer appropriate for today's learning environment, as the models are based on a top-down, behaviouristic and subject matter expert-driven approach to learning, rather than a constructivist and learner-centred approach. Current ID models are moving away from linear ISD approaches to models that acknowledge the interrelatedness and concurrency of all activities of design (Smith & Ragan, 2005). The need for instructional designers to recognise changing educational theory and practice has led to the revision of the ID competencies. The International Board of Standards for Training, Performance and Instruction (IBSTPI) Instructional Design competencies were created in 1986, but in recognition of the rapid developments in technology-mediated approaches to learning and teaching these competencies were revised in 2000 (Richey, Fields, & Foxon, 2001). The revision was also in recognition of several developments in the major theories that underpin the instructional design field over the past 15 years. The new version contains 23 competencies and 127 performance statements, and reflects the influence of advanced technologies, team-based design, and business management skills, among other things. It is unlikely that many IDs would be sufficiently experienced and qualified to meet all the IBSTPI competencies, although there is a trend towards certification in the ID field. While there is an increase in the numbers of IDs in education and industry, there is such wide variation in work duties, modes on occupational entry, educational preparations and career paths that Richey, Fields, & Foxon (2001) suggest that ID should be regarded as an emerging rather than an established profession.

Keppell (2004) notes that IDs now apply a range of ideas from cognitive and social-constructivist theories and draw on a repertoire of learning designs when working with content experts. The instructional designer in this chapter is experienced with the use of a range of ID models and her practice was informed by educational theory and ID literature (Gagne, 1985; Jonassen, 1999; Laurillard, 2002; Reigeluth, 1999; Smith & Ragan, 2005; Vygotsky, 1978). The university in this case has a strong distance education tradition based on independent learning, using self-contained and predominantly print-based learning packages. The blended initiative has provided an opportunity to reconceptualise the way distance education has been designed and delivered. The initiative came at a time when there was a reduced number of IDs and the traditional approach of IDs working individually with subject matter experts was no longer resourced. The ID was interested in applying a community of practice approach in her ID role, and the opportunity arose with the implementation of the hybrid initiative, as outlined in the context section of the case description.

Emergence of the Concept of CoP

The term "communities of practice" emerged from Lave and Wenger's (1991) study that explored the concept of "situated learning" in the apprenticeship model. Through practice in the community the novice moves from peripheral to full participation in the group activities. Lave and Wenger (1991) viewed the acquisition of knowledge as a social process, and this idea will be explored further in this chapter when reflecting on the nature and purpose of conversation in communities of practice (CoPs).

Wenger, McDermott, and Snyder (2002) describe CoPs as:

> *Groups of people who share a concern, a set of problems, or a passion about a topic, and who deepen their knowledge and expertise in this area by interacting on an ongoing basis. ... (As they) accumulate knowledge, they become informally bound by the value that they find in learning together. Over time, they develop a unique perspective on their topic as well as a body of common knowledge, practices, and approaches. They also develop personal relationships and established ways of interacting. They may even develop a common sense of identity. They become a community of practice.* (pp. 4-5)

Communities of practice (CoPs) take a variety of forms depending on their context, however they all share a basic structure. Wenger (1998) suggests that a community of practice is a unique combination of three fundamental elements. These elements are a *domain* of knowledge that creates a common ground and sense of common identity, a *community* of people who care about the domain and create the social fabric of learning, and a shared *practice* that the community develops to be effective in their domain. In industry, communities of practice emerged as a means of facilitating the growth and implementation of new knowledge. Knowledge management emerged in the mid-1990s (Ponzi & Koenig, 2002) as a way to deal with the explosion of information and a climate of continuous change. However, many of the knowledge management strategies implemented by management proved ineffective, for example, complex databases became digital graveyards of unused information. Heldreth and Kimble (2002) argue that more recently there has been recognition of the importance of subtler, tacit types of knowledge that needs to be shared and that CoPs have been identified as being a group where such types of knowledge are nurtured, shared and sustained. Tacit knowledge is highly personal, and is understood by the individual without being articulated. It is hard to formalise and therefore difficult to communicate to others as it is unvoiced or unspoken. Within a community of practice the acquisition of knowledge as a social process (Lave & Wenger, 1991; Vygotsky, 1978) is supported by positive feedback from participants in this case study in their evaluation of the CoP approach. The ID in this case study has an interest in the use of communities of practice as an approach to working with groups of subject matter experts to facilitate course design. She participated in the "Foundations of Communities of Practice" workshop (http://www.cpsquare.org/edu/foundations) and is a member of CPSquare (http://www.cpsquare.org/) an international group of people involved in communities of practice across a range of professionals. The discussion of the cultivation of the CoP will be grounded in the context of the unfolding story of instructional design practice in this case study.

Case Study: Implementing a Pedogogical Framework for Designing Hybrid Courses: A CoP Approach

Context: An Australian Distance Education University

The university in this case study has offered distance education for more than 25 years and has approximately 25,000 enrolments, including over 7,400 international students. It offers under- and post-graduate programs both on-campus and nationally and internationally using flexible delivery. Many academics employed at the university have industry and/or on-campus teaching experience, but little or no experience in flexible learning, and some employed directly from industry for their subject matter expertise have no formal educational background when they commence their academic role. Part of the ID's role is to facilitate the design of learning and teaching strategies into the distance learning course, and to introduce faculty to the distance learning production processes. This role demands a sound knowledge of ID theory and sensitivity to the concerns of academics moving into a new, distance-teaching role. This role can lead to tension, as lead-in time lines for developing quality distance learning materials are much longer than time-lines for preparing materials to present in an on-campus lecture. Some academics unfamiliar with the distance education timelines can feel that they have lost academic autonomy. In an on-campus context academics can plan their own preparation timelines for lectures and tutorials, and the presentation is usually a private interaction between the academic and students. Preparing distance education materials often require several months lead-in preparation time, and these learning materials are open to peer scrutiny. In this context, the ability to interact effectively with faculty staff, and promote ID theory and practice (which often means "more work" to time stressed staff) is a key ID skill. Also, the ability to listen and tease out, then build on the educational practice of content experts is an essential ID skill needed to work effectively with subject matter experts (SMEs) across a number of faculties. Keppell (2000) notes a number of principles for interacting with subject matter experts. These include clarifying the roles and expectations of the client/SME, adapting the interview format to the SME, developing generic questions to utilise in the interview and use mapping strategies to reorganise the content. The need for ID sensitivity to the beliefs and practices of faculty staff is also articulated by Crawford (2004), who highlights that negotiation is an essential part of the design process.

The Traditional Institutional Approach to Instructional Design

In this case study, instructional designers (IDs) were located in the Distance and e-Learning Centre (DeC) and worked across a range of Faculties with subject matter experts to design new, online and blended/hybrid courses, or those courses undergoing major revision. The instructional designer, co-author of this chapter, has over 15 years experience in designing learning both in higher education and at a government health training institution. In the 1990s IDs focused only on distance (off-campus) learning, working closely on a one-to-one basis with faculty content experts and members of the DeC development team to design and deliver distance learning materials—based on ID and distance learning theory. IDs were usually allocated to work with a particular faculty, but remained physically located in the DeC building. Figure 1 shows the institutional organisational structure and interface between the Faculties and DeC in the development of distance learning materials.

The approach generally used by IDs was the "generator" model (Figure 2) where IDs work closely with subject matter experts (SMEs) in the initial stages to design a course blueprint outlining the key learning and teaching strategies to achieve the planned learning outcomes of the course. The blueprint addresses the "big picture" design environment by taking the course specification and designing the framework of the course, including learning/teaching strategies, assessment, module topics and learning resources. In close collaboration with the ID, the subject matter expert develops a sample module for the course. Once the sample module is completed the ID provides feedback and makes recommendations (if required) to improve learning outcomes. Once a final draft is agreed upon, this sample module is fast tracked through the production system and provides a model for the writing of subsequent modules and, ideally, detailed ID feedback is usually not required.

This approach has proven more effective than the "transformer" approach, which generally means IDs are given materials already completed by subject matter experts. IDs are then faced with the difficulty of redesigning (transforming) materials that authors believed were near completion. The distance learning materials were designed for independent learning, using an approach based on distance education theory and practice where students were expected to build their discipline knowledge through interaction with content. Faculty provided feedback on assessment and in some cases offered telephone tutorials, a range of media resources or campus-based residential schools. Of course the generator model is an idealised model. In reality the success of this approach depends on context and personalities, not just on the application of a model of practice. Since the mid-1990s, changing pedagogy and the increasing availability of technology has meant that other educational options beside print-based distance learning courses were needed to meet changing stakeholder expectations. In response to these changes an online initiative was launched in 1997. IDs

Figure 1. Organisational structure and interface between the Faculties and DeC in the development of distance learning materials (Used with permission of the Distance and e-Learning Centre, University of Southern Queensland)

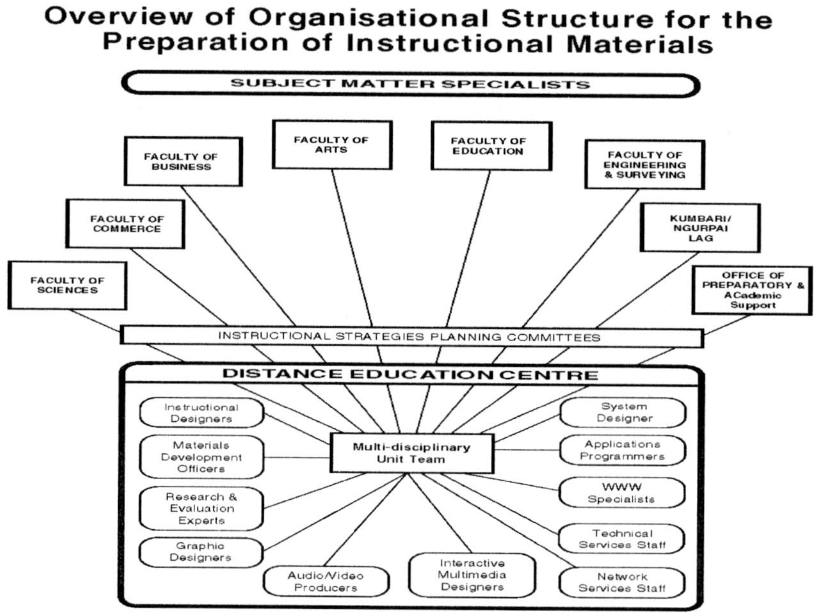

participated in the design and development of online courses and the training of faculty in the application of online pedagogy and technology. After several offers it became clear that many online courses did not meet the needs and expectations of academics and students. In 2003, a number of hybrid initiatives were implemented to blend on- and off-campus learning, reconceptualise approaches to learning based on changed pedagogy, and to take advantage of emerging technology.

Evolving Instructional Design Practice within the CoP

The usual practice for designing distance courses at the institution was for the instructional designer to be assigned to work with individual subject matter experts (SMEs) to design distance materials. However, in 2003 the implementation of a "hybrid" (or blended learning) initiative and a new production software by management, plus a reduced ID team, lead to the introduction of IDs working with groups of academics for course design as a cost effective alternative to the past practice of IDs mainly working with individual course leaders. As part of an initiative to build faculty expertise in learning and teaching and the use of technology, the ID author worked with a group of five SMEs who had volunteered to be part of the hybrid initiative. These SMEs had a range of academic experience, from over 15 years to just two years teaching, and their discipline background included law, tax, finance and accounting. The SMEs were responsible for the creation and operation of courses

Figure 2. Instructional design generator model (Used with permission of the Distance and e-Learning Centre, University of Southern Queensland)

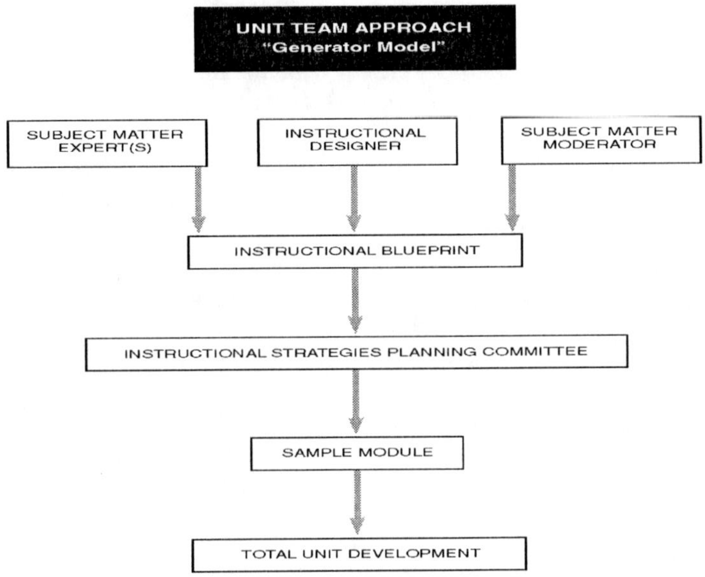

that were offered by distance, online and on-campus mode within a Bachelor of Business degree and postgraduate Master of Business Accounting (MBA). Until the implementation of the hybrid initiative in 2003, most courses had been offered externally as print-based packages, with Web access to supporting learning materials. For some courses external students also had access to telephone tutorials and the option of a residential school during semester. Courses were also offered to on-campus students who attended lectures and tutorials, and also had access to Web materials. Students also had an option to purchase the external printed course package.

While the institution has a strong distance education tradition based on independent learning (using self-contained and predominantly print-based learning packages) the hybrid initiative provided an opportunity to reconceptualise the way distance education has been designed and delivered. Existing instructional design models that had proved effective for the design of print-based learning materials were considered inappropriate for the design of hybrid learning environments. Wenger (1998) suggests that, "because the world is in flux and conditions always change, any practice must constantly be reinvented" (p. 94). The challenge was to introduce subject matter experts to the key principles of constructivist pedagogy, and to provide a framework for the application of technology to support learning design decisions. An additional challenge (or opportunity) for the ID was how to foster the acceptance of the hybrid initiative and facilitate accompanying growth in professional expertise, all within a context of declining resources. When implementing the hybrid initiative, the ID role changed from working with individual subject matter experts to a community of practice approach.

Brokering a Pedagogical Framework in a Faculty CoP

This case study reports on how the instructional designer assumed a brokering role to introduce an element of ID practice (Mayes & Fowler, 1999; Mayes, 2002), pedagogical framework, to a group of five subject matter experts within a community of practice. Brokering can be defined as connections provided by people who can introduce elements of one practice into another (Wenger, 1998). When establishing the CoP the three elements of the community of practice, domain, community and practice were not formally articulated, however they all functioned together to create an ideal structure to foster the implementation of the hybrid initiative. The domain was the design of hybrid learning courses, while the core community included the instructional designer and five subject matter experts. The practice was the existing knowledge and tools the community had for the design of distance learning courses. The designer introduced the Mayes framework as a boundary object (Wenger, 1998) to the SMEs in order to provide a conceptual and organisational framework to focus the design and development process with the faculty community of practice. Wenger (1998) defines boundary objects as "artifacts, documents, terms, concepts, and other forms of reification around which communities of practice can organize their interconnections" (p. 105). The Mayes framework (1999, 2002) was used as a boundary object in this study to introduce course leaders, with little or no previous background in blended design and development, to the key principles of constructivist pedagogy, and to provide a framework for group discussion about the application of technology to support learning design decisions. The following sections will articulate the pedagogical aspects of the Mayes framework and how it was used to facilitate the design, development and evaluation of blended courses within the community of practice.

The Mayes Pedagogical Framework

Put simply, this design framework asks subject matter experts to put aside their tendency to think in terms of content coverage, and to start with identifying what really needs to be learned. These learning outcomes are matched with learning and teaching activities—what the students are actually going to do—which are placed at the centre of the design. The feedback learners will receive on their performance of these activities is an integral part of the activities themselves. It is when designing the feedback loop that the key principles of social constructivist thinking must be grasped. It must be appreciated that the social aspects of learning bring into focus the extent to which an individual learner is part of a learning group, and the extent to which that group can be considered as an emerging community of practice. So, as well as feedback from tutors, the designer must think carefully about engagement with peers.

The framework is made as understandable as possible to subject experts who may have only a limited interest in pedagogy by identifying three stages of learning and representing them as a learning cycle. There is quite a long tradition in learning theory of doing this (Rumelhart & Norman, 1978; Fitts & Posner, 1967; Kolb, 1984). Mayes' contribution is to describe these in a way that makes it easy to map onto types of learning technology. The framework is described in terms that address conceptual learning, rather than skill acquisition, though it is possible to re-frame the description in a way that would be suitable for training, rather than education. Each stage directs attention to an essential aspect of pedagogy: the analysis of what is to be learned, the tasks that will allow the intended outcomes to be achieved through feedback and reflection, and the situating of these outcomes through dialogue with tutors and peers. Described like this we see that the real advance on traditional ISD is in the emphasis on dialogue and the engagement with peer learning.

- **Conceptualisation:** Refers to the users' initial contact with *other peoples' concepts.* This involves an interaction between the learner's pre-existing framework of understanding and a new exposition.
- **Construction:** Refers to the process of building and combining concepts through their use in the performance of meaningful *tasks*. Traditionally these have been tasks like laboratory work, writing, preparing presentations, and so forth. The results of such a process are products like essays, notes, handouts and laboratory reports.
- **Dialogue:** The testing and tuning of conceptualisations through discussion, argument and reflection. In education, the goal is testing of understanding, often of abstract concepts. This stage is best characterised in education as *dialogue*. The conceptualisations are tested and further developed during conversation with both tutors and fellow learners, and in the reflection on these.

Most learning technology provides access to *courseware,* normally interpreted to mean the computer-based delivery of learning materials. The simple term is too general since it obscures differences both in the pedagogy and in the associated technology. Here, a classification is offered, based both on the way the courseware is originated, and on its mapping to types of learning. *Primary courseware* is intended mainly to present subject matter. Increasingly, primary courseware will be Web-based. *Secondary courseware* describes the environment and set of tools by which the learner performs learning tasks, and the tasks (and task materials) themselves. *Tertiary courseware* is material that has been produced by previous learners, in the course of discussing their learning tasks with peers or tutors. It may consist of outputs from assessment. One kind of tertiary material will be compiled from the questions, answers and discussion that will typically be generated by a computer conference.

Primary courseware comes in many forms, some of which will involve impressive interactivity in simulated environments. The learner may explore the exposition, and may even be

Figure 3. (Re)conceptualisation cycle (Mayes, 2002)

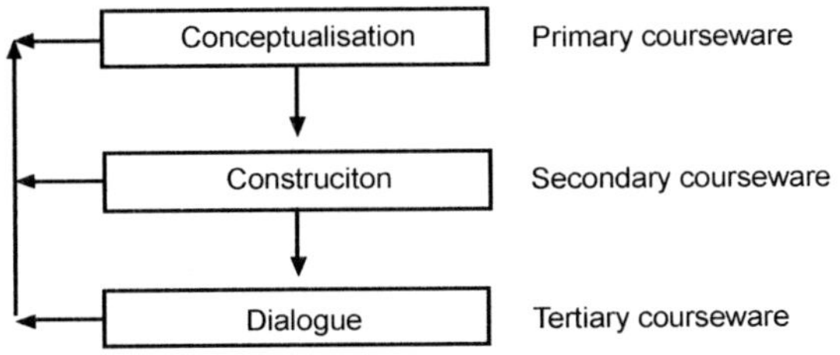

able to pose "what if" questions of the software. Nevertheless, the purpose of the primary courseware is to offer subject matter resources. Secondary courseware, on the other hand, directly supports the learner's task-based learning activity. So a task environment in which learners use search tools to explore Web content would be regarded as secondary courseware. The key to this stage is to ensure that the tasks follow constructivist principles of learner identification with the task, and active problem solving.

It is with tertiary courseware, however, that attention is drawn to the social dimension of learning. Tertiary courseware is a new conception of courseware in which the defining characteristic is the encouragement of dialogue and the "re-use" of the dialogues of other learners. The idea of tertiary courseware seems important because it offers a way in which computers might be able to provide a partial experience of dialogue in educational situations where it is simply not possible for teachers to engage in one-to-one tutorial conversations with students. The effectiveness of the idea depends on the validity of the concept of *vicarious learning*: the extent to which learners can benefit by being shown examples of the learning experiences of others. Mayes, Dineen, McKendree, and Lee (2001) describe how dialogues recorded during "task-directed discussions" by previous learners were valuable for new learners. This idea—that learners can benefit from accessing the outputs of the learning of previous learners—contrasts with the traditional approach to instructional dialogue by assuming that there is considerable scope for learning without being a direct participant.

This aspect of the framework links directly with the approach of communities of practice. Wenger (2005) has recently depicted an important aspect of the approach as the "horizontalisation" of learning. Vicarious learning depends for its effect on the extent to which one learner identifies with another, seeing the other's approach to learning as relevant and interesting. A common identity defines a community of practice: in this case a community of learners who have expertise in the practices of learning. Moreover, the community can be situated in a particular subject area and at a particular level of mastery. The important requirement for vicarious learning to occur is that a learner accessing tertiary courseware should see it as having been generated by learning experiences of others with whom the new learner is able to identify, that is, a member of a community of learners to which the new learner aspires to be a legitimate participant. The learning resources produced by the previous learners are not the quality-controlled materials produced by teachers: their essential quality is not accuracy but validity. They must illustrate the real business of learning and what the new learner will gain most from them is less to do with mastering a subject and more to do with learning how to learn.

Fowler and Mayes (2000) took this argument into the realm of relationships: relationships between teachers and their students, between students and their peers, and between learners and others who have a significant influence on their approach to learning. In the general approach of networked learning we see various ways in which learners situate their experiences, their tasks and their growing knowledge. Much of this is not developing as conventional pedagogy—if by that term we imply the deliberate design of educational procedures—but as informal learning, facilitated by the rapid emergence of Web tools that enable learners to connect with others sharing similar learning interests or tasks anywhere on the Internet, and which are referred to as *social software*. This is facilitating the bottom-up development of learning communities on a scale that goes completely beyond our previous institution-bound concepts of educational groups. Learners form online communities spontaneously by combining one-to-one (e-mail and instant messaging), one-to-many (discussion tools, blogs and podcasts), and many-to-many (wikis) communication modes. Through these rapidly emerging tools, encouraging all users to share their own developing understanding of an area through social bookmarking and folksonomy, peer communication and collaboration becomes possible on a global scale and we start to glimpse a completely new kind of e-learning, in stark contrast to the conventional quality-controlled learning directed by top-down software, in which users' roles are circumscribed by the rigidities of institution-based virtual learning environments.

In summary, this framework encourages us to see that each stage of learning should be supported by a different form of technology. The main value of this analysis is to emphasise where in the learning cycle the support most needs to be directed. This offers a pedagogical rationale for designing the technology, and incidentally makes it became obvious where we should not waste our resources. Thus, multimedia and Web content support conceptualisation and a range of task support software maps onto construction. Dialogue can be conducted through computer-mediated communication (CMC), videoconferencing and mobile telephony, which can then be captured and stored. Each kind is important; a fully supportive learning environment requires all three. The underpinning pedagogy is constructive alignment (Biggs, 1999). The design principles require that learning activities, including both tasks (secondary) and dialogue (tertiary), are addressed before resources are devoted to the design of learning materials.

Issues Relating to the Implementation of Mayes Pedagogical Framework

In this case study, management organised a number of university-wide information sessions on the hybrid initiative, and IDs and other Distance and e-Learning Centre staff were co-opted to implement the initiative. The hybrid initiative was a top-down management initiative, designed to support the use of technology in learning and teaching, although many subject matter experts were already using a range of media and technology to enhance their courses. In the context of this case study, senior management of one faculty called for "volunteers" to pilot the hybrid approach. The ID author worked with a group of faculty SME volunteers to initiate a community of practice approach for implementing the hybrid initiative. The faculty volunteers saw value in participating in the initiative as a means of adding learning value to their courses. Wenger, McDermott, and Snyder (2002) argue that value is a key to community life because most participation is voluntary. Early value comes from focusing on the current problems and needs of community members (Wenger, McDermott, & Snyder, 2002) but as the community grows it develops a systematic body of knowledge that members can easily access. As the SMEs were unfamiliar with the hybrid approach, the initial meeting of the CoP focused on clarification of the meaning of hybrid delivery and the discussion of a suitable design framework for the hybrid courses. The discussions focused on the management initiative of using a hybrid approach for "delivery," and what that meant to academic staff working at the coalface and the use of technology to enhance learning and teaching, and constructivist and collaborative learning theory. In this case study, the ID was a community coordinator, acting as a broker to share instructional design theory and practice with the group to facilitate hybrid course design and to foster the professional development of the participating course leaders. As part of the broker role (Wenger, 1998), the idea of using a design framework was introduced by the designer to the group and members were asked if they had an educational or ID model/s that they used or preferred. After some discussion the group reached a shared agreement that the Mayes framework (1999; 2002) (serving as a boundary object) would assist in conceptualising the effective use of hybrid technology and inform the design process.

Participation in the hybrid initiative was on top of SME's existing workload, so in the second meeting the ID moved the pedagogical discussion about hybrid delivery to actual implementation of the design phase. The instructional designer generated and circulated a table using the Mayes framework to enable individual subject matter experts to individually reflect on, and document, existing and planned learning strategies, and to consider how these were mediated by technology. Table 1 provides an example of a completed framework.

Subject matter experts documented their planned hybrid learning and teaching strategies either using the framework or an adapted version that suited their pedagogical and development focus. These plans were tabled and discussed in the group meetings. This process was of particular value to community members, as they shared knowledge and benefited from colleagues feedback within their domain of practice. As the community discussed the shared designs, and considered how learners would undertake the learning activities, it began obvious that some members lacked the necessary technical knowledge or skills to implement their design. The designer asked SMEs to prepare a personal professional development plan, using the table based on the Mayes framework, to document existing or desired technical expertise that would allow them to implement the learning strategies they had planned. The discussion and sharing of desired staff development support alerted the group to the need for institutional support for the development phase of the process. A senior faculty member was invited to the meeting to discuss resourcing issues. No additional resources had been made available to faculty staff for the hybrid initiative; however, resources were available from the media and production sections of the Distance and e-Learning Centre for technology enhancements. Lack of resources for the implementation of the hybrid projects caused some disenchantment with the initiative and group meetings ceased, although interaction between members of the CoP continued on an informal basis. From this stage the ID worked with three individual subject matter experts to implement the planned course designs. Two of the five courses were unable to proceed, owing to workload or other professional issues.

Table 1. An example of a course structure in the Mayes framework

Course Code:	**Course Name:**	**Course Leader:**
Courseware	Existing	Planned
Primary	Print study book, selected readings Face to Face lectures PowerPoint lectures- WebCT & CD Set text book	Further audio New readings
Secondary	SA Questions & Feedback F2F tutorial tasks Interactivity-especially database and multimedia on the lecture presentation Adobe and E-reader tutorial	Possibly quizzes, crosswords Recorded lectures Answers to tutorial questions Tip of the week Library tutorial Course planner Exam notes proforma
Tertiary	WebCT online discussion groups (size?) Tutorial discussion groups	Weekly discussion topics Formative assessment Faculty funding?

The community coordinator role of the ID included a number of roles outlined by Wenger, McDermott, and Snyder (2002, p. 80) in their discussion of the critical role of a community coordinator. These roles included identifying important issues in the domain, planning and facilitating community meetings, linking community members, crossing boundaries between organisation units, brokering knowledge assets (the Mayes framework) and building practice. The role also included discussing constructivist learning theory and recent developments in hybrid learning with the group, as well as facilitating the professional development of the participating course leaders. This facilitation, or "change agent" role (Schwier, Campbell, & Kenny, 2004) is an emerging trend in IDs' roles—where IDs have an increasing responsibility in facilitating the discussion of status quo pedagogy and the application of technology to enhance learning.

Evaluation of the CoP Approach and the Use of the Mayes Framework

The subject matter experts (SME) were interviewed and asked to reflect on the community of practice approach and the application of the Mayes framework for the design of blended courses. Several themes emerged from the data, and the findings indicated that the SMEs all found the use of the model beneficial for conceptualising and designing learning environments. Each SME mentioned that the Mayes framework served as a particularly useful boundary object in the CoP context, where it served as the framework around which the community could organise their interconnections (Wenger et al., 2002). The Mayes framework provided a sound starting point for the design discussions and provided a useful planning strategy. One course leader noted that, *"it was a daunting task"* to know where to start with the hybrid process, and that the framework provided a place to start, *"so we could work out what things to do first, second, third. If you don't have that it just becomes a jumbled mess."*

Each of the SMEs interviewed commented positively on the CoP process, and mentioned that the Mayes framework provided a common point of reference for community interaction and knowledge building. Firstly it provided a context for pedagogical discussions, and secondly it provided a common framework for a shared discussion of the design for individual courses. Wenger, McDermott, and Snyder (2002) suggest that mutual engagement around joint enterprise is an ideal context for leading-edge learning. One course leader, whose course is offered in a number of teaching modes over three semesters, and involves a group of academics, mentioned that the framework was particularly useful for arriving at a consensus about learning activities and preparing a planned development strategy within the teaching group. Another course leader commented that working in a CoP was one of the benefits of the planning process and that *"interacting with others was beneficial."* While the community was active there was a sense of being involved in a learning community, and this process has continued informally among community members at the end of the scheduled meetings.

The subject matter experts indicated that the framework seemed to mirror the intuitive design processes of experienced educators. When reflecting on its use one SME commented:

I found it quite intuitive. I could see very quickly that this framework would complement my approach to doing things. It was a useful means of organising thoughts and breaking things into primary, secondary and tertiary. This gives it structure that I can relate to immediately. It takes ideas that are fairly nebulous and puts them into some sort of structure. I think as an organising structure—that's its primary strength.

The SME was articulating what Wenger (1998) has termed "reification." Wenger (1998) suggests that, "the concept of reification very generally refers to the process of giving form to our experience by producing objects that congeal this experience to 'thingness.' In so doing we create points of focus around which the negotiation of meaning becomes organised" (p. 58). Another SME commented on the use of the Mayes framework saying that:

I like a framework that is concrete, that I can make something of, and that gave me questions to think about, but also seems to have logic in it. I can see the relevance of what I would like to do and it makes sense to me with my intuitive sense, with having done very little formal education. I thought, this is something I can work with, and as soon as the ID was talking about it I began to think about how it could be implemented, and I also used elements of this thinking for the departmental retreat, as a prompt for course leaders to take time out and rethink their subject in a different way.

SMEs found the framework made the key principles of constructivist pedagogy understandable, and that it also clarified how the use of technology could be used where it demonstrably adds value to the learning experience. An SME commented that:

The framework was very efficient at conceptualising and preparing learning tasks. There is an endless amount of technology, but this framework is very useful in saying this particular technology is very useful and we will chose that because it seems to fit into what we are doing. We can see how the technologies we have chosen are going to improve how the students go about learning.

One SME reflected on the use of other instructional design approaches and commented on the changing approaches to ID.

In the early days when I was first working with an ID, we talked about modeling and scaffolding and the removal of scaffolding. It seemed to be a lot of what the academic did, and when they thought the student was ready they took something away. But this (Mayes framework) is much more about listening to the student as well, and that influencing the way the academic did things. It also acknowledged that students are talking with each other and learning, so you're looking at setting up a learning context in which there was that sort of dialogue going on.

The SMEs were all positive about the application of the Mayes framework as it made the principles of constructivist pedagogy readily understandable. Through the process of reification (Wenger, 1998) it provided a framework for discussion, sharing and building community knowledge and also provided an effective organising structure for the design of hybrid courses.

Addressing the Issues

In this case study, one of the issues that concerned SMEs was the lack of consultation at the grass roots level about the hybrid initiative, and they were concerned about how it would impact on existing methods of learning and teaching. The SME members of the CoP were all volunteers, keen to explore different approaches to learning and teaching; however, lack of consultation and resourcing of the initiative caused some disenchantment. The management should consult with faculty staff at the department level and provide opportunities for informed discussion and stakeholder input and feedback before major change initiatives are implemented. An incremental approach, with pilot studies, evaluation and opportunities for feedback from all stakeholders, including students is recommended. Lack of resourcing was an issue, as SMEs undertook their involvement in the hybrid process on top of an already demanding workload. Reasonable allocation of resources, particularly workload time, is essential to ensure commitment by SMEs. Lack of time also meant that the formal meeting times to explore and extend knowledge generated in the CoP did not continue after the initial five meetings, although informal discussions were maintained.

The conceptualisation and implementation of the CoP process would have benefited from a longer development phase. More discussion of the CoP approach would have clarified the roles of different members of the CoP, and perhaps lead to a more sustained community. Of course, Wenger (2002) notes that we are all members of personal and professional CoPs, often without any understanding of communities of practice as presented in the literature. However, discussion and clarification of the concept and processes may have increased the sustainability of the CoP. It is always a difficult judgement call for an ID to decide how much additional information to introduce when working with SMEs. Goodyear (2005) argues that while there is substantial unmet demand for useable forms of design guidance, it is generally expressed in ways that emphasise academics' strong sense of being time-poor. The focus of the group meetings was the design of hybrid courses, so apart from one meeting to introduce the idea of communities of practice to the faculty, no formal discussions about the CoP approach were undertaken in the meetings. More discussions about the CoP approach may have meant that the group sustained more structured links and discussions about the educational philosophy informing their practice, however owing to time pressure, discussions concentrated on the design of hybrid courses. The perceived pressure to move from exploring SMEs' beliefs about what constituted good learning and teaching to initiating the design of courses meant that the table to document individual course design (*Table 1*) was introduced by the ID before each SME had articulated their educational philosophy. Balancing the need to progress the design process efficiently, against structured opportunities to explore and clarify ideas, is a constant challenge for IDs working with time-poor SMEs. Based on the experience and evaluation of the CoP process in this case study a number of instructional design principles were identified and are articulated below.

Instructional Design Principles

1. **Establish the underlying beliefs about learning and teaching:** It is important that there is an initial discussion of beliefs about learning and teaching and desired learning outcomes. This clarifies the pedagogy underpinning the learning and teaching approach and provides the foundation for designing effective learning environments. Too often SMEs are seduced by the glitz of new technology applications, and think, *"I'll have one of those for my course."* Clarification of the SME's educational philosophy and how it can be best applied to the specific learning context draws the SME focus away from "end products" to essential learning activities. Designing learning and teaching activities is the crux of the Mayes framework. Hopefully it can be assumed that instructional designers come into such a discussion with a solid grounding in educational and ID theory, and are competent in the range of ID competencies, such as those outlined by International Board of Standards for Training, Performance and Instruction (Richey, Fields, & Foxon, 2001). In this case study the Mayes framework served as a boundary object (Wenger, 1998) and evaluation indicated it provided a foundation for the conceptualisation and design of the hybrid courses.
2. **Establish roles and expectations:** When working with an individual SME or members of the CoP it is necessary to establish how the participants will contribute to the joint enterprise and move towards achieving the planned outcome of the project. A flow chart of the design, development and implementation steps clarifies the process and provides a visual overview on which to base discussions about timelines and participant roles.
3. **Effective communication and organisational skills:** It is essential that the IDs have effective communication and organisational skills. The ability to prompt a SME to articulate their educational philosophy, to listen and then feedback and extend that philosophy, as it relates to learning theories, provides the foundation for the design process. Keppell (2000) also comments that the importance of the communication process between the ID and SME cannot be overemphasized. The ability to communicate effectively builds the foundation for an effective working relationship, which is also essential for the smooth operation of the project. In this case study the ID had already established a close working relationship with most of the group members. This helped the acceptance of the framework by the SMEs, based on an existing positive professional relationship with the ID, and a belief that it would inform and expedite the design process.
4. **Nurture the CoP:** The community of practice should be nurtured and supported both formally by institutional power brokers and informally by knowledge sharing, contribution of time and resources, and by networking across a range of face-to-face or electronic contexts. Wenger, McDermott, and Snyder (2002) suggest that while communities of practice form naturally, organisations need to become more proactive and strategic about developing and integrating them into institutional operations.
5. **Locate the design project within the institutional context:** The ID must be attuned to realities of the SME educational goals and working environment, as well as having an understanding of management priorities. The ID can be in a situation where management is expecting the ID to implement an institutional initiative without the full support of people working at the coalface. Early discussions with SMEs will clarify

issues and expectations, and the ID needs to reach a working alignment between institution-wide goals and those of the SME. An example in this case study relates to the recent focus in Australian universities to increase research output, particularly in the area of learning and teaching. Evaluation and reflection on practice is an important part of an educator's role, be they ID or SME. By working with SMEs to develop research projects and publications relating to the design project the ID can both inform the design practice and value add to the ID and SME's professional profile.

6. **Use a pedagogically sound but simple framework for the design process:** It is assumed that instructional designers have a solid grounding in educational and ID theory, and use a pedagogically sound framework that is appropriate for the design process. This achieves two goals. Firstly, it ensures that the design of the learning environment is based on sound pedagogical principles. Secondly, using such a framework provides the basis for a shared understanding of the design process and facilitates the community of practice interactions. In this case study the Mayes framework provided an efficient and effective framework for shared communication with SMEs and for the design of flexible learning environments. The underpinning pedagogy of the Mayes framework is constructive alignment (Biggs, 1999) and it focuses on the activities of the learners at each stage of learning. The framework enables the SME to conceptualise the learning activities at each level—primary (conceptualisation), secondary (construction) and tertiary (dialogue). The framework is not linear, as is the case in the ADDIE model, as each stage of learning is iterative and informs and enhances the other stages in an iterative process. The authors perceive that its lack of prescriptive detail means it provides a systematic design structure that can be flexibly applied across a range of applications. The application of the framework in a range of contexts is undergoing further research.

Conclusion

In the case study reported here the framework was used as a starting point for discussion between the instructional designer, who was supporting the course redesign, and the course leaders. An interesting instructional design question for further study is whether this framework might be developed into a more comprehensive design tool, where educational issues such as level of study and pre-requisite knowledge, as well as more fine-grained pedagogical techniques, might be addressed. At present its main effectiveness probably stems from its initial simplicity and if it is to be elaborated into a more detailed design vehicle then this top-level simplicity must be protected.

There is hardly a course leader anywhere in higher education who is not at least considering whether their provision might be enhanced by the introduction of technology in some form. Nevertheless, Zemsky and Massy (2004) suggest that the e-learning innovation cycle has stalled at the innovator and early adopter stages. A community of practice approach builds on personal and discipline expertise and informs and sustains the change process. It provides an environment for sharing and building knowledge, exchanging new ideas and exploring innovations that are grounded in practice, while supported by a community of like-minded colleagues. The case study reported here has focused on a comparatively neglected but crucial aspect of the application of technology in learning and teaching: the process by which the teachers themselves come to take ownership of the technology enhancement. It is important that the teachers reflect on their own learning, and accept that taking responsibility for learning outcomes within the context of a wider community of learners is the key both for themselves and for their students. This is a critical aspect that goes to the heart of the design process in higher education.

References

Aycock, A., Garnham, C., & Kaleta, R. (2002, March). Lessons learned from the hybrid course project. *Teaching with Technology Today, University of Wisconsin System Online Journal, 8*(6), 1-6. Retrieved August 17, 2003, from http://www.uwsa.edu/ttt/articles/garnham2.html

Biggs, J. (1999). *Teaching for quality learning at university.* Buckingham: Society for Research in Higher Education/Open University.

Crawford, C. (2004). Non-linear instructional design model: Eternal, synergistic design and development. *British Journal of Educational Technology, 35*(4), 413-420.

Eklund, J., Kay, M., & Lynch, H. (2003). E-learning: Emerging issues and key trends: A discussion paper. *Australian Flexible Learning Framework.* Retrieved May 27, 2006, from www.nfer.ac.uk/latest-news/ontheweb/pdfs/feb04.pdf

Fitts, P.M., & Posner, M.I. (1967). *Learning and skilled performance in human performance.* Belmont, CA: Brock-Cole.

Fowler, C.J.H., & Mayes, J.T. (2000). Learning relationships: From theory to design. In D. Squires, G. Conole, & G. Jacobs (Eds.), *The changing face of learning technology.* Cardiff: University of Wales Press.

Gagne, R. (1985). *The conditions of learning.* New York: Holt, Rinehart and Winston.

Gayeski, D.M. (1998). *Out -of-the box instructional design: Moving from assembly-line models to non-linear performance models.* Retrieved May 27, 2006, from www.lightlink.com/omnicom/t&disd.html

Goodyear, P. (2005). Educational design and networked learning: Patterns, pattern languages and design practice. *Australasian Journal of Educational Technology, 10*(1), 82-101.

Gordon, J., & Zemke, R. (2000, April). The attack on ISD. *Training,* 43-53.

Hildreth, P.J., & Kimble, C. (2002). The duality of knowledge. *Information Research, 8*(1), paper no. 142. Retrieved April 6, 2005, from http://InformationR.net/ir/8-1/paper142.html

House of Commons Education and Skills Committee. (2005). *Report on the UK e-University.* Retrieved April 6, 2005, from http://www.publications.parliament.uk/pa/cm200405/cmselect/cmeduski/205/205.pdf

Ikenberry, S.O. (1999). The university and the information age. In W.Z. Hirsch & L.E. Weber (Eds.), *Challenges facing higher education at the millennium.* Phoenix, AZ: Oryx Press.

Jonassen, D.H. (1999). Designing constructivist learning environments. In C.M. Reigeluth (Ed.), *Instructional-design theories and models volume II: A new paradigm of instructional theory.* Mahwah, NJ: Lawrence Erlbaum Associates.

Keppell, M. (2000). Principles at the heart of an instructional designer: Subject matter expert interaction. In R. Sims, M. O'Reilly, & S. Sawkins (Eds.), *Learning to Choose: Choosing to Learn. Proceedings of the 17th Annual ASCILITE Conference* (pp. 317-326). Lismore, NSW: Southern Cross University Press. Retrieved August 6, 2005, from http://www.ascilite.org.au/conferences/coffs00/papers/mike_keppell.pdf

Keppell, M. (2004). Legitimate participation? Instructional designer-subject matter expert interactions in communities of practice. *World Conference on Educational Multimedia, Hypermedia and Telecommunications, 1*, 3611-3618.

Kolb, D.A. (1984). *Experiential learning.* Englewood Cliffs, NJ: Prentice Hall.

Laurillard, D. (2002). *Rethinking university teaching: A conversational framework for the effective use of learning technologies* (2nd ed.). London: Routledge Falmer.

Lave, J., & Wenger, E. (1991). *Situated learning: Legitimate peripheral participation.* Cambridge, UK: Cambridge University Press.

Mayes, J.T., & Fowler, C.J.H. (1999). Learning technology and usability: A framework for understanding courseware. *Interacting with Computers, 11*, 485-497.

Mayes, J.T, Dineen, F., McKendree, J., & Lee, J. (2001). Learning from watching others learn. In C. Steeples & C. Jones (Eds.), *Networked learning: Perspectives and issues.* London: Springer.

Mayes, J.T. (2002). Pedagogy, lifelong learning and ICT. *Electronic Journal of Instructional Science and Technology, 5*(1). Retrieved February 15, 2003, from http://www.ipm.ucl.ac.be/ChaireIBM/Mayes.pdf

Merrill, M.D., Li, Z., & Jones, M.K. (1990). Limitations of first generation instructional design (ID1). *Educational Technology, 30*(1), 7-11.

Ponzi, L., & Koenig, M. (2002). Knowledge management: Another management fad? *Information Research, 8*(1). Retrieved July 11, 2006, from http://InformationR.net/ir/8-1/paper145.html

Rumelhart, V.E., & Norman, D.A. (1978). Accretion, tuning, and restructuring: Three modes of learning. In J.W. Cotton & R.L. Klatzky (Eds.), *Semantic factors in cognition.* Hillsdale, NJ: Lawrence Erlbaum Associates.

Reigeluth, C.M. (1999). What is instructional design theory and how is it changing? In C.M. Reigeluth (Ed.), *Instructional-design theories and models volume II: A new paradigm of instructional theory.* Mahwah, NJ: Lawrence Erlbaum Associates.

Resnick, L.B., & Resnick, D.P. (1991). Assessing the thinking curriculum: New tools for education reform. In B.R. Gifford & M.C. O'Connor (Eds.), *Changing assessment: Alternative views of aptitude, achievement and instruction.* Boston: Kluwer.

Richey, R., Fields, D., & Foxon, M. (2001). *Instructional design competencies: The standards* (3rd ed.). Syracuse, NY: Eric Clearinghouse on Information and Technology.

Schwier, R., Campbell, K., & Kenny, R. (2004). Instructional designers' observations about identity, communities of practice and change agency. *Australasian Journal of Educational Technology, 20*(1), 69-100.

Smith, P., & Ragan, T. (2005). *Instructional design* (3rd ed.). New York: Wiley.

Vygotsky, L.S. (1978), *Mind and society: Development of higher psychological processes.* Cambridge, MA: Harvard University Press.

Waddoups, G.L., & Howell, S.L. (2001). Bringing online learning to campus: The hybridization of teaching and learning at Brigham Young University. *International Review of Research in Open and Distance Learning, 2*(2). Retrieved August 17, 2005, from http://www.irrodl.org/index.php/irrodl/article/view/52/108

Wenger, E. (1998). *Communities of practice: Learning, meaning, and identity.* Cambridge: Cambridge University Press.

Wenger, E. (2005). Learning, technology, and community: A journey of the self. In J. Cook & D. Whitelock (Eds.), *ALT-C 2005: Exploring the frontiers of e-learning: Borders, outposts and migration, 12th International Conference of the Association for Learning Technology*. University of Manchester, UK.

Wenger, E., McDermott, R., & Snyder, W.M. (2002). *Cultivating communities of practice.* Boston: Harvard Business School Press.

Young, J.R. (2002, March 22). Hybrid teaching seeks to end the divide between traditional and online instruction. *The Chronicle of Higher Education.*

Zemsky, R., & Massy, W. (2004). *Thwarted innovation: What happened to e-learning and why.* University of Pennsylvania: The Learning Alliance for Higher Education.

Zemke, R., & Rossett, A. (2002). A hard look at ISD. *Training, 26-34.*

Chapter X

Delivering Online Expertise, Online

Stephen Quinton, Curtin University of Technology, Australia

Abstract

This chapter describes two strategies for delivering educational design expertise and online professional development via the Internet. The issues and difficulties pertaining to the design and application of online staff development are examined in terms of the factors and needs that were observed during the implementation phases. The professional development initiative focuses on staff development Web sites which aim to inspire instructional design staff to understand the implicit teaching and learning goals used by lecturers and to assist lecturing staff to increase their awareness of instructional design methodologies. This approach allows participants engaged in online developments to share a common pool of understanding and expertise. The chapter concludes by identifying the potential advantages of the Web-based professional development strategies.

Introduction

It is generally accepted that learning management systems (LMS) are useful for online teaching. However, there are many aspects of online learning that need to be learned before teaching in this new environment. For instance, there are lecturers who are reticent to engage in online learning delivery because they do not have the appropriate skills, are too busy or do not have sufficient time. On the other hand, some lecturers possess the skills and competencies to teach online but lack access to suitable teaching resources appropriate for their teaching area. Given the diversity of needs and skill levels, it is argued that university staff require convenient, on-demand access to start-up advice, high quality Web resources, and ongoing, up-to-date online professional development support.

Online delivery platforms such as WebCT and BlackBoard offer a well-integrated, consistent approach to the development and distribution of electronic learning materials. A useful analogy is to think of these technologies as a workbench comprised of tools for combining text, graphics, video, and audio files in ways that allow lecturers to adapt selected teaching content to the online environment. Most LMS Web development tools include "wizards" that guide the user in the creation of online teaching materials. For the novice, this means that the task of designing Web material can be accomplished with little or no expertise in writing HTML code. However, regardless of the sophistication of the available tools and facilities, leveraging this technology for teaching and learning purposes requires practitioners to develop a range of skills and competencies that extend beyond the capacity of many LMS platforms and enable the transfer of sound teaching practices to the online environment.

If academic staff are to succeed in the transition to online teaching, then support for any related shift in educational practice should be holistic in scope, responsive in nature, and sensitive to changes in academic roles and responsibilities. This chapter details two staff development programmes currently available to staff at Curtin University of Technology. It describes the complex task of delivering online educational design expertise and flexible learning strategies to academic staff. The issues and difficulties of Web-based online staff development are discussed in relation to just-in-time access to guidelines and procedures and the practical examples that assist staff to enhance the quality of teaching and learning in the online environment. The chapter concludes with an overview of future refinements and a summary of the key factors that may assist other institutions in establishing similar approaches to online staff development.

Background

University staff are currently facing an enormous challenge to provide high quality learning experiences to their on-campus and off-campus students due to declining resources and an increasing demand for greater flexibility in teaching delivery options. At the same time, academic teaching practices are under considerable pressure to keep pace with rapid developments in information and communication technologies (ICT) that are shaping students' expectations of what they believe is a university education. These emerging pressures inevitably compel universities to institute appropriate professional development programmes and to enhance academic staff skills.

The demands imposed on university support centres responsible for academic staff development have escalated in recent years. In addition to a continuing need to improve the quality of face-to-face tuition (Ramsden, 1992), there are emerging pressures to teach online as universities seek to incorporate the use of ICT into their academic programmes (Oliver, 2001; Paloff & Pratt, 1999). It is becoming essential that programmes offered by staff development centres are responsive, cost effective, and incorporate the vision needed to meet the increasing demands and challenges confronting the education sector over the coming decade. The difficulty however, is that the research literature indicates that staff in universities are not fully prepared for a large-scale transition to online teaching.

To address this issue, Oliver (2001) Curtin University of Technology researchers have been exploring professional development programmes for online learning. In this context, a comprehensive review of the literature on the use of ICT in teaching and learning and professional development issues has been conducted over the past five years. The aim of this research was to provide high quality development programmes and support strategies that will assist academic staff to teach online using effective pedagogical practices. In addition, due to the increasing demands on staff time, the researchers have provided support that is readily available, user friendly, and reflects current advances in the use of ICT in teaching and learning. Given the difficulties many academics must cope with during the course of their normal working day, it is essential that they be provided wth convenient access to a responsive professional development programme that meets their immediate needs.

To allow for the broad diversity of staff and student preferences, flexible delivery through e-learning has been identified as one of three priority areas in the University Teaching and Learning Plan. At Curtin, online design and development expertise is made available to staff in several ways: a centralised service provided by the Educational Design and eLearning (EDeL) unit located within the Learning Support Network; support teams established within the University's four teaching Divisions; and the expertise of early-adopters working independently in the teaching schools. In addition, two key strategies support online professional development needs which include the Flexible Learning and Delivery (FLaD) and the WebKit support Web sites that provide an integrated approach to educational design support for staff involved in online teaching and learning. This approach emphasises a focus on pedagogical strategy and content development. The aim is to encourage instructional designers and lecturing staff to explore the broader issues and roles of educational/instructional design. At the same time, staff become familiar with the development guidelines and procedures for ensuring the quality of online design at Curtin. The two sites aim to sensitise instructional design staff to the implicit teaching and learning goals of lecturing staff and to raise the level of instructional design expertise of lecturing staff.

Literature Review

The Roles of Academic Staff

An important aspect of the research undertaken involves the analysis of academic staff roles and competencies in the use of ICT as applied to their teaching and learning practices. We are exploring the changing roles of academic staff as they move from face-to-face to online teaching and the implications of these changes for the planning of professional development programmes. It is clear from this research that the number of roles undertaken by university lecturers is steadily increasing (Bess, 1998). This trend is supported in a comparison of the six roles identified for lecturers conducted in 1985 (McKeachie, 1986) with the eight roles for lecturers using online materials in 2001 (Goodyear, Salmon, Spector, Steeples, & Tickner, 2001), as outlined in Table 1. In this table, the roles of face-to-face lecturers are aligned with those of online lecturers. While it is no surprise that the technologically focussed roles have changed significantly, there is also considerable overlap in the roles of university lecturers as disciplinary experts, facilitators of student learning and student advisors.

The roles of instructional designer, site facilitator and proctor, librarian and graphic designer Should also be included in the list. Kemshal-Bell (2001) for example, describes three roles of online teachers, which include technical, facilitation, and management roles. Furthermore, university teaching and learning practices have changed from a teacher-directed approach to a student-centred, self-directed approach (Ramsden, 1992; Biggs, 1990) that has significantly altered the ways teachers and students relate to one another. The changes in staff and student roles and relationships are reflected in an analysis of teacher and student roles involved in online courses as provided by Collins and Berge (1996), which are summarised below:

Table 1. The changing roles of university lecturers

Six roles of lecturers in 1985 (McKeachie, 1986)	**Eight roles of online lecturers in 2001** (Goodyear et al., 2001)
• **Expert** - presents knowledge • **Formal Authority** - sets the learning goals • **Ego-Ideal** - role model for developing positive attitudes to learning • **Facilitator** - attends to the learning environment • **Socialising Agent** - attends to students' intellectual and social development needs • **Person** – provides a human link with the student and recognises student's values and interests	• **Content-Facilitator** – facilitates an understanding of course content. • **Researcher** – produces new knowledge to teach • **Assessor** – provides grades, feedback, and validation of learners' work • **Process Facilitator** - facilitates a range of online activities supportive of student learning • **Designer** – designs effective online learning activities • **Technologist** - makes technological choices to improve the environment made available to learners • **Advisor-Counsellor** – offers advice or counselling to students • **Manager-Administrator** – manages learner registration, security, and record keeping

- Teachers have become expert questioners, consultants, guides, and resource facilitators rather than providers of answers and students have become active constructors as opposed to passive receivers of knowledge,
- Teachers are designers of student's learning experiences rather than the sole provider of content and students have become complex problem-solvers instead of memorisers of facts,
- The teacher presents multiple perspectives on topics, emphasising the salient points whereas the students are encouraged to view topics from multiple perspectives, refine their own questions, and seek out their own answers,
- The teacher emphasises the acquisition of learning strategies (both individually and collaboratively) while students work as group members on collaborative/cooperative assignments and group interactions,
- The teacher no longer has total autonomy over the learning activities and students have become autonomous, independent, self-motivated managers of their own time and learning processes,
- Teachers now provide the initial structure to students' learning activities, encouraging increased autonomy and self-direction to emphasise open discussion of students' work,
- A move from total teacher control of the teaching environment to sharing with students as fellow learners where the focus is on knowledge application rather than observance of the teacher as the benchmark for expert performance.

As suggested by the above discussion, the changes in roles, skills and competencies required of university lecturers have implications for the provision of professional development support programmes. The key, issues to be considered includes the need to:

- **Create challenging learning environments:** Lecturers must engage students and provide meaningful activities and challenges that clearly relate to the required learning outcomes (McInnis, 2001). Students are more likely to "opt out" of an online course than a face-to-face course if they do not perceive it to be relevant to their needs (Salter & Hansen, 1999). It is important that professional development programmes address this issue and assist staff to devise challenging, engaging, and supportive online learning environments.
- **Attend to pedagogical issues:** The new technologies may compel academics to examine their pedagogical approaches to teaching and learning and devise more innovative strategies to enhance students' online learning experiences. This in turn presents a challenge for professional development services to integrate current advances in pedagogical practices into their staff development programmes.
- **Work as a team:** New technological innovations are encouraging academics to adopt a team approach to their teaching and learning practices (Ellis & Phelps, 2000; Burford & Cooper, 2000; di Corpo, 2001). As lecturers work in teams to collaborate on the production of learning materials, there is an increased need to teach collaborative

skills as an integral part of online professional development programmes (di Corpo, 2001).

- **Support both students and staff:** Lecturing staff require support for managing the impact of technology on teaching and learning and to develop new ways to work together (di Corpo, 2001; Faire, 1994; Herrington & Oliver, 2001; Loucks-Horsley, 1997; Macchiusi & Trinidad, 2001). Thus, it is critical to ensure that students are adequately equipped to cope with the rapidly changing learning and working environments (Hicks, Reid, & George, 1999).
- **Identify new directions for professional development programmes:** It seems that the introduction of new technologies has prompted a critical reflection and re-evaluation of the way university teaching has been delivered in the past. This new awareness leads to questions that are crucial to the planning of successful professional development programmes. These questions include:
    - **How should universities respond at an institutional level?** Universities have been struggling to adapt to the changing environment in which they operate (Adams, Marshall, & Cameron, 1999). An essential aspect of responding to change is to provide the infrastructure required to enable staff and students to utilise new technologies (Atkinson & Brown, 1997). Another aspect to consider is that institutions must examine their strategic options for the future (Reid, 1999), and provide a framework for staff to make those options a reality (Popisil & Willcoxson, 1988). For example, a high technology solution could include the use of reusable online learning resources that permit a more flexible and responsive learning environment without demanding high levels of technical expertise from staff and students (Quinton, 2001; Oliver, 2001).
    - **To what extent are changes occurring in teaching and learning due to the new technologies?** The introduction of new technologies is just one of several factors influencing the way universities function. Another factor is the constantly changing perspectives on the nature and purpose of teaching and learning. A third factor is the changing context in which both lecturers and learners operate and the resultant effect on teaching and learning practices. For example, lecturers are already collaborating in teams to develop new ways of teaching in the online learning environment (Trinidad & Albon, 2001).
    - **To what extent are face-to-face teaching and online learning different facets of a broader teaching process?** There has been many debates on whether lecturers must learn to view face-to-face and online learning as part of their repertoire of tools of trade, and to use these tools appropriately to meet the divergent needs of their students (Bryant, Scoufis, & Cheers, 1999). By working collaboratively, lecturers become more efficient in their area of expertise and interest while making productive use of the expertise and interest of their colleagues (Bess, 1998). Insofar as there are overlaps between the traditional and online teaching modes, the integration of online methodologies with professional development for face-to-face teaching presents a feasible option.
    - **How can the introduction of new technologies improve the overall quality of teaching and learning?** As noted, the application of the learning process to the online mode can lead to improvements in the quality of traditional face-to-face

teaching by providing opportunities for reflection and evaluation (Campbell, McGee, & Yates, 2000; McShane, 1999; Torrisi Steele, & Davis, 2000). Harnessing reflective practices and the power of discourse through the provision of opportunities for mentoring and the dissemination of research findings may lead to other useful avenues for professional development centres to improve the quality of teaching and learning in universities.

Moving Staff Development to Beyond Online Competency

The Web can facilitate access to highly effective learning environments that promote three essential attributes of a productive online learning community: the active construction of knowledge; positive interpersonal relationships; and rich discursive interactivity. It is well documented for example, that in collaborative face-to-face classrooms, learners share ideas and elaborate on new information as they actively engage in supporting each other to develop the skills needed to apply higher order thinking strategies, form new hypotheses, and reflect on what they learn. The importance of providing opportunities for communication, participation and interaction in Web environments to support cognitive development is also well documented (McCracken, 2004). Lecturers that understand how to elicit and manage positive online social dynamics are well equipped to encourage creative knowledge building activities that extend the learning opportunities and build new foundations on which more elaborate communal structures will emerge (Woods & Ebersole, 2003). In addition, online learning communities provide students with the opportunity to engage in effective, independent learning activities. Thus, the provision of academic support is critical to ensuring electronic learning environments are inclusive, accessible, instructive, and responsive to changing staff and student needs.

Enhancing Staff Online Expertise

Often, academics have a limited understanding of the implications in creating Web environments and exploiting the associated technologies. The initial transition period, or the amount of time required from commencement of conversion of an existing teaching unit to when they are comfortable with working on their own in an online environment, can for many academics be the most difficult area to overcome. Therefore, convenient access to efficient training is needed to get them started. It is argued therefore, that the tools used by academics should be:

- Readily understood,
- Easy to use (intuitive),
- Available on demand.

In addition, educational design and delivery practices must be responsive to emerging global challenges as indicated by:

- Increasing competition for courses and students,
- Diminishing restrictions due to time and space factors,
- Changes in the nature of intellectual work resulting from advances in ICT,
- Accelerating pace of knowledge developments,
- An increasing focus on knowledge, information management and creative thinking for economic advantage,
- A decreasing need for individual retention of information and an increasing value in what the individual knows and the skills required to apply/enhance that knowledge.

As a result, there is a need to recognise the crucial interdependence between the way higher education is organised and the way learning is deployed particularly given that the role of ICT is undergoing dramatic change in several key areas:

- Information technology has become central to determining strategic change in higher education,
- The capacity to deliver genuine "flexible" learning is fast becoming a priority (and a reality),
- Hardware and software are no longer the only influencing factors—the chosen technology must support educational and pedagogical integrity.

Addressing the Problems Arising from the Introduction of New Technologies

Apart from the issue of technology skill requirements, any move by universities to shift learning to the online environment poses a threat to the traditional roles of academics. Moreover, the potential to source university services externally may tempt administrators to cut costs by reducing staff numbers and replacing them with lower paid, less skilled staff (Young, 1997). The introduction of online learning within universities places demands in terms of additional workloads and skills development on existing staff (Adams, Marshall, & Cameron, 1999; Herrington & Oliver, 2001; Kemshal-Bell, 2001; McInnis, 1999). Above all, every staff development programme should not increase existing staff workloads to unacceptable levels. One way to overcome these problems is to encourage staff to collaborate in teams to maximise the use of limited resources (Bess, 1998; di Corpo, 2001; Paulson, 2002).

The value of formalised instructional design support for the efficient and effective deployment of online delivery programmes is now accepted as crucial to ensuring successful student learning outcomes. However, it is known that the development of online learning solutions in universities tends to lack ready access to the same levels of resources and specialist expertise made available within commercial enterprises. For the most part, academic staff become developers of online learning materials in difficult circumstances, usually prompted by university directives to "go online" and often supported or guided by an instructional designer, a Web developer or a colleague with some technical knowledge of Web technologies. The problem that arises is that standards in design, development and delivery vary, and in many instances, quality and content may be compromised by a complex combination of timeframes, funding, competency levels, and access to expert support.

Despite these problems, there are potential benefits that could encourage staff to adopt new technologies. Foremost are the benefits to students in gaining more flexible and responsive learning opportunities (McInnis, 2001). The new technologies offer the potential for learning experiences that are tailored to the individual needs of students in ways that are difficult to achieve in face-to-face settings. Furthermore, teachers who are introduced to online learning often find that their traditional (face-to-face) teaching improves as a result (McShane, 2000). Staff can benefit from the provision of professional development support that assists them to realise the full potential of the new technologies. A useful strategy is to continually monitor and review the requisite skills for both face-to-face and online teaching and learning. In this way, the successful implementation of online teaching and learning and associated support programmes can be built upon existing teaching practices so that staff may gain proficiency in online course developments (Bennett, Priest, & Macpherson, 1999).

Case Description

Programme Aims and Outcomes

The key features of the FLaD and WebKit sites were derived as a result of the background study and literature review. Following the research study phase was the design and development stages of the Web sites, which took place over a period of three years: eighteen months for the FLaD site and three years for the WebKit. One instructional designer was selected for the WebKit development and two instructional designers were appointed to the FLaD site. One project manager assumed responsibility for managing both teams to ensure overall consistency and cohesiveness of the two sites. Both sites were officially released to staff during semester one in 2005. A number of factors were involved in the design of both sites:

- The issues and findings derived from the research studies,
- Ongoing consultation with staff located throughout the campus to obtain advice and constructive feedback on the design and layout of the site and provide suggestions on how the site may be refined to better reflect staff needs,
- Enlisting the support of a small group of lecturers who evaluated both sites at various stages during the design/development phase and refined the display layout, features, content, and navigational aspects,
- An iterative design approach was adopted where the concepts, assumptions and experience gained from all previous prototype developments were continually evaluated, and the results were applied to the next stage of development.

In light of the above factors and considerations, the general aims of the FLaD and WebKit Web-based staff development strategies were to assist university unit coordinators and lecturers gain the necessary skills and competencies in:

- Understanding the essential aspects of the educational design and development of online teaching unit(s),
- Sourcing/developing the most appropriate content required for online learning,
- Planning, identification, and reaching agreement on the online development deliverables, and the parties responsible for those deliverables,
- The effective facilitation and management of widely dispersed learners engaged in the online medium.

The core aim is to provide staff with ready access to a comprehensive Web-based expertise and resources facility that will assist them to design and develop online teaching units. The Web sites not only offer a comprehensive set of practical, "hands-on" guidelines, procedures, and examples to initiate and progress the design process, but also serve to establish useful benchmarks for evaluating online teaching units during their delivery. Ultimately, the goal of the educational design process is to provide learners with multiple opportunities for achieving quality learning outcomes given the diversity of potential difficulties and demands they may encounter during their learning experiences. The staff development programme outcomes underscore a broad range of advantages and benefits for staff, the most immediate of which include:

- Enhance online teaching and learning activities within the broader campus community (an online staff development Web site can be linked as an additional resource to other related on-campus teaching programmes),
- Engender greater awareness of alternative understandings and experiences in global online learning practices,
- Foster research and creative thinking through "on-time" exposure to comprehensive literature and innovative examples,
- Broaden students' learning experiences through increased interaction with lecturing staff who have been equipped with the necessary expertise to design and facilitate innovative online environments.

The flexible learning and delivery (FLaD) Web site was designed to provide a comprehensive support facility for academic and instructional design staff that will assist them to deliver effective online learning solutions. In essence, the site aims to encourage staff to adopt proven best practice standards in online learning design. It also provides ready access to information and tools that encourage a project team approach to educational design, where the focus is on techniques and methods aimed at promoting active student involvement leading to the development of higher order thinking skills.

The second strategy involved the WebKit site, which expanded the online staff development programme to include a range of user-friendly Web resource development tools. These tools comprise special purpose "tools" that enable staff to produce sophisticated, pedagogically sound, interactive online teaching resources. The site addresses a wide range of online development needs while ensuring the output of staff work meets high educational standards. In its current form, the WebKit aims to: ease the task of migrating existing classroom and paper-based teaching units to the online environment; achieve greater efficiencies in Web page development; reduce costs in terms of time and resource creation; encourage increased staff participation in the conversion of existing teaching units to the online environment; and introduce innovative methods for ensuring quality learning outcomes.

The FLaD Site

Strategically, the flexible learning and delivery (FLaD) Web site aims to aid in the implementation of Curtin's Teaching and Learning Plan (2006-2008) in terms of promoting and encouraging the flexible delivery of Curtin's degree courses. Its targeted audiences are instructional designers and academic staff developing learning materials for online delivery. In essence, the FLaD site is an online resource for staff involved in flexible learning delivery using online and distance education technologies. It covers a diverse range of topics such as:

- How to get started in online flexible delivery,
- Developing material for online flexible delivery,
- Enhancing flexible teaching and learning,
- Flexible teaching in the online and other modes,
- Using learning management systems such as WebCT and BlackBoard,
- Student support and information.

The FLaD site comprises three main sections: Schools and Divisions; Procedures and Forms; and the Sample Gallery. All sections reflect the diverse levels of flexible online delivery at Curtin and articulate the core strategies for the implementation and delivery of online learning at each level. A brief description of each section is provided below:

1. **Schools and divisions:** This section is intended for staff members who are interested or involved in online learning and delivery by presenting guidelines for developing flexible teaching materials. For staff with more experience, information and advice is provided on how to enhance their online teaching and learning materials.
2. **Procedures and forms:** This section outlines a project-based methodology for the design, development and delivery of online learning materials. It features documents that can be used to create (and manage) effective online learning environments.
3. **Sample gallery:** The sample gallery provides users with examples of online learning materials that have been developed in Curtin's schools and divisions. It is intended

to provide staff with an idea of the scope and diversity of online learning in a higher education context.

Schools and divisions: This section of FLaD recognises the need to cater for two key dimensions in online learning delivery in higher education:

- Excellence in teaching practices and learning design,
- ICT competency.

In the current educational technology climate, it has become increasingly critical to adopt a set of procedures and practices that promote a minimum standard in the quality of learning materials offered online and in the quality of teaching that occurs in the Web-based delivery medium. The expertise in both these areas has long been the domain of instructional designers. However, not all academic staff have the option of accessing full-time instructional design expertise. For these reasons, this section of FLaD was devised to provide online design advice and guidance to academics embarking on online delivery. It is written from an instructional design point of view to present best practice approaches to the design, development and delivery of flexible online learning resources, and covers all relevant stages from design through to delivery as outlined below:

Stage 1. Getting started targets:

- Preparation of content material for online delivery,
- Skill sets required to develop online learning resources,
- Types and quality of content required for the external delivery of degree course provisions through the online medium, that is: unit outlines, study guides, readers, and university policy statements,
- Incorporation of Curtin's outcomes-focused education policy in the development of online materials,
- Copyright issues relevant to the delivery of online learning material.

Stage 2. Enhancing online delivery targets:

- Methods and strategies required to enhance flexible delivery through the incorporation of universal design principles, videotaped lectures (iLectures), and interactive multimedia.

Stage 3. Delivering flexible learning through online targets:

- Teaching practices suited to all delivery modes including the online environment,
- Supporting students living in widely distributed locations,

- Incorporating and facilitating online collaborative learning through discussion groups, video cameras, and related technologies,
- Assessment strategies specific to the external, online delivery and distance education modes,
- Evaluation of the quality and effectiveness of online learning resources and subsequent updating/revision.

Curtin also offers external programmes through its distance education (DE) and the Open Universities Australia (OUA) provisions. Approximately one-third of these programmes are delivered online using the WebCT and BlackBoard Learning Management Systems. With this in mind, the Schools and Divisions section of the FLaD site provides guidance in the use of Curtin's LMS delivery platforms covering the developmental and administrative aspects of:

- Unit creation and use of authoring tools,
- Releasing online units for delivery,
- Student administration,
- Records management and assessment records,
- Training and support in the use of a LMS.

As a resource for academic staff, the FLaD site also serves as a means of exposing staff to the instructional design imperatives of the higher education sector in relation to a student-centred learning context. The practices and approaches it proffers are based on feedback derived through a range of external studies and online student evaluation surveys. This aspect of the Schools and Divisions section ensures that best practice in instructional design principles align with identified student needs such as flexibility and portability of learning content and the timely provision of well-structured, clearly articulated support for students studying online.

Procedures and Forms: This section offers a project methodology aimed at encouraging a more structured approach to the design and development of online learning content. While recognising that online development within a University can be initiated by early-adopters, it is the lack of a pre-planned project management approach that often leads to incomplete projects or delays in the delivery of online learning materials. A well-structured project management methodology can assist to track and monitor such projects and provide insight into the effective fulfillment of the project scope given the known limitations, the available budget, the expected delivery deadlines, and the anticipated quality of the final deliverables.

In addition to project management strategies, the Procedure and Forms section presents a project lifecycle process for the development of online learning materials. It lists recommended steps to initiate effective methods for gaining support and advice on how to manage key tasks within the development cycle. While its primary audience are instructional designers, who in general apply project management principles to the design and development of online learning resources, the facilities and tools provided in this section are also useful for any academic staff member aspiring to develop their own materials for online delivery. A useful, unexpected advantage of this section is that it informs academic staff about the valuable contribution instructional designers make to the successful design of online learning solutions. A key element of this section is the provision of guidelines, forms and checklists to ensure that all materials made available for online development comply with established University guidelines and procedures. The main features include:

- **Project proposal form:** This form sets out the general requirements of the proposed unit development in terms of educational outcomes, resource deliverables, and budget allocations. It also establishes an agreed plan of action by delineating and describing the roles of the academic, the instructional designers, and the support staff.
- **Educational design plan:** The purpose of the online educational design plan is to assist:
    - Academic staff to plan and develop the educational design aspects of their online unit/s.
    - Academic staff in identifying and sourcing the content required for the online unit/s.
    - Instructional designers with identifying project deliverables and the parties responsible for the agreed deliverables.
    - Instructional designers with defining the key milestones for all project deliverables in relation to all involved parties.

  The educational design plan also provides an outline of the proposed design procedure in relation to: aims; objectives; learning outcomes; and the recommended educational design, content and assessment methods. It builds on the information provided in the Project Proposal form by detailing all project design specifics along with the essential teaching/learning micro-strategies.
- **Unit development checklist:** The unit development checklist is used by academic staff to ensure that the content material is complete and appropriate for online (and/or print-based) delivery. In addition to content, it also covers referencing and copyright clearance requirements.
- **Unit maintenance checklist:** A checklist of items to ensure that the units are reviewed and maintained for currency of information, copyright, references (including links to Web sites), and completion of the project activities as agreed to in the project plan.

Sample Gallery: The sample gallery provides best practice examples of how Web technologies and multimedia can be leveraged to facilitate effective online flexible delivery. The samples provided demonstrate:

- The use of media (video, audio, FLASH interactions/animations) in the presentation of engaging learning materials and activities (for example, micro-simulations),

- Examples of effective interface design for intuitive navigation and well-structured content,
- The convergence of print, digital, and audio-visual media in the delivery of flexible learning solutions.

While promoting best practice in online design and delivery approaches, the sample gallery also presents an effective dimension for demonstrating that online and flexible delivery tasks are achievable.

The WebKit Site

As technology increases in complexity and sophistication, so too does the task of designing effective teaching environments. This in turn places greater pressure on staff to sustain technological proficiency. Many universities have responded to the technical skill requirements of online teaching and learning by providing minimal levels of specialist staff and resources to support the development of online materials. The skills required for online delivery continue to expand as technology increases in complexity and sophistication (di Corpo, 2001). As noted in Table 1, a direct consequence has been that the range of skills required of university lecturers has steadily expanded over the years. The increasing pressure to develop online competency skills (both for staff and students) has led to concerns that the educational issues underpinning instructional design will be overshadowed by the demands placed on staff to master the new technologies (Atkinson & Brown, 1997). The danger is that a narrowed focus on technical mastery combined with a corresponding reliance on support from overworked technical staff may result in lecturing staff neglecting the essential pedagogical aspects of their educational design practices and thereby lead to a decline in the quality of the teaching and learning experiences offered to students (Bennett et al., 1999).

A useful strategy to ensure staff will retain control of their teaching and learning practices while simultaneously introducing them to new technologies is to make available a "kit" for creating high quality online teaching resources. This kit may comprise "tools" that assist staff to create online resources such as interactive quizzes, learning activities, and case studies alongside related assessment exercises. Such a kit can reduce the technical demands placed on staff while enabling efficient online material development and encourage increased participation in the conversion of existing teaching units to the Web environment. Once freed from the need to master the associated technology, staff are empowered to focus upon the pedagogical aspects of the educational resources they are creating (di Corpo, 2001). A toolkit approach to online resource development shifts the lecturer's focus from dealing with the specifics of technology application to an examination of the educational assumptions underlying the design of a unit. It also encourages explorations of what is possible and desirable in terms of student interactions and assessments. The components of a kit approach should not be tied to any particular technology or proprietary delivery platform and is therefore adaptable to changing technologies.

The WebKit strategy supports the above principles by: applying innovative technological solutions to online teaching and learning developments; promoting collaborative practices that incorporate reflective practice and action research approaches; encouraging support for curriculum practices that are responsive to the expectations of all stakeholders; and initiating a "learning partnership" ethos in which the diversity of students' needs is central. Specifically, WebKit is a readily accessible, easy to use campus-based Web site that promotes the design, development, and evaluation of Web content for all teaching modes. It is also a staff development facility that complements the aims of the FLaD site. In brief, the WebKit site includes: educational design advice (online evaluation and assessment resources); Web page design guidelines (checklists, policies, and procedures with links to the FLaD Procedures and Forms section); and provides access to various Web-based resources to assist staff to create pedagogically rich learning resources.

As well as providing additional resources for lecturers already developing online teaching units, the WebKit site also assists other lecturers to make the transition to the online medium. WebKit has been developed to accommodate the diversity of academic needs and skill levels described earlier while providing convenient, on-demand access to start-up advice, Web resources, and up-to-date support. In addition, the WebKit site is designed to encourage lecturers to participate in its ongoing development by sharing resources with other colleagues. It therefore affords a means of establishing a repository of discipline specific resources. In principle, the WebKit facility offers a readily accessible, intuitive local Web site to assist in the practical aspects of design, development, and evaluation of Web content. At this stage in its development, the WebKit site incorporates:

- Design advice in terms of online developments, teaching and learning issues, assessment and evaluation guidelines,
- Online design templates and examples,
- A resource database (such as graphics, video, animations, sounds, icons, and buttons),
- A toolbox of software utilities to assist staff to create interactive teaching resources.

All tools and utilities in the WebKit site are selected for inclusion using research-based criteria derived through agreed standards and specifications for online teaching. Consistent with the research conducted thus far, the toolkit facilitates ease of use for staff in terms of:

- Purpose, both as a resource tool and relevance to educational practice,
- Ease of operation and modification to suit the required unit content and learning objectives,
- Seamless adaptation and/or conversion of teaching materials to a Web page format,
- Potential to enhance the delivery of pedagogically effective online learning materials.

To this end, the site features six essential elements of Web design implementation considered fundamental to the effective delivery of online teaching. For each element, examples of good and poor design are provided. The six elements include: educational design; resource development tools; guidelines; interactive tools; assessment; and evaluation. At this stage in its development selected staff test the site and provide evaluation feedback.

Evaluating the Benefits and Issues

The following summarises the benefits that are expected to emerge from an online approach to delivering staff development programmes. Each of the benefits listed serve as a means of defining what criteria will assist to evaluate the effectiveness and value of the facilities as made available for staff use. The most promising advantages for university staff are anticipated to:

- Ease the task of accessing resource design and development expertise,
- Simplify the development and modification of resources to facilitate relevance and adaptability to unit objectives,
- Enhance staff competence by utilising technology to manage complex development tasks,
- Engage staff with divergent competence and interest levels in a flexible manner,
- Provide incentives for staff to become actively involved in Web page design,
- Promote collaboration among staff through their contributions of examples,
- Ensure adaptability and/or compatibility with existing proprietary platforms such as WebCT and BlackBoard,
- Permit a capacity to incorporate current work practices into online delivery practices without creating undue difficulties and increasing workloads,
- Provide a practical means of ensuring technical consistency as well as ensure hardware/software compatibility is maintained,
- Deliver an effective additional strategy for achieving high quality educational outcomes.

Other benefits not directly related to staff development needs have been identified as follows:

- A reduction in Web page development time and conversion of traditional teaching units to an online medium. Reduced time requirements automatically translate to concurrent reductions in costs.
- A reduced need for technical staff to be continually involved in the direct provision of support, advice and ongoing maintenance to lecturers within the schools.
- The emergence of a broader research climate. At present, several research projects are underway:

- Dynamic and learner initiated hypertext links to facilitate higher levels of comprehension,
- Rapid Web development methods and procedures,
- Development of "intelligent" concept analysis tools to facilitate the teaching of complex concepts in an online environment,
- The viability and usefulness of a database model for the management and provision of reusable learning objects.

In terms of evaluating the benefits to be derived from the staff development approaches outlined in this case study, it is emphasised that both the FLaD and the WebKit sites are still being appraised by university staff. However, each site is in a state of continuous development and a number of new ideas and features have emerged that will contribute to the ongoing design of the Web sites. An essential aspect of this iterative refinement process will be the evaluation of the effectiveness and usefulness of the sites as a staff development strategy. To this end, a range of factors and methods have been noted for future application.

Identified Principles of Practice

The successful integration of the staff development outlined in the preceding pages is contingent upon the need to conduct research studies that aim to devise new models of online implementation and learning resource development. In this regard, it is emphasised that the practical outcomes of an online staff development programme should support the provision of:

- An improved quality of service to the University through:
    - A comprehensive, streamlined consultative and staff development service,
    - An integrated resource development package (FLaD and WebKit),
    - Efficient utilisation of resources to avoid unnecessary duplication,
    - Research partnerships to devise new teaching and learning innovations and strategies.
- An informed contribution to the broader university decision making processes,
- A fully integrated quality assurance and evaluation process for all modes of educational delivery,
- An expanded range of cost effective Web-delivered online development tools to improve staff competence in online learning design,
- Solutions for improving online teaching and learning based on the appropriate and efficient use of educational technologies,

- In-house specialist services to ensure the university is able to retain control of related IP/copyright/marketing rights.

Conclusion

I have argued the feasibility of using online support and resource sites as a strategy for staff development. While not expected to be a perfect substitute for the physical presence of a qualified staff development specialist, there are clear benefits for both staff and students in implementing a Web-based environment as an integral part of the overall professional development experience. The FLaD and WebKit sites represent a comprehensive, unified strategy for prompting instructional designers and lecturing staff to explore the broader arena of online educational design and to continually refine the established guidelines and procedures that are essential for improving the quality of design and the intended learning outcomes. Equally important, the sites aim to inspire instructional design staff to consider the needs of lecturing staff. I further submit that the staff development models outlined in this chapter provide a broader, more holistic, creative, and flexible framework for structuring the online learning process. This view is further premised on the need to enhance staff and students' online experiences by devising collaborative learning environments that are inclusive, evolutionary, and facilitate conceptual thinking as a necessary part of the learning process. As in all applications of this type, the effectiveness of ICT in contributing to learning will be a function of how well the technology supports a particular model of learning and the appropriateness of that model to the required learning outcomes. The brief analysis undertaken in this chapter of the roles, skills and competencies required for academic staff to make the transition to online teaching suggests that the current approaches and methods for delivering courses online will need to be continually revised and refined. In my view, given that most university lecturers will remain involved in face-to-face modes of teaching, there may be more efficient ways of providing professional development programmes that aim to improve the quality of all modes of teaching in higher education.

References

Adams, M., Marshall, S., & Cameron, A. (1999). *Strategic academic program development: Heads of schools' perceptions of the role of professional development.* Paper presented at the Cornerstones: What Do We Value in Higher Education? HERDSA Annual International Conference, Melbourne, Australia. Retrieved May 22, 2006, from http://www.herdsa.org.au/branches/vic/Cornerstones/pdf/AdamsM.pdf

Atkinson, R., & Brown, A. (1997, February). Online units: What infrastructure services are required? In R. Pospisil & L. Willcoxson (Eds.), *Learning Through Teaching, Proceedings of the 6th Annual Teaching Learning Forum* (pp. 6-11). Murdoch University. Retrieved from http://lsn.curtin.edu.au/tlf/tlf1997/atkinson.html

Bennett, S., Priest, A.M., & Macpherson, C. (1999). Learning about online learning: An approach to staff development for university teachers. *Australian Journal of Educational Technology, 15*(3), 207-221.

Bess, J.L. (1998). Teaching well: Do you have to be schizophrenic? *The Review of Higher Education, 22*(1), 1-15.

Biggs, J.B. (1990). *Teaching: Design for learning.* Paper presented at the Annual Conference of the Higher Education Research and Development Society of Australasia (HERDSA), Griffith University, Brisbane, Australia.

Bryant, M., Scoufis, M., & Cheers, M. (1999, July 12-15). *The transformation of higher education in Australia university teaching is at a crossroad.* Paper presented at the Cornerstones: What do we value in Higher Education? HERDSA Annual International Conference, Melbourne, Australia.

Burford, S., & Cooper, L. (2000). Online development using WebCT: A faculty managed process for quality. *Australian Journal of Educational Technology, 16*(3), 201-214.

Campbell, N., McGee, C., & Yates, R. (2000, December 2-4). *It is not out with old and in with the new: The challenge to adapt to online teaching.* Paper presented at the Open learning 98: Offering new directions. Proceedings of the 3rd International Conference on Open Learning, Brisbane, Qld Australia. Retrieved May, 26, 2006, from http://www.unisanet.unisa.edu.au/cccc/papers/non_refereed/campbell.htm

Collins, M., & Berge, Z. (1996). *Facilitating interaction in computer mediated online courses.* Paper presented at the FSU/AECT Distance Education Conference, Tallahassee, Florida. Retrieved May 22, 2006, from http://www.emoderators.com/moderators/flcc.html

di Corpo, S. (2001). *Supporting academic staff to use learning technologies: The instructional designer as staff developer.* Paper presented at the Moving Online Conference II: A conference to explore the challenges for workplaces, colleges and universities, Conrad Jupiters Gold Coast, Queensland, Australia. Retrieved May 22, 2006, from www.ecu.edu.au/conferences/tlf/2002/pub/docs/Kulski.pdf

Ellis, A., & Phelps, R. (2000). Staff development for online delivery: A collaborative, team based action learning model. *Australian Journal of Educational Technology, 16*(1), 26-44.

Faire, M. (1994, July 3-6). *Improving the practicum: The professional development needs of lecturers, associate teachers and student teachers.* Paper presented at the 24th Annual Conference of the Australian Teacher Education Association, Brisbane, Queensland.

Goodyear, P., Salmon, G., Spector, J.M., Steeples, C., & Tickner, S. (2001). Competences for online teaching: A special report. *Educational Technology, Research and Development, 49*(1), 65-72.

Herrington, J., & Oliver, R. (2001). *Online learning: Professional development for the changing role of the lecturer.* Paper presented at the Moving Online Conference II., September 2-4, 2001. A conference to explore the challenges for workplaces, colleges and universities, Conrad Jupiters Gold Coast, Queensland, Australia.

Hicks, M., Reid, I., & George, R. (1999). *Enhancing online teaching: Designing responsive learning environments.* Paper presented at the Cornerstones: What do we value in higher education? Melbourne, Australia. Retrieved May 29, 2006, from http://64.233.167.104/search?q=cache:x45xjHq0kxEJ:www.herdsa.org.au/branches/vic/Cornerstones/pdf/Hicks.PDF+Enhancing+online+teaching:+designing+responsive+learning+environments&hl=zh-TW&ct=clnk&cd=2

Kemshal-Bell, G. (2001). *The online teacher*. Final report prepared for the Project Steering Committee of the VET Teachers and Online Learning Project. Sydney: TAFE, NSW.

Loucks-Horsley, S. (1997). *The role of teaching and learning in systemic reform: A focus on professional development*. Paper presented at the Annual Forum of the National Institute for Science Education, Washington, DC. Retrieved May, 2006, from http://teech.terc.edu/papers/papers/susanlh.htm

Macchiusi, L., & Trinidad, S. (2001, February 7-9). Information and communication technologies: The adoption by an Australian university. In *Expanding Horizons in Teaching and Learning. Proceedings of the 10th Annual Teaching Learning Forum*. Perth: Curtin University of Technology. Retrieved July 12, 2006, from http://lsn.curtin.edu.au/tlf/tlf2001/macchiusi.html

McCracken, H. (2004, Spring). Extending virtual access: Promoting engagement and retention through integrated support systems. *Online Journal of Distance Learning Administration, VII*(I), Nos. 1, 3. Retrieved May 22, 2006, from http://www.westga.edu/%7Edistance/jmain11.html

McInnis, C. (1999). *The work roles of academics in Australian universities*. Canberra: Department of Education, Training and Youth Affairs (DETYA).

McInnis, C. (2001). *Signs of disengagement? The changing undergraduate experience in Australian universities*. Melbourne: Centre for the Study of Higher Education, Faculty of Education, University of Melbourne. Retrieved May 29, 2006, from http://eric.ed.gov/ERICDocs/data/ericdocs2/content_storage_01/0000000b/80/27/98/c5.pdf

McKeachie, W.J. (1986). *Teaching tips: A guidebook for the beginning college teacher*. Lexington, MA: D.C. Heath.

McShane, K. (1999). *Academics online: A study of academics adapting to Web-based teaching*. Paper presented at the Australian Association for Research in Education and the New Zealand Association for Research in Education Joint Conference, Melbourne, Australia. Retrieved May 29, 2006, from http://www.aare.edu.au/99pap/mcs99609.htm

McShane, K. (2000) The online academic: Case study narratives of change and resistance. In R. Sims, M. O'Reilly, & S. Sawkins (Eds.), *Learning to Choose: Choosing to Learn. Proceedings of the 17th Annual ASCILITE Conference* (pp. 351-362). Lismore, NSW: Southern Cross University Press.

Oliver, R. (2001). *Assuring the quality of online learning in Australian higher education*. Paper presented at the Moving Online Conference II, Goldcoast, Australia. Retrieved May 29, 2006, from http://elrond.scam.ecu.edu.au/oliver/2001/mocpaper.pdf

Paloff, R., & Pratt, K. (1999). *Building learning communities in cyberspace: Effective strategies for the online classroom*. San Francisco: Jossey-Bass.

Paulson, K. (2002). Reconfiguring faculty roles for virtual settings. *The Journal of Higher Education, 73*(1), 123-140.

Pospisil, R., & Willcoxson, L. (1988, July 5-8). *Online teaching: Implications for institutional and academic staff development.* Paper presented at the IEdTech '98: Education and technology: Planning for progress, partnership and profit: Conference proceedings: The Biennial Conference of the Australian Society for Educational Technology, Perth, Western Australia.

Quinton, S. (2001, November 12-15). *Meaningful learning in a complex information environment.* Paper presented at the 9th International Conference on Computers in Education/SchoolNet 2001, Seoul, Korea.

Ramsden, P. (1992). *Learning to teach in higher education.* London: Routledge.

Reid, I. (1999). Beyond models: Developing a university strategy for online instruction. *Journal of Asynchronous Learning Networks, 3*(1), 19-31.

Salter, G., & Hansen, S. (1999). *Modelling new skills for online teaching.* Paper presented at the ASCILITE '99: Responding to Diversity. The 16th Annual Conference of the Australian Society for Computers in Learning in Tertiary Education, Brisbane, Queensland, Australia. Retrieved May 22, 2006, from http://www.ascilite.org.au/conferences/brisbane99/papers/salterhansen.pdf

Torrisi Steele, G., & Davis, G. (2000). A website for my subject: The experiences of some academics' engagement with educational designers in a team based approach to developing online learning materials. *Australian Journal of Educational Technology, 16*(3), 283-301.

Trinidad, S., & Albon, R. (2001). *Tapping out new rhythms in the journey of learning.* Paper presented at the Expanding Horizons in Teaching and Learning: Teaching and Learning Forum, Curtin University of Technology, Perth, Western Australia. Retrieved May 22, 2006, from http://cleo.murdoch.edu.au/confs/tlf/tlf2001/trinidad.html

Woods, R., & Ebersole. (2003). Becoming a "communal architect" in the online classroom: Integrating cognitive and affective learning for maximum effect in Web-based learning. *Online Journal of Distance Learning Administration,* 6(1). Retrieved May 29, 2006, from http://www.westga.edu/%7Edistance/ojdla/spring61/woods61.htm

Young, J.R. (1997). Rethinking the role of the professor in an age of high-tech tools. *The Chronicle of Higher Education, Inc.* Retrieved May 29, 2006, from http://crab.rutgers.edu/~goertzel/rethinkingroleofprofessor.htm

Chapter XI

Bridging the Instructional Designers and Lecturers in Technology Education: A Framework for Cultivating a Community of Practice

Samuel Ng Hong Kok, Institute of Technical Education, Singapore

Tang Buay Choo, Institute of Technical Education, Singapore

Myint Swe Khine, Murdoch University, Australia

Abstract

This chapter examines an initiative to create educational technology (ET) Champions and leaders within a higher education institution in Singapore. It examines how the concept of communities of practice was applied to an initiative for transforming teaching and learning through educational technology. Instructional designers coached ET Champions in the principles of creating learning objects who later returned to their respective colleges to work with other lecturers. ET Champions progressed through five stages, which included peripheral, legitimate, core, strategic and transformational membership. Each stage required support and guidance within the community.

Introduction

How people learn and the conditions under which they learn has inspired research that has generated different theories. For instance, cognitive theories emphasize learning as an individual endeavor (Gagne & Medsker, 1996). In recent years learning has been seen as a social phenomenon that is situated in a social context. The social nature of cognition and situated perspective can be traced back to the work of Vygotsky (1978) who conceived that cognition begins at the social level and transcends to the individual level. This view is supported and further enhanced by the account of Lave and Wenger (1991) who stated that learning is a process of participation in communities of practice. Participation is at first legitimately peripheral and increases gradually in engagement and complexity until the person is a full member of the community.

Traditionally, instructional design has been described as a system of procedures for development in education and training programs in a consistent and reliable fashion. It is a complex process that is creative, active, and iterative. Instructional designers believe that the use of systematic design procedures can assist in making instruction more effective, efficient, and relevant. Instructional design also requires a team that may consist of a subject matter expert, instructional designer and other production personnel (Gustafson & Branch, 2002; Litchfield & Keller, 2002). Instructional designers may also combine their role with managing the project, which is often beneficial, but at other times confusing to other team members. Communication between the subject matter expert and instructional designers can sometimes be challenging due to a misunderstanding of roles. Ideally each team member should contribute his or her expertise to the design process to enhance the project quality.

The emphasis on communities of practice with collaboration and shared responsibilities has influenced the creation of learning organizations. The role of instructional designers has also been influenced by this trend and they are often involved in fostering a community of practice in a training organization or institution. Instructional designers may lead and manage large-scale instructional development which involves regular communication, mentoring and professional development of team members. Communities of practice may also be ideal vehicles for leveraging tacit knowledge because they enable person-to-person interaction and engage a whole group in advancing their field of practice. As a result, this interaction process may assist in dispersing insights about collaborative thinking across the entire organization (Wenger, McDermott, & Snyder, 2002).

Community of Practice

The notion of community is not a new concept, as a natural part of human behavior consists of socializing and interacting with other people in a variety of environments and circumstances. The concept of communities of practice leverages on the sharing of the diverse experiences between people of similar interest. In addition, the advancement in information and communication technologies makes it possible for individuals to form their community and share their experiences and learn from each other (Saint-Onge & Wallace, 2003).

Case Description

Context

During the 1990s, educational institutions throughout the world began to recognize and exploit the potential of technology. Technology, if properly used, can assist in providing high quality education with increased flexibility and accessibility. In 1998, the Institute of Technical Education (ITE), a post-secondary technical educational institution in Singapore, formulated its first IT Master plan. This plan aims to transform its geographically distributed colleges into a vibrant community of connected learning colleges. Our division, the Educational Design and Technology Division (EDT), was dedicated to the realization of this vision. Like other educational institutions that have embarked on this journey, a first step was to recruit core educational technology staff to assist in implementing this vision. These staff included instructional designers, multimedia designers and multimedia programmers and they were expected to provide leadership in the application and integration of educational technology into teaching and learning.

It is important to articulate our vision before examining our implementation process. Firstly, our management believed that we needed a core group of lecturers to support the learning colleges and to ensure the sustainability of the effort. These lecturers required educational technology capabilities that enabled them to both lead and support initiatives. Secondly, as a result of this belief, the 'instructional designers' main responsibility was to:

- lead and guide academic staff in the design and development of media-rich learning objects; and
- the development of core educational technology capabilities at the college level which would assist in supporting and sustaining the transformation effort.

Thirdly, to fulfill these two responsibilities a conscious effort was made to cultivate a community of educational technology (ET) leaders, which consisted of instructional design professionals at EDT and selected lecturers (whom we call ET Champions) from the colleges. Guided by the instructional design professionals, these ET Champions learned relevant instructional design and educational technology skills to be effective in their role. Figure 1 summarises our approach to harnessing and exploiting the potential of technology to provide high quality education with increased flexibility and accessibility.

Why Cultivate a Community of Educational Technology (ET) Leaders?

The main role of the ET Leaders community, consisting of instructional design professionals at EDT and ET Champions, is to drive, support and sustain ITE's effort in exploiting technology to transform pedagogic practices at the colleges. The instructional design professionals at EDT are process experts while the ET Champions are content experts from different

*Figure 1. The Institute of Technical Education's approach to developing a community of educational technology change agents**

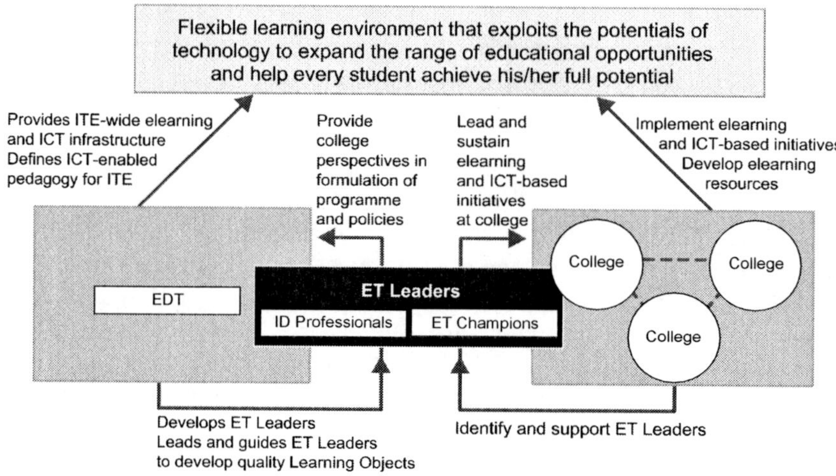

* *Note: When the ITE's IT masterplan was first conceptualized in 1998, ITE had 10 geographically distributed campuses organized into two different networks. Today, with the addition of one new regional campus in 2004, there are 11 distributed campuses re-organized into three colleges (with the original two networks forming two colleges and the regional campus forming the third college).*

subject domains. ET Champions are selected from the lecturing community and their role is to guide fellow lecturers at the colleges to develop e-learning resources and implement other teaching and learning initiatives. The instructional design professionals guide the ET Champions to learn the skills, knowledge and authentic practices needed to perform their role. In short, the instructional design professionals are responsible for enculturating the ET Champions into the community, thus developing them into ET leaders at the college level. Our approach required the team to reflect on our views about knowledge and our beliefs about how people learn. In addition this exploration into the concept of communities of practice provided an approach that we could utilize to prepare ET Champions for the role of ET leaders. The reasons for choosing this approach include:

Authentic context: We believe that knowledge resides in the individual as well as groups of people that share a context in which the knowledge is used (Damarin, 1996). This socio-cultural perspective of learning emphasises the importance of social and authentic contexts, and joint collaborative activities for effective learning and practice (Rueda & Dembo, 1995). In the social and authentic setting of a group's practices, the joint collaborative activities facilitate learning, thinking and social mediation in relation to new knowledge within a context. In other words, context has a fundamental, rather than merely facilitative, role. It is the change process within a context that is essential when ET Champions acquire new competencies and practices in the ET Leaders community (Lerner & Kaufman, 1985; Rogoff, 1990).

Furthermore, we share the view that competence or knowledge is a duality, consisting of two complementary aspects, *hard* (or explicit) and *soft* (or tacit) knowledge (Brown & Duguid, 1996; Wenger, McDermott, & Synder, 2002; Saint-Onge & Wallace, 2003; Hildreth, 2004). While new ET Champions can learn the *hard* aspect through codified, articulated, disseminated and demonstrated instructions from the instructional design professionals, the learning of the *soft* aspect requires them to interact with more experienced members within a community (Brown & Duguid, 1996). In other words, as suggested by Brown & Duguid (2000), engagement in the practices of a community of practice allows learners to learn both implicitly and explicitly. Cultivating a community of ET leaders thus provides an authentic context for the ET Champions to acquire both implicit and explicit skills and knowledge expected of their role.

Identity forming: Wenger (1998) suggested that individual learning involves engaging in and contributing to the practices of his/her communities. This view suggests that learning is a process of social participation situated in the practice of a community. It involves active participation in the practice of the community so that one can become an identified member of that community (Lave & Wenger, 1991). The process of identity-forming entails acquisition of the skills and knowledge that enables one to be involved in new activities, perform new tasks and functions, and take on new responsibilities within a community. Such identity-forming has implications for the ET Champions who need to gain legitimacy and recognition of their role as ET Leaders.

Continuous learning: Participation in a community of practice involves constant fine-tuning between experience and learning. The community not only serves as a fertile learning context for new ET Champions but also for the continual generation of new insights that may be transformed into new knowledge (Wenger, 1998). Through joint participation, the ET leaders should be able to pool their expertise and share their experiences to improve current practices. They should also generate new ideas resulting in increased individual capabilities and improved organizational performance (Saint-Onge & Wallace, 2003). In this rapidly changing educational climate, especially in e-learning and ICT-related areas, the ability to continuously learn and increase capabilities is crucial in our colleges.

Brokering: The ET Champions will return to the colleges as ET leaders to transfer their learning to the Lecturers' communities. While leading the Lecturers' communities in developing e-learning resources and implementing ICT-based initiatives, they still continue to actively participate in the practices of the ET Leaders community to learn and acquire relevant skills. In other words, they are members of two communities, that is, Lecturers and the ET Leaders communities. The ET Champions need to "travel back and forth" to connect the two communities by coordinating and aligning their interests and perspectives. In short, they are "brokers" (Wenger, 1998). Having the ET Champions performing the brokers' role has the advantage of minimizing "arrogant perception" (Damarin, 1996) that might be present if this role were performed by the instructional design professionals at EDT. But more significantly, having come from the Lecturers' communities themselves, ET Champions already have the established social capital of trust, mutual understanding, respect, and shared values (Cohen & Prusak, 2001) This shared perspective should make it much easier for the ET Champions to engage with their fellow lecturers in using educational technology to transform their pedagogic practices.

Figure 2. Sustaining ICT-based initiatives at the college level through ET Champions

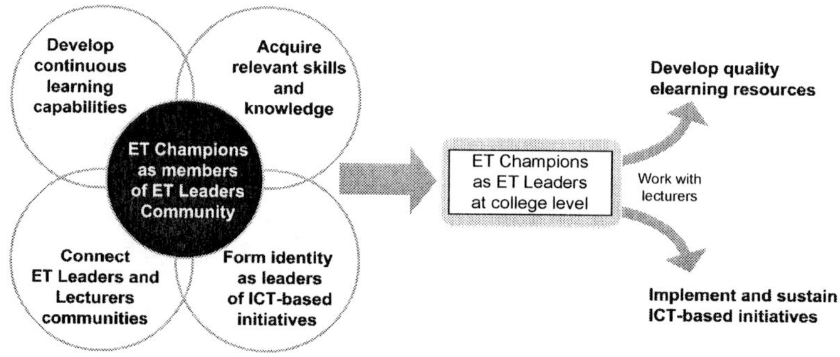

In summary, cultivating a community of ET leaders provides a social and authentic context for the ET Champions to acquire relevant skills and knowledge and form an identity through learning within a community of practice. It will also enhance their capabilities through community support and provide a bridge between the lecturers and instructional design professionals at EDT, that is brokers. As illustrated in Figure 2, this approach reflects our belief that learning involves becoming part of a community through participation in socially organized activities or practices.

Supporting and Cultivating a Community of ET Leaders

The Initial Years (1999 to 2001): Enculturating new ET Champions

In 1999, ITE started recruiting instructional design professionals to be ET leaders at EDT. The first task facing the instructional design professionals was to design a programme to enculturate ET Champions into the practice of the ET leaders' community. This would enable them to guide lecturers in the development of quality e-learning resources and to lead the implementation of ICT-based initiatives. A six-month ET Champions attachment programme was developed with the following structure:

Phases	Duration	Expectations
Pre-programme briefing	0.5 day	Develop common understanding of purpose, objectives, curriculum and expectations of the programme
Training with close guidance	3 months	Develop one learning object
Independent Practice	3 months	Develop two more learning objects

Guided by our belief in situated learning perspectives, such as cognitive apprenticeship (Collins, Brown, & Newman, 1989) and legitimate peripheral participation (Lave & Wenger, 1991), the programme—based on the following principles—was implemented in July 2000 with six selected lecturers attached to EDT.

1. **Engagement in authentic activities:** The community of ET leaders used the widely adopted ADDIE model (Kruse, 2005) of instructional design to develop learning objects. The main focus of the ET Champion attachment programme was to enculturate the ET Champions into the community through engagement in this practice. To ensure active and authentic engagement, care was taken to identify the main task in each stage of the ADDIE model and divide it into sub-tasks that are situated in the overall social practice (Brown & Duguid, 1996). For example, the main task in the analysis stage was to analyse the selected module of study in order to identify learning objects to be developed. This main task was divided into the following sub-tasks:
   - Identify content of the module
   - Group related content into adequate chunks
   - Arrange chunks of content into an appropriate sequence
   - Specify the instructional objective for each chunk of content
   - Identify chunks suitable for development into interactive multimedia learning objects
   - Prepare an Initial Design Document stating the goals, content selection considerations and outcomes for the use of educational technology in teaching and learning.

   We also considered that new ET Champions joining the community would have minimum knowledge of instructional design and educational technology. To address this factor we provided formal training sessions in the first three months of the programme so as to provide them with the foundational knowledge and skills that they could apply when engaged in the authentic activities. During these three months, they were guided through a series of structured learning cycles, one for each stage in the ADDIE model, similar to the experiential learning cycle described by Kolb (1984), as illustrated in Figure 3.
2. **Team learning (Senge, 1990):** ET Champions were placed into multi-disciplinary teams to develop learning objects. These teams were lead by an instructional designer, and supported by multimedia designers and programmers. The ET Champions served as content experts in the team. This enabled the team to socially negotiate the development of learning objects and work through an authentic activity involving decisions concerning design and authoring methods. These collectively generated solutions became shared knowledge, which was added to the community. Furthermore, at the end of each phase of the development process, each ET Champion would showcase his/her work to other ET Champions and instructional designers. During these showcase sessions, "stories" and ideas were swapped, and insights were added to the community.
3. **"Stealing" of knowledge (Brown & Duguid, 1996):** During the initial stages new ET Champions were guided through introductory design tasks. The instructional design professionals also modelled complex and cognitively challenging design tasks for the ET Champions. This process provided new ET Champions with the opportunity to observe how instructional design experts performed learning object development. This also assisted ET Champions to obtain a better understanding of expert performance. As they gained more knowledge and became more confident, they were encouraged

Figure 3. Experiential learning: First three months of ET Champion Attachment Programme

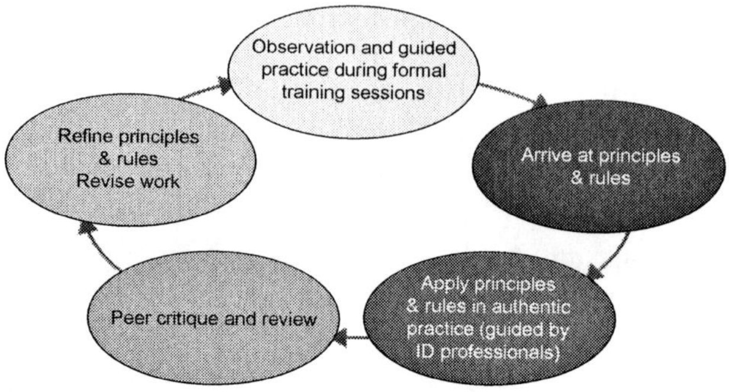

to undertake more challenging tasks. In addition, when the programme was extended to one year in July 2001, there were a mix of new and experienced ET Champions in each team and the community. This arrangement provided new ET Champions with a learning environment where they could legitimately participate in the practice. This allowed them to experience how practitioners performed their role and allowed them to gain an insight into their expertise, that is, to legitimately steal knowledge from the more experienced members (Brown & Duguid, 1996). Because instructional design is essentially about problem-solving and inventing new solutions (Schwier, Campbell, & Kenny, 2004) a large part of competence remains implicit or tacit. This legitimate participation process allowed new ET Champions to pick-up both the hard and soft knowledge and skills of learning object development.

4. **Customised coaching and scaffolding efforts:** Different ET Champions entered the community with different levels of expertise. The curriculum of the programme had to provide different levels of individualized coaching and scaffolding efforts to each ET Champion. The instructional designers would ascertain each ET Champion's level of expertise in order to recognize his/her Zone of Proximal Development (Vygotsky, 1978) and structured an appropriate level of scaffolding for him/her. As the ET Champion gained more expertise, the support was withdrawn gradually so that the ET Champion would be more self-directed and independent in their learning.
5. **Reflection and articulation of learning skills:** As they engaged in the community's practice throughout the programme, ET Champions were provided with opportunities to articulate their thoughts, and problem-solving and decision-making processes. For example, in their teams, they explained their problems, solutions, requirements and decisions to other team members. Review sessions held at the end of each phase of the development process encouraged them to think about how they approached the learning and tasks. ET Champions were encouraged to write in their reflective journals and instructional design professionals responded to entries in the journal. This process encouraged metacognitive skills for continuous learning.

6. **Adopt appropriate technology tools to support performance:** Technology tools can expand the scope of the ET Champions and facilitate their engagement in authentic practice of the community. For example, providing ET Champions with authoring templates created by our multimedia programmers reduced the learning time required by ET Champions to learn complex authoring skills. The use of MindManager (a mind-mapping tool) facilitated their cognitive process skills in performing content analysis.
7. **Multiple practice for expertise development (McLellan, 1996):** Initially designed as a six-month programme, the programme was extended to one year in July 2001, as a result of useful feedback gathered during and after each implementation. The ET Champions strongly expressed their desire for more practice opportunities to sharpen their skills and to ensure that the skills became more developed. While the extension permitted more opportunities for ET Champions to develop more learning objects, it also allowed ET Champions to gain more self-confidence and control, thus moving them into a more autonomous phase of performance.

The Maturing Years (2002 to 2004): Supporting the Growing Community

During this phase, new ET Champions were enculturated into the community through the ET Champion Attachment Programme while, at the same time, more members returned to the colleges. Older members advanced to higher levels of participation, taking on new roles and responsibilities. New issues and challenges surfaced as a result. One key challenge facing the community was to support the different needs of members at different levels of participation. At the same time, new insights and opportunities arose as a result of organisational changes within ITE and new developments in educational technology. Various measures and strategies were introduced in response to the demands of these new challenges, opportunities and insights. Some of these included:

1. **ET Champion dialogue sessions:** There was frequent exchange and modification of ideas and beliefs systems through dialogue among members. Such mutual engagement and negotiation/re-negotiation of joint enterprise (Wenger, 1998) were often informal and ad-hoc. As highlighted by Davenport and Prusak (1998), such informal and ad hoc communications is an essential part of interaction within a community. However, with more ET Champions stationed at the colleges, there was a need to have formal dialogue sessions with all ET Champions. In 2002, quarterly ET Champions Dialogue sessions were introduced to complement the informal and ad-hoc dialogue among members.
2. **Knowledge sharing initiatives:** As suggested by Wenger (1998), any community of practice will produce artifacts, tools, stories, procedures, and concepts that reify different aspects of, and eventually become part of the practice. Over time, while participating in the practice and negotiating meaning, a number of resources (both physical and cognitive) were created by the ET Champions. Hence there was a need to provide platforms for sharing and disseminating the resources. *Knowledge Sharing Sessions, Knowledge Forums* and the development of a *Reusable Folder* were sharing initiatives that were launched.

Knowledge Sharing Sessions, a bi-monthly event initiated in 2002, started as a platform for enhancing the expertise of ET Champions through sharing. In this session instructional design professionals shared new insights into the use of existing tools, new instructional strategies and emerging technology tools. In 2004, as more ET Champions became more central within the community, this platform evolved into one where they could share their experiences and new knowledge (both tacit and explicit) with members in the community.

Knowledge Forum also started in 2002 with the initial purpose of providing a platform for members stationed at EDT to raise problems encountered during their work. In the forum new members invited solutions from others and shared new approaches. As more ET Champions became ET leaders this platform was extended to all members (both at EDT and colleges) as a platform for sharing and disseminating knowledge generated through their participation in the practice.

Reusable Folder, initiated in 2003, is a platform for disseminating objects that are the result of the reification process—a process described by Wenger (1998) as producing objects that congeal our experience into "thingness." Examples of the reification process include finding solutions to the instructional design problems, which included interactive activities, animations and graphics. These solutions were created by the ET Champions, together with the instructional design professionals at EDT, and their creative knowledge was embedded in the design. These valuable knowledge objects could be reused by other members to enhance practice. To enhance the value of the *Reusable Folder* the instructional design professionals at EDT re-purposed many of the interactive activities into templates, which we termed *Practice Objects*. These assisted the ET Champions to guide lecturers through learning object development.

3. **Mediation tools:** As pointed out by Vygotsky (1978), an individual's activity is mediated by tools within the practice. When appropriate tools are used, performance can be greatly enhanced. As such, there was a continuous effort to identify, create and disseminate new tools to facilitate the practices of the community. Examples include *Macromedia Flash Action Scripting, Video Editing Software, 3-D Graphics Software, Microsoft PowerPoint 2000, Game Manager* and *Courseware Evaluation Rubrics*. The first three tools listed above are available in the market while the last two tools were developed by the community.

   Game Manager is a tool developed in 2004 by our multimedia programmers and designers for the creation of interactive game-based activities. The game ideas were generated by ET Champions as they engaged in the activity of learning object development.

   Courseware Evaluation Rubrics is a tool developed by our Instructional Designers to assist ET Champions to guide lecturers in learning object development.

   Like the *Reusable Folder* mentioned earlier, these two tools also serve as boundary objects (Star & Griesemer, 1989; Wenger, 1998), which are used by the ET Leaders and members of the Lecturers' communities.

4. **Activities for enhancing expertise:** Recognising that knowledge and competence is a duality with both hard (explicit) and soft (tacit) aspects, it was essential that ET Champions learned both aspects for effective performance. To assist this learning,

workshops or informal training sessions were undertaken when new tools were identified.

In addition, an *eNewsletter* (named inTouch) was launched in 2003 to update members on the latest trends and developments in EDT and the educational technology field.

5. **ET units at colleges:** In July 2003, an ET Unit, staffed by five ET Champions (designated as eLearning Specialists), was established at each of the two colleges. Two impending organisational developments at that time prompted this move. Firstly, colleges would be given more autonomy in their strategic planning and operations. ET Champions were needed to define ICT-based practices and design new programmes and initiatives at the college level. Secondly, we wished to advance students toward greater autonomy and flexibility through online learning. We planned to develop at least one module per course into a full e-learning module in 2004. There was a need to equip our ET Champions to lead this planning and implementation. The establishment of the ET Units resulted in the creation of a boundary practice (Wenger, 1998), which served as a form of brokering between the ET Leaders and Lecturer communities.

The Transforming Years (2005 - onwards): Transforming the Community

2005 was a transition year, as funding for the five-year IT Master Plan would end. Due to this discontinued funding the one-year ET Champion Attachment Programme was discontinued. In addition, colleges were encouraged to be more autonomous in their operation. ET Champions needed to take on more responsibility in defining ICT-based pedagogy, formulating plans and conceiving new initiatives. ET Champions needed to play a central role in the ET Leaders' community to transform practices and to ensure the sustainability of the community.

To prepare ET Champions for this new role, EDT worked with ET Champions on various innovative projects to assist them in acquiring the skills and knowledge needed to re-define and transform the practices of the community. Some of these projects included:

1. **Situated Learning Pedagogic Practice:** This is a series of projects that explore the design of situated learning environments from the vocational education perspective. The first project in this series identified a set of design elements essential to a situated learning environment from the vocational training perspective (Seow & Tang, 2005). Subsequently, a set of generic principles for each element was identified to guide the design and selection of learning activities. Customizing this set of generic design principles for customer service content and applying the ITE pedagogic model (Leong & Chia, 2000), a new instructional model (named situated learning instruction model for customer service skills) was developed.
2. **E-lesson:** This project aims to develop an instructional design framework to guide lecturers to design appropriate activity-centred multimedia packages to promote problem solving, collaboration and deep learning amongst ITE students. The multimedia packages attempted to motivate students through meaningful tasks by immersing students in real-world tasks.

Developing communities capable of transformation involves "agents of change." Our strategies for cultivating the community provided support to ensure that members accessed resources to make decisions and take appropriate actions according to their own designs. Table 1 provides a summary of the strategies introduced and the main thrust behind the introduction of these strategies.

Lessons Learned

In this section, we reflect on our experience and attempt to highlight insights gained and identify practices that we could adopt when cultivating future communities of practice. We found the following ideas to be valuable:

1. **Declared intention:** Our community exhibited many characteristics of a formal, highly structured, or engineered community described by Saint-Onge and Wallace (2003). The organizational purpose of the community was clearly defined and communicated to the members but we still needed to clearly define this intention to our new members. ET Champions joining the community needed to be able to see the value of the community and needed to develop a greater sense of ownership for the joint enterprise. Mutual trust could be established through the sharing of stories and experiences.

   In retrospect, if we were to start again, we would define our community using the three elements, Domain, Community and Practice, espoused by Wenger, McDermott, and Snyder (2002), as follows:

   - **Domain:** Expertise in instructional design and educational technology
   - **Community:** ET leaders working together with the common goal of enhancing the quality of teaching and learning through the application and integration of educational technology to expand the range of educational opportunities available
   - **Practice:** Shared repertoire of experiences, stories, tools, best practices in instructional design and educational technology. In short, the declared intentionality of the community would indicate to members that they would need to take responsibility for the community's shared future as a place where they could work in synergy to continually create and change their reality.

2. **Changing roles and varying support:** The value of community of practices as a vehicle for learning became more apparent as we progressed through the three development stages of cultivating the community. We were able to see improvement in each ET Champion's performance as they progressed through the different levels of participation within the community. They were able to engage actively in the practices of the community and contributed to the joint enterprise in response to their concerns and needs.

   As espoused by Lave and Wenger (1991), our ET Champions assumed different identities as they were enculturated into the community. They began as newcomers, and

Table 1. Cultivating ET Leaders Community: New measures and initiatives introduced

Thrusts	**New measures and initiatives introduced**		
	The *Initial* years (1999 – 2001)	**The *Maturing* Years (2002 – 2004)**	**The *Transforming* years (2005 - onwards)**
Need to enculturate new ET Champions into the community	2001 – *Enhancing expertise*: ET Champion Attachment Programme		
Need to equip ET Champions with both implicit and explicit knowledge needed to harness capabilities of new technology tools		2002 – *Enhancing expertise*: Short professional development programmes on new technology tools	
Need to keep ET Champions aware of new ways of using existing tools, instructional strategies and emerging technology tools		2002 – *Knowledge sharing*: Knowledge Sharing Sessions (by ID professionals at EDT)	
Need to provide platform for ET Champions at EDT to surface problems, invite solutions and discuss ideas as they engaged in learning object development		2002 – *Support negotiation*: Knowledge Forum (within EDT only)	
More ET Champions at colleges. Need to complement informal ah hoc dialogue with formal sessions		2002 – *Support negotiation*: ET Champions Dialogue Sessions	
More ET Champions at the colleges performing core duties expected of a "trained" ET Champion, i.e., sustaining and leading ICT-based initiatives		2003 – *Knowledge sharing*: Knowledge Forum (extended to all members, both at EDT and at colleges) – *Support Performance*: Game Manager & Courseware Evaluation Rubrics	
More ET Champions at the colleges performing core duties expected of a "trained" ET Champion, i.e., sustaining and leading ICT-based initiatives		2003 – *Knowledge sharing & support performance*: Resuable Folder	

continued on following page

Table 1. continued

Thrusts	**New measures and initiatives introduced**		
	The *Initial* years (1999 – 2001)	**The *Maturing* Years (2002 – 2004)**	**The *Transforming* years (2005 - onwards)**
More ET Champions at the colleges performing core duties expected of a "trained" ET Champion, i.e., sustaining and leading ICT-based initiatives. Need to encourage them to explore emergent technology tools and trends		2003 – *Enhancing expertise*: eNewsletter	
More ET Champions involved in strategic planning at college level, introducing new programmes and initiatives.		2004 – *Knowledge Sharing*: Knowledge Sharing Sessions (began to include sharing by ET Champions)	
More ET Champions involved in defining ICT-based pedagogy at the college level. Need to equip them with skills and knowledge to assist them to redefine and transform the practices of the community			2005 – *Encourage innovation*: Innovation Projects

Table 2. Expected contributions of ET Champions at different levels of participation

Roles (Levels of participation)	**Expected contributions (Nature of participation)**	**Identity**
ET Champion during first 3 months of ET Champion Attachment Programme	Participate at the **peripheral level**, developing one learning object under the close guidance of instructional design professionals at EDT.	Peripheral Member
ET Champion during the next 9 months of ET Champion Attachment Programme	Begin to participate more confidently in the community's **legitimate** practice of developing learning objects. Develop between four to seven learning objects, mentored by instructional design professionals at EDT. Scaffolds provided by instructional design professionals were withdrawn gradually as ET Champions gained more expertise and confidence.	Legitimate Member
ET Champion back at colleges after one-year of attachment at EDT	Performing the **core** duties expected of a "trained" ET Champion: • Guide lecturers in developing learning objects. • Share knowledge and expertise in eLearning facilitation and learning objects development with lecturers. • Lead lecturers in the implementation of ICT-based initiatives.	Core Member
ET Champions with some experience guiding lecturers in developing learning objects	Involved in **strategic** planning for ICT-based initiatives and defining ICT-based pedagogy at the college level. Lead the implementation of ICT-based initiatives at the college level. Develop new training programmes for lecturers to equip them with the skills for learning object development and the facilitation of e-learning.	Strategic Member
ET Champions with experience defining ICT-based pedagogy at the college level	Re-define and **transform** ICT-based pedagogy at the college level.	Transformative Member

then moved through the different levels of participation to eventually become central participants in the community. Initially, we identified 3 levels of participation based on the one-year attachment programme: *first 3 months, next 9 months and post-attachment*. As more ET Champions returned to the Lecturers' community to lead, we were able to delineate the post-attachment level based on the kind of contributions made by the ET Champions. This was expanded to five levels of participation. The "identity" we accorded to ET Champions at each level of participation is summarized in Table 2.

Since the majority of the members were brokers engaged in both the ET Leaders' and Lecturers' communities it is appropriate to examine these levels of participation from the perspective of practice-based connections (Wenger, 1998). We identified two distinct paths, depicted in Figure 4, which ET Champions could progress through at the

Figure 4. Levels of participation within the ET Leaders community

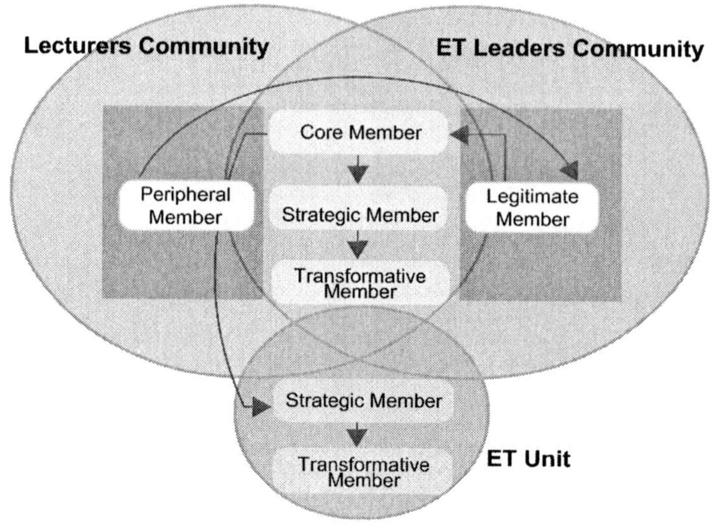

different levels of participation. After being core members they could participate as strategic or transformative members either within the *overlap* of the two communities or at the *boundary* in the ET Unit. These paths reflected, to some extent, the career paths available to our lecturers defined by our Human Resources Division. Lecturers (or ET Champions) who opted for the Teaching Track are likely to take the path within the overlap while those who opted for the Specialist Track are likely to join the ET Units.

The identities assumed by the ET Champions during the enculturation process enabled us to relate more specifically to the varying concerns and needs. Our support varied as the needs of the ET Champions and the community changed over time. Table 3 shows the concerns and needs of each identity and the support provided in response to their needs.

3. **Communities of practice are living organisms:** Our ET Leaders' community could be likened to a living organism, which followed a dynamic lifecycle of development (Wenger, McDermott, & Snyder, 2002). However, unlike the five stages of development identified by Wenger et al. (2002) our community progressed through three distinct stages: *Initial, Maturing and Transforming* stages. In the initial stage we understood the organisational mandate for developing a core group of lecturers to transform pedagogical practices at the colleges. We also knew that lecturers had to be seconded from their Lecturers' community into some kind of ET Leaders' community. In other words, we were clear that ET Champions would be brokers of two communities, exchanging ideas, concerns, needs and expertise from one community to the other community for mutual benefit and development.

   From the initial stage, through the maturing and into the transforming years, the ET Champions' brokering role gathered momentum. Initially, the main focus of the ET

Table 3. Enculturation of ET Champions: Support provided to each level

Identity	Concerns	Needs	Support
Peripheral Member	How to acquire the basic skills & knowledge to develop learning objects?	• Direct and close support/guidance from instructional design professionals	Enhance expertise – first 3 months of ET Champion Attachment Programme
Legitimate Member	How to improve skills and knowledge to develop quality learning objects?	• Coaching with fading scaffolded by instructional design professionals • Access to more experienced ET Champions • Ideas on harnessing capabilities of existing and emerging technology tools to develop learning objects	• Enhance Expertise – next 9 months of ET Champion Attachment Programme • Enhanced Expertise – Access to sharing by more experienced members (e.g., Knowledge Forum, Knowledge Sharing Sessions) • Negotiation platforms – Access to Knowledge Forum & ET Champions Dialogue to get help from more experienced members
Core Member	How to guide lecturers in learning object development? How to lead ICT-based initiatives at the college? How to harness the capabilities of existing and emerging technology tools to support the lecturers?	• Indirect support in terms of tools and resources (e.g., Reusable folder, Game Manager) • Ideas and guidance in harnessing capabilities of existing and emerging technology tools to support the lecturers • Access to more experienced ET Champions	• Enhanced Expertise – Workshops and informal training sessions on emerging technology tools or new ways of using existing tools • Enhanced Expertise – eNewsletter • Enhanced Expertise – Access to sharing by more experienced members (e.g., Knowledge Forum, Knowledge Sharing Sessions) • Negotiation platforms – access to Knowledge Forum & ET Champions Dialogue to obtain assistance from more experienced members • Support Performance – Access to tools (e.g., Game Manager) and Knowledge Objects (e.g., Reusable folder) by more experienced members

continued on following page

Table 3. continued

Identity	Concerns	Needs	Support
Strategic Member	Determine new initiatives to introduce at the college level? How to develop new ways to enhance the practice?	• Ideas and guidance in harnessing capabilities of existing and emerging technology tools to support the lecturers • Platform for sharing new knowledge created	• Enhanced Expertise – Workshops and informal training sessions on emerging technology tools or new ways of using existing tools • Enhanced Expertise – eNewsletter • Facilitate sharing – Platform (e.g., Knowledge Sharing Sessions and Knowledge Forum) for sharing new knowledge created
Transformative Member	How to generate innovative ways of doing things? How to transform current practices to harness the potential of ICT to support flexible learning and expand the range of educational opportunities?	• Skills in research & development • Ideas of emerging technology tools and trends in educational technology • Platform for sharing new knowledge created	• Enhanced Expertise – Research & Development Methodology • Enhanced Expertise – Workshops and informal training sessions on emerging technology tools or new ways of using existing tools • Enhanced Expertise – eNewsletter • Facilitate sharing – Platform (e.g., Knowledge Sharing Sessions and Knowledge Forum) for sharing new knowledge created • Encourage innovation – Engage ET Champions in innovative projects

Figure 5. EDT as boundary practice

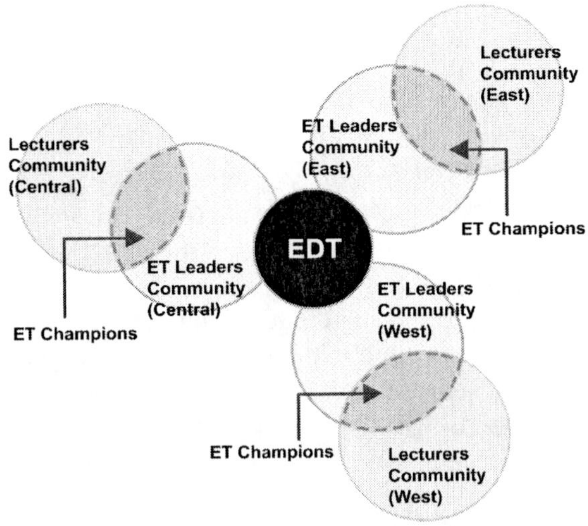

Champions was to connect the needs and expertise of the two communities. As the colleges embarked on major initiatives such as developing one online module in each programme, some ET Champions began to take on more responsibility. As a result, a group of community leaders emerged at the college level, leading and coordinating the other ET Champions' effort in supporting and guiding the lecturers. As the scope of such coordinating work expanded, the ET leaders reviewed their existing practice during the ET Champions Dialogue sessions. As a result of these discussions the concept of establishing ET units at the colleges was adopted.

Currently, there are three ET Units (one per college) staffed by ET Champions or eLearning specialists. The "brokering practice" of these community leaders is gaining momentum and is beginning to transform the community. We are beginning to see the ET Leaders' community evolving into two levels of brokering. The first level would be ET Champions at the college, connecting lecturers in the Lecturers' community with the e-learning Specialists in the ET Unit. The second level would be the instructional design professionals at EDT, connecting the three ET Units at the three colleges. Under this new structure, EDT's role would be similar to that of a boundary practice, which connects and aligns the practices of the three ET Units with the ITE's mission, vision and values (Wenger, 1998). *Figure 5* illustrates this eventual state of transformation of the ET Leaders' community.

In summary, our experience with cultivating the ET Leaders community led us to identify four steps in cultivating a community of practice.

1. **Define intention:** Firstly, we need to define the intention and value from the perspectives of the community. In other words, we need to define the domain, community and practice (Wenger, McDermott, & Snyder, 2002) of the community.

2. **Identify levels of participation:** As highlighted by Wenger, McDermott, and Snyder (2002), a community architecture should provide for different levels of participation. Members need to be aware of the different levels of participation and the roles and responsibilities at each level. Identifying and defining different levels of participation is a crucial step before proceeding to the next step. In the case of our ET Leaders' community, we initially identified three levels of participation, namely Peripheral, Legitimate and Core. As the community grew and the focus of the community expanded, two more levels (Strategic and Transformative) emerged.
3. **Recruit members:** Potential members of our ET Leaders' community were identified by the management at the college level and formally appointed. We would continue to adopt this practice in our future efforts to cultivate new communities of practice. However, instead of merely informing new members of their role we designed a means to clarify (and perhaps redefine) the scope of the community.
4. **Enculturate members by providing different levels of support:** New members need to be enculturated into the community and appropriate support needed to be provided to facilitate this process. As communities evolve, the scope of their domain, the structure of the community and the nature of the practice might change. When this happens, the type of support provided should also change. One pattern we noticed in our ET Leaders' community (as shown in Figure 5) is that support was needed at all levels and different levels needed different types of support. This is illustrated in Figure 6. This figure depicts the type of support required from the perspective of members at different levels of participation. For example, as we have more ET Champions (Core Members) stationed at the colleges, initiatives targeted at supporting performance (for example, *Game Manager* and *Reusable Folder*) were introduced or extended to Core Members stationed at the colleges.

Figure 6. Support required at each level of participation

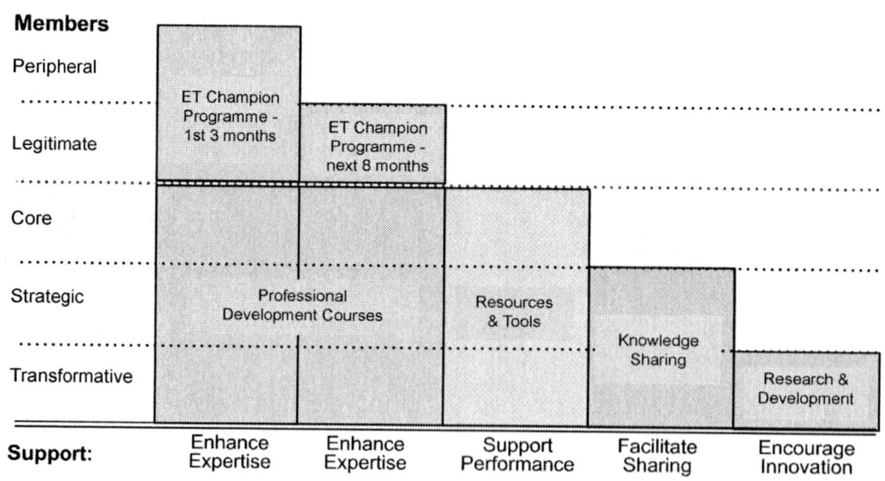

Figure 7. Framework for supporting and cultivating the community

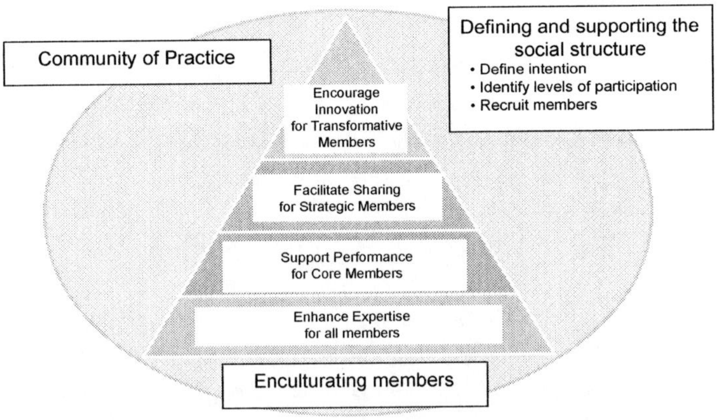

Conceptual Framework for Supporting and Cultivating the Community

As a conceptual framework can serve as a useful tool in guiding others who are considering a similar approach, we attempted to depict the steps discussed above in the form of a conceptual framework shown in Figure 7.

The circle represents the community and the strategies in the outer part of the circle represent strategies for defining the community's intention and social structure. The pyramid inside the circle depicts the type of support to be introduced at different stages of the enculturation process for new members. For example, at the beginning of the enculturation process, support for enhancing expertise should be provided. When Core Members emerge, resources and tools (such as Game Manager in the case of the ET Leaders' community) targeted at supporting performance should be provided.

Looking Ahead

Our ET Leaders' community is unique in that its main focus was to serve a strategic purpose of the organization to cultivate a group of brokers with membership of two different communities. This enabled the colleges to be empowered with greater autonomy to develop the ITE's brand of education. In any organization there exists many Communities of Practice that are often interrelated with overlapping memberships. These allow the transfer of knowledge and learning through these social links. ITE is no exception. There is an expanded scope to capitalize on the network to support the division's effort in creating a vibrant community of connected learning colleges. The aim is to continue to support high quality education with increased flexibility and accessibility. The ET leader's community is the first step in enhancing linkages within the network of practices to support this vision. In the near future, we will harness our experience to start more communities.

References

Brown, J.S., & Duguid, P. (1996). Stolen knowledge. In H. McLellan (Ed.), *Situated learning perspectives* (pp. 47-56). Englewood Cliffs, NJ: Educational Technology Publications.

Brown, J.S., & Duguid, P. (2000). *The social life of information.* Cambridge, MA: Harvard Business School.

Brown, J.S., Collins, A., & Duguid, P. (1996). Situated cognition and the culture of learning. In H. McLellan (Ed.), *Situated learning perspectives* (pp. 19-44). Englewood Cliffs, NJ: Educational Technology Publications.

Cohen, D., & Prusak, L. (2001). *In good company.* Boston: Harvard Business School.

Collins, A., Brown, J.S., & Newman, S.E. (1989). Cognitive apprenticeship: Teaching the crafts of reading, writing, and mathematics. In L.B. Resnick (Ed.), *Knowing, learning, and instruction: Essays in honor of Robert Glaser* (pp. 453-494). Hillsdale, NJ: Lawrence Erlbaum Associates.

Damarin, S.K. (1996). Schooling and situated knowledge: Travel or tourism? In H. McLellan (Ed.), *Situated learning perspectives* (pp. 77-87). Englewood Cliffs, NJ: Educational Technology Publications.

Davenport, T., & Prusak, L. (1998). *Working knowledge. How organizations manage what they know.* Cambridge, MA: Harvard Business School.

Gagné, R.M., & Medsker, K.L. (1996). *The conditions of learning training applications.* Florida: Harcourt Brace & Company.

Hildreth, P.M. (2004). *Going virtual: Distributed communities of practice.* Hershey, PA: Idea Group Inc.

Kolb, D.A. (1984) *Experiential learning.* Englewood Cliffs, NJ: Prentice Hall.

Gustafson, K., & Branch, R. (2002). What is instructional design? In R. Reiser & J. Dempsey (Eds.), *Trends and issues in instructional design and technology* (pp 16-25). Upper Saddle River, NJ: Merrill Prentice Hall.

Kruse, K. (2005). *Introduction to instructional design and the ADDIE model.* Retrieved August 13, 2005, from http://www.e-learningguru.com/articles/art2_1.htm

Lave, J., & Wenger, E. (1991). *Situated learning: Legitimate peripheral participation.* Cambridge: University of Cambridge Press.

Leong, P. & Chia, C.M. (2000). The ITE pedagogic model-facilitating learning in technical education. Paper *presented at the 2nd Asia-Pacific Coference on problem-based learning.*

Lerner, R.M., & Kaufman, M.B. (1985). The concept of development in contextualism. *Development Review*, *5*, 309-333.

Litchfield, B., & Keller, J. (2002). Instructional project management. In R. Reiser & J. Dempsey (Eds.), *Trends and issues in instructional design and technology* (pp. 168-182). Upper Saddle River, NJ: Merrill Prentice Hall.

McLellan, H. (1996). Situated learning: Multiple perspectives. In H. McLellan (Ed.), *Situated learning perspectives* (pp. 5-17). Englewood Cliffs, NJ: Educational Technology Publications.

Rogoff, B. (1990). *Apprenticeship in thinking: Cognitive development in social context.* New York: Oxford University Press.

Rueda, R., & Dembo M.H. (1995). Motivational processes in learning: A comparative analysis of cognitive and sociocultural frameworks. *Advances in Motivation and Achievement, 9*, 255-289.

Saint-Onge, H., & Wallace, D. (2003). *Leveraging communities of practice for strategic advantage.* Burlington, MA: Butterworth-Heinemann.

Schwier, R.A., Campbell, K., & Kenny, R. (2004). Instructional designers' observations about identity, communities of practice and change agency. *Australasian Journal of Educational Technology*, *20*(1), 69-100.

Senge, P. (1990). *The fifth discipline: The art and practice of the learning organization.* Bantam Doubleday Dell Publishing Group, Inc.

Star, S.L. & Griesemer, J.R. (1989). Institutional ecology, 'translations,' and boundary objects: Amateurs and professionals in Berkeley's Museum of Vertebrate Zoology, 1907-1939. *Social Studies of Science,* (19), 387-420.

Vygotsky, L.S. (1978). *Mind in society: The development of higher psychological processes.* Cambridge: Harvard University Press.

Wenger, E. (1998). *Communities of practice: Learning, meaning, and identity.* Cambridge: Cambridge University Press.

Wenger, E., McDermott, R., & Snyder, W.M. (2002). *Cultivating communities of practice: A guide to managing knowledge.* Boston: Harvard Business School Publishing.

Chapter XII

Designer Communities: Developing a Knowledge Base of Strategies, Tools, and Experience

Sarah Lambert, University of Wollongong, Australia

Christine Brown, University of Wollongong, Australia

Abstract

This chapter highlights the importance of developing and sustaining a knowledge base among designers to enable the collective sharing of strategies and tools for communication within project teams. This chapter identifies and discusses the need to capture collective wisdom of designers who work in close proximity within the same university. It examines a case study of a project that illustrates changes in the design context in relation to types of projects (CD-ROM, Web-based, learning management systems) and discusses these trends through the eyes of two designers. It also discusses the trend away from large standalone projects to networked "learning objects." It examines these trends in relation to a number of strategies that support the learning design community and its work.

Introduction

Designers are often required to immerse themselves within temporary project communities to develop teaching and learning interventions using CD-ROM and Web-based approaches. As part of this community they need to be effective communicators of project needs, processes, products and outcomes with all members of the team. As each project is unique, designers build a rich repertoire of strategies to handle the challenges they face which are often relevant to subsequent projects. This chapter looks through the eyes of two designers who have become part of a localised designer community within the University of Wollongong (UoW), Australia. The designers illustrate their perspectives through a case study that typifies changes in the nature of their design work. In particular, the types of projects have changed over time as well as the project size, scope and outcomes. These factors have implications for the designer's role, which are further elaborated within the chapter. In addition, the designer's role within the community, re-usability of design patterns and output, and the nature of production teams are also discussed. This chapter suggests that there is a trend away from large projects to a broader range of smaller developments in-line with current thinking about "learning objects."

The key objective of the chapter is to highlight the importance of developing and sustaining a knowledge base among designers to enable the collective sharing of strategies and tools for communication within project teams. This chapter identifies and discusses the need to capture collective wisdom of designers who work in close proximity within the same university. While this seems obvious, it requires substantial energy and discipline to facilitate this exchange in a busy work environment where designers have their own allocation of projects, and have difficulty allocating time for professional development activities. Jonassen & Reeves (1996) acknowledge that those who design and develop multimedia products learn a great deal—possibly more than those who access them as a learning resource. Therefore if the design/production team are to share transferable elements of their collective experience, these have to be recorded and circulated among relevant design communities. This chapter will also discuss project specific and team community factors associated with the case study to highlight the challenges associated with the designer's role and the strategies adopted to address those challenges. It will also identify some of the structures that need to be instigated to allow designers to store and share this knowledge. The goal is a sustainable developer community that is continually learning.

The following case typifies a period of transition from a culture of large multimedia project development to an environment where many smaller and typically Web-based projects were developed. This transition required a more substantial project management infrastructure and extra management staff who could potentially collect valuable data on production processes to facilitate strategy and tool sharing among design teams.

Tradewinds Phase 1: CD-ROM (1998-2002)

This case traces the development of an interactive role-playing game involving the Dutch East India Company of 17th century Southeast Asia that simulates the sea-faring trade in precious spices, metals and fabric (see Figure 1). It was developed in close association with two academic staff within the Faculty of Arts at the University of Wollongong.

Factors Concerning the Nature of the Project

Purpose

The prime purpose of the project was to assist users to understand the history and politics of European colonial trading with Southeast Asia. Although the game was applicable for a wide range of adults, it was designed for use in teaching history and politics courses at the University of Wollongong.

Project Scope and Size

Originally the game was designed to simulate trading for one season on a single ship. Further iterations of the game examined trading over multiple seasons to simulate the ongoing career of an employee in the Dutch East India Company. The content included historical data about buying and selling commodities in 17th century Southeast Asia, a substantial bank of historical images including etchings and maps, and a range of 3-D modelled images that were animated into scenes, such as sailing the high seas and pirate battles. The highly visual nature of the material was considered vital to user engagement with the simulation. The production team needed to maintain a focus on the educational needs of users in the context of rich historical content.

Figure 1. Tradewinds role-playing trading game CD-ROM

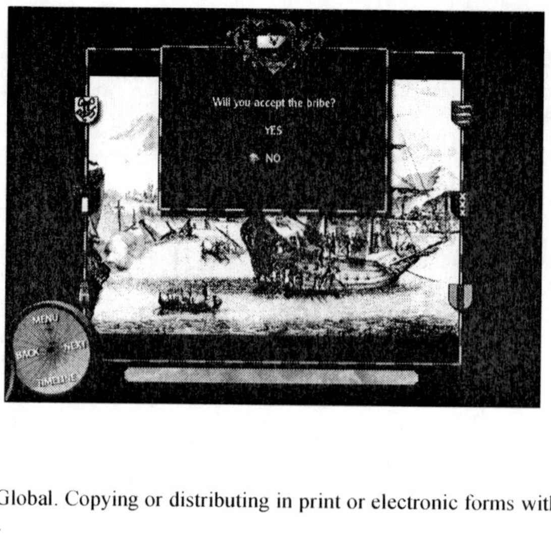

A further challenge to emerge with the growth in project scope was the need for additional funding to complete all aspects of the project. This project initially attracted $AUD35,000 production funding in 1998-99 from the Committee for University Teaching and Staff Development (CUTSD). This Australian federal government competitive grant scheme allowed the project team to complete the historical write-up, image collection and development of the trading game and animations. However, many strands within the planned structure remained undeveloped at the end of Phase 1 of development. Pressure from management and funding bodies to complete and show outcomes was a normal part of the project context given the degree of funding.

The Nature of the Output Mode

Phase 1 (1998-2002): The design was based on the use of CD-ROM delivery.

Factors Concerning the Project Community

Duration of Immersion in Project Community

Neither of the authors was involved in *Tradewinds* during Phase 1 development. Three designers provided design input to the project community for short periods of time with no overlap.

Size of Team and Specificity of Role

The graphic designer, senior programmer and two Arts' academics formed the core team. The graphic designer and senior programmer were continuously involved and adopted multiple team roles. Educational designers who worked in a consultative role were based in the Academic Staff Development Unit, though they were frequently working in faculties across Wollongong and its satellite campuses. Four production staff also contributed to the team on a short-term basis throughout the project.

Changes in Team Composition

The sporadic role of the educational designers was a challenge for Phase 1 of *Tradewinds'* development. As they were not located in the production unit they were unable to contribute time to the project due to other competing roles. The senior programmer and graphic designer overcame this lack of involvement by working directly with the academic staff as opposed to relying on the educational designers to fulfil this role.

Pattern of Communication Between Team Members and Content Experts

Communication between the educational designers and the Flexible Learning Services (FLS) production staff was also a challenge. During this phase, the prime mechanism for the game development was direct communication between the programmer and one of the Arts' academics.

Opportunity for Ongoing Relationship Through a Series of Projects

As the project was incomplete by the end of Phase 1, additional funding was needed to allow the project to continue.

Issues and Challenges

Maintaining momentum for this complex project was not always easy as there was a wealth of information, and the design and navigation were difficult within the *Tradewinds* project. Sometimes the designers needed to place the project aside and work on other projects before completing aspects of the design. In retrospect these are common feelings in the middle of a large development project. Iterative development is simply part of the process. Sometimes simple solutions might work, and at other times discarding weeks of work and going back to the proverbial "drawing board" may be the only option for project quality. What follows is a snapshot of the production unit—Flexible Learning Services—in 2000. It provides the necessary context to understanding the steps taken to address the issues raised, and in particular to further the development of *Tradewinds* through an alternate funding avenue with its own set of conditions.

Context Snapshot: Flexible Learning Services (2000-2002)

In 2000, Flexible Learning Services focussed on a broad range of projects. There was a team dedicated to developing CD-ROM based multimedia products, involving graphic-design and video production staff. There was also another team working on Web-based products—some of which required 100-200 hours of production time. The larger Web sites targeted support for generic skills such as academic writing and study skills. Two other large projects were associated with the unit itself—the Flexible Learning Services Web site, and the development of a Web-based project management database.

Supporting this environment were several major funding sources including CUTSD grants (Committee for University Teaching and Staff Development – Australia-wide competitive government grants) and ESDF grants (Wollongong University-based competitive Educational Strategies Development Fund grants). There was also a funding pool to support the development of Wollongong's South Coast Educational Network (SCEN). SCEN was necessary to support the Arts and Commerce faculties, who were the first to teach at the University's satellite campuses in Nowra, Bateman's Bay and Bega. These annual funding sources permitted a small number of large projects to be completed over one or two years. They also permitted subject matter experts (typically UoW academics) to "buy-out" some of their marking and/or tutorial time to work on projects.

In addition to these funding sources, "service agreements" were established between CEDIR and the faculties. This faculty service agreement (FSA) model permitted an increased number of academics to engage in smaller projects to support teaching innovation and excellence.

The faculties ranked priority projects and CEDIR supported development work to the limit of their allocation of staff time. Although UoW academics were the subject matter experts, under this model they were required to conduct projects as additional teaching load since there was no option for tutorial or marking "buy-out." FSA project timelines were restricted to six months per project. Many projects were carried over into the next session due to their overly ambitious aims. The production unit also needed to adjust to a trend away from large projects to smaller projects. Project records from this period provide an indication of the balance between large and small projects. Using total hours worked on the project (by the production staff) as a simple indicator of project size, Table 1 shows how many small, medium and large projects were completed during the period January-July in 2000.

FSA projects made up the majority of small and medium sized projects, while the majority of large projects were funded by grants. The biggest category was large projects.

For production staff this was both a buoyant period with award-winning high-profile projects and a turbulent time as projects needed to be regularly re-scoped and re-negotiated and some projects remained unfinished. Staff burnout and turnover were perennial issues and academic staff turnover had an impact on the production community, particularly when subject matter experts left the university resulting in discarded production work on some projects. Such realities were part of a trend experienced by many tertiary resource development units. It was felt that management expertise and research was required to find solutions through policy, funding and organisational structure (Bates, 2000).

Project initiation of sessional FSA projects relied on the availability of busy academics who had ambitious plans that needed to be revised to complete a realistic development. Buoyed by the acceptance of the FSA program, a restructure of CEDIR in 2002 saw the creation of a Learning Design Unit within FLS. This new unit was charged with ensuring the educational quality of the products developed. The Learning Designers led the projects, and the role required both educational design and project management skills. Simple repeatable routines to elicit information from clients, to scope shorter time-frame projects, and to record outcomes of meetings were developed and shared by the learning designers. Like many instructional designers, we struggled to balance the multiple tasks or "hats" the role required (Hakkinen, 2002; Liu, Gibby, Quiros, & Demps, 2002), and tried to define our role within the development community.

Published literature of this time discussed the role of the instructional designer within the development team. The role underwent a professionalisation, with discussion of common

Table 1. Number of projects semester 1, 2000 (viewed by size and funding source)

January - July 2000	**Small**	**Medium**	**Large**	**Total**
	<15 hrs	**15-60 hrs**	**>60 hrs**	
*Grant supported	0	4	11	15
FSA supported	8	8	8	24
Total	8	12	19	39

* *Note: CUTSD, ESDF, SCEN grants*

techniques and tools (Althauser & Matuga, 1998; Collis & Nikolova, 1998; Keppell, 2001). Papers critically reviewed current models of educational multimedia software development and provided new solutions. For example, Shabajee argued for explicit consideration of values and beliefs as the first step in project development (Shabajee, 1999). This work discussed the role of epistemology, pedagogy and psychological assumptions on the usability of educational multimedia resources (Shearer, 1997).

Around this time, universities were beginning to invest in the potential of learning management systems such as WebCT or Blackboard, and teachers began to adopt these as a way to develop and maintain their teaching resources, which was independent of central resource production units. Innovators explored the possibilities of the communication and collaboration afforded by network-based learning. These constructivist developments were identified and differentiated from projects driven by the discipline knowledge (Agostinho, Lefoe, & Hedberg, 1997; Wegerif, 1998). To differentiate our role from such trends, the title of "learning designer" was chosen rather than instructional designer to emphasise that we were creating contexts for learning, not sequential instructions for students. Generally instructional design models were reconceptualised during this period, as growing interest in constructivism favoured less restrictive and more non-linear instructional design models (Crawford, 2004).

During this period, evaluation routines were established to determine client satisfaction with our process, as well as students' satisfaction with the usability of the products we developed for them in partnership with academic clients. With a rising trend towards smaller projects funded via the faculty service agreement, the *Tradewinds* project was continued in 2002.

Tradewinds Phase 2: Web-Based (2003–2005)

Factors Concerning the Nature of the Project

Project Scope and Size

During Phase 2 of development, plans for a major CD-ROM title with possible commercial prospects were curtailed in favour of a more modest Web-based game and information Web site. This Web site would be accessible to students any time during their course via WebCT (see Figure 2). The content was divided into more manageable chunks and used to support face-to-face teaching activities. The game survived the transition to the Web environment, but the animations and other media-rich features were casualties of the transition.

The FSA provided an ongoing source of support to "finish" the project in five six-month stages from 2003-2005. The product was continuously used throughout this development period. In the latter FSA review cycles, additions to the site included lecture notes, URLs, and online activities submitted by the discussion forum. This transition made the ongoing maintenance of the product easier, as the text was no longer constrained within a CD-based

Figure 2. The Web interface of Tradewinds in Phase 2

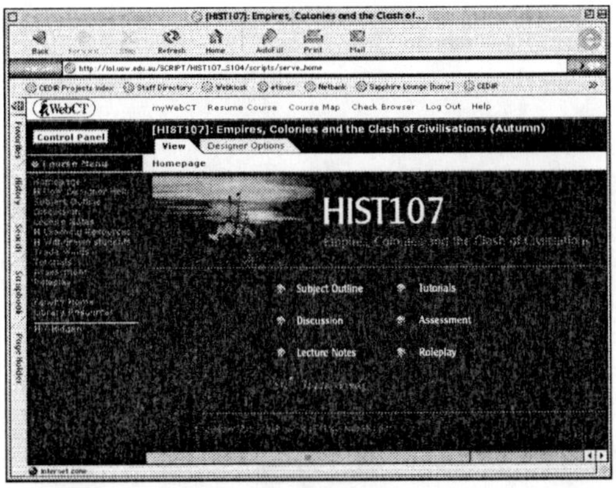

product. It could also be edited by less technically minded staff with basic Web-page editing software. Similarly, each module or feature of the Web site was a more manageable "chunk," with the potential for re-use in other courses.

Factors Concerning the Project Community

Duration of Immersion in Project Community

In the last three years of the project, a full-time learning designer from the Learning Design Unit (one of the authors) joined the team and managed the transition to the Web-based module.

Size of Team and Specificity of Role

The graphic designer, senior programmer and two Arts' academics remained in the core team, joined by the learning designer and a new Web programmer. During Phase 2 the learning designer also became the production team co-ordinator.

Changes in Team Composition

Figure 3 shows the production staff roles in Phase 1 and Phase 2 of the project. The second phase was characterised by a stable team with more long-term contributors than short-term contributors, reversing the trend for Phase 1.

Opportunity for Ongoing Relationship Through a Series of Projects

The staff development aspect of this project was quite significant, as the content experts' design and production expertise developed considerably over the project time. The content

Figure 3. Production staff involved in the Tradewinds project

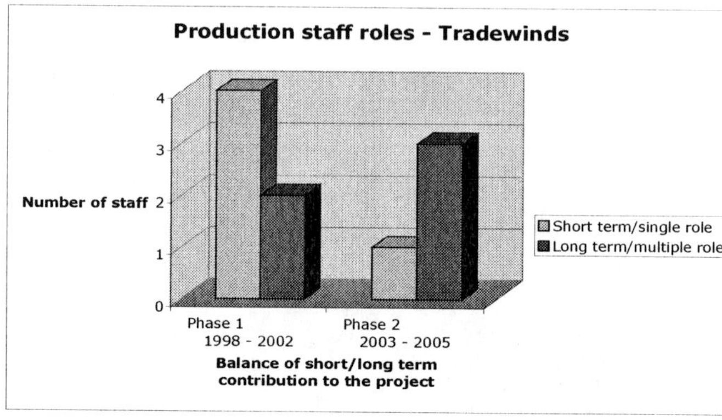

experts were also involved in other design and production projects. There were significant opportunities once the project moved to sessional faculty service agreement cycles. The team worked on a different focus each session. One of the clients was employed in a facilitation role within the Arts Faculty and became a team member of a range of different projects in that faculty. Long-term professional relationships were formed. What follows is a discussion of the trends within our development community, anchored to several key concepts in educational design literature, and a description of some of the accompanying structural changes to FLS.

Elements of Change

As we have seen, in the period of the *Tradewinds* project, substantial changes have occurred within the teams and structure of the central resource development unit as well as within the university and the broader context, which included the use of the Internet and learning management systems.

Standalone Content and Active Learning

During this period there was a shift away from standalone CD-ROMs to engaging students through peer learning. Phase 2 of the *Tradewinds* project can be seen to be part of a wider acceptance of social-constructivist perspectives. It suggests that social interaction plays a fundamental role in the development of cognition that exceeds what can be attained alone (Vygotsky, 1978). *Tradewinds* grasped this concept by focussing on game-play as central to the student experience and extended the possibilities of learning by dialogue into the online collaborative environment of the discussion forum. In the discussion forum students shared responses and acted as moderators in the discussion groups.

Another practical consideration influencing the shift from CD-ROM-based projects is the issue of ownership and maintenance. Once the CD-ROM is delivered, the academic cannot change the text or activities until the next major revision. This limitation is not popular with academics who may update their lectures each session and expect to be able to update their resources at the same time. The use of learning management systems or simple Web pages to deliver resources allows the academic to update the material without the need for additional production assistance.

Importance of Academic Staff Development

The process of co-design with the academic in this way carries a parallel agenda of academic professional development (Lambert, 2003). The cyclical nature of FSA support permits academic subject experts to progressively expand their repertoire of strategies to engage learners in meaningful ways, informed by reflection and evaluation of the project. If new designers work with the academic subject experts, they should be able to tap into the history, artefacts and evaluation data of past FSA cycles. This requires a central repository of such information and a process to gather, maintain and update its contents.

Reusable Learning Objects

While there are many technical definitions of learning objects, we prefer: "the smallest autonomous pedagogical unit that cannot be broken into smaller sub-units; examples could be lecture slides, quizzes, and audio tracks" (Lukasiak, Agostinho, Goodes, Bennett, Lockyer, & Harper, 2004, p. 467). Within the *Tradewinds* package there are a number of maps, information, and Web pages that would be considered reusable learning objects. However, separating content from context to produce reusable content has limitations. If we consider that the learning occurs in the learning interactions, then a resource separated from its learning context or activity may deliver no learning at all (Bradley & Boyle, 2004). One solution is to develop repositories of learning designs or sequences of learning tasks to supplement repositories of reusable learning objects (Agostinho, Lefoe, & Hedberg, 1997; AUTC, 2003; Lukasiak, Agostinho, Goodes, Bennett, Lockyer, & Harper, 2004). Another approach may include information about appropriate learning tasks as part of the "meta-tag" information that comes with the learning object itself (Jonassen & Churchill, 2004).

As the professional debate continues, the learning designers in FLS have considered this trend and developed smaller reusable learning objects within learning designs. This has diminished the likelihood of design as top-down architecture for CD-ROM development, and has increased the focus on the design of smaller modular learning objects. This means that we are working closely with academics to determine learning tasks and objects appropriate to their learning context. It also demands more strategic discussions with academics conducting curriculum review to identify the resources most likely to have widespread application and therefore high reusability.

Change in Project Team Structure

The establishment of the learning design unit within FLS heralded a new team structure. The placement of the learning designers within the production unit provided a degree of team continuity and rapport not experienced when the developers had worked in a more consultative way. The learning designer could liaise directly with academics and engage the production staff when required. Given the trend towards increased project numbers involving more modular resource development and close co-design with academics, the Learning Designers could not sustain their multiple projects effectively, resulting in the hiring of a client liaison officer (CLO), who became a key communication contact.

Development of Learning Designer Specialisation

During 2003, both authors were associated with the learning design unit of FLS, having sought the ability to balance work across more moderate sized projects. There was a common desire for the intellectual stimulation of developing professional relationships with a range of subject matter experts across more than one subject domain. Working from the "home-base" of the FLS production unit provided a community of designers to exchange lessons learned from each project via sharing at monthly staff meetings.

Although the learning designers had begun a dialogue about the nature of the learning design role, including a sharing of client meeting support tools, it became clear that differences in background and expertise created differences in approaches to projects. Over time the learning designers have become more articulate in expressing their areas of expertise. Figure 4 illustrates how the learning design role developed. It suggests that the learning designer has a speciality as well as a common ground at the core of the role, to maintain a consistent quality service. While some work documented ad-hoc sharing of common tools, it became clear that a more systematic collection of project experiences and outcomes was the next step. A system to document and allow sharing of speciality knowledge would be useful to share with academic clients and faculty members upon project completion. In addition, this bank of corporate knowledge would form the foundation for the learning design team and future staff changes.

Strategies to Support the Production and Designer Community

In order for designers to capitalise on the benefits of experience beyond the individual level, it is necessary to share with the designer community. Typical methods of sharing with the wider designer community include conference presentations, journal articles, and books that specifically target designers. Of equal importance is the recognition of the need to nurture local designer communities. These are often the most relevant source of ideas to deal with problems in the local context.

Figure 4. Areas of specialty associated with the role of learning designer

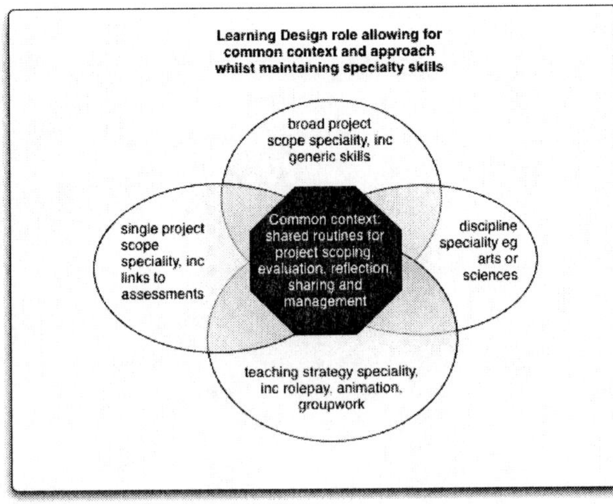

To achieve this goal, the *Flexible Learning Services Showcase* database of educational multimedia was developed in 2003. This database contains detailed cases or examples of work undertaken at UoW by teaching academics in partnership with CEDIR Learning Designers and resource development teams. It includes screen-shots or images of the products developed for teaching and workload information regarding development time. Comments regarding the application of the product to teaching, and in some cases evaluation of its use, are included. Users can search for examples by faculty, type of project or technology outcome, or year produced. Figure 5 shows the homepage of the Web site, with the pull-down menu for project scope activated. This allows users to search for projects of subject, program, university-wide or even community-wide scope.

During 2003-2004, FLS staff spent approximately 1,200 hours developing approximately 50 subjects/projects each year. Showing new clients a range of recent projects with common context or needs was an often repeated and successful strategy to scope new projects. To support this approach a resource was needed to capture a snapshot of our projects so we could share the results with others (see Figures 5 and 6). At this time it is very important to give academics a clear guideline as to the time necessary to undertake such projects, and the database documents these details.

Further data, such as project timelines, workload, and evaluation notes, can also be added and displayed in the database. Since implementing the FLS case database, the learning designers have been able to more effectively assist academics to plan for their own subject improvements by giving examples of good practice from within and outside their discipline, and indicating a probable timeline for developing such products. An unplanned but very welcome outcome is the ability to support a range of staff development programs across campus with a variety of concrete examples, and in some cases, create communities of practice around teaching strategies like collaborative learning or virtual experiments, which flourish across disciplines.

Figure 5. The homepage or search screen for the FLS Case database

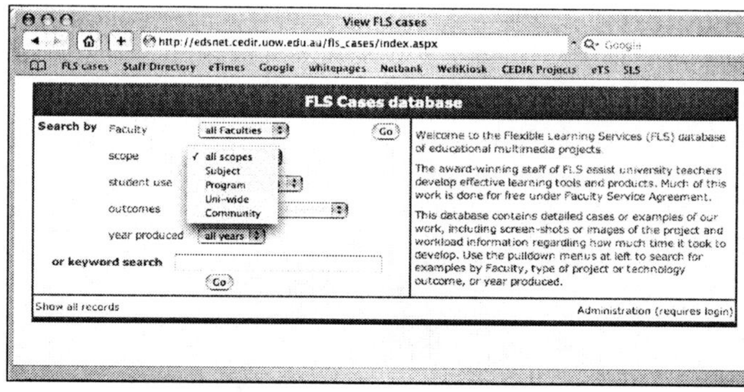

Figure 6. The minimum (compulsory) data required to add a project case to the FLS Case database

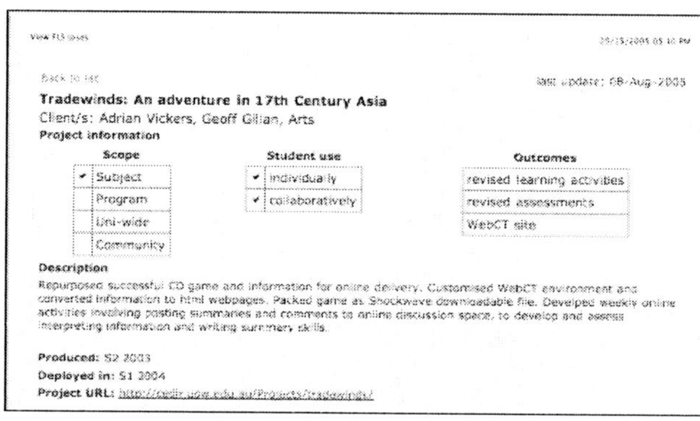

In addition to the FLS case database there are archived collections of finished projects including code and original interface designs, parts of which may be recycled. There are also folders of support material for clients and learning designers that give examples of models and methods for holding a project initiation meeting, to specifying edits to a Web site, or reviewing products for accessibility and usability. We share a common context for our work, and designers aim to keep up-to-date with the policies and guidelines that intersect with their areas of specialty, sharing these at particular staff development forums. Figure 7 represents these items as elements within the learning designer home base of the production community.

These systems form a strong platform of support for the whole production unit to work within. They provide a continuity of quality service over time, so there is less impact from staff changes as processes and project histories are documented. It is the kind of corporate memory that is useful for our work and is critical to the sustainability and quality of our unit. We are confident about promising each client a quality process of partnership for educational resource development as continuity and quality is built into the system. The learning design

Figure 7. Production community as the central point of reference across many communities

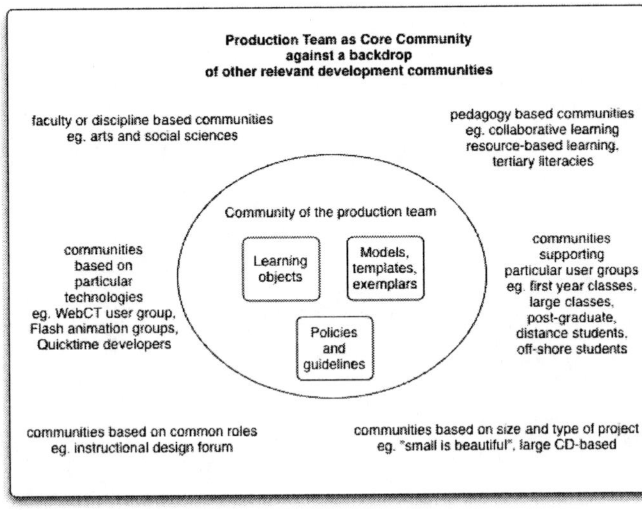

staff are part of a community located in a production environment supported by a number of repositories of re-usable learning objects, as well as models, templates and exemplars which can be shared (see Figure 7).

Context Snapshot: Flexible Learning Services (2005)

The Flexible Learning Services was previously dedicated to CD-ROM production and is now working predominantly on Web-based sessional projects—typically small and modular in nature, targeting a single subject within a discipline. Most projects are supported by the faculty service agreement rather than grant funding, which limits the opportunity for academic partners to "buy-out" tutoring or marking time, so development work is usually completed in parallel with teaching. Meetings with academics are held in the preparation period for teaching. In this way it is often possible to facilitate and support reflection on teaching and subsequent implementation of changes that would otherwise be completed by the teacher on their own. Larger projects target the development of program, faculty or university-wide resources to support graduate attribute skills. The project outcomes provide resources, supports, and enhanced designs for teaching and learning.

Following evaluation, some projects return for further development work, allowing for modular enhancement over one to two years. The academic partners on these and many sessional projects form a community with the learning designers and production staff. Table 2

Table 2. Number of projects Semester 1, 2005, viewed by size and funding source

January - July 2005	**Small**	**Medium**	**Large**	**Total**
	<15 hrs	**15-60 hrs**	**>60 hrs**	
Externally funded	7	1	4	12
FSA supported	18	13	6	37
Total	25	14	10	49

Table 3. Change in total number of projects viewed by size and year

	Small-Medium	**Large**
Jan - July 2000	20	19
Jan - July 2005	39	10
% Change 2000 to 2005	**+95%**	**-74%**

provides a breakdown of projects in Session 1, 2005, according to their size (as determined by FLS staff learning design and production hours) and the nature of funding.

The large FSA projects listed here are video productions and a few large Web projects. The external organization collaborations funded the remaining larger Web sites with significant illustration and animation features. Table 3 summarises the change in project numbers from 2000-2005.

Table 3 indicates that since 2000, the number of large projects has decreased by 74%, while the number of small-medium projects has increased by 95%. This is not just a change in numbers, but also a change in how we define a small to medium project. In addition a significant component of the work may be completed between the learning designer and the academic partner or client. These projects are characterised by strong staff development outcomes. For example, the client learns how to restructure a course for partial online delivery for the first time, in partnership with a learning designer (Lambert, 2003). In some instances, production staff such as graphic designers, Web programmers or video producers may be asked to complete graphics and illustrations, or to transform the text worked by client and learning designer into html for delivery via a WebCT learning module.

The rise in popularity of WebCT at UoW has also been a significant factor in the type of projects undertaken. The Strategic Plan for e-Teaching and e-Learning (Wollongong, 2005) indicates that approximately 40% of subjects in 2005 are taught in blended mode (face-to-face plus online presence), or up to approximately 60%, if subjects taught at off-shore or satellite campus locations are included in the figures. WebCT has made it possible for many academics to manage their own e-teaching developments including moderating an online discussion, adding lecture or practical notes, providing revision quizzes or practice exams, and linking to Web sites and other supporting material. In this context, the larger projects are now either broader in application than a single subject (such as generic skills), or large simulation/animation projects developed with Macromedia Flash technology, which

Figure 8. Comparison of FLS staff numbers and roles for 2000 and 2005

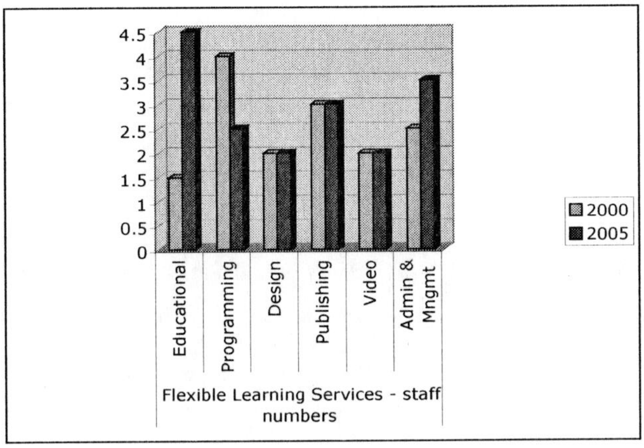

demands development processes not unlike the traditional CD-ROM development process. Staffing needs have reflected these changes, and now the composition of our production team has changed. For instance, there are more learning designers and flash animators and fewer desktop publishers and html programmers (see Figure 8).

Between 2000 and 2005 the number of staff focusing on educational issues has increased (from 1.5 to 4.5 staff members), while programming staff has decreased. The ratio of production to educational staff is more balanced, reflecting the kind of service we now offer. Also, to cope with a larger number of smaller projects, the project management needs have increased, reflected in the slight increase in the number of administrative and management staff.

Conclusion

The authors have made the transition from a relatively constrained and defined role within a few large projects as independent designers, to a broadly defined role across many projects. This has been accompanied by the need to adapt within multiple communities to the relevant practices and processes. This progression has eventuated due to changes within the production environment, and been enabled by the development of a designer community as the key anchor for professional development.

Two designer perspectives have been integrated in this chapter to emphasise the benefits that accrue from creating a foundation community to share communication strategies in support of the design process. Within CEDIR, at the University of Wollongong, there is a developing project community whose evolving common language allows discussion about development in blended learning environments, learning management systems and the need for staff development. As we move in wider circles and enter other communities, we find commonality in the way these organizations are undertaking small projects similar to the trends at Wollongong. In addition we are able to converse about project design with a common language as a result of the work we have undertaken to focus on the development of designer communities. Our aim is to sustain a community that is continually learning.

References

Agostinho, S., Lefoe, G., & Hedberg, J. (1997). *Online collaboration for effective learning: A case study of a postgraduate university course.* Paper presented at the AUSWEB97.

Althauser, R., & Matuga, J.M. (1998). On the pedagogy of electronic instruction. In C.J. Bonk & K.S. King (Eds.), *Electronic collaborators: Learner-centred technologies for literacy, apprenticeship, and discourse* (pp. 183-208). Mahway, NJ: Lawrence Erlbaum Associates Inc.

AUTC. (2003). *Products of the AUTC project on ICT-based learning designs.* Retrieved November 30, 2003, from http://www.learningdesigns.uow.edu.au/index.html

Bates, A.W. (2000) *Managing technological change: Strategies for university and college leaders.* San Francisco: Jossey Bass.

Bradley, C., & Boyle, T. (2004). The design, development, and use of multimedia learning objects. *Journal of Educational Multimedia and Hypermedia, 13*(4), 371-389.

Collis, B., & Nikolova, I. (1998). Flexible learning and design of instruction. *British Journal of Educational Technology, 29*, 59-72.

Crawford, C. (2004), Non-linear instructional design model: Eternal, synergistic design and development. *British Journal of Educational Technology, 35*(4), 413-420.

Hakkinen, P. (2002). Challenges for design of computer-based learning environments. *British Journal of Educational Technology, 33*(4), 461-469.

Jonassen, D.H., & Reeves, T.C. (1996). Learning with technology: Using computers as cognitive tools. In D.H. Jonassen (Ed.), *Handbook of research for educational communications and technology* (pp. 693-719). New York: Macmillan.

Jonassen, D., & Churchill, D. (2004, April/June). Is there a learning orientation in learning objects? *International Journal on E-Learning*, 32-41.

Keppell, M. (2001, Summer/Fall). Optimizing instructional designer - subject matter expert communication in the design and development of multimedia projects. *Journal of Interactive Learning Research*, 209-219.

Lambert, S. (2003, December 7-9). Learning design at the university of Wollongong. In G. Crisp, D. Thiele, I. Scholten, S. Barker, & J. Baron (Eds.), *Interact, Integrate, Impact: Proceedings of the 20th Annual Conference of the Australasian Society for Computers in Tertiary Education* (pp. 293-303). Adelaide.

Liu, M., Gibby, S., Quiros, O., & Demps, E. (2002). Challenges of being an instructional designer for new media development: A view from the practitioners. *Journal of Educational Multimedia and Hypermedia, 11*(3), 195-219.

Lukasiak, J., Agostinho, S., Goodes, J., Bennett, S., Lockyer, L., & Harper, B. (2004). A framework for the flexible content packaging of learning objects and learning designs. *Journal of Educational Multimedia and Hypermedia, 13*(4), 465-481.

Shabajee, P. (1999). Making values and beliefs explicit as a tool for the effective development of educational multimedia software: A prototype. *British Journal of Educational Technology, 30*(2), 101-113.

Shearer, D., Hall, P. & Melchior, E-M. (1997). *Usability in multi-media development.* Paper presented at the CAL'97, Exeter.

University of Wollongong. (2005). *eTeaching business plan 2005-2010*. University of Wollongong.

Vygotsky, L.S. (1978). *Mind in society: The development of higher psychological processes.* Cambridge, MA: Harvard University Press.

Wegerif, R. (1998). The social dimension of asynchronous learning networks. *Journal of Asynchronous Learning Networks, 2*(1), 34-49.

Section IV

Faculty and Departmental Context

Chapter XIII

Terms of Engagement: A Case Study of Instructional Designers in a Faculty of Law

Len Webster, Monash University, Australia

Patricie Mertova, Monash University, Australia

Abstract

In this chapter we tell a story of a discipline-specific instructional design unit located in a Faculty of Law of a large Australian university. This unit is engaged in the instructional design and development of a variety of units/subjects, courses and projects for undergraduate, postgraduate and professional practice programs as well teaching a Graduate Certificate in Law Teaching. Other activities in this specific community of practice include assisting staff with new approaches to their teaching, developing longer-term relationships with teaching staff and fostering reflective practice. The story of practice will attempt to describe the challenges and ways in which this small "band" of instructional designers has embedded themselves in the life and directions of a Law Faculty.

Introduction

Instructional design practice and research are eclectic. They draw on a range of disciplines, theories and models. This chapter takes a further step in this eclectic practice by considering the terms of engagement for a small discipline-based education unit within a Faculty of Law. In this endeavour, it employs a more human-centred and narrative perspective. It, therefore, highlights the human factors essential to success in working in another discipline. These factors were previously not considered as instructional design strategies and features. Instructional design is not alone in progressing this view, as many other disciplines have sought to incorporate human factors and human centredness into their strategies to achieve an improved outcome.

This chapter underlines the benefits of a discipline-based human-centred approach to instructional design within a Faculty of Law. The argument for such an approach is situated in the current debate about the need for the restructuring of the present legal education, and also for the provision of teaching support to legal academics. Some of the issues that the community of instructional designers have faced, will be shown in the experiential stories of the director of this instructional design unit and an instructional design team member. These stories will be counterbalanced by a story of a law teacher and his experience with law-specific instructional design.

The Education Unit described in this chapter is engaged in the design and development of a variety of units/subjects, courses and projects for undergraduate, postgraduate and professional practice programs. It also offers a discipline-based teacher professional development program and a Graduate Certificate in Law Teaching. Other activities in this specific community of practice include, for instance, assisting staff with new approaches to their teaching. This story of professional practice will attempt to describe the challenges and ways in which a small "band" of instructional designers have embedded themselves in the life and directions of a Law Faculty. It will examine the ways in which the unit has managed to establish integrity and credibility in an often adversarial, suspicious and reluctant to change practice environment.

The first of these challenges was the actual establishment of the discipline-based unit within a university that had previously located this type of support centrally. The second challenge was defining the ways in which the unit would relate to the Faculty and also the existing central support units. Other forces that may have impacted indirectly on the unit's establishment within a community of practice included the dramatic increase in online learning, and the blurring of boundaries between on-campus and off-campus learning and teaching. At the same time, universities were tackling the issue of adoption of "immature," large-scale online management systems, with increasing access for all teachers to a form (albeit restrictive) of online materials and resources. These factors contributed to a rethink and changes in teaching approaches by the academic staff, and escalated the need for "in-context support." The higher education sector we work within is complex and dynamic, with reduced funding and increased entrepreneurial needs.

The third challenge was the establishment of the unit within the Faculty. The unit was faced with differing degrees of acceptance: some academics have welcomed such support whereas others were strongly against the unit, which was perceived as an intrusion to their traditionally developed practices. Finally, it needs to be pointed out that the issues and challenges that the instructional designers had to face were frequently of a non-traditional instructional design nature. This chapter therefore highlights the holistic, human-centred nature of instructional design. Instructional design does not exist in isolation from the political and cultural issues related to the environment in which the instructional design is undertaken, and that these may be the issues that are frequently hindering instructional designers' work.

Significance of a Discipline-Based Approach to Teaching in Higher Education

The relevance of discipline-based approaches has been debated in the higher education literature. For instance, Healey (2000a) argues that within the higher education context there is a growing demand on the development of the scholarship of teaching according to the needs of the individual disciplines. He perceives that the core of the development of subject-based teaching should include: application of the principles of good practice on disciplinal basis, development of the status of teaching, building interconnection between research and teaching, as well as research into the pedagogies of the individual disciplines. However, he also acknowledges that sharing information about one's disciplinal teaching practices with practitioners from other disciplines is important for the development of the scholarship of teaching.

His disciplinal approach argument is supported by Boyer (1990), Rice (1995) and Biglan (1973). Boyer (1990) argues for a disciplinal approach as a key to fostering standards, rigour and respect to the teaching scholarship. Rice (1995) remarks that improvements to teaching of a particular discipline have to be rooted in the intellectual substance of that particular discipline. Biglan (1973) even cautions about the limitations to the transferability of practices from one area into another with a different subject matter.

Jenkins and Healey (2000) suggest that institution-based generic teaching and learning programs for new teachers in higher education are a common occurrence in many countries, and acknowledge the need for them. However, they also argue that there is a need to supplement such courses by discipline-based courses, and point to the fact that individual disciplines have their particular concerns, which cannot be addressed from a generic perspective. Healey (2000b) suggests that the combination of teaching methods and approaches varies between disciplines, and that the teacher should focus on assisting the students to learn the knowledge, skills and discourse of the particular subject. He further argues that the learning goals often vary between disciplines. Donald (1997) supported this argument by suggesting that the social sciences and humanities emphasise critical thinking and communication skills, whilst physical and life sciences focus predominantly on the learning of facts and principles.

These arguments formed the basis for the development of a discipline-based approach to teaching law in our higher education setting. To accomplish this, the Dean of the Faculty formed an Education Unit within the Faculty with an overarching task of supporting law-based teaching and assisting in continuous improvement of its quality.

Benefits and Challenges of a Discipline-Based Approach to Teaching in Higher Education: Example of the Graduate Certificate in Law Teaching Course

The overarching benefit as well as the main purpose of establishing an educational development unit within a particular faculty was the focus on the teaching and educational issues related to the particular discipline, in this case law. This approach enables the instructional design and development to focus on the specific disciplinal teaching and learning issues, rather than focusing on generic teaching and learning issues. To balance this focus, it is also necessary to recognize the potential risks of focusing on one discipline without accounting for the educational issues of other disciplines. There has been an attempt to achieve a balance between the needs and operations within a discipline and the advantages in collaborating with other disciplines. From its commencement, the Educational Unit has cooperated with the Centre within the Faculty of Medicine, Nursing and Health Sciences. Both Units have perceived benefits in cross-disciplinal cooperation in areas such as use of resources across faculties and widening curricular scope (Lawson, Kiegaldie, Webster, Jolly, & Thomas, 2004).

Since its beginnings, in 2000, the Unit has successfully run a significant number of discipline-specific flexible, online, predominantly distance learning courses. One such discipline-based course is the Graduate Certificate in Law Teaching (GCLT). It was specifically designed for those teaching law and law-related subjects at tertiary level who wish to enhance their professional teaching practice. This two-year Course is offered part-time and flexibly delivered—partially face-to-face and partially online using computer and other communication technologies.

There were a number of benefits of this course. For instance, the development of a community of teachers within the Faculty became evident soon after the commencement of the course. Teachers discussed issues relevant to their discipline and higher education within the formal structures of the course. In addition they also continued to informally discuss issues relevant to their teaching in the corridors and staff rooms of the university environment. There was a supportive group structure where issues could be discussed in a non-threatening environment.

Assessment tasks were also aligned with participants' own teaching and many of the projects and pieces of assessment work were incorporated or trialed in their teaching allocations, immediately bringing benefits to the students in a relatively short timeframe. These improvement projects are often difficult to initiate in higher education settings due to the competing demands of research targets and other priorities. The development and implementation of this course can also be viewed as a quality development project within the Faculty, as well as providing a structured and contextualised approach to staff development.

For the law teachers, the gaining of a formal qualification has been perceived as a further benefit. This qualification has provided them with a formal higher education teaching qualification that they could transfer to other academic positions, both nationally and internationally. This would acknowledge their teaching in countries where a higher education teaching qualification is becoming mandatory.

Finally, the developers of this course who had previously worked in educational development at a Central University level, the course provided a meaningful long-term relationship with the Faculty staff on which to build teaching expertise. The satisfaction of this longer-term relationship and the benefits of a structured course seemed more efficient and had greater impact than short-duration generic teaching and learning programs.

Apart from benefits, there were also some challenges perceived whilst running the course. One of the key challenges of this particular online course was to encourage the individual law teachers to share their understandings of teaching and learning practices. In addition, creativeness, innovativeness and openness to review was encouraged throughout the course. The course encouraged the learners to network, and transfer understandings from one "sub-community" of practice culture to another.

Strategies that were adopted in the development and running of the GCLT Course to ensure relevance to the discipline included:

- Continuing involvement of selected Faculty of Law staff in the key stages of course and unit design, implementation and evaluation;
- Encouraging experienced and recognized teachers (i.e., recipients of the Vice Chancellor's Distinguished Teaching Award) of the Faculty of Law to teach in the Course;
- Using feedback from the previous course to inform the quality development process for the next offering of the course.

Appreciation of the Discipline-Based Approach by the Law Teachers' Community of Practice: Example of the Assessment of the GCLT Course

Arguably, the significance of a discipline-based approach to teaching was expressed by the law teachers themselves who demanded running a law-specific course for teacher professional development. This discipline-based approach differed from the University-based generic course of teacher development for teachers from a wide range of disciplines. Also, a majority of the GCLT course content was specifically focused on law-related teaching issues, rather than issues that would apply to tertiary teaching in general.

The course has been evaluated on a unit-by-unit basis using online evaluation software *E-valuate-IT*, where students submitted their surveys online after completing individual units. The surveys consisted of multiple-choice and open-ended questions. Overall, the evaluation of the GCLT course was positive. The participants felt that the course had encouraged them to reflect on their own teaching practices by exposing them to the feedback of others, and made them more open to trying new teaching methods, including flexible and online delivery. Some participants have found that the online environment is an effective organisational tool for their teaching and learning. They also appreciated the friendly and stimulating environment of the online mode complemented with face-to-face sessions.

At the end of the course, the students were asked to write their reflections on their experience with the course. Their reflective stories offered valuable feedback in terms of positive features of the course but also identified areas where some alterations should be made. Apart from the general appreciation of the disciplinal focus of the course, the participants in this first cohort identified some significant positives, including the flexible delivery of the course, which was perceived generally as "very helpful" and well-suited to their diverse teaching, research and administrative responsibilities. They appreciated the fact that they could manage their workloads around their "other less flexible commitments," and this provided them with time to reflect on unit materials and come back to them later if they needed to. They found the Web-page structure for the units "easy to work with," and considered the readings, activities, and so forth, incorporated into each Module "self-contained," and the accompanying information sufficient "without being too cluttered." They also appreciated the information sharing and feedback within their groups, and being able to access other group members' work online or in face-to-face sessions. Appreciation of the cooperative aspect of the group work was also mentioned, and many pointed out the significance of the combination of the online work with face-to-face sessions, as many thought that each of these would not work particularly well with each other. Another very positive outcome of the course was that the students continued reflecting on and discussing their teaching approaches with their law colleagues even outside their classes. A few participants in the first cohort also identified some areas that needed improvement, such as the technical issues. Participants sometimes experienced problems in accessing the course and its individual parts online. This was mostly due to a consequence of the inevitable complex system downtimes that occur.

The Worldviews of the Law Teacher and the Instructional Designer: Two Distinctive Communities of Practice

Through teaching the GCLT course and discussing law-related teaching issues with law academics, we observed certain distinctive features in their worldviews. For instance: What was unique about their disciplinal views and their own worldviews of teaching and learning? A worldview according to Henson (1992) is the perception of reality based on central assumptions, concepts, and premises shared by members of a culture or subculture. Worldviews are encompassed in the stories that are told. Stories are one mechanism that reveal these views. We will illustrate these views through stories in the section on "Stories of Experience," where we introduce the stories of professional experience of the director of an instructional design unit, an instructional designer, and a law teacher.

The worldview or mindset of the law teacher has been shaped by the context in which legal education developed, and changed. For a long time discontent with legal education has been expressed in countries like Australia and the U.S. This concern has been expressed by Blasi (1995), Henderson (2003) and Schultz (1992). Blasi (1995) expressed concern that the knowledge of the "lawyering expertise" is not broad ranging within legal education. Law academics are knowledgeable about how lawyers acquire expertise in solving doctrinal problems, but neglect problem-solving abilities, expertise and judgment. He further argued that the majority of law faculties train novice lawyers for large legal firms. This means that the current educational system has the capacity to train legal clerks, scholars, law review editors and appellate advocates, but has largely ignored other areas of law. Blasi suggested that there was a disjunction between legal education and the legal profession, which some legal academics perceive as disturbing while others accept it as the status quo. The following is an alarming comment of a legal academic (quoted in Blasi) who accepts the status quo:

Law professors are not paid to train lawyers, but to study the law and to teach their students what they happen to discover. (Blasi, 1995, p. 326, note 5)

Blasi proposed that under the current conditions of high complexity and uncertainty, lawyers should be trained for the widest possible range of settings, and thus the teaching methods should reflect a wide range of perceptions and knowledge.

Henderson (2003) supports Blasi's view. By examining student perceptions of legal education, she points to law students' common complaints about what they learn and how they are taught. Students, for instance complain about:

- the over-emphasis on corporate and private-practice courses within the curriculum;
- lack of regular and meaningful feedback on their work;
- a grading system being minimally reflective of students' intellectual and lawyering capacities;
- issues addressed and skills taught at law schools being far removed from the everyday problems of lawyering practice, and so forth.

However, these concerns are also expressed by law academics, administrators and professional organizations. Henderson (2003) suggested that in many instances academics get blamed for the current state of legal education, which she found inadequate considering the large class sizes and also the pressure on academics to produce scholarly publications. Henderson perceived that part of the problem of the current legal education is that its educational purpose has changed: in the past the students formed a fairly homogenous group, whereas at present students form a highly diverse group in terms of age, class or gender. Another significant issue focuses on the institutionalization of legal education, that is, that present-day law schools are fundamentally academic institutions. She observed that the current practices of most law schools are based on tradition, not on a regular assessment of the needs of the public, students and the legal profession. She ascribed this factor to a combination of institutional inertia and financial disincentives for change. She proposed the restructuring of the law curriculum and pedagogy to focus on students' lawyering capacities, such as judgment capacity, communication capacity, and aspects of legal reasoning beyond case analysis. Henderson suggested that it is important that students develop these capacities in conjunction with learning legal doctrine and theory. She proposed the significance of continuous professional development of legal academics and teaching support for academic staff.

Many of the issues mentioned by Blasi and Henderson are further supported by Schultz (1992). She also highlighted the need for bridging the gap between legal education and the profession:

we cannot really teach students how lawyers think without teaching them at the same time what lawyers do. Thinking like a lawyer is a much richer and more intricate process than collecting and manipulating doctrine ... (p. 48)

Schultz (1992) highlighted the fact that current legal education should match the complexity of the legal world in which the students will need to function after they graduate. She also argued for the necessity of teaching "skills" and "substance" as complementary not separate skills:

What is known and understood is useless if it cannot be communicated effectively. Conversely, the communication process cannot be taught and refined without understanding what is to be communicated. (p. 66)

All the issues mentioned by Blasi, Henderson and Schultz have impacted on our Faculty of Law and thus shaped the worldview(s) of the law academics. In terms of the current trends within the Faculty of Law itself, we have also perceived a fairly strong tendency toward training students for large corporate and private firms. Students tend to complain about the lack of timely feedback, and they also find the issues addressed in classes are often removed from the everyday "lawyering experience." We are aware of large class sizes, and the pressure on academics to produce scholarly publications, which frequently prevents them from improvement and innovation in their teaching techniques. We agree with Henderson that some legal academics do not view any need for change or improvement in their teaching which supports the concept of the institutionalization of legal education. Therefore, some academics perceive law as purely an academic discipline.

If we compare the two communities of practice: law teachers and designers, we have observed some differences in their worldviews. Instructional designers are frequently comfortable in going into largely undefined domains of knowledge. They are often used to thinking broadly and attempt to see the bigger picture outcomes rather than the detailed analyses. This may not be the case of all instructional designers, but at least some will relate to such a perspective.

In comparison, the following are some observations that might be considered a part of the worldview of law academics that we have identified as contributing to the difficulty of instigating changes within legal education over the recent years:

- Looking for specific direction versus exploration;
- Having an adversarial approach;
- Requiring detailed direction;
- An emphasis on legal analysis at the expense of other practical legal skills.

There are also many outstanding teachers in our Faculty, who are faced with many challenges, including increased workloads; and their leadership and teaching has often been inspirational.

A Matrix of Activity of the Educational Unit: Multiple Aspects of Instructional Design

In a changing tertiary education climate that is dominated by funding issues, it is useful for a unit engaged in support to be independent and self-funded. We also found that credibility is achieved by having a teaching load in one's own right. To this end, the Education Unit in the Law Faculty have been engaged in a matrix of activities that ranged from teaching our own award courses, involvement in governance of the faculty, strategic projects, quality development, evaluation and course and unit development. The following is an overview of the range of activities in which the Unit has been engaged.

Teaching: A Professional Development Project for Law Teachers – Graduate Certificate in Law Teaching

The Graduate Certificate in Law Teaching was established, designed and taught by our unit. It has been developed for professionals involved in the teaching of law and law-related subjects. This qualification is recognised as a discipline-specific qualification as well as satisfying academic staff appointment probation requirements. The GCLT has been positively received by academic teaching staff.

Faculty Strategic Projects: Graduate Diploma in Legal Practice, Skills and Ethics

We were successful in a Faculty tender to develop a national program for legal professional accreditation with the Graduate Diploma in Legal Practice, Skills and Ethics. This provides students with the practical legal training to assist them to develop professional practice skills and gain professional accreditation on completion of their initial law degree.

Faculty-Wide Programs: Skills, Ethics and Research Program

This is a faculty-wide program, integrated through all four years of the undergraduate law degree. The Skills, Ethics and Research Program differs from other LLB units in that it is practice-oriented and the units are either integrated with host units or taught online.

Professional Development: Program for Judges

The unit developed an online program to assist judges and magistrates in their professional development with an emphasis on practical skills, recent legal developments, and related issues. The first program had the topic of "disability" as its focus. This program was developed for judges to enable them to identify discrimination against a person with disability, but also to respond to disabled participants in the court system. Aspects of this program have been particularly appreciated including the flexibility of the program, the way in which the program has built the students' awareness of the issues related to disability and the court system, and also the way the program has encouraged the students to instigate change. It has positioned the Faculty in good standing with its professional base.

International Projects: An Example of an Inter-Disciplinary Collaborative Online Program

In conjunction with another university, the unit collaborated in the development of an online program on the Psychiatry of Intellectual Disability offered by the Faculty of Medicine, Nursing and Health Sciences. This unit explores ways in which the specificities of any particular social, cultural and political context affect the learning experience of the program, and in their psychiatric practice with patients with intellectual disability. It has also generated an understanding of the need for a reflective approach to the teaching of the psychiatry of intellectual disability.

Quality Development

An important component of the development and design of all our programs, courses and units is the aspect of quality development. In our endeavour to constantly improve and monitor the quality of our programs, courses and units, we have found some useful tools, such as an online evaluation software E-valuate-IT. We employ this software to evaluate individual units and programs. E-valuate-IT enables us to create surveys for individual units, parts of programs or whole programs, depending on our particular need. After finishing a unit or a program the survey for that particular unit or program is distributed to individual students who can then fill in and submit their surveys online at a time that best suits them. When the students have submitted their completed surveys, E-valuate-IT enables us to generate a report on the basis of the submitted data.

Role in Faculty Governance

The role of instructional design and educational development was consolidated with the appointment of the director of the unit to the faculty portfolio for flexible learning, multimedia and information technology. This role oversees one of the six main organisational portfolios of the Faculty of Law. The director is a member of the Faculty Executive Committee, a member of the Dean's Team and has responsibilities that cover all key performance indicators (KPIs) of the faculty's strategic plan in the areas of information technology, flexible learning and multimedia.

The examples above represent a sample of the diversity of projects that the Education Unit has engaged in over a four-year period. The axis of activity might best be described as: governance, teaching, strategic projects, research, and course and unit development (the latter being a prime focus of traditional instructional design in tertiary education). In many of these activities, a leadership and management role is required. We perceive that it has been this diversity that has assisted us to establish ourselves in the discipline in which we work. It has further reinforced the teamwork required for success in complex projects in the higher education arena today.

Stories of Experience: Instructional Design Unit Director, Instructional Designer and a Law Teacher

In this section we will present three different stories of professional experiences concerning discipline-based instructional design: a story of the director of an instructional design unit, an instructional designer who has worked within that unit, and a law teacher who has undertaken the Graduate Certificate in Law Teaching (GCLT) program run by the unit. Our aim is to provide several "snapshots" of work within a discipline-based instructional design unit, including the receiving side of their services/support.

To disclose the individual professional experiences, we have chosen a story format, as we believe that stories enable us to present experience holistically in all its complexity and richness. Stories also recognize the temporal notion of experiences; the fact that experiences are not static and that they are influenced by other developments over time. What we reveal in our stories is always selective because our minds are selective, and thus they always choose aspects of our experience, which are significant or critical to us, and which we will subsequently attend to or disclose (Bell, 2002).

Story of the Director

It was one of those memorable phone calls that remain clear in my mind today, although it is now more than five years ago. As I listened to my phone messages, one caught my attention. As I recall the words were: "It's the Dean of Law here, I wondered if we might catch up to talk..." Within a few months I was a newly appointed Director of an Education Unit within the Faculty of Law.

From first contact it was evident that the Dean (who was also my supervisor) was highly supportive of instructional design. He acknowledged the specialized role of instructional design in supporting staff in development of their learning and teaching resources. He certainly had a vision for the future of the law undergraduate learning experience as well as postgraduate, professional practice and ongoing professional legal training.

Perhaps most important was the preparedness to allow the role to evolve. Although initially the brief was to support flexible learning, the involvement and roles broadened. My initial role description reflected the broad basis of the role in the faculty and it soon moved to forming a unit. The first appointment was made only a few months from my commencement in the Law Faculty. This occurred as a consequence, I like to think, of the shaping of the "human factor" that such functions have. There is no doubt that getting the right person is paramount, but then a degree of flexibility is needed to let the final shaping occur. Over a period of 12 months this occurred with a number of new directions incorporated into the formation of a unit.

As a consequence my assigned duties later broadened to:

- *establishing the unit within the faculty;*
- *contributing to the development, implementation and ongoing support of faculty policy for flexible learning;*
- *developing collaborative and positive relationships with Faculty staff to encourage adoption of flexible learning approaches;*
- *encouraging team-based approaches to development of flexible learning within the faculty;*
- *providing educational development advice regarding faculty flexible learning projects and initiatives;*
- *supporting legal education qualification provision through the Graduate Certificate in Law Teaching;*
- *contributing to staff development opportunities for faculty staff in flexible learning.*

(Stories of Professional Practice, 2005, extract)

Story of an Instructional Designer

It is now two years since I left the faculty. In looking back I have found the work I undertook there has been one of the primary influences on the way I operate in a different position in a different university with different staff.

What was Critical about the Graduate Certificate in Legal Practice, Skills and Ethics Project?

From my perspective the project brought together so many people who were walking in so many different shoes. The two universities involved had—in some respects—very different agendas, despite their "partnership," and the law firm had offices in each capital city and these reflected the culture and lifestyle of that city. Despite being a "National" company, each office was in many ways a world unto itself and this was recognizable in the students with whom we were working. And finally, within our own Law Faculty, the unit was not necessarily seen as belonging or having a shared entity. I did not get to know many of the "old hands" of the faculty very well. I had the pleasure of working with relatively "new blood," fairly new lecturers who, whilst they did carry the traditions of the law as a discipline, had not yet been moulded into an "academic" tradition.

If I was to note one particular characteristic, which "stood" out in the complexities with which we were working, it was the simple nature of change and change resistance. My experience did not indicate that the challenges arose because, as developers we were different and in many ways "unknown" with regard to law, but rather that academic tradition, and the generally perceived view of what an academic was, created far more resistance to our work than the factor of the discipline. I note this in reflection from my multiple experiences in an Education Faculty and currently working as a change agent. The work of educational development is extremely uncomfortable for a traditional academic who is used to dealing with the "teaching" part simply through the passive transmission of content as a "Sage on the stage." Flexible, online and alternate ways of teaching and learning take time, and often more time than the development and delivery of a passive content-focused one-hour lecture. In the eyes of the traditional academic, their priorities are research and other individual activities, which will promote their name and reputation, with teaching being seen simply as a minor priority which they have to do in order to bring money into the faculty.

Context

"Living" in a law faculty full-time, I think, would be different to being the "part-time" visitor. In some ways, I "lived" a chameleon life at that time. Many in my own Education Faculty were not quite sure what it was that I did. They could relate to my teaching responsibilities, and they knew I would always try and help them with "technological" things, but for the most part, the majority did not have real understanding of the nature of discipline teaching and learning per se. They too were predominantly disciplinary content specialists with the face-to-face mode of classroom presentation thrown in as the "teaching method." And this was perfectly understandable as the classes they dealt with were primary and secondary education.

Challenges and Strategies

In relation to what I have said above, I never felt uncomfortable with the law lecturers. As a major strategy I have learnt over the years—I am quite willing to play the role of the "novice"—when it came to the content. I would also play the role of the "student" so that when they were delivering and developing, I would ask—as a student—what and how, and so forth, they intended for me to learn...

Yes there were some who had no understanding of their students—but this was rare. Yes, there were times when some thought of us as "glorified general administrative staff"—but these were even fewer.

If I had one last comment it would be that lawyers were in the main easier to work with than educators. They did not have the pre-conceptions of educators ... For example, because I am an educator I am an expert in all things educational. They were willing to share and willing to learn ... and I think in most cases enjoyed "teaching" me!

(Stories of Professional Practice, 2005, extract)

Story of a Law Teacher (Reflection on the Graduate Certificate in Law Teaching Program Undertaken with the Unit)

From a personal point of view, self-reflection normally involves me reviewing all the doubts I have about my teaching abilities. I question whether my teaching is really improving at all. Do I do enough to facilitate learning, or am I a boring, uninspiring teacher? I suppose this is the whole idea behind reflective practice, and I certainly hope that the process of worrying about these things ensures that I am a more effective teacher!

The taxonomies we looked at are a useful reminder of the ideals of teaching and learning. I know I tend to assume that I know what these ideals are, but if pressed I doubt if I would be able to express all the considerations in, for example, Bloom's taxonomy. So reviewing some of these theoretical checklists certainly helped me to reflect on what, why, and how I do things (or don't do things). Certainly, one thing the course has helped with is to suggest some ideas as to alternative ways of conducting teaching and learning.

The subject's focus on learning outcomes forced me to actually think about what students should be taking out of courses, rather than simply focusing on my own teaching practices. This encouraged me to think quite critically about what law schools generally expect their students to learn, and how this measures up against my opinions of what life experiences students will have once they leave law school. There is a fundamental tension between these two expectations that I doubt will be resolved in the near future. Perhaps this needs to be a more express component of the subject. Assessment works the same way. I don't believe that exams are an effective form of assessment, yet they are so entrenched in law school culture.

Moving on from my reflections on some of the content of the course, I now want to consider my overall learning experience in this subject. First, I think the flexibility built into the subject was a bonus. Having the subject taught as an "intensive" certainly made it easier to fit into my schedule than would otherwise have been the case. The meetings were held at a good time, and seemed to be of an appropriate length for our purposes—that is, I think we were able to say everything we needed to say on each topic during the time provided.

I want to combine my reflections on the online aspect of the subject with our consideration of technology as a learning tool. I must admit I am very wary of the hype that surrounds promotion of technology as being automatically an improvement on, or different to, how things have been done in the past. In other words, technology must serve education, rather than the other way around.

Following on from this last point, and returning to my overall learning experience in this subject, I think it was the face-to-face meetings in this subject which brought everything together. At one level, the meetings were useful for getting concerns about my experience of teaching off my chest, for engaging in self-reflection. I think I would have been less effective at reflective practice without this interaction. At another level, our discussions enabled some comparing and contrasting of experiences and techniques that was extremely beneficial. I certainly felt able to be quite open about my criticisms of law school curriculum and assessment, although at times I was probably being annoyingly opinionated! These sessions alone would not have been sufficient, which I think goes to the point about the integration of different elements into a holistic learning experience. The combination of assessable and non-assessable tasks, the available materials, and the subject Web page, were all essential elements of the learning experience in the subject.

(Stories of Professional Practice, 2005, extract)

The three stories have attempted to provide a picture of how a discipline-based instructional design unit, in this case law-based, functions. The story of the director has portrayed the experiences of how it all started and developed and also reflected on the inevitable managerial side of discipline-based instructional design. The instructional designer has provided a "window" on the day-to-day practice of the actual discipline-based instructional design, and the law teacher has given a reflection on how the instructional design endeavours were received by the law community. The story of the director has highlighted the fundamental facts of sustaining an instructional design unit within long-established practices of a tertiary discipline, such as law. The instructional designer has also perceived the more institutional issues (such as being perceived as new, bringing about a change into long-accepted practices). The law teacher has admitted there is a need to reform current legal education, and that he appreciated the endeavours of the instructional design unit (e.g., the combination of flexible online teaching with the face-to-face mode of instruction, and the encouragement of reflection and critical thinking).

Issues of Acceptance

The story of the law teacher has emphasized the fact that there is a pressing need for instructional design support within the law discipline. The stories of the director and instructional designer have pointed out that the traditional instructional design issues have played only a minor part in their professional endeavours. The major issues focused on the institutional and political issues that have significantly impacted on their practice, because these were the fundamental issues of their "existence" within the discipline. Five years after establishment of the instructional design unit, it is still not possible to say that we have obtained the full support of all faculty staff and at times we feel we are walking on the "cliff edge" of existence. However, the experiences of our team do highlight a number of principles of acceptance.

The first is to be seen as teachers in our own right, equal to other academics, sharing the same challenges, pressures and systems as they do. We elected to do this through the establishment of an accredited course in teacher education for the discipline, the Graduate Certificate in Law Teaching. We replaced more traditional staff development approaches with this teaching responsibility and were brought into contact with many of the new and younger teachers in the faculty.

Our activities led us to engage with the professional community. This engagement was achieved by being involved in key projects of the faculty that led to postgraduate training and professional accreditation. This positioning with the professional practice base of the community in which we were situated led to further projects and in some cases successful tenders that brought income to the faculty. A cumulative effect of the above two issues was the generation of some funds for the faculty, which was beneficial to our standing in the faculty.

Perhaps the most important issues in relation to acceptance were the human factors. Much of this related to forging new relationships and working in a collaborative and cooperative manner. This entailed working with both general and academic staff as well as leadership at all levels. Communication is a key skill for any instructional designer and our context in a discipline-based learning and teaching environment was no different.

When selecting teaching staff for the projects we were engaged in, we were careful that the teachers were always acknowledged as experts in the particular field of law. We took considerable care in ensuring this role was clear and respected, and that it was an important feature of the teamwork we were trying to inspire. It seemed necessary that the teachers had the respect and a sense of being valued in what they were trying to achieve.

Finally, there was the timeliness and value of the advice that we were able to provide. We were able to draw on resources and offer advice. This ranged from ways of evaluating their subjects and courses to various instructional features and strategies that assisted them in achieving their stated outcomes. Perhaps the most valued aspect of this advice included safeguarding and preventing academics from making mistakes that could possibly damage their academic credibility amongst their peers.

In summary, we constantly worked on the acceptance factor of our unit and our own work. The recent incorporation of the unit's instructional work into the faculty leadership structure has been a substantial step towards recognition and faith put in us by the faculty.

Conclusion

This story has attempted to shed some light on the "life" and functioning of a small instructional design unit within a Faculty of Law of one large university. The story started from the acknowledgment of the significance of discipline-based instructional design, which led to the establishment of the instructional design unit.

Benefits of a discipline-based approach to teaching in higher education include:

- establishment of a community of law teachers
- immediate incorporation of some of the assessment tasks into their own teaching allocations
- gaining of formal qualification, or provision of long-term relationships with faculty staff with the designers.

All these factors have been highlighted through the example of the Graduate Certificate in Law Teaching course. Some challenges (such as sharing of understandings between the academic staff belonging to different "sub-communities" within the faculty) have also been identified. An appreciation of the discipline-based approach has also been indicated through the assessment of the law teaching course. It was highlighted that the law teachers demanded the running of the course. They appreciated its flexibility, information sharing and group feedback and the combination of online and face-to-face modes.

The story has compared the worldviews of a law teacher and instructional designers. These stories were set against the background of the current legal education issues, which influence the mindset of law teachers. The story has also taken us through a range of projects and aspects of work of the instructional design unit (strategic projects, national projects, project evaluation, unit's role in the faculty governance). This chapter has briefly examined three stories of the director, an instructional designer and a law teacher. We also examined the issues of acceptance of the unit within the law faculty, which remain the most pressing issues impacting on our instructional design practice. The factors that have assisted us to gain acceptance and be valued by the law community include the "diversity of activities" and having "equal academic standing and responsibilities" to other academics in our faculty. This story has many further chapters.

References

Bell, J.S. (2002). Narrative inquiry: More than just telling stories. *TESOL Quarterly*, *36*(2), 207-213.

Biglan, A. (1973). Relationships between subject matter characteristics and the structure and output of university departments. *Journal of Applied Psychology*, *57*(3), 204-213.

Blasi, G.L. (1995). What lawyers know: Lawyering expertise, cognitive science, and the function of theory. *Journal of Legal Education*, *45*(3), 323-398.

Donald, J. (1997). Improving the environment for leading: Academic leaders talk about what works. In M. Healey (Ed.) (2000a), Developing the scholarship of teaching in higher education: A discipline-based approach. *Higher Education Research and Development*, HERDSA, *19*(2), 169-189.

Boyer, E.L. (1990). *Scholarship revisited.* Princeton, NJ: Carnegie Foundation for the Advancement of Teaching.

Healey, M. (2000a). Developing the scholarship of teaching in higher education: A discipline-based approach. *Higher Education Research and Development, HERDSA, 19*(2), 169-189.

Healey, M. (2000b, February 4). How to put scholarship into teaching: What good practice needs to be shared and understood. *Times Higher Education Supplement.*

Henderson, B.R. (2003). Asking the lost question: What is the purpose of legal school? *Journal of Legal Education, 53*(1), 48-80.

Henson, L. (1992). *The momina theme of life: Developed biblically, theologically and contextually.* Master of Arts program. School of World Mission, Fuller Theological Seminary, Los Angeles.

Jenkins, A., & Healey, M. (2000). Getting disciplined: Geographic perspectives. *HERDSA News, 22*(1), 11-13.

Lawson, M., Kiegaldie, D., Webster, L., Jolly, B., & Thomas, I. (2004). Educating professionals: Synergy in developing an online unit about assessment and evaluation for legal and health professional educators. *Educacion Medica, 7*(3), 109.

Rice, E.R. (1995). Foreword. In R.M. Diamond & B.A. Adam (Eds.), *The disciplines speak: Re-warding the scholarly, professional, and creative work of faculty* (pp. v-vii). Washington, DC: American Association for Higher Education.

Schulz, N.L. (1992). How do lawyers really think? *Journal of Legal Education, 42*(1), 57-75.

Stories of Professional Practice: A collection of stories. (2005). Faculty of Law, Monash University.

Chapter XIV

Introducing E-Learning in a Traditional Chinese Context

Pamela Pui Wan Leung, Hong Kong Institute of Education, Hong Kong

Abstract

This chapter describes an attempt to introduce e-learning to a group of language teacher educators in a traditional Chinese context. It reports on the strategies adopted in a one-year teaching development project, responses of participants, typical instructional designs generated and the causes for innovation-decision. It argues that even in a context with a strong transmission tradition, an ordinary member can still function as a "change agent" in diffusing teaching innovation and developing a focused learning community. By revealing the process and results of the attempt, the author hopes that other practitioners can continue to explore feasible ways of stimulating active learning in both teachers and students. Lessons learned from this study may also enable instructional designers to gain a better understanding of how to promote their work in similar cultural contexts.

Introduction

Despite a long history of being an international city, Hong Kong has a dominant Chinese population. Chinese is the official language and Chinese Language is a core subject in the school curriculum. Because of the ethnic background of the society, learning or teaching Chinese has never been confined to the study of the language system. Instead, it covers a broad scope of literature and culture, which includes the transmission of traditional values and the cultivation and appreciation of Chinese culture in its entirety. As a result, teachers of the subject have generally been perceived as relatively conservative or resistant to innovation.

With the rapid development of information technology, various disciplines are under pressure to adopt online facilities to promote learning. Although the use of technology does not imply an automatic enhancement in learning quality, the emergent shift to a new mode of communication is gradually transforming learning and challenges the traditional ways of teaching and learning Chinese in Hong Kong. Among the eight local tertiary education institutions, which have all embraced e-learning of some kind, none of their Chinese language related units seem to be making an effective use of online facilities. Lecturing, group discussion and tutorials are the key learning activities in the course descriptions. Teaching and learning of Chinese appear to be conceptualized mainly in terms of traditional face-to-face teaching approaches.

In order to generate a meaningful environment for learning Chinese with information and communication technologies (ICT), this chapter makes a novel attempt to introduce e-learning to a "community of practice" (Wenger, McDermott, & Snyder, 2002) in Chinese language teacher- education. It reports on the strategies used by the author for introducing e-learning ideas to a group of teacher educators of Chinese, responses of participants, typical ways of "blended learning" (Bates & Poole, 2003) and the causes for the innovation-decision.

The case study examines the ways in which e-learning can be possibly introduced in a context with a strong transmission tradition. The approach is particularly meaningful because the course participants were either in-service teachers or prospective teachers. Their e-learning experiences can have a profound impact on their future instructional designs, implying ultimate changes in the teaching and learning of the traditional school subject. Once the seeds of e-learning are sown in the field of Chinese, fellow practitioners can continue to explore feasible ways of stimulating students to learn more actively. The lessons learned from this implementation may also serve as a reference for instructional designers promoting their work in similar cultural contexts.

Background

The role of ICT has become prominent in most education sectors because it increases access and flexibility for both learners and teachers. A review of the literature shows that ICT can facilitate active learning, provide meaningful experiences and promote lifelong learning (Damoense, 2003; Grabe & Grabe, 2004). By combining online learning with face-to-face approaches, "blended learning" suits most learning needs in various contexts (Aldrich, 2004; Bastiaens, Boon, & Martens, 2003; Bates & Poole, 2003; Jochems, van Merriënboer, & Koper, 2003). Yet partly because of the technical skills required for establishing an e-learning environment, some teachers still follow the transmission model of instruction, resulting in limited student participation and limited student responsibility in the process of learning and teaching.

In recent years, more well-designed and user-friendly e-learning management systems have assisted online teaching and learning. To optimize learning effectiveness through technology, the Hong Kong Institute of Education (HKIEd) launched an online system (Blackboard) on-campus in 2003. It was through this opportunity that the author learned about the value of adopting ICT in fostering deep learning. Since then, e-learning has become an integral part of the teaching activities of the author. Nevertheless, similar changes did not take place automatically in other modules taught on the same campus. In particular, because most new technologies were first launched in English, the teaching and learning of Chinese and related subjects were perceived as a conservative domain to which technology was least relevant.

To persuade colleagues teaching Chinese that it is worth using the online facilities to stimulate active learning, this author volunteered to launch a teaching development project. It was hoped that more teaching members could make use of the learning support tool to create meaningful learning and teaching experiences, and in the long run, set examples for practitioners in the field.

The process of introducing e-learning to language teacher-educators in this case echoes Rogers' (1995) notion of diffusion of innovation. According to Rogers, the rate of adoption of innovations depends on a range of variables including perceived attributes of innovations by individuals, types of innovation-decision, communication channels, nature of the social system and extent of the change agents' promotion efforts. As the "diffusion" process in this case was generated mainly from an enthusiastic member, not all variables suggested by Rogers (1995) were applicable to the process. Nevertheless, the results of this study show that an ordinary member can become an effective change agent within the social system and cultivate a small "community of practice" (Wenger et al., 2002). In one year, e-learning has progressively diffused across programmes, optimizing student learning of Chinese and related subjects.

Although packaged with new technologies, the true value of e-learning should not be limited to grasping technological skills. Bates and Poole (2003) reiterate that the question of teaching with technology is about serving learners and not about using technology. To succeed in implementing e-learning, Jochems et al. (2003) suggest that pedagogical, technological and organizational aspects have to be taken into account.

The literature has repeatedly emphasized the importance of pedagogy in e-learning (see Seale, 2003). Good (2001) identifies many required components of e-pedagogy and suggests that the e-learning pedagogue needs to include conventional pedagogy, online awareness, the ability to plan and manage events online, comprehension of the current and future potential of technology, and the ability to interweave technology into the instructional design. Bates and Poole (2003) suggest that key elements of quality in teaching with technology include content, course planning, instructional design, media production, support and moderation of the learning experience, student administration, course evaluation and maintenance. Overall, the pedagogical considerations behind online activities should be no less than those behind face-to-face teaching. The core concern is about how technology can be used effectively to assure quality learning. The question to follow is: what is valued as learning in different disciplines?

In general, there are different orientations to pedagogy, for example, traditional pedagogy, social constructive pedagogy and transformative pedagogy (Cummins, 2005). The traditional pedagogy focuses on transmission of information and skills, whereas within social constructivist approaches, learners are encouraged to construct meanings and become cognitively engaged in challenging projects and activities. Nevertheless, both traditional and constructivist pedagogies tend to focus on instructional rather than the social dimensions. By contrast, transformative pedagogy aims to prepare students to participate fully in shaping their societies. Although Cummins (2005) argues that a transformative pedagogical orientation works the best for promoting academic language learning, he also suggests that it is more appropriate to see these three orientations as points on a continuum.

To promote e-learning in a discipline dominated by traditional approaches to teaching, it seemed more appropriate to introduce alternatives such as the social constructivist approaches. Rosenberg (2001) argues that successful e-learning depends on building an appropriate strategy that optimizes the technology in growing and sustaining a new learning culture. In particular, the foundation for establishing such a learning culture lies in drawing a clear distinction between *"instruction"* and *"information"* (p. 13). If teachers cannot distinguish between the need for information and the need for instruction, and how they work in tandem, e-learning may be confined only to technology-delivered learning.

Following the above line of thinking, the teaching development project reported here "shepherded" members' evolution from transmission of knowledge to technology-enhanced teaching and learning. A few strategies, based on the principles for cultivating communities of practice developed by Wenger, McDermott, and Snyder (2002, p. 51) have been useful in "spreading" e-learning among a group of teacher-educators of Chinese. In this chapter, e-learning refers to learning through ICT such as computers, Web pages, virtual classrooms, and so forth. The focus is on specific learning outcomes rather than transmission of specific knowledge. Since most members were beginner users, e-learning was still perceived as technology-delivered learning, but the ultimate aim of this project was to introduce technology-enhanced learning in Chinese language and related subjects.

Case Description

The Context: Institutional Mission, Departmental Tradition and Individual Enthusiasm

Established in 1994 by combining the former Colleges of Education, the HKIEd is the only government funded higher education institution dedicated solely to the upgrading and professional development of teacher-education in Hong Kong. The Institute provides master and undergraduate degree, post-graduate diploma and a range of in-service programmes to around 7,000 pre-service students and serving teachers. Trained graduates from the Institute serve the more than 2,000 early childhood, primary and secondary schools in Hong Kong.

The prime focus of the Institute is on teacher-education. All programmes offered are relevant to the local education context. Chinese language is a core subject in the school system. The Department of Chinese is the largest academic unit with around 60 teaching staff, offering more than one hundred modules in language, literature, culture and language teaching methods for participants who aim to become educators in the early childhood, primary or secondary sectors. In general, traditional Chinese teaching emphasizes knowledge-telling from the teacher to students, and teaching by the teacher as an example. Following the traditional approaches, teachers in a Chinese context are not likely to adopt teaching innovations which appear to reduce the transmission of knowledge and set "poor examples." Therefore, practices in the Chinese department situated in a Chinese context may represent a particular cultural thinking about teaching and learning.

Because of the ethnic background, Chinese is the first language of most Hong Kong people. In addition to developing language skills, Chinese language education has its widely recognized mission of fostering traditional Chinese thoughts and thinking in students. Often, traditional Chinese values and moral thoughts are conveyed through exemplary writings of distinguished authors. Therefore, teaching materials are mainly derived from literary works, and the teaching approach leans towards a transmission model. Understandably, most teachers of Chinese, including teacher-educators, were taught and trained to teach in this tradition.

Although Chinese studies are occasionally considered as "traditional" in a negative sense of being old-fashioned, the teaching staff of the Department of Chinese enjoys a very good reputation among course participants. Their subject expertise and commitment to quality teaching are highly respected. However, given the limited hours of contact and the extended requirements for teachers under the ongoing education reform, teaching expertise of individuals within the transmission tradition alone can hardly facilitate participants to meet the new expectations of learning and teaching in a dynamic era. In fact, similar problems also exist in other departments.

The need to assure that the quality of teacher-education meets the needs of future teachers is unquestionable. The HKIEd launched its first online management system called NextEd in 2001. However, due to various reasons, the system had not motivated academic staff to use the e-learning environment. In 2003, Blackboard was introduced by the newly established Centre for Integrating Technology in Education. Workshops for staff and students were organized and more members of the Institute learned about the operation of the new technology. Most participants in the training workshops were mainly enthusiastic individuals looking for stimulating ways of fostering students' engagement in the learning process. There was no Institute policy that made it a requirement for teaching staff to teach with the new technology, but there were opportunities for academics to expand their teaching repertoire with it. For instance, there was financial and technical support for staff to contextualize the use of the information management system in different disciplines.

Fascinated by the "magical" functions of the new technology, this author and a few enthusiastic colleagues had adopted the online system primarily for saving the cost of printing lecture handouts. There was no open exchange of experiences in using the new teaching resource for promoting learning, perhaps no one had ever thought about its ultimate educational value.

Serious discussions on the topic began only when the application for a departmental staff development project was supported by the Institute in fall 2004.

Although the Department supported the funding application, the author as an ordinary member initiated the project. The author perceived such an opportunity as an invaluable chance to learn and obtain support, which would eventually benefit both members in the Department and course participants. In response to the local education reform, the need to improve the quality of teaching was widely accepted among the members. To make a genuine difference from the existing practice, members were encouraged to work collaboratively to gain mutual support. Because the idea was proposed by an ordinary member with frontline practical experiences, the project focused mainly on consolidating members' conceptions of alternative approaches to learning and the computer literacy required for using the technology. Most members welcomed this "practical approach," which unlike the "top-down" policies, they found useful and easy to follow.

Methods: Cultivating a Community of Practice

Establishing a Secure Learning Atmosphere

Compared with disciplines taught in English or languages other than Chinese, the development of computer literacy among staff teaching Chinese and related studies is relatively slow. This was partly because most computer operations were first launched in English and most Chinese teachers are less proficient in English. On the other hand, even when Chinese software became popular, it is laborious to learn to input Chinese because the structure of traditional Chinese characters is very complex. Users have to memorize different parts of a character represented by different keys on the keyboard. Typing Chinese is much more complex than typing English. As a result, most Chinese teachers are not motivated to develop computer literacy in Chinese. With the development of various input methods, the situation has changed progressively in the last decade. More Chinese teachers are beginning to use computers and the "diffusion" of ICT in the discipline has become easier.

To introduce the online teaching aid in such a context, nothing could be taken for granted and every step had to be handled carefully to avoid misunderstandings. First, the author had to reiterate that it was a departmental project, and it belonged to the department as a whole. All members were welcome to join and there was no pressure on individual members. The only condition was that members were expected to commit to sharing their experiences in teaching with the technology. As long as members were willing to try, the project was available to provide assistance. The project itself was a learning activity, which aimed to enhance professional development.

Arranging a Mediator Between Technology and Subject Teaching

For members who were less familiar with information technology, it was crucial to convince them that information technology can be a useful tool in teaching and learning. With the funding obtained, the project employed an assistant to provide prompt technical support door-to-door to members' offices. The members welcomed this because they could receive direct advice on solving their particular problems. They did not even need to spend extra time on attending training workshops because the assistant could attend on their behalf and informed them of the techniques that were most relevant to their teaching. More importantly, because technical assistance could be provided on an individual basis, members could learn at their own pace without feeling embarrassed for burdening the advanced users in the Department. At the end, the assistant became an in-house consultant in teaching with technology, helping members to transform teaching materials into digital formats, demonstrating the operation of the system in class, preparing operational guidelines in Chinese, and clarifying uncertainties about communicating with course participants through the online system. In essence, the assistant's individual support contributed directly to fostering members' confidence in using the perceived-to-be complex information management system. In our experience, a technical assistant with a subject background was a significant benefit in the diffusion of the teaching innovation.

Creating Opportunities for Self-Actualization

Teacher-educators' commitment to teach well is not in doubt. The members were eager to participate in the project to set examples for course participants. Lasting for 12 months, the project period covered two regular semesters and a summer semester. Preparation and promotion were needed in the first semester when members were not familiar with the technology. From the second semester onwards, most members could experiment with the technology fairly independently. They also liked to share their own experiences because they wanted to know what went on in other classes. The workflow was similar to the development of an action research project.

As shown in Table 1, in the early stages the project sought to explore members' needs and general perceptions. Then there were two departmental seminars to prepare members for making their innovation-decisions. The core project team made an attempt to keep members well informed of the action plan and to encourage them to choose strategies that suited their teaching. We also disclosed the steps and results of the pre-project survey. Through the semi-formal departmental sharing, the less experienced members could learn about the possibilities and challenges of teaching with technology and how different they are from the traditional practice. At the same time, "in-house" and public presentations offered opportunities for the experienced members to develop a sense of identity in promoting good practices on dif-

Table 1. Major activities of the teaching development project

Stage	Activity
I	A pre-project questionnaire survey for teaching staff
II	Departmental seminars in the first semester
III	First round of focus groups with course participants
IV	Departmental, institutional and international presentations
V	A post-project questionnaire survey for teaching staff
VI	Second round of focus groups with course participants

ferent occasions. In the second semester, some members were invited to share the wisdom in their teaching with a wider audience. Lastly, the project also obtained feedback from the course participants through focus groups and created a "win-win" situation for the members to reflect on their practice. Our experiences not only led to improvement of teaching in the department, but also contributed in a more general way to the teaching of Chinese.

Hatching a Frame of Reference for Examples to Generate

In the process of introducing the new technology, the project team was aware of the importance of learning about the application of ICT. Without a distinct concept of how technology can be used to facilitate teaching and learning, the objective of using technology could easily be reduced to using technology for its own sake. During the project, Salmon's (2003) model of teaching and learning online through computer mediated communication (CMC) was popular on the HKIEd campus. The author then played a role of elaborating the "trendy idea" in the department. Although the notion of CMC was novel to many members, Salmon's (2003) comprehensive framework did provide a set of step-by-step procedures for users to follow. It covers five stages of development "access and motivation, online socialization, information exchange, knowledge construction, development" and their relations to the level of interactivity. Members with different experiences could easily find a position which best described the level of their practice and achievement. As a result, the model served as the main frame of reference for the project.

Nevertheless, the most effective way of situating Salmon's (2003) theoretical framework in context is to provide concrete examples. Convincing examples should demonstrate that the framework is applicable to various aspects of teaching in a specific discipline. Evolving naturally, the author approached members who showed interest in making better use of the new technology for developing examples of practice. Eventually, we set-up a core team of four members to develop examples in teaching Chinese linguistics, literature, culture and teaching methods. Besides developing examples, the core team also worked toward a sharing session at an international conference at the completion of the project. The team members collected and analyzed messages from online discussions in the relevant modules, reviewed the relevant literature, and became involved in frequent informal idea exchanges. Although the team did not know a great deal about ICT or CMC, it practiced cooperative learning under a simple belief, that is, as long as the instructional designs were in-line with the learning objectives, they were teaching alternatives.

Regardless of the levels of learning achieved (Salmon, 2003), the four team members all exemplified different ways of adopting the online system for creating additional learning opportunities. The instructional designs not only reflect the extent of adopting ICT in each case, but also indicate the members' innovation-decisions as subject experts. The designs are not detailed lesson plans but they represent the members' judgments of when and how to incorporate ICT into teaching particular subjects. The characteristics of each attempt are illustrated in Figures 1-4.

Figure 1 represents a core team member's first attempt to enrich his teaching with CMC. The module was "Introduction to Modern Chinese Language and Culture," which aimed to foster student ability to analyze how culture is represented by language use. The participants were Year One student teachers from various backgrounds, for example, arts, science,

Figure 1. An initial attempt to prepare students for online learning in a culture module

10 face-to-face lectures	Open Forum 1	To propose a topic for the study of language culture
		Online moderation
		Face-to-face feedback in class
	Open Forum 2	To identify a tentative essay topic
		Online moderation
		Face-to-face feedback in class

commerce, and so forth. For the students, studying specific topics on Chinese culture in higher education was a new experience and most of them were typical passive knowledge recipients. Given the typical nature of the module and the characteristics of the participants, the members aimed to explore more learning opportunities with ICT. He expected to achieve three objectives:

- To familiarize the participants with the operation of the e-learning system
- To facilitate the participants' grasp of the concepts of "culture" and "language culture"
- To foster an active learning atmosphere among the participants.

At the end of the module, these three objectives were guiding principles for evaluating the results of the "teaching experiment."

In addition to the weekly face-to-face lectures, the member familiarized his class with the new mode of learning by initiating two consecutive online open forums. The themes of the forums were designed to engage participants in the post-lecture discussion on cultural topics. Through online discussions, he hoped that the participants could clarify and consolidate their ideas for the term essay. The "layers" of each forum indicate a cycle of communication between the member and the participants. On the one hand, the member played a central role as an online moderator, promoting meaningful online discourses and balancing their participation. On the other hand, he sought every in-class opportunity to clarify any misunderstanding in the face-to-face context. Although the students operated at a lower level of socialization, the participants still relied on the tutor's guidance and instructions. The new technology enabled him to understand what the participants had learned and it allowed him to provide prompt feedback and monitor their learning progress. He was satisfied with the participants' performance in pursuing the deeper meaning of cultural phenomena discussed in face-to-face lectures.

The second example related to the teaching of a linguistic module by the author. The module "Chinese Grammar and Logic in Linguistics" is for Year Two participants. It aims (1) to provide basic grammatical knowledge of Chinese for the participants and (2) to foster their ability to analyze student writing from a meta-linguistic perspective. Corresponding to these objectives, the participants have to complete a written examination and submit an analysis of primary student writing for assessment.

It was the second time I taught the module with ICT. In the previous year, I set up a group-based learning platform to provide regular online exercises on grammatical categories and a discussion forum for the participants to ask questions. Although most participants (over 90%) finished (and redid) the 22 online exercises, their response to the discussion forum was poor. To better facilitate conceptual understanding, active learning and knowledge building (Bates & Poole, 2003; Berg, 2004) and "mediate" participant attitude toward the learning of the subject (Laurillard, 1993), I revised the online setting to focus on mediating learning through CMC.

Among the four parallel groups taking the module, I was responsible for teaching one group of participants. In order that all participants of the module could benefit from CMC, the teaching team agreed to minimize the extra workload of other tutors. I set-up discussion venues for different occasions: there was a macro-forum, which was open to all tutors and groups. There was also a group-based forum for each group chaired by individual tutors. Last, within Group 3, I arranged two specific online tasks to stimulate discussions among the group participants (see Figure 2). As the main content of the module comprised knowledge of modern Chinese language, the participants needed to grasp the basic linguistic concepts before they were able to discuss the application of those concepts. This application included analyzing language structures, and consisted of a sequence of online multiple-choice exercises, which were designed to prepare the participants for discussion. Again, the online exercises were much better received than the discussion forums. Most participants completed the exercises after each lecture for revision. The discussion forums became venues for the participants to question the correct answers and obtain feedback in the exercises. Overall, although I attempted to promote exchange of learning experiences across groups, without a basic teacher-student relationship, responses in the macro-forum were not satisfactory. The participants appeared to attach only to their group tutor and peers within the same group. The online facilities in this case functioned merely to motivate the participants to study the subject content. It will certainly take much more time than 10 weeks of lectures for the participants to develop a meta-language for discussing the appropriateness of using the Chinese language.

Figure 2. A pattern for promoting online discussion in a linguistic module

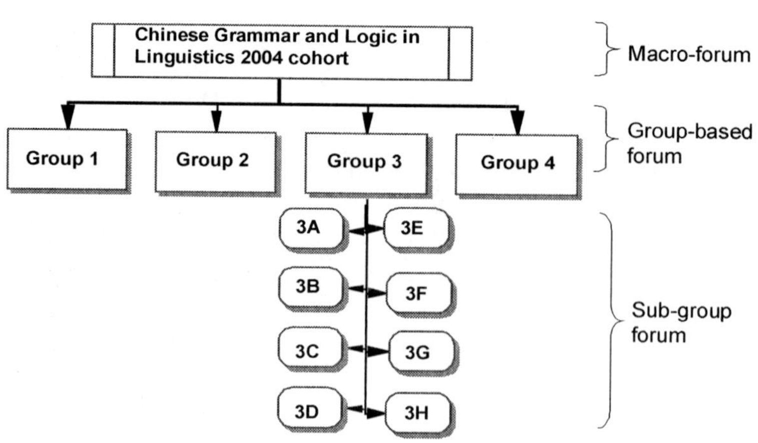

According to Salmon (2003), the next two examples reached the higher levels of learning, that is, information exchange and knowledge construction. As shown in Figure 3, the third example was about a Putonghua (Spoken Mandarin) methods module provided for Year Two student teachers before they attended teaching practice. The module aimed to familiarize the participants with different language teaching approaches and deepen their understanding of the underlying principles. The major activities in the module include try-out teaching and peer review of try-out teaching. The member was willing to experiment with ICT because most participants in the past were passive and the teaching of the module was ineffective even in small groups. The design was in fact based on the old content of the same module.

In order to extend classroom learning and enhance interactions with the participants, the member organized a sequence of "blended learning" activities. Before the try-out teaching, she uploaded video clips of actual teaching by in-service teachers online for the participants' observation and review. The participants then had to complete a prescribed review form for recording afterthoughts on the observation. Throughout the module, the participants worked in small groups both during the face-to-face lectures and online. They took turns and played different roles as teacher, pupil, observer and assessor.

Within each group, the participants exchanged their views in the process of developing an "instructional design" for try-out teaching. Once a group completed the discussion and the design draft was refined, the member then commented on the soft copy and returned it to the group concerned for follow-up in the face-to-face discussions. At the same time, another group would comment on the peer design. After a few rounds of revision, the member uploaded the final version of the design for sharing among the participants. In addition to the instant feedback on try-out teaching in class, all the participants could review the teaching processes because the member uploaded the recording after class. In particular, the "teaching group" had to review the recording for reflection, and the "commenting group" had to provide online feedback for peer-assessment.

Figure 3. An instructional design for online learning in a methods module

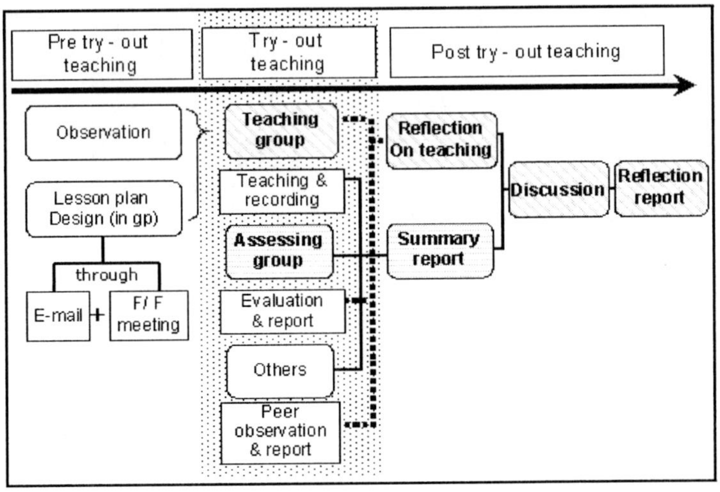

Although a similar practice had been in place without the online facilities, the use of the online facilities now provided a systematic approach. If time allowed, this member could design more effective principles for guiding the participants through the observation, lesson design, try-out teaching and peer review of the teaching process. The accumulated records of discussions allowed the participants to review and reflect on the development of their understanding of teaching. This relatively successful experience has strengthened the member's confidence in using technology in her teaching.

The fourth example was a design for learning in a children's literature module (see Figure 4). Similar to the third example, the member guided the participants through a carefully structured process from individual learning to collaborative learning. After reading extensively on a set of prescriptive poems, each participant identified one favorite poem, articulated their initial thoughts and shared these thoughts with other students in a small group of four. Each group then needed to negotiate and decide on one best poem and report on the discussion result. The member's role in monitoring the learning process was to provide the reading materials, to moderate discussion and organize the discussion results for online sharing. In Bates and Poole's (2003) words, it was a facilitative, observant but background role, focusing on the students' own thinking processes and collaborative learning. As the participants possessed various personal views in analyzing literary works, CMC facilitated them to broaden their perspectives in sharing with others. Because the subject content did not require as much fundamental knowledge for discussion as in the linguistic or culture modules, there was no right or wrong answer and the participants were more confident about expressing their thoughts and feelings. When a consensus was reached within a group, the participants developed a relatively comprehensive view of literary analysis. According to the member, the participants became more critical in reading other literary works as well as poems. While this last example was the most mature in bringing the participants to a higher level of learning (knowledge construction), it constituted only a small part of the module learning. The member made use of the online facilities not only to supplement additional references for the module, but also to provide supportive conditions for the participants to construct their own way of analyzing and appreciating literary texts. The example demonstrated the great

Figure 4. An instructional design for online collaborative learning in a literature module

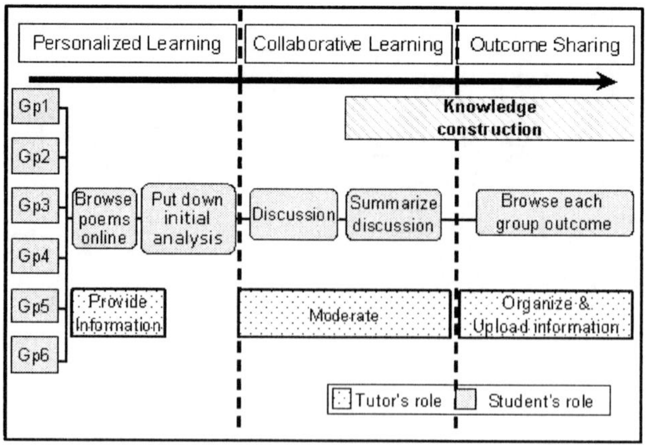

potential of CMC in engaging the participants in meaningful dialogue, which formed an integral part of learning, particularly in literary subjects.

The above preliminary instructional designs, which are generated from authentic teaching situations, are remarkable outcomes. As subject matter experts, the core team demonstrated how to recreate the learning potential inherent in lectures of varied nature, that is, culture, linguistics, teaching methods and literature. Our attempts set concrete examples for both fellow colleagues in the Department and teachers of Chinese in general. The essential message was that the quality of learning in these modules could be enhanced with ICT, and the kinds of learning enhanced through ICT might not occur in traditional approaches to teaching. Therefore, the teaching of these Chinese subjects should not be confined to the transmission model.

Evaluation

Undoubtedly, online learning has progressively encouraged both the tutors and the participants to reflect on the role of traditional teachers. Although the core team of the project provided examples of technology-enhanced learning in Chinese, not every member in the Department perceived the same need to make any change. Throughout the project, the causes for innovation-decision were investigated through focus groups with course participants, and questionnaire surveys of members in the Department.

On the participant side, we conducted two rounds of focus group discussions at the end of each semester to collect qualitative feedback on online learning. Forty-seven representatives from modules using the online system attended. Given a tutor's clear expectations and commitment in the communication process, the participants in general welcomed the increased flexibility and the extended interaction with tutors. Some participants reflected that they were motivated by peer responses and had become more attentive in live lectures. Among the available online functions, the increased sources of references online, such as hyperlinks to relevant Web sites, were considered the most exciting. Many participants browsed the online modules and downloaded teaching materials [Use_Lit104][1]. Some were willing to participate in or watch open online dialogues [SelfMo_Pth308]. Accordingly, they were able to learn more independently at their own time and own pace [SelfMo_Cult407]. In addition, some participants seemed to have gained a better understanding about their role and responsibilities in online learning. For instance, a representative at the focus group remarked:

He (the tutor) did not participate (in online discussion). I suppose he did not want to interfere with the discussion among us...If he did, no one would continue the discussion. [TRole_Cult307]

Compared with modules not using online learning, these modules encouraged the participants to think more deeply through online discussions. Our findings are consistent with studies in the literature (e.g., Inglis, Ling, & Joosten, 2002; Saunders & Pincas, 2003; Spector, 2005).

Nevertheless, as this is a novel practice, different sorts of related problems reported in the literature also existed (e.g., Jochems et al., 2003; Mortera-Gutierrez, 2004). Some participants admitted that online learning required a higher level of self-discipline. If they were not committed in the discussion process, learning would not occur automatically. Since the participants met almost every day and attended weekly lectures, they often queried the necessity and effectiveness of communicating online. The following are two typical remarks:

A ten-minute discussion with the tutor in lecture might mean thousands of words online (I wonder if the online discussion is cost-effective...). [Time_Lit208]

Once it took me more than an hour to read all the messages. I had not logged on the forum for only one week (It was not easy to cope in the online learning environment). [Time_Pth905]

Repeatedly, the major hindrances for the participants to appreciate learning online were time and commitment. In some cases, the participants thought that neither they nor the tutors were prepared to adopt the facilities for teaching and learning. According to these participants, much so-called online learning does not have much substance. Some tutors did not update the teaching materials regularly and did not seem to care about online discussion, suggesting that online learning was "incorporated" mainly because it was "fashionable." Most tutors seemed to be able to manage the basic operation of the system. However, other than delivering the teaching materials online, they had not been able to do much else.

On the other hand, it was evident from the focus group discussions that most participants were passive knowledge recipients. They looked to the tutors as sources of information and authority. They wished to receive nicely typeset handouts instead of having to print out only the most relevant online information [Info_Lit108]. For instance, if handouts were disclosed online beforehand, some participants would be less motivated to attend the lecture [Dmotiv_Pth106]. The participants' perception of learning as receiving knowledge (information) from the tutor was further verified by their neglect of the introduction of the online system. Some participants had never attended any training workshop nor had they read any user manuals, although some of those were translated into Chinese especially for them. Worse still, those who were not familiar with Chinese input methods perceived CMC as a complete waste of time and an obstacle to their study. Many participants did not respond to e-mails.

As would-be or serving teachers, the participants' learning experiences would affect their teaching in different ways. ICT has started to have a major impact across different educational sectors. The in-service participants who refused to adopt our new learning initiatives did not use the online system in their serving schools. They insisted that traditional teaching is more direct and they could not afford extra time to adapt to the new system. Nevertheless, they did realize that the new initiative was attractive to students. They could see students discussing online if the discussion forum was managed by other people. By and large, managing online learning in addition to daily teaching was perceived as an extra burden among schoolteachers of Chinese. For instance:

I seldom used (online communication facilities). We met everyday. Why couldn't we distribute the assignments and notes straight away and work at once? [Com_Pth809]

If I start an online forum, I will have to respond from time to time but I really have no time. I think the idea of online learning is good, the Institute tutors used it well, but I might not follow... In my school, only the panel chairs responded at discussion forums. I hardly responded, unless the question was explicitly addressed to me. [Com_Pth110-112]

Surprisingly, some in-service participants were more experienced in using online facilities than the tutors because a number of primary and secondary schools had long adopted online learning. In these schools, students could submit their work online and the teachers could provide feedback by various electronic channels. However, according to a participant, school students were not motivated to open-up themselves at discussion forums. This might be due to the different stages of personal development. Most secondary school students were interested in chatting casually but not in discussing serious topics. The participant's concern was that school students would not tell the teacher the truth [SSt_Pth709].

We have found that most participants indicated that exchanging ideas with peers was stimulating and stated that they would try this approach with their students in their future practices.

On the teacher side, the core team conducted two questionnaire surveys to collect the 58 members' perceptions of using the online system in the Department. The first one was in September 2004. A total of 55 members returned the questionnaires (response rate = 94.8%). The second one, conducted in June 2005, attracted only 24 respondents (response rate = 41.3%).

Since the introduction of the online system in 2003, there has been a continual increase in the number of tutors involved. In 2003-2004, only 25.8% (n=15) teaching staff in the Department registered twenty modules for online learning. In 2004-2005, about 75.8% (n=44) staff and 172 modules were involved in learning online. This seems to suggest a rapid increase even though most of the modules were offered in two different semesters respectively.

Initially, most members adopted the online system because it saved the cost of printing handouts and facilitated communication. The online system was often used to post announcements and display course materials. The main concerns among these members were technical skills and copyright related to digitalizing materials for uploading purposes, and so forth. Towards the end of the project, six members (25% of respondents) reported that they had incorporated online learning in six modules (i.e., a total of 36 modules). Concerning the amount of time spent on managing the online learning environment, 14 respondents (58.3%) indicated that they spent less than four hours per week to monitor the participants' learning. For these members, the most challenging aspect was the poor response from the participants. Among the enthusiastic members, the online system has become an integral part of their teaching, 18 respondents (75%) indicated that they would continue to use the system because it is user-friendly and convenient. Six members (25% of respondents) insisted that they would not adopt online learning at all because they were satisfied with their teaching and had no extra time to develop online learning.

Regarding the incorporation of online learning and its impact on module learning and teaching, feedback from the tutors and feedback from the participants were mutually complementary. At the initial stage of adapting to the change of the role of traditional teachers, both parties needed to know more about the potential of the new technology before they could strike a balance between fashion and function. Obviously, this teaching development project has boosted the spread of the innovation. The increase in the number of enthusiastic members in the Department indicates that the nature of learning in the discipline has been gradually transformed, and changes to the role of traditional teachers have subtly taken place. Given more time and examples, more and more experienced subject experts should be able to make use of information technology in enhancing the quality of learning in the Chinese modules. Those members who refused to change must face the reality that learning is becoming more dynamic and they are risking the possibility of missing out on opportunities for innovation and improvement (Saunders & Pincas, 2003).

Conclusion

This chapter described how to cultivate a community of practice in Chinese language teacher education through a teaching development project, and examined the causes for innovation-decisions.

In terms of changes to the overall on-campus models of teaching and learning, the project did not seem to have accomplished much. Online activities were supplements to live lectures and the Blackboard system was mainly used for provision of online materials. However, the impact of the introduction of e-learning on traditional teaching should not be underestimated. Most users in the first place might be distracted by the prefix "e" (for electronic or technology) in "e-learning," but as time goes by, more people understand that the focus should lie in the root of the word "learning" (Oliver, 2003). The pedagogic potential offered by online facilities to improve aspects of face-to-face lectures does not involve the technology, but the alternative modes, knowledge, skills and even attitudes to learning that participants can develop. In this project, the spread of the innovation stimulated not only the subject tutors but also the course participants to reflect on the role of teachers that they play.

To conclude, despite a strong transmission tradition, an enthusiastic "insider" (Wenger et al., 2002) was possibly an effective "change agent" in introducing teaching innovation such as incorporating online learning into traditional teaching. In addition to personal enthusiasm, the "change agent" had to be highly sensitive to the teaching and learning traditions in the context. Special attention has to be paid to the planning, resourcing and the implementation of the project through the principles of EACH:

*E*stablishing a secure learning atmosphere

*A*rranging a mediator between technology and subject teaching

*C*reating opportunities for self-actualization

*H*atching a frame of reference for examples to generate.

Because the members could try out the innovation before they fully committed themselves to adopting it, they were less resistant to its introduction (Rogers, 1995). As a result, the project established a collaborative learning environment to facilitate both cognitive and social scaffolding (Trinidad & Pearson, 2004), enabling members in a teaching department to become progressively more involved in the project and sustain their commitment and interests. To gain quality and efficiency for the spread of innovation, it was important to treat the members (teachers) as learners. As Oliver (2003) suggests, teachers cannot "learn" simply by being told what the technology is, they have to gain experience and contextualize it within their own practice in order to make sense of it. In Davison's (2005) words, "Practice is an effective teacher, and community of practice an ideal learning environment" (p. 10).

An effective way to support learning in a community of practice is to provide a variety of authentic examples. Often, the examples may not necessarily be flawless. As long as an example is developed in the direction of establishing a peer collaborative learning process for all participants, it is relevant. The four preliminary instructional designs outlined in this project are not individual lesson plans. Rather, they illustrate the core team's attempts to structure activities for participant learning throughout the course of particular studies. Ranging from individual work to group exchanges, the integrated online components were carefully organized to maximize the effectiveness of learning collaboration. The participants tackled different tasks after lectures and increased knowledge and critical skills through interactions with peers and the tutor. In most cases, they understood some preliminary data, grasped some basic skills, applied their understanding and arrived at some generalizations. The instructional designs in this case were stimulants rather than sample standard practices. With good planning and realistic expectations, both teachers and learners can benefit from the online learning environment.

References

Aldrich, C. (2004). *Simulations and the future of learning: An innovative (and perhaps revolutionary) approach to e-learning*. San Francisco: John Wiley & Sons.

Bastiaens, T., Boon, J., & Martens, R. (2003). Evaluating integrated e-learning. In W. Jochems, J. van Merriënboer, & R. Koper (Eds.), *Integrated e-learning: Implications for pedagogy, technology and organization* (pp. 187-198). London; New York: Routledge Falmer.

Bates, A.W., & Poole, G. (2003). *Effective teaching with technology in higher education: Foundations for success* (1st ed.). San Francisco: Jossey-Bass.

Berg, G.A. (2004). *The knowledge medium: Designing effective computer-based learning environments*. Hershey, PA.

Cummins, J. (2005). Using information technology to create a zone of proximal development for academic language learning: A critical perspective on trends and possibilities. In C. Davison (Ed.), *Information technology and innovation in language education* (pp. 105-126). Hong Kong: Hong Kong University Press.

Damoense, M.Y. (2003). Online learning: Implications for effective learning for higher education in South Africa. *Australian Journal of Educational Technology, 19*(1), 25-45.

Davison, C. (2005). Information technology and innovation in language education (introduction). In C. Davison (Ed.), *Information technology and innovation in language education* (pp. 3-22). Hong Kong: Hong Kong University Press.

Good, M. (2001). On the way to online pedagogy. In J. Stephenson (Ed.), *Teaching and learning online: Pedagogies for new technologies* (pp. 165-174). Sterling, VA: Stylus Publishing.

Grabe, M., & Grabe, C. (2004). *Integrating technology for meaningful learning* (4th ed.). New York; Boston: Houghton Mifflin.

Inglis, A., Ling, P., & Joosten, V. (2002). *Delivering digitally: Managing the transition to the knowledge media* (2nd ed.). London: Kogan Page.

Jochems, W., van Merriënboer, J., & Koper, R. (Eds.). (2003). *Integrated e-learning: Implications for pedagogy, technology and organization.* London; New York: Routledge Falmer.

Laurillard, D. (1993). *Rethinking university teaching: A framework for the effective use of educational technology.* London: Routledge.

Mortera-Gutierrez, F. (2004). Faculty best practices using blended learning in e-learning and face-to-face instruction. In G. Richards (Ed.), *Proceedings of World Conference on E-Learning in Corporate, Government, Healthcare, and Higher Education 2004* (pp. 845-850). Chesapeake, VA: AACE.

Oliver, M. (2003). Looking backwards, looking forwards: An overview, some conclusions and an agenda. In J. Seale (Ed.), *Learning technology in transition: From individual enthusiasm to institutional implementation* (pp. 147-160). Lisse/Abingdon/Exton, PA/Tokyo: Swets & Zeitlinger.

Rogers, E.M. (1995). *Diffusion of innovations* (4th ed.). New York: The Free Press.

Rosenberg, M.J. (2001). *E-learning: Strategies for delivering knowledge in the digital age.* New York: McGraw-Hill.

Salmon, G. (2003). *E-moderating: The key to teaching and learning online* (2nd ed.). London; New York: Routledge Falmer.

Saunders, G., & Pincas, A. (2003). *Learning on-line on campus.* Winchcombe, UK: Learning Partners.

Seale, J.K. (Ed.). (2003). *Learning technology in transition: From individual enthusiasm to institutional implementation.* Lisse/Abingdon/Exton, PA/Tokyo: Swets & Zeitlinger.

Spector, J.M. (2005). Time demands in online instruction. *Distance Education, 26*(1), 5-27.

Trinidad, S., & Pearson, J. (2004). Implementing and evaluating e-learning environments. In R. Atikinson, C. McBeath, D. Jonas-Dwyer, & R. Phillips (Eds.), *Beyond the Comfort Zone: Proceedings of the 21st Annual Conference of the Australasian Society for Computers in Learning in Tertiary Education* (ascilite) (pp. 895-903). Perth, Australia.

Wenger, E., McDermott, R., & Snyder, W.M. (2002). *Cultivating communities of practice: A guide to managing knowledge.* Boston: Harvard Business School Press.

Appendix

I. A Sample Mission Statement Extracted from the Official Web Site of a Department of Chinese of a University in Hong Kong (http://www.hku.hk/chinese/)

The primary role of the Department of Chinese is to promote the understanding of Chinese language, literature and history; to further the ability of students in the use of the Chinese language; and to study the development of Chinese civilization and its place in the modern world.

II. Questions Used in Pre-Project and Post-Project Surveys for Faculty Members (originally in Chinese)

Pre-Project Survey

1. Have you ever used the e-learning system provided by the Institute?
2. In how many modules you taught, have you made use of the e-learning system?
3. Have you incorporated e-learning again when you teach the same module? If so, in how many modules have you done so?
4. Which technical functions of the e-learning system have you used?
5. What are the effects of adopting the e-learning system?
6. Can the system support the educational technologies you used to use?
7. What are the educational technologies you used to use?
8. How much time per week would be needed for you to maximize the function of the system in enhancing teaching?
9. What are the difficulties in using the e-learning system?
10. What measures have you adopted to overcome these difficulties?

Post-Project Survey

1. Have you used the e-learning system provided by the Institute in this academic year?
2. In how many modules you taught, have you made use of the e-learning system?
3. Please rank the technical functions of the system according to the frequency you used.
4. Please rank the effects of adopting the e-learning system according to their importance in your teaching.
5. How much time per week have you spent on maximizing the function of the system in enhancing teaching?
6. Please rank the difficulties in using the e-learning system.

7. What measures have you adopted to overcome these difficulties? Was it successful? Why?
8. Will you continue to use the system in your teaching? Why?
9. Has this project influenced your decision on using the system? How?

III. Questions Used in Focus Group Discussion with Course Particpants (originally in Chinese)

1. How often do you visit the online platform of your module(s)?
2. How long do you spend on each visit?
3. Which technical functions of the platform do you use most?
4. Which of these functions do you find most useful? Why?
5. Have you encountered any difficulty in using the platform? Why?
6. Do you have any suggestion for overcoming these difficulties?

IV. A Sketch of the Use of the E-Learning System in the Chinese Department in this Case:

Academic Year	Module registered	Staff involved
2003-2004 [whole year]	20	15
2004-2005 Semester I	89	44
2004-2005 Semester II	83	38

Note: There were altogether 61 teaching staff at the time of survey. Most of the modules offered by the Department were taught in the first semester of 2004-2005. The decrease of modules registered for using the e-learning system in the second semester correlates with the actual number of modules then offered.

Endnote

1 All focus groups were tape recorded, transcribed verbatim and coded according to the module types and the themes emerged in the discussions. For instance, [Use_Lit104] indicates that the theme was on the use of ICT in learning and teaching, and the opinion was from a participant in a literature module, which appears in line 104 of the record. Other coding categories quoted are as follows:

- Themes Emerged in Focus Groups:

  [SelfMo] Self-motivated

  [TRole] Tutor's role

[Time] Time

[Info] Course information/Teaching material

[Dmotiv] Demotivated

[Com] Communication

[SSt] School student

- Module Types:

[Lit] Literature

[Pth] Putonghua (Mandarin/Spoken Modern Chinese)

[Cult] Culture

Chapter XV

Exploring the Nardoo: Designing Problem-Based Learning Experiences for Secondary School Students

Sue Bennett, University of Wollongong, Australia

Abstract

This chapter examines how instructional designers work together in teams to solve problems. It examines the advantages and disadvantages of a team approach to instructional design. This case will explore how a team of instructional designers worked together to create Exploring the Nardoo, *a multi-award winning CD-ROM developed by the University of Wollongong's Educational Media Laboratory (emLab). The case describes key issues related to the design and development of the package from the perspective of a faculty-based multimedia unit, which was established with a strong emphasis on advancing research through innovations in design.*

Introduction

Instructional design is often a process by which an individual designer works closely with a subject matter expert to collect and adapt content for the development of instructional materials. Examples of the types of problems solo designers might face are included in cases (Ertmer & Quinn, 2003), descriptions of design paradigms (Visscher-Voerman, Gustafson, & Plomp, 1999), and instructional design books (Reigeluth, 1999). Research into the instructional design process is also available in works such as the early research by Perez and colleagues (Perez & Emery, 1995; Perez, Johnson, & Emery, 1995) and, more recently, Keppell (2000). Comparatively, little attention has been paid to questions about how teams of instructional designers work together. For example, what happens when instructional designers work in teams to solve problems, and what are the advantages and disadvantages of a team approach to instructional design?

This case will explore how a team of instructional designers worked together to create *Exploring the Nardoo*, a multi-award winning CD-ROM developed by the University of Wollongong's Educational Media Laboratory (emLab). The case describes key issues related to the design and development of the package from the perspective of a faculty-based multimedia unit, which was established with a strong emphasis on advancing research through innovations in design. The case is based on extensive primary research by the author, which was originally carried out to develop an online case for students in a postgraduate course at the University of Wollongong. The data collected and analysed to develop the case included interviews with four of the instructional designers on the team, archival documents and research papers.

This case offers a unique perspective of this well-known project by revealing the experiences of the designers, which provides a behind-the-scenes view of the negotiations and decisions made during the development of the project. The case sets these experiences within the real-life situation of the project, and describes the strategies the designers used to address the problems and how these led to the solutions chosen. The case also draws out principles that can be derived from these experiences and the "lessons learned" by these instructional designers. These will provide insights for other instructional designers grappling with similar issues or situations. The case also explores the "communities of practice" concept from a different perspective by considering the community of practice created by the project team and the influences of external communities of practice with which team members identify.

Background

The notion of "communities of practice" was first introduced by the work of Lave and Wenger on situated learning (Lave & Wenger, 1991). In their conceptualisation, a person builds expertise by gradually becoming a part of a community of practice. This process moves the person from legitimate peripheral participation to full participation. These ideas have sparked interest in how learning environments can be designed to provide "contexts in which learners ... can practice the kinds of activities that they will encounter outside of schools" by situating "authentic activities within the environmental circumstances and surroundings that are present" in the real world (Barab & Duffy, 2000, p. 30). Understanding the nature of these communities and how they are established and maintained is of particular interest in the areas of professional preparation and professional development, for which the notions of enculturation and knowledge sharing seem particularly relevant. This is evidenced by the recent interest in *online* communities of practice (cf., Barab, MaKinster, Moore, Cunningham, & the ILF Design Team, 2001; Conceição, Sherry, & Gibson, 2004; Cox & Osguthorpe, 2003; Herrington, Herrington, & Kervin, 2005). Communities of practice are also being suggested as a strategy to foster the exchange of ideas and the formulation of new thinking in business and government (Snyder, Wenger, & de Sousa Briggs, 2004; Wenger, 2004).

In essence, the "community of practice" concept invites alternative ways to think about how knowledge is shared and created by groups of people. Communities of practice exist in a myriad of forms, and may be formal or informal in their membership and means of interaction. A key characteristic is that "people in communities of practice share their experience and knowledge in free-flowing, creative ways that foster new approaches to problems" (Wenger & Snyder, 2000, p. 140). Some communities exist for a limited time, for example to solve a particular problem. Other communities are more persistent, perhaps formed because of the mutual interests or concerns of their members. All communities of practice are underpinned by common beliefs, practices and assumptions, many of which are implicit (Barab & Duffy, 2000).

Communities of practice are also relevant to understanding how instructional designers work. Instructional design often occurs within a team context; this is particularly so for large projects and those that require specialist technical and production input. The collective effort required involves instructional designers working with subject matter experts, graphic designers, programmers and audio-visual specialists. This usually requires collaboration between team members from different organisations, or from different groups within an organisation. While such teams may be created formally by management, they often have a more informal beginning as members are gathered because of their expertise and availability. Wenger and Snyder (2000) suggest that such groupings are more likely to become a community of practice. These project teams become communities of practice.

In addition, the members of the project team will also identify with other communities of practice that align with their professional expertise. Working on design projects enables members to apply their professional knowledge and skills, but also to develop new knowledge and then disseminate this back to their community of practice. In this way the professional community is sustained and transformed, a further characteristic identified by Barab and Duffy (2000). These notions of communities of practice are considered in this case from the perspectives of four instructional designers who worked as part of a larger team on a major educational multimedia project.

Case Description

Context

In the early 1990s there was a great deal of interest and activity in designing interactive multimedia for education, and an emerging awareness of the potential of Internet-based learning. Teachers and designers had begun to discuss how constructivist approaches to learning might be realised using the new technologies that were becoming available. There had, however, been little implementation of these ideas. Most multimedia applications of the time still reflected the instructional tutorial model associated with earlier modes of computer-assisted learning. It was into this environment that *Investigating Lake Iluka* was released in 1994. This CD-ROM based resource presented learners with a simulated lake environment. It allowed students to explore various ecosystems, and make physical, chemical and biological measurements while investigating ecological issues. Following *Investigating Lake Iluka's* release, its designers from the University of Wollongong's Faculty of Education were approached by the New South Wales Department of Land and Water Resources to create a similar package. This initiated the development of *Exploring the Nardoo.*

Exploring the Nardoo brought together a government department and a faculty-based design and development unit to create a learning resource aimed at secondary school students. The work was carried out by a multi-disciplinary team, which included instructional designers, subject matter experts, graphic designers, programmers and audio-visual consultants. The project drew together a range of expertise, with team members bringing their own values and assumptions to the project. Furthermore, the design team included instructional designers who were also research and teaching academics within the Faculty, and instructional designers who were secondary school teachers. While a community of practice formed within the context of this project team, the participants also identified with other communities of practice, such as communities focusing on instructional design, educational research, school education, scientific research, public dissemination of science, graphic design, and technical development. This created a complex dynamic that fostered innovation and, on occasion, produced conflict.

Initiation of Project

The project began in early 1994 with discussions about the nature of the proposed project and the budget. The Department of Land and Water Conservation (DLWC) wanted to develop a CD-ROM package to complement a wider campaign to improve awareness of water conservation issues. The target audience would be secondary school students, who would then hopefully take the message home to their families. Having been impressed with *Investigating Lake Iluka*, the DLWC envisaged a similar resource. The university-based designers, however, saw the project as an opportunity to improve on their previous work and to implement some new ideas. The initial discussions took place between two key personnel from the university and several representatives from DLWC. After extensive consultation over a period of three months, a project proposal was produced that formalised the basis for contractual arrangements between the parties. This document established the timeline, stages and milestones; provided a detailed costing; identified technical issues; and described the expertise of the proposed design team (which drew on the team that created *Investigating Lake Iluka*). In essence, this proposal represented the shared understanding developed in the initial stages of the project, and once it was accepted the project could begin.

Design of the Product

The basis for the design of *Exploring the Nardoo* is underpinned by two key principles: (1) that the package would support learning through setting the information and activities within a relevant context; and (2) that learning would be driven by exploration and problem-solving.

The first of these principles was applied through the way information was structured and presented in the package. Drawing on the concept of an "information landscape" (Florin, 1990), the package is centred around an inland water catchment. The catchment is presented through four time periods, ranging from a pristine environment through to the present day, and in four regions along the river's length. The river is presented graphically, and learners can investigate various locations by clicking on objects embedded in the landscape, such as a town or a factory, to access related information. This information may take the form of radio, newspaper or television stories, the results of measurements within the river, or descriptions about plants and animals found in the area. By navigating from the source to the mouth, learners can explore the way different activities impact on the river environment. By moving through the time periods, learners can see how those activities have changed with habitation and development of the valley. Learners can also visit the Water Research Centre, which is represented using an illustrated office interior. By clicking on objects in the office, learners can access further information. In implementing the information landscape approach, the designers hoped to create an intuitive interface encouraging learners to explore a source of rich information presented in a variety of realistic formats.

The second key design principle—that learning should be driven by exploration and problem solving—is integrated through a range of water management investigations, related to both natural events and human impact. These investigations are supported not only by the information made available through the landscape, but also through a number of support tools and strategies. Guides in the form of three staff members in the Water Research Centre introduce the scenario and invite learners to choose from the investigations. They also offer guidance and suggestions based on the investigation selected. Simulations allow learners to explore issues related to blue-green algae, dam management and household water use by entering and manipulating variables. As learners move through the river environment they can gather information and personalise their notes using a personal digital assistant (PDA)—an innovative tool originating from the program. The PDA allows students to copy, paste and type in text, and to link to other types of media. An integrated presentation tool allows learners to develop a comprehensive response to an investigation that can incorporate the textual, graphic, audio and video resources they have collected. In addition, genre templates are provided to scaffold learners' argumentation.

Design and Development Process

After the acceptance of the proposal, the team spent four months on an initial period of design work. They first developed a design brief. The main purpose of this document was to identify links to the curriculum and to map these, in general terms, to the problems and the accompanying support tools and strategies. These ideas were developed further and incorporated into a design statement, which described the overall scope and nature of the package and its features. As the first project milestone, the design statement was an agreed sign-off point and, like the project proposal, it represented the shared understanding at that stage of the project. This document was the result of much consultation with the DLWC and a great deal of discussion amongst the members of the design team.

Prior experience both as educators and as designers of educational software had taught the team that learning resources are only used when there are clear links to the curriculum, enabling teachers to more easily see the applicability of the resource to their teaching. Furthermore, research and evaluations conducted on the use of *Investigating Lake Iluka* in the classroom had helped the design team to identify some deficiencies in the package that they could address in the design of *Exploring the Nardoo*. Feedback from both teachers and students indicated that the problems needed to be introduced at the beginning of the package and be easily accessible to encourage the learners to get involved with the tasks. Students also wanted to be able to edit their notes directly in the package and to incorporate the media resources. The copy-and-paste notes feature from the earlier package was transformed into a sophisticated multimedia notebook and presentation tool that allowed learners to edit their text and link to portions of resources as quotes. Another issue was that students needed more support in solving the problems, and so the guides and genre templates were introduced.

The designers also drew inspiration from the emerging literature associated with constructivism, situated learning, interactivity and the role of computers as cognitive tools. They began to put some of the ideas from this body of conceptual literature into practice. Technology was also changing rapidly and this allowed new technical options to be considered. As the literature and technology were developing, so were the ideas of the team and these impacted on the design of *Exploring the Nardoo*. For example, one designer indicated that the team had lengthy discussions about the best way to convey the context and that they talked about the nature of the river landscape at nearly every meeting in the early stages of the design. The underpinning concept and usability issues were hotly debated. This process enabled the team to consider a broad range of alternative options as a means of encouraging innovative thinking. In the words of one designer, *if you don't start broad and then narrow it in and don't pay attention to ideas as they come along, you can miss some good ideas*, and *you need to have a store of ideas that you can tap into in case something doesn't work.*

The PDA also became a significant focus for design discussions. Initially, the designers saw the PDA as an extension of the note collection feature in *Investigating Lake Iluka*, which was based on a book metaphor. It soon became apparent, however, that with the text editing and presentation functionality needed in the PDA, it would be more like a hand-held electronic device. At the time, the Apple Newton had recently become available, along with a range of other hand-held electronic organisers, games and devices. Team members brought in pictures from catalogues to generate ideas for the appearance and functionality of the PDA. As it took shape the PDA also became the solution to two other problems the team was having with the design. It became a means to play audio-visual resources, and so eliminated the need for the Water Research Centre to contain an extra room intended for this purpose. This move simplified the structure of the package and reduced the amount of graphic design work needed. The PDA was also adopted as a means of navigating through time periods in the river environment, replacing an earlier design idea which would have seen learners navigating through vertical layers and digging further down to go back in time. Opinions had been divided on the usefulness of this metaphor, despite considerable discussion about it and testing of the concept on paper. Both of these PDA functions represented a significant departure from the realism of the information landscape, a dilemma that, as one of the designers suggested, demonstrates the tension between being true to a metaphor and "stretching it to take advantage of what a computer can do." This stretching of the metaphor is also apparent in the hot links and scrollable windows used in an on-screen representation of a book in this package.

In describing the process by which *Exploring the Nardoo* was created, the designers repeatedly recalled the need to be flexible and adaptable during the process. It is apparent that the designers were driven by the desire to introduce further innovations beyond what they had achieved in their earlier work, but also beyond what had been developed by others. They convey a sense of this project as breaking new ground in terms of design, and because there were few precedents, there was often no obvious design solution. One of the designers reflected that there were many possible ways in which some design problems could have been solved, and he found this both exciting and scary.

It is also clear from the way this project is described that the development work occurred concurrently with the design. During the early stages of the project the focus had been on the design work that would be formalised in the design statement, however the team needed to take care that it could deliver the design ideas proposed. The designers realised early in the project that the commercial multimedia authoring software they had used to create *Investigating Lake Iluka* was too limited to support many of the new features they envisaged for *Exploring the Nardoo*. At the time, the only solution was to develop their own software tools, which would allow much greater design freedom. And so, even in the early stages of the design, the programmer was testing the viability of some of the functionality proposed. After the design statement had been submitted and signed off by the DWLC, the challenge of implementing the design really began. At this stage there was simultaneous design and development as new ideas were tried and compromises were negotiated.

Nine months of work was required to develop the first prototype, which was the second project milestone and sign-off point. After a further four months, formative evaluation with school students was conducted. It was during these stages in particular that some of the constraints became apparent and impacted on the design of the product. All of the designers interviewed spoke of both the wealth of design ideas developed and the enormous content resources provided by the client. It was a challenge to the whole team to determine what would and what would not be included in the package. The budget was the most obvious limitation and this in turn limited the amount of time that could be devoted to the project. This meant that some content was not included; for example, only three of the six planned simulations were included in the final version. Some features were also modified, for example the simulations that are included contain fewer hints than the team had planned.

Team members also had to develop some new skills to achieve the project goals. For example, the main graphic designer had only just begun to use some of the software tools required and was having difficulty keeping pace with the project requirements. A decision was made to bring in another graphic designer on contract to assist. Advances in the technology also meant that the programmer had new challenges as well as new opportunities. At the time, drag-and-drop functionality was just beginning to be widely used, but there was a significant problem in implementing across platforms. A delay of around five months ensued while this was being resolved. Changes in the nature of the project also meant that some priorities changed. The most obvious example of this was the influence of the publisher—who the team had started negotiations with while developing the prototype. This added pressure on the team to ensure that the product was commercially viable. As a result, the project team was required to develop an increased level of teacher documentation to accompany the CD-ROM.

Almost two years after the proposal had been accepted, the package was launched. The end result was a package that was published commercially in Australia and the United States, but which also had significant research and development outcomes. The design ideas have been the subject of academic publications, and the product has received awards and accolades internationally.

Roles and Teamwork

A major project of this size requires a range of design, production and technical experts. This case, however, focuses on the experiences of the instructional designers. There were four key members of the instructional design team. Three were staff members of the university (two of whom were former teachers), and one was a secondary school teacher on secondment. Two of the designers were continuously involved throughout the project and they took responsibility for the project management and coordination. Two other designers were heavily involved at specific stages and focused on particular aspects of the project. One, for example, led the development of the simulations, and the other worked closely with the subject matter experts on the content. Two other academics had input into the design and were more peripherally involved, rejoining the team at various times to provide feedback on design ideas, often providing a "reality check" for those more closely involved in the project.

Each designer had their own perspective on the project, depending on the nature and level of their involvement, but also on their backgrounds. Three of the designers had significant experience in secondary science teaching, although two had since moved to university positions. This gave these members a good understanding of a teacher's perspective of the characteristics of an effective learning resource, and of what teachers would need from a package like *Exploring the Nardoo.* The academic members of the team were also committed to furthering the research agenda in the design of interactive multimedia for education. This was the main driver of innovation, which ensured that *Exploring the Nardoo* was not simply a copy of *Investigating Lake Iluka* with different content. Furthermore, while there was an underlying commitment to the key design principles, the academic designers had different expertise and views. For example, one designer had particular expertise in interface design that was called upon at various times during the project. This mix of perspectives ensured that there was constant questioning of ideas throughout the project, and that design decisions were well justified.

As well as working with each other, the instructional designers were part of the wider project team that included subject matter experts, graphics designers, programmers and audio-visual experts. All of the designers were multi-skilled in that their expertise extended beyond instructional design. For example, all were experienced users of educational technology in their own teaching, and most also brought highly developed technical skills and production knowledge to the project. Some team members also had background knowledge in science that was also relevant to the nature of this project. These factors were highly beneficial to the functioning of the team because the designers were better able to communicate to the scientists who acted as the subject matter experts and with the multimedia and computing specialists.

Despite this, however, there were times when the priorities of the team members and their views of what was most important to the project differed from one another. This was perhaps most obvious in the relationship between the designers and the two subject matter experts. The scientists from the DLWC were heavily involved in identifying, selecting and creating content. The instructional designer carried out significant re-writing of existing information to make it suitable for secondary school students, and reworked a significant amount of material into alternative formats such as newspaper stories or TV news items. This was an involved process, requiring that the subject matter experts checked the revised content to ensure that it was accurate. Comments from the designers indicate that although these subject matter experts gradually came to understand a lot about the overall process and the complexities involved, they were still very much focussed on maximising the amount of content in the product. The design team, on the other hand, were more concerned with "getting the interactivity and navigation in place."

Challenges, Strategies, and Solutions

Exploring the Nardoo posed two main challenges for the design team. The first was in fostering innovation within the constraints of money, time, skills and technical limitations. While these constraints need to be managed and addressed in any project, they pose particular challenges when innovation is a key goal. As noted by the designers on this project, innovation requires open-mindedness, adaptability and compromise. Open-mindedness ensures that there is a culture in which ideas can be shared and debated in a constructive way. A range of perspectives on any problem is valuable, as is a degree of risk-taking. Adaptability and compromise are essential features when either the ideas or their implementation do not work or cannot be achieved within the constraints. All of these are characteristics of the process by which *Exploring the Nardoo* was designed and developed, and contrast markedly to the simplified versions of instructional design that regularly appear in text books. While these models may alert readers to the types of activities that occur during the process, they do little to convey the messiness and uncertainty that are features of innovations such as the one discussed here. Most notably such models often separate design and development, whereas in the case of *Exploring the Nardoo* these activities were inextricably entwined.

The other significant challenge for the designers was working with a diverse team. Just like other educational multimedia products, be they CD or Web-based, *Exploring the Nardoo* required the input of a wide variety of experts. The initial task for the project leaders was to assemble the right project team. In this case many of the key players had been involved in the previous project, but this new project also introduced new members with different knowledge and skills. It was a distinct advantage that the instructional designers were multi-skilled, and it is likely that the enhanced communication that resulted enabled the project participants to build a shared understanding more easily. The project documents, such as the brief and design statement, became expressions of that shared understanding. These were not detailed design specifications, but they were sufficient to articulate the agreed scope and nature of the project. As one designer noted, however, even when ideas were committed to paper, there were still times when the client (DLWC) would have a very different interpretation. The team addressed this by mocking up screen representations of the package in the early stages to make those ideas more concrete. The lead designers also worked hard to manage expectations through continuous consultation with DLWC, formal and informal face-to-face meetings, and e-mail messages. These provided important forums for addressing the multiple perspectives and the sometimes competing priorities of the team members.

Principles

There are five principles that emerge from this case that may be relevant to other designers. These are offered below as the "lessons learned" from this project.

Assess and Address Constraints

Every instructional design project must be completed within particular constraints. Some of these, such as the budget and timeframe, are inherent in the project and easy to identify from the outset. Others become important because of changes or events that occur during the project, such as the introduction of a new software standard that requires a different approach or new skill to be learned. All constraints impact on a design in some way, and instructional designers need to continually assess constraints throughout a project and work with other team members to address them.

Identify Underlying Instructional Design Principles and Goals

The underlying instructional design principles and goals should be identified in the early stages of a project. Significant deliberation and discussion is needed to ensure that all team members develop a sound understanding of these principles and goals. The agreed principles and goals can then guide specific design decisions, and help the team to maintain consistency across the project. This is particularly effective when projects are large, and when individuals or sub-teams take responsibility for parts of the project.

Be Open to Adaptation of the Design

Instructional designers need to be receptive to adaptations in the design. This is important at the beginning of a project when the scope and nature of the design is being negotiated. At this stage adaptations come from the multiple perspectives of the team members and from mock-ups to test new ideas. Trying to restrict the design at this stage may mean that innovative ideas are discarded. Adaptations are often necessary partway through a project—perhaps as a constraint becomes apparent, or when a particular design idea cannot be achieved or is rejected during formative evaluation.

Establish and Manage Open Communication

Open communication among team members that is respectful of others' perspectives is essential to projects that are developed by diverse teams. This can be achieved when the contribution of ideas is valued and when all members feel able to provide input. This may be established by bringing all members of the team together at various times, and using strategies to maintain communication between meetings when sub-teams may be working on a particular aspect of the project. Continuous communication with the client, who may not have prior experience in working on a similar project, can help to manage their expectations and inform them about the process.

Use Documentation as a Communication Strategy

Various types of documentation can be part of an effective communication strategy for design teams. The most obvious form of documentation is the formal project document that is submitted for review and becomes a milestone for sign-off. These documents represent agreements about the project and usually detail the scope of the project and its key features. They can become reference points during discussions and debates about the design. Other forms of documentation that might be shared include mock-ups of graphic design options, key points from meetings, and e-mail communications. Documents can be easily shared between team members and provide a means to record decision-making amongst the group.

Conclusion

The case has described some of the experiences of four members of the instructional design team on the *Exploring the Nardoo* project. This project is of interest because it involved a number of designers working together within a larger team that included subject matter experts and production specialists. Further, the project was a vehicle for innovation in the design of interactive multimedia for science education. Innovation on the project was supported by the nature of the team, in particular the multi-skilled instructional designers, and by the flexible and iterative process that combined design and development throughout. This case highlights the role of effective communication strategies and reference to underlying design principles as part of that process.

When viewed in terms of the communities of practice concept, it is possible to see that this project, and others like it, create a community of practice and also interact with other communities of practice. In terms of the project itself, the participants were engaged in a joint enterprise that over time developed particular ways of communicating and collaborating, shared understandings of the problem, and common resources and practices. Participants were also members of other communities and these influenced their goals and perspectives. Participants brought with them some of the culture of the communities they identified with, such as being a member of an educational technology research community, or as a classroom teacher. It is also evident that the design practices developed as part of this project were fed back into the communities through presentations and publications.

Acknowledgment

The author would like to thank the members of the *Exploring the Nardoo* design team who shared their perspectives and reflections on the project.

References

Barab, S., & Duffy, T. (2000). From practice fields to communities of practice. In D.H. Jonassen & S.M. Land (Eds.), *Theoretical foundations of learning environments* (pp. 25-55). Mahwah, NJ: Lawrence Erlbaum Associates.

Barab, S., MaKinster, J.G., Moore, J.A., Cunningham, D.J., & the ILF Design Team. (2001). Designing and building an on-line community: The struggle to support sociability in the inquiry learning forum. *Educational Technology Research and Development, 49*(4), 71-96.

Conceição, S., Sherry, L., & Gibson, D. (2004). Using developmental research to design, develop and evaluate an urban education portal. *Journal of Interactive Learning Research, 15*(3), 271-286.

Cox, S., & Osguthorpe, R. (2003). Building an online instructional design community: Origin, development and the future. *Educational Technology, 18*(5), 44-48.

Ertmer, P., & Quinn, J. (Eds.). (2003). *The ID casebook: Case studies in instructional design.* Englewood Cliffs, NJ: Merrill/Prentice-Hall.

Herrington, A., Herrington, J., & Kervin, L. (2005). The BEST site on the Internet: An online resource of beginning and establishing successful teachers. In P. Kommers & G. Richards (Eds.), *Proceedings of EDMEDIA 2005 World Conference on Educational Multimedia, Hypermedia and Telecommunications* (pp. 2646-2651). Norfolk, VA: Association for the Advancement of Computing in Education.

Keppell, M. (2000). Principles at the heart of an instructional designer-subject matter expert interaction. In R. Sims, M. O'Reilly, & S. Sawkins (Eds.), *Proceedings of the 17th ASCILITE Conference* (pp. 317-326). Lismore, NSW: Southern Cross University Press.

Lave, J., & Wenger, E. (1991). *Situated learning: Legitimate peripheral participation.* Cambridge: Cambridge University Press.

Perez, R., & Emery, C. (1995). Designer thinking: How novices and experts think about instructional design. *Performance Improvement Quarterly, 8*(3), 80-95.

Perez, R., Johnson, J., & Emery, C. (1995). Instructional design expertise: A cognitive model of design. *Instructional Science, 23*, 321-349.

Reigeluth, C. (Ed.). (1999). *Instructional theories and models*. Mahwah, NJ: Lawrence Erlbaum Associates.

Snyder, W., Wenger, E., & de Sousa Briggs, X. (2004). Communities of practice in government: Leveraging knowledge for performance. *The Public Manager, 32*(4), 17-21.

Visscher-Voerman, I., Gustafson, K., & Plomp, T. (1999). Educational design and development: An overview of paradigms. In J. van den Akker, R. Branch, K. Gustafson, N. Nieveen, & T. Plomp (Eds.), *Design approaches and tools in education and training* (pp. 15-28). Dordrecht, Netherlands: Kluwer Academic Publishers.

Wenger, E. (2004, January). Knowledge management is a donut: Shaping your knowledge strategy with communities of practice. *Ivey Business Journal,* pp. 1-8.

Wenger, E., & Snyder, W. (2000, January/February). Communities of practice: The organizational frontier. *Harvard Business Review,* 139-145.

Chapter XVI

Multi-Disciplinary Collaboration to Unravel Expert Knowledge: Designing for Effective Human-Computer Interaction

Elspeth McKay, RMIT University, Australia

Jennifer Martin, RMIT University, Australia

Abstract

This chapter introduces project management as a pivotal tool that underpins successful information systems design. It argues that the strength of the human-dimension of human-computer interaction (HCI) is often omitted by system designers. It discusses some of the issues that arise when dealing with a multi-disciplined project team. These include dealing with a non-conventional learning context, the challenge of designing an appropriate learning design and instructional architecture. Furthermore, the authors hope that understanding the underlying principles of effective conflict management throughout the process of systems design will inform others of a better communication methodology for dealing with difficult behaviour when designing an information system. It is also hoped that this discussion will assist in the understanding of the intricate and interactive relationships that arise between the different elements of HCI.

Introduction

The process of designing computerized information systems involves many different types of design techniques. Instructional designers play an important role in user-centered interface design, capturing and designing appropriate learning content and media selection. There are many examples of projects where the simplest conceptual notion blossomed into a complicated technical nightmare for an educational systems developer. Perhaps it is because of this that systems analysis and design has been called a black art (McKay, Thomas, & Martin, 2004). In some quarters it has become fashionable to follow the so-called principles of user-centered design to focus on the cognitive factors that are involved in human-computer interaction (HCI). A multi-disciplinary collaborative project team was formed to develop an innovative computerized information system for people wishing to find work. This specialized information system was intended to target users who may have experienced some type of challenging event that caused an interruption to their lives, leaving them with low self-esteem and lacking the confidence to find suitable employment.

The typical project management challenges that affected project outcomes included: teasing out the experts' knowledge into everyday language, dealing with difficult people, unexpected changes to the project's focus, awkward authorware tools, and project development hurdles that defy even the most experienced system developer. To illustrate how these influences impacted upon the instructional design process, a case study is presented in this chapter, setting out the principles of instructional design that guided the project. We define instructional design as the professional practice of constructing an appropriate context for a specialized learning context. The development of the pilot information system did not run smoothly and conflict management strategies were required to complete the funded project on time.

The specific objective of this chapter is to reveal the necessity to draw on instructional design principles for taking a fine-grained approach to match the learning context with the target user needs. The common axiom that a one-size-fits-all approach to instructional strategies can be adopted for an information/skill development system, simply is not appropriate when seeking ways to encourage the long-term unemployed back to work. This chapter reveals how difficult it was to implement a sound instructional design framework for an information system in a vocational rehabilitation community. There are many competing issues that converge within this type of recovery-oriented community, including the policies and practice of the existing service providers. Lack of funding for these service providers was a common reason expressed by this group for the current dilemma facing people wishing to return to work after a long absence.

The environmental context for this research project is explained in the background section of this chapter. In this first section, there is clarification of the multi-disciplinary project team roles within the project. In the overview section, we outline the functionality of the prototype information system and the outcomes from the user trial. The case description section articulates the context for implementing effective HCI for vocational rehabilitation as a community of practice. The non-conventional learning context of this project raises awareness for the special circumstances that surround this research. We propose that there is a dilemma for the instructional designer to choose the appropriate learning design in this type of skill renewal context. In addition, there is a separate challenge to devise an appropriate instructional architecture. This design view relates to the cognitive processing that is expected. As such it sets the background for the type of architecture that integrates the learning content and instructional strategies employed by the information system developer. This activity is much the same as we experience in developing specifications with an architect when building a house. Added challenges for the instructional design relate to knowing how to capture the human-dimension of HCI in this type of customized information system. Although this discussion is much easier to articulate with the benefit of hindsight, rather than during the actual event, our conflict resolution strategies were an afterthought rather than a proactive approach to maintain quality project outcomes. The principles section reveals the lessons learned from the project. This is where we propose that the human-dimension of HCI involves many interacting forces. These can be seen as the nexus for information system's use and the context of the information and communications technologies that drive the instructional platform. With such a complex range of interacting HCI components, we choose to describe the weakest side of our project that had a direct impact on the research outcomes. This includes the desire for effective multi-disciplinary communication and a suitable model for conflict resolution strategies. We conclude the chapter with a discussion of the implications arising from our work for instructional design, and improvements for multi-disciplinary collaboration. Enhancement of the human-dimension in HCI and instructional design may require a complementary partnership.

Background

The project brief involved the design of an effective HCI information system (proof-of-concept) as a customized learning environment for finding appropriate employment opportunities for the long-term unemployed. Looking for work involves a synthesis of decisions relating to many separate job-seeking tasks. It requires discrimination of how an individual's skills match the job description, whether the salary offered is acceptable, and whether the location of the work and the logistics of arranging transport are suitable. These job-seeking tasks are even more difficult for the disabled, and despite the Web Access Initiative (WAI, 2002), this type of specialized Web-enabled work-searching system designed as vocational rehabilitation tools does not exist. The target system users included young adults requiring vocational re-training/rehabilitation following some type of traumatizing event. This event may have resulted in a dramatic change in their everyday environment. Hence this project had immediate application within a community-based vocational training programme.

A range of computer-supported collaborative learning systems appears to be taking a ubiquitous approach to fulfilling the socio-economic need for re-skilling the general population. As there are no specialized job-searching systems that cater for such a disabled community, an opportunity exists among educational technologists to devise a customizable e-learning platform that promotes inclusive job-seeking strategies that assist people seeking suitable employment as well as providing a life-long learning resource.

In 2003, a one-year university research grant was awarded to a multi-disciplinary project team. This team was represented by three professional communities of practice: psychology, social work and information systems. The academic team members at an Australian University consisted of two subject matter experts (SMEs), a professor of psychology (disability studies), and an associate professor of social work with a comprehensive record of community practice. The role of instructional designer and overall project management was performed by the information technologist with formal postgraduate instructional design qualifications and cognitive performance assessment and evaluation experience. A multimedia system developer was also employed to build the system.

The strength of this academic research project team lies in the combined expertise of the team. In the past, they have utilized HCI to articulate their instructional design framework for several projects. Their projects involved investigations into various instructional strategies that can be employed to develop various customized learning shells that accommodate young people recovering from the residual effects of a mental illness, who may need help in finding ways to regain cognitive skills (McKay, Martin, & Izard, 2005). The age group of their participants ranged from 15 to 25 years representing a range of scholastic experiential awareness that included interrupted school education to unfinished undergraduate studies.

Despite following a sound instructional design framework based on the first principles of instruction, as described by Merrill (2002b, 2003); misunderstandings still arose between the academic team members and the system developer that negatively impacted project outcomes. The short-term goal of the project was to generate a working model that would deliver sufficient functionality to demonstrate the benefits of customizing a work-searching information system for building self-esteem in a vocational rehabilitation setting. The middle-term goal was to secure sufficient interest and funding from a community service provider/industry sector partner to attract government sponsorship. The longer-term goal was to build the complete information system for providing a fully interactive specialist Web portal. The information system was called the Electronic Work-finding Requirements Awareness Programme (eWRAP).

Information System Overview

According to the SMEs, an essential feature of the system was to make access to the information easy. For this reason, the system utilized touch-screen technology to enhance accessibility to the information. This meant that the system should function without a keyboard and mouse. Extensive discussion with a target user group revealed that the home page should welcome the user through an audio greeting that could be toggled to a textual description as an alternative (see Figure 1). There was a design requirement to ensure that navigation was simple and user-friendly. To return to the login screen, the user should only need to press a close button to finish a session. Re-entry to the system also needed to be simple.

The instructional designer worked tirelessly with a fictitious personal profile generated by the SMEs to unravel their expert knowledge and design appropriate screen chattels. For instance, a simple press of each key option was designed to deliver a sub-level menu. The screen chattels were always on display, including: an orientation button (top of screen), audio/text toggle button, page navigation mechanisms, back button (previous screen), a home page button, and the full menu of key job-seeking options displayed along the bottom edge of the screen. This framework presented an intuitive/inquisitive approach to information where the user has complete control over where they may wish to go next. In keeping with the 5-star principles of instruction (Merrill, 2003) the prototype offers video-on-demand (VOD) (Okamoto, Matsui, Inoue, & Cristea, 2000). These vignettes presented/showed the user everyday activities related to health and safety issues, preparing for an interview (Figure 2), typical job environments, and benefits of socializing at work. Four categories of work were offered (professional, community, health and education, and trades and services); VOD

Figure 1. Prototype login screen

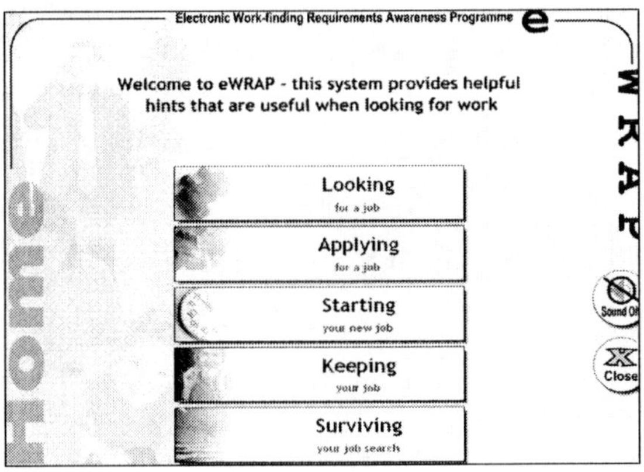

Figure 2. Video on demand

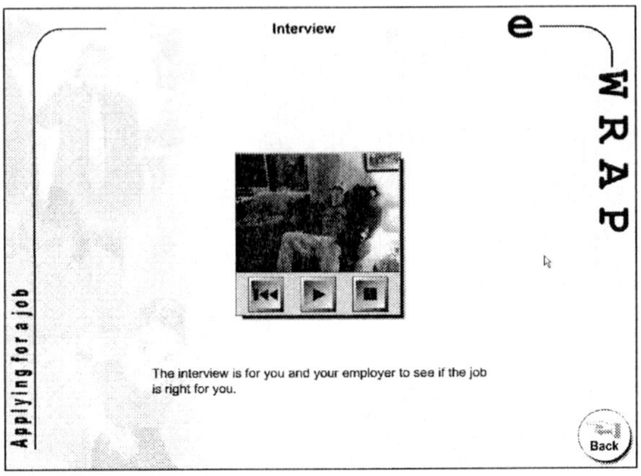

buttons are located beneath each category. The focal point of the prototype was the interactive job selection module: a comprehensive employment knowledge repository including a job vacancy listing and specific position descriptions.

User Trials

A pilot study was completed over a four-month period. Arrangements were made with appropriate people, already known to the team, to test system components as they were progressively finished. Preliminary qualitative feedback, including that of several non-computer users, was very positive. The users found the system easy to use, informative, and could relate to the characters in the various VOD vignettes. An example of the comments from the participants included: *"the person applying for the computer position reminded me of people I know, it made me think that behaving like that is not good,"* and, *"I can see that wearing suitable clothing is important for an interview."*

This section has provided the context to orient the reader. It has also defined the multidisciplinary nature of the project team, and summarized the functionality of eWRAP. The discussion now focuses on the instructional design issues during the information system development.

Case Description

Due to the complex mix of cross-disciplinary team members, it was perhaps inevitable that this project experienced many problems. The cultural rules and customs associated with each team member's professional practice would need to be fully understood by all team members. This meant that we needed to initially understand the reasons for building such a specialist information system. The system needed to be an effective tool for people recovering from mental illness, who have never been employed. To design the information system it was necessary to investigate how this group suffers negative effects of long-term unemployment. The outcome of this initial research was conducted by the SMEs and translated into a linguistic framework, which needed to be understood by all project stakeholders. Therefore, the project culture required a common language in which the SMEs could advise on Web-based employment services that would provide open, flexible and distributed access for people who may experience difficulty in returning to work after a long absence.

To establish the parameters for this custom-built information system, the instructional designer initiated a preliminary investigation of the user needs and a work-finding task analysis that was conducted by the SMEs (Caplan, 2004) to unravel their expert knowledge. This investigation revealed that work force accessibility emerges as an important social issue. Furthermore, among unemployed Australians seeking work, 19% have a disability, and may be disadvantaged in accessing information for gaining employment. Finding work is never an easy process. Job-seekers are expected to wade through several disparate information sources, which may include newspapers, telephone canvassing, computer listings, and Internet browsing. This process is more difficult for people who are trying to find their way back into the working world after an episode of mental illness.

The findings of the work-finding task analysis suggested that looking for work is a complicated process. The job-seeking process requires the performance of problem-solving activities that need to conceptualise the relationship between the skills needed for a job and the employment environment. This is not an easy process for people who have experienced a mental illness. People may experience a profoundly disrupted ability to think, feel and relate to others and the environment in usual ways. People who have been mentally ill may need assistance to overcome delusional thinking (Frey, 2002), where the real context surrounding their skills and abilities is distorted. Moreover each time this experience is negative, it serves to promote an already lowered self-esteem, another unfortunate legacy of mental illness (Torrey, 1983). Looking for work involves a synthesis of decisions relating to many separate issues, including: work ready skills (task analysis), employer requirements (formal and informal behaviours), remuneration (part-time/full-time/voluntary), location (distance-to- travel from home), and transportation (familiarity and convenience issues).

These decisions require a motivated attitude towards finding work, which may not always be characteristic of this target audience. Unfortunately, lack of motivation is another residual affect of mental illness and medication. Motivation has been described by many instructional designers as an outcome of learning, meaning a clever arrangement of situations for learning to promote feelings of competence and efficacy (Gagne, 1985; Merrill, 2002a; Smyslova & Voiskounsky, 2005). It was clear to the academic project team that the context for this information system should provide a dual role for the users; finding appropriate work and to facilitate high-quality learning experiences through an enhanced instructional tool designed for vocational rehabilitation programmes. The human performance technology issues for this information system are not unique; the right factors to develop problem-solving skills occupies many of the human performance models used to transform the work force in general. However, the "bringing together" of all these disparate decisions is often too much for people recovering from mental illness. Failure can rapidly de-motivate such fragile people leading to a further spiral downwards, re-enforcing their isolation from the workforce. People with a diagnosis of a mental illness often experience high levels of social disadvantage and stigma (Epstein & Olsen, 2001), which can result in an overwhelming sense of fear and isolation for the individual. More recently, there has been an increase in the range of initiatives within community mental health settings that integrate both mental health and vocational rehabilitation programmes. Work is the key to recovery from mental illness as it contributes to improved levels of self-esteem (Rogers, 1995; Kakutani, 1998). In an account of a small business established and run by four people with psychiatric diagnoses who had previously been long-term unemployed, the Kakutani findings indicate improved levels in self-esteem as well as increased motivation. She concludes that, for chronically mentally ill clients, employment is the best rehabilitation goal. However, the process to achieve this takes time and effort, but it is possible (Kakutani, 1998, p. 115).

The instructional design framework for eWRAP now included: a linguistic culture that was understood by all stakeholders, the work-finding task analysis that located the critical entry level requirements, and an awareness for the need to promote unique and sensitive motivational strategies. An innovative approach to vocational rehabilitation was emerging.

Non-Conventional Learning Context

Armed with this background and context for assisting people to find suitable work (Honey, 2000), the academic team held several meetings to scope their project. Aspects of this project have been published elsewhere (McKay & Martin, 2002; McKay, Thomas, & Martin, 2003; McKay et al., 2004). These earlier publications focused on the social science aspects of the project's educative environment. The target profile of the users for this information system could be described as non-conventional, insofar as their preparation, behaviour, and expectations may not be conventional (Macias, DeCarlo, Wang, Frey, & Barreira, 2001). As such, these manuscripts were written specifically for the research community interested in universal access to information systems. In contrast to this earlier literature, this chapter concentrates on the instructional design issues that challenged the developers of the information system as they worked alongside the content specialists. The SMEs played an important role in the concept development stage of the project. It was critical to unravel the SMEs expert knowledge and to clarify the user requirements based on the clinical experience and professional practice of the experts. The SMEs met with the instructional designer to formalize the plan to deliver effective instructional strategies that inform education and training opportunities for renewing work readiness skills. It was expected that further recommendations of appropriate vocational rehabilitation strategies, which inform stakeholders involved in assisting the long-term unemployed, would emerge throughout the project. Moreover, the primary aim of the information system would provide enhanced job-seeking resources to benefit many people ordinarily not included in mainstream programmes.

Designing an instructional architecture for online learning environments requires an understanding of the users' information needs and possible mental models in each particular learning domain. For this purpose, a design-persona was developed as the user-archetype, becoming the hypothetical participant who journeys through the learning materials (McKay et al., 2004). A design-persona assists the learning system development process by bringing the learner to life as a reference point. It gives an identity to someone who plans to participate in an online learning programme. To generate this unique design-persona, the project team conducted a brainstorming session to identify the main features of the persona. The subsequent features included: age, gender, current state of health, schooling achieved, past employment opportunities, housing, usual travel mode, socializing patterns, life-skills, smoking habits, and so forth. The design-persona was given a name (Jill). It is this naming process that brings the design-persona to life. Decisions on the learning environment were then made by the project team through the hypothetical eyes of this design-persona.

A great deal of project development time was wasted devising this conceptual persona called Jill, to lessen the possibility of the research team's subjectivity during the system's design decisions. In happier circumstances, each time a decision on system functionality was raised, the team should have been able to use the context of Jill's profile to answer the system's technical requirements. Instead, it was recognized that scope-creep had taken over; the project manager tried in vain to keep the developer from launching into solving longer-term goals.

While understanding the non-conventional learning context refocused the project team; this facilitated an empathetic awareness to devise appropriate instructional mechanisms. As such, instructional design principles lead to the next step in the information system development process.

Challenge of Designing an Appropriate Learning Design

We need to be clear about how to differentiate between learning and instruction (Heinich, Molenda, Russell, & Smaldino, 2002). One prevalent learning design is the passive absorption view; learning in this view is about assimilating information; while instruction is about providing information to learners. Some call this a transmission view of teaching (Mayer, 2001; Souza, 2003). Learning environments that rely on lectures or videotapes to transmit information generally reflect this view. However, due to the difficulties of short concentration expected with the target users, this learning design was considered by the instructional designer as inappropriate.

Moreover, the specialized nature of the vocational rehabilitation audience for this information system required a cognitive approach towards implementing an appropriate learning design. It was important to provide a safe and comfortable environment in which the users could construct knowledge in a social context. However, Hung & Nichani (2001) advocate for appropriate or internalized knowledge building by individuals in community-based learning environments. Otherwise, only a collective identity is achieved (Hung & Nichani, 2001). As a consequence, our learning design would require an individualized context that included a social context of workplace examples that supported the construction of new or refreshed knowledge (Kang & Byun, 2001). The anticipated wide-range of non-conventional learner attributes of the target users, meant the emphasis for this information system would need to focus on the active processes learners may expect to use to construct their new knowledge (Pedroni, 2004). This construction requires an integration of new incoming information from the environment with existing knowledge in memory. In the cognitive view, learning is about active construction of new knowledge by interacting with new information and instruction is about promoting the psychological processes that mediate that construction. Moreover, there was a high level of stigma anticipated by the project team from the target user towards learning per se, brought about by inadequate views of learning in their past experience.

The instructional designer cautioned the project team on the care required in the choice of attention getting strategies employed for their non-conventional learning environment. Until more is known about the interactive effects of instructional format and cognitive performance in an online context (McKay, 2000a), screen display techniques were to be kept simple and uncluttered by screen motion and animated movement. Therefore a more holistic view of learning was brought forward by the instructional designer to tap into both cerebral hemispheres to attract benefits from both the analytical and visual orientation of the target users (McKay, 2006). According to Riding (2002), researchers in general are aware of learners' cognitive or learning style differences—and the implications for instructional design. He describes a model of assessing the position of an individual on two basic dimensions of cognitive style. In the first, the VERBAL-IMAGERY dimension depicts the way people prefer to represent information during thinking. This is often referred to as cognitive style. By drawing on Pavio's work, Riding suggests that some people think in terms of mental pictures (the visualisers), while others think in terms of words (the verbalisers) (Riding, 2002). Riding points out that people are capable of utilizing either cognitive mode. He says that some people have a tendency to use only one mode—visual or verbal. A person's preferred cognitive style affects performance in both the perceptual and conceptual domains of the learning process. A more effective learning strategy would facilitate active integration of both these cognitive styles. According to Riding, personal choice and the task at hand may influence cognition. People will naturally revert to the easiest thinking mode according to what they are doing at the time. Past experience may also play an important role in this dimension.

The second dimension is called WHOLIST-ANALYTIC that identifies people's mode of processing information that is not changeable. Riding believes this cognitive dimension is inherent and may hold true over time. Cognitive style is therefore made-up of the combination of these two basic dimensions, which Riding believes are independent. There is a common belief that imagers will learn better if offered visual material and that verbalisers will learn best with text. However, common beliefs can lead researchers and courseware designers down the wrong path (McKay, 2000a, 2000b).

The active construction of knowledge is commonly accepted as a mechanism for learning (Kang & Byun, 2001), and this construction can be fostered through diverse instructional environments. eWRAP provides a dual role; learning in the sense that strategies would be employed to ignite relearning of specific tasks such as preparing for work (making lunches, choosing the best transport to arrive on time, how to manage the social aspects of the working environment, etc.). The eWRAP instructional strategies would also provide critical information about finding work (listing the employers and their job vacancies, example video clips showing various work environments, etc.). This means that the design must account for an individual's cognitive processing of learning/instruction. This is separate from the technological mechanisms or system architectures that are required to facilitate the information system.

A decision was made by the project team to employ receptive and guided discovery architectures (Clark, 2003). In the receptive architecture, the work-finding information system would provide the user with information in the form of words and pictures, both still and animated. The emphasis is often implemented as tell-and-ask and cannot be considered as instruction (Merrill, 2002c); while guided discovery architecture would be employed to encourage exploration of the information system.

Challenge of Designing an Appropriate Instructional Architecture

Research evidence points to prior experience as a significant learner characteristic influencing learning (Heltne & Bagley, 2004). Recent literature on learning focuses on the integration of new content with prior knowledge in memory (Clark, 2003). Therefore, novices may have minimal relevant prior knowledge. As a result, their cognitive processes are different from an experienced learner with substantial background experience. Consequently, novices might benefit from different instructional methods more than experienced learners (Bagley & Heltne, 2003). It was expected that the target users in this project might have varying degrees of experiential knowledge of how to look for work. In this sense, most of them would be considered as novice job-seekers. Even if they had worked prior to becoming ill, they may have been absent from the workforce for a long time. In this sense, the information system would be expected to identify these types of users and implement a fast tracking of the instructional strategies (McKay et al., 2005).

Originally it was felt by the project team that the target users with relatively little background knowledge would benefit from an instructional context offering directive architecture. This would provide information in small chunks and offer frequent practice opportunities. Moreover, people with greater prior knowledge of how to gain employment have much more to draw upon when using this type of information system; they would be able to manage larger chunks of information. In ordinary circumstances, based on what they already know, they would be able to make better choices about their instructional needs. Due to the problems the target users may have developed through being unemployed for long periods this expectation would not be appropriate. The Merrill (2002c) notion of "don't just tell me, show me," was frequently adopted. This means that eWRAP maintains consistency, with guidance and relevant media using visual metaphors, and voice descriptions offering the user a choice to turn-off the audio description and read a text-based version of the same material. As such, the eWRAP instructional architecture offers differentiated instructional strategies for novice and experienced job-seekers (Bagley & Heltne 2003). This type of instructional architecture emphasizes the human-dimension of HCI; where the requirements for human information processing is directly synchronized with the dialogue techniques associated with the information and communications technologies that drive the information system.

Challenge of Dealing with the HCI Design Implications

It was anticipated that this project would capture the efficiencies of HCI to enhance job searching for people undergoing vocational rehabilitation programmes. There are some Web-based employment services that claim to provide open, flexible and distributed access for people who may experience difficulty in returning to work after a long absence. Therefore an immediate challenge for the academic team members was to provide evidence for this type of enhanced Web-mediated work-searching information system that provided a safe and appropriate learning design. A number of other problems also bubbled to the surface early in the project development. The first dilemma was to clarify the people who will benefit most from such a system, while another was the fact that the environmental context of this research project was unique. As described earlier, it set out to address the needs of people who suffer negative cognitive effects from long-term unemployment, not those with physical disabilities. Consequently, the project team held many meetings with the SMEs and the system developers. It was established that the system would need to be designed to embody an educative role to enhance the self-confidence of people (of all age groups) who may have been out of work for many years, or who may have never experienced paid employment.

It soon became obvious that the fledgling system was suffering from exponential growth. The system developer began adding new functionality, which increased the scope of the project. As a result of this rapid expansion, the next dilemma facing the project team was to re-map the development schedule. The short-term goal was in place to develop a relatively small prototype of the information system with sufficient functionality to demonstrate the benefits of a programme for building self-esteem in vocational rehabilitation. The longer-term goal would provide the work-searching Web-portal to link understanding employers offering appropriate job opportunities with unemployed people who require substantial assistance in finding and maintaining work. However, shifting the system development extenuated the weaker side of the project management. It was also at this point that interdisciplinary communication became difficult.

Challenge of Multi-Disciplinary Collaboration

Combining the expertise from disparate disciplines was a major challenge for the project team. There were continual competing tensions between the academic team members interested in the end-user requirements, the system developer's aspirations for widening their product brief, and the project manager's interest in completing a successful project on time and within budget. Imperative ethical issues arose from the clinical psychology and social science perspectives that would permeate into every aspect of the system's design methodology. As a result, an extensive amount of time was spent in weekly project team meetings with the academics and the system developer to finalize the design-persona.

There was also considerable confusion with the roles and responsibilities of team members in relation to specific tasks. For example, it was difficult to determine who should write-up the system specifications that would be used to build a workable pilot prototype. The system specifications were developed by the project manager with the expectation that the system developer understood their obligation to populate the prototype with appropriate content. This meant that the design and delivery of visual metaphors and textual captions were to be implemented according to the agreed specifications. Even though these responsibilities were specified in an agreement between the university and the system developer, many problems arose because of communication difficulties between stakeholders. The project manager's requests for compliance testing obligations were refused by the system developer. The unfortunate dissonance this created for the project team meant that the system developer delivered a system framework devoid of content. Consequently, a second multimedia system developer was enlisted to complete the interactive database. However, the earlier problems relating to non-delivery of specified technical requirements of the prototype were already well entrenched, which resulted in a low-quality product. This has also jeopardised the longer-term project goals to fund the development of a Web-portal. In hindsight, proactive development of effective communication, conflict management and prevention strategies could have improved the outcome.

The Case Description section of this chapter identified the non-conventional learning context of this project. It explained the nuances between the learning design and the instructional architecture. These important issues discussed the multi-disciplinary collaboration that was needed for capturing the SMEs' knowledge and professional practice to facilitate the human-dimension of HCI. The next section of this chapter articulates some of the instructional design principles from this project, which may be relevant to other communities of practice.

Principles

There were valuable lessons from this project. Tighter project management was needed to prevent the project functionality/scope creep. Although the brainstorming sessions produced a number of useful outcomes: a shared linguistic/cultural framework for the multi-disciplinary team members, a meaningful design-persona (Jill), and agreement on the information system's screen chattels (visual metaphors, and the colour and size of the text captions, etc); the project's scope was allowed to creep outside the project tolerances. When the full extent creep was recognized (too late), the project manager tried in vain to keep the information system developer from focusing on longer-term goals outside of their project brief.

The multi-disciplinary nature of the instructional design requires the instructional designer to adopt an understanding of the communities of practice. This means developing a respectful and empathic attitude that continually navigates the knowledge acquisition process in other disciplines. The discussion now focuses on the solutions for dealing with the collaborative relationships across diverse disciplines, to include: the complex nature of the HCI environment, effective communication strategies to encourage and promote knowledge sharing and prevent a demarcation of discipline ownership.

Multi-Disciplinary Instructional Design Framework

Choosing the most suitable model for HCI is a difficult process (Preece, 1994, 2002). In this project the instructional designer experienced a similar difficulty. For instance, instructional design, which should perhaps be a starting point for courseware design, may only be referred to when describing the selection of instructional strategies to *justify* an approach taken by a courseware developer. To exasperate matters even more, the highly visual nature of multimedia and the semantic distinctions of certain words can cause problems amongst experienced information system developers working within an unfamiliar paradigm. Consequently certain planning activities that should occur during the design phase of a computerized information system were affected in this project.

In established design disciplines (architectural design, graphic design) the term *design* is well understood. In these fields, the need for time to be spent on initial documentation for specifications is well accepted. However, the same cannot be said for HCI and information systems design. Moreover, in disciplines that are not inherently visual (computer software design and mechanical engineering) the use of the word design is often misunderstood. Information systems developers need to understand when to use this term as a noun to describe the results from the processes. It has been suggested elsewhere that it is more often used as a verb to describe their performance when carrying out their system designer role (Inglis, 2003).

HCI is not new and the recognition of the sweeping effects that the information and communications technologies bring to our everyday lives is only now becoming apparent. Although the Association for Computing Machinery was established in 1947 (see http://www.acm.org/) the proliferation of HCI has only occurred during the last decade. Insufficient research has been conducted into the interacting relationships of HCI. People building computerized information systems have struggled for many years to define these interactive relationships. Figure 3 attempts to distil these components in the HCI context. To be successful in this techno-learning environment, an instructional designer must consider all these components to deliver their specific end-user requirements.

Figure 3. Human-computer interaction (Adapted from Preece, 1994, p. 16)

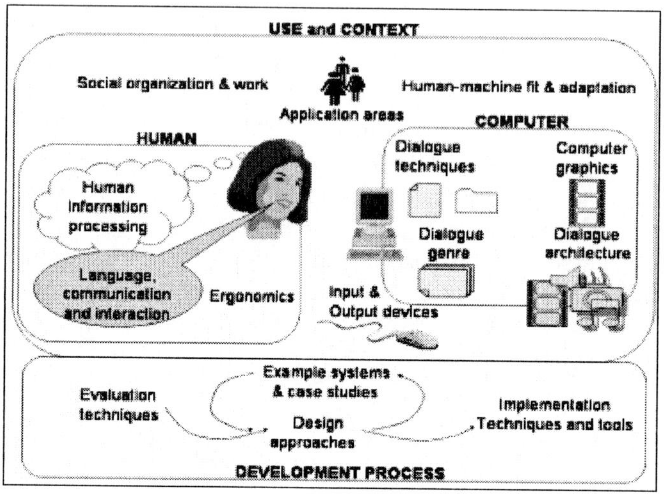

By condensing a large number of disparate disciplines into one model, it soon becomes apparent that we must find ways to work across the traditional boundaries of individual disciplines. Thereby one can expect the synthesis of rich intellectual resources that may otherwise be lost when the approach to information system's design concentrates on a single paradigm (see also, ACM SIGCHI, http://www.acm.org/sigchi/). This project is typical of the emerging interest in satisfying the human-dimension of HCI. As we found, there were times when paradigmatic conflict arises. We offer the following strategies to alleviate multi-disciplinary communication difficulties that include a model for conflict prevention and resolution, and how to deal with difficult behaviours and emotions.

Effective Multi-Disciplinary Communication

Multi-disciplinary collaboration requires skilful communication between partners that transcend disciplinary boundaries. This includes strategies for effective conflict prevention and resolution. Skilful communication requires quality relationships with people that take account of values and beliefs and identify areas of possible conflict. This is communicated in verbal and non-verbal behaviors that are face-to-face as well as via e-mail. Whilst e-mail is a fast and efficient means of transmitting messages it does not provide opportunities to observe and respond to a person's non-verbal behavior including posture, facial expression, movement and tone of voice. It also removes the listening component of understanding a person's verbal messages and the opportunity to check for congruency between verbal and non-verbal communications.

Effective multi-disciplinary communication requires an understanding of the different cultures within each discipline. Guiding principles are:

- Prepare yourself to find out about different disciplines
- Recognize and face fears and concerns
- Recognize differences between your own discipline and those from different disciplines
- Recognize differences among members of different disciplines—avoid stereotyping
- Recognize different meanings in verbal, non-verbal and e-communications
- Follow cultural rules and customs according to each discipline (Martin & Hess, 2004).

Preparation involves taking the time to find out about the different disciplines and interests of the discipline representatives. It is about being open to new possibilities and being aware of areas that are confusing or unclear due to disciplinary differences. It is about recognizing differences and facing fears. Within HCI these are often about the use and application of new technologies by different discipline areas. Sometimes people feel awkward when they ask basic questions in front of informed users. This difficulty may create a barrier for further clarifying communication. This may also result in miscommunication and people working with what is known to them, within the comfort zone of their own particular disciplines. In addition, timelines may be developed that request disciplines to provide expertise at different times of the project, which may accentuate the disparate discipline knowledge for the project. This is not multi-disciplinary collaboration in a true sense; the disciplines are still predominantly working in isolation albeit on different component parts of the same project. Effective multi-disciplinary communication moves beyond this approach to a model of active collaboration by members of different disciplines throughout the project. This provides continuity across all disciplines and provides opportunities for joint learning and teamwork. A free-flowing exchange of information should occur across disciplines to enhance communication and increase the likelihood of creative solutions that integrate knowledge from different disciplines. This is particularly important for complex problem-solving, as solutions generally do not sit within discreet disciplines. Therefore, we propose the following model for implementing an information/educational/training system with complex instructional design issues.

Model for Conflict Prevention and Resolution

In this particular case study effective partnerships were required across the diverse disciplines of information technology, psychology and social work. It soon became apparent that different words had different meanings and that common meanings and understandings within a discipline no longer applied. Conflict developed between people who felt that some members were not doing what they were meant to do. This occurred because everybody felt they had already completed their share of the project. It not only involved contractual arrangements but also reputation. The importance of professional reputation cannot be under-estimated in an industry that relies on recommendations for further contracts. In this case study, conflict developed due to a lack of a common language understanding and its associated expectations. This resulted in frustration and at times intense emotions. It also meant that the end product did not match the expectations of the project team even though the designers felt they had fulfilled their project responsibilities. After the original contract concluded, another system developer was contracted to complete work on the project. Because of the initial project confusion and miscommunication about the end-product requirements, the product still failed to meet the project teams expectations.

Agreement and project design: A successful agreement must be seen to be fair and equitable across all disciplines. This requires a common multi-disciplinary vision. The clarification of the rights and entitlements and an understanding of respective sources of power and leverage are necessary. Guidelines for the open exchange of information and for the transfer of technology need to be standardised. Standards and general criteria can establish behavioural frameworks that can be adapted to the values and culture of each discipline. Agreement by multi-disciplinary parties to binding commitments and obligations includes general and operational policies and principles as well as enforceable detailed regulations and sanctions. More detailed policies might include integrated multi-disciplinary activity. It is important that multi-disciplinary agreements address shared concerns, demonstrate value for the members of each discipline participating in the project and are responsive to the communities the project is designed to assist.

Implementation and follow-up: Strategies aimed at the enforcement of multi-disciplinary agreements are necessary. This requires the recognition of joint and individual responsibilities of each discipline. The restructuring of existing organizations, or the establishment of new organizations and structures, may be required. Feedback mechanisms need to be built into communications, within and between disciplines and project participants. The ability to implement preferred options will be determined by the availability of financial and other resources. It is important that an action plan is developed with tasks assigned to particular people. A timeframe for implementation and resource allocation is needed alongside review or monitoring mechanisms. These measures will lead to greater confidence in a multi-disciplinary project, which will hopefully result in more cooperation and commitment in future collaborations. However, even as the famous axiom says, the best-laid plans of mice and men often go awry; we understand it is helpful to have a fallback approach to deal with difficult behaviours and emotions.

Dealing with the Difficult Behaviours and Emotions

An analysis of power is central to effective conflict resolution and successful project outcomes. Co-operative power (that is power with) is required for success rather than power over other project team members from other disciplines. This is perhaps the main difference between working within one's own discipline and working across disciplines. Within disciplines there is usually a hierarchy in terms of status, expertise and leadership functions. However in a multi-disciplinary team, roles and status in terms of the management of the project are often unclear. Whilst project members may be expert in their own particular discipline area they may also be considered a novice in another's discipline areas. This raises the question of whose discipline holds most expertise in the particular project design. This is a contentious issue and may be seen differently according to the perspective of each discipline. A worst-case scenario involves a diverse team of discipline experts who each try to exert power over each other. Often people give up power to others where there is a valued relationship or respect of person's particular expertise. They may be persuaded or perhaps rewarded/punished for non-compliance.

Effective multi-disciplinary communication is the most critical task that a project team should address. Understanding how the different cultures interplay amongst various team members should assist in producing a quality outcome. Crossing the boundaries of one's own discipline can be difficult, but it is necessary for the success of any project. In the initial stages of the project, it is vital that the development team adopts strategies to face the fears and concerns that surface from an unfamiliar paradigm. In hindsight, we have demonstrated that the omission of this factor from the project's design framework weakened the outcome of the end product for all stakeholders. In our case, while the academic team members were acquainted with each other's expertise, the multimedia system developer and other external stakeholders were unfamiliar with other disciplines.

This chapter has disseminated a design framework to unravel multi-disciplinary expert knowledge. The multidiscipline nature of the research drew out important aspects of disability studies within psychology and social work to innovate this specialist knowledge in a form relevant to the human-dimension of HCI. As such, our project surfaced some interesting and challenging aspects for the instructional designer. These included a challenging non-conventional learning environment. From our experience with this project, we also propose strategies for dealing with the multi-disciplinary collaborative knowledge sharing.

Summary and Conclusion

Taking the short-cut approach to project management/instructional design does not work. One of the challenges for an instructional designer is to articulate the principles of instructional design to all project team members throughout the life of a project. When customizing a learning environment that lacks a clear instructional design framework, the problematic issues that arise along the way may reflect a continual reinvention of the project management wheel! Even with the best intentions, information systems development expertise, professional integrity, and legal agreements to ensure developer/client requirements are met, implementing a project can still be ineffective. Instructional designers play an important role in user-centered interface design, developing appropriate learning content and media selection. The specific objective of this chapter focused on the necessity to examine instructional design principles for matching the learning design with the target user needs.

To offer new options for Web-mediated courseware design, this chapter presented an example of designing a HCI application that involves information and communications technologies as the delivery vehicle. The essence of this work reflects the importance of the interacting relationships amongst the various HCI components as identified by Preece (2002). In respect to the ways in which these variables form dependent relationships, the lessons learned from this project may provide valuable experiential knowledge to inform an effective instructional design framework applicable for educational system's design.

Implications for Instructional Design

The purpose of this chapter was to discuss the process of courseware design. In particular, the case study revealed the extra care the project manager/instructional designer needs to employ to understand the context. When not managed carefully, the end product quality may be ineffective for the target audience. This chapter demonstrated that effective online courseware design is not merely a replication of paper-based materials. The full context of the system must be thoroughly investigated before one pixel is added to the e-melting pot called HCI. In the last decade research work has entered the literature on the interactive effect of preferred cognitive style and instructional format (McKay, 2000a; Riding, 2002). Dealing with the human-dimension of HCI means project teams need to be familiar with conflict resolution practice. Moreover, while the documentation on the computerized (e-learning) forum is mounting; there is little attention to instructional design from the more artificial intelligence-oriented researchers. Finally, unless there is an evaluation and an analysis of the interactive effects of each HCI component shown in Figure 3, the courseware designer may continue to develop flawed systems when attention is not paid to the human-dimension of HCI.

Improvements in Multi-Disciplinary Collaboration

The high costs often associated with online courseware design can escalate unless the project is carefully managed. In addition, effective conflict prevention and management strategies must also be incorporated into the design brief. The complexity of the human-dimension in a multi-disciplinary project should not be underestimated. In hindsight, our team can determine where the project made mistakes. The first instance was during the development of the agreement. Protection of both parties was not properly addressed. Implementing information and communication technology tools is a complex undertaking that should not be under-estimated. It is difficult to anticipate when conflict amongst team members/stakeholders may arise. It is vital to establish a conducive project culture in the early stages of the project in an attempt to minimize conflict. Agreements must therefore offer each party sufficient comfort to express themselves according to their own paradigmatic culture. The turning point for this project took place when the first system developer was not able to deliver the system complete with the agreed technical requirements. This meant that all trust evaporated between all parties. The project team was unable to obtain a quality end product for their target audience and the system developer's reputation was tarnished.

Another issue that is important for an effective design framework relates to the need to examine the interrelationships of all HCI components to prevent escalating costs. This refers to the interaction between the human-dimension, the computer equipment, and the development process (Preece, 1994). The design framework must address how the social organization of the paradigm relates to the way the information processing occurs in the system. Questions need to be asked about the expectations of the interactions between the discipline language and the implemented communication tools. The system architecture specifications are an integral feature of any project that involves HCI.

Finally, it is important to install appropriate evaluation techniques to ensure that the project stays on track to deliver a successful end product that is on time and within budget. The results from the example described in this chapter confirm that the multi-disciplinary and multisensory approach for navigating the knowledge and information presented through HCI is here to stay. We call for more research that investigates the human-dimension of HCI, especially in relation to how people cope with the instructional strategies that are heavily involved with multimedia. Effective instructional design is critical if the digital divide is to be reduced in the years to come (McKay, 2005). Since the earliest time in our recorded history, humans have shown each other how to do things; adapting the instruction according to differing contexts. It will be through capturing this ability (for reuse) that HCI will really come of age. Vocational training will become commonplace- available for all. This chapter has demonstrated that project managers/instructional designers must have exceptionally good communication, analytic, problem-solving and conflict resolution skills to obtain optimum results from multi-disciplinary collaboration.

Acknowledgment

This work would not have been possible without the funds awarded to the project team by the RMIT University's Virtual Research Institute – Small Grants Scheme – 2003.

In relation to this manuscript, the authors wish to thank the book chapter reviewers for their helpful advice and opportunity to improve on our original submission. In addition we are grateful for the tireless proofreading performed by Keven Asquith.

References

Bagley, C.A., & Heltne, M. (2003). *Cooperative teams.* Paper presented at the Collaboration Conference, Bloomington, MN.

Caplan, D. (2004). The development of online courses. In T. Anderson & F. Elloumi (Eds.), *Theory and practice of online learning*. Canada: Athabasca University.

Clark, R.C. (2003). *Expertise, learning, and instruction: Building expertise* (2nd ed.) (p. 256). MN: International Society for Performance Improvement.

Epstein, M., & Olsen, A. (2001). Mental illness: Responses from the community. In G. Medows & B. Singh (Eds.), *Mental health in Australia.* Melbourne: Oxford University Press.

Frey, D. (2002). *Feature story: Since my first break: An update*. Janssen Site: Mentalwellness.com. Retrieved January 12, 2006, from http://www.mentalwellness.com/stories/break.htm

Gagne, R.M. (1985). *The conditions of learning: And theory of instruction* (4th ed.). NY: Holt/Rinehart/Winston.

Heinich, R., Molenda, M., Russell, J.D., & Smaldino, S.E. (2002). *Instructional media and technologies for learning*. Upper Saddle River, NJ: Person Education.

Heltne, M.M., & Bagley, C.A. (2004). *Enhancing creativity through e-Learning with collaborative technologies*. Paper presented at the International Conference on Computers in Education - Acquiring and Constructing Knowledge through Human-Computer Interaction: Creating new visions for the future of learning.

Honey, A. (2000, Winter). Psychiatric vocational rehabilitation: Where are the customers' views? *Psychiatric Rehabilitation Journal, 23*.

Hung, D., & Nichani, M. (2001). Constructivism and e-learning: Balancing between the individual and social levels of cognition. *Educational Technology, 41*(3), 40-44.

Inglis, A. (2003). *Which future of instructional design in a world moving to e-Learning?* Paper presented at the eLearning Conference on Design and Development: Instructional Design - Applying First Principles of Instruction, Melbourne, Australia.

Kakutani, K. (1998, Fall). New life espresso: Report on a business run by people with psychiatric disabilities. *Psychiatric Rehabilitation Journal, 22*(3).

Kang, M., & Byun, H.P. (2001). A conceptual framework for a Web-based knowledge construction support system. *Educational Technology, 41*(4), 48-53.

Macias, C., DeCarlo, L., Wang, Q., Frey, J., & Barreira, P. (2001). Work interest as a predictor of competitive employment: Policy implications for psychiatric rehabilitation. *Administration and Policy in Mental Health, 28*(4), 279-297.

Martin, J., & Hess, L. (2004, September 1-3). *Chinese culture and recovery from mental illness*. Paper presented at The Mental Health Services Conference of Australia and New Zealand, Gold Coast Convention Centre, Broadbeach, Queensland.

Mayer, R.E. (2001). *Multimedia learning*. NY: Cambridge Press.

McKay, E. (2000a). *Instructional strategies integrating the cognitive style construct: A meta-knowledge processing model (Contextual components that facilitate spatial/logical task performance)*. Unpublished doctoral dissertation (Com. Sci. & Info. Sys.). Deakin University, Geelong, Australia. Retrieved January 13, 2007, from http://www.tux.lib.deakin.edu.au/adt-VDU/public/adt-VDU20061011.122556/

McKay, E. (2000b). Measurement of cognitive performance in computer programming concept acquisition: Interactive effects of visual metaphors and the cognitive style construct. *Journal of Applied Measurement, 1*(3), 257-286.

McKay, E. (2005, October). Human-computer interaction closes the digital divide: A multicultural, intergenerational ICT case study. *Information Age, National Journal of the Australian Computer Society*, 16-20.

McKay, E. (2006). Human-computer interaction passes on the wisdom: Intergenerational knowledge sharing. In K. Cagilitay (Ed.), *Affective and emotional aspects of human-computer interaction: Emphasis on game-based and innovative learning approaches*. IOS Press. ISBN: 1-58603-572-x. ISBN: 1572-4794, 207-216.

McKay, E., & Martin, J. (2002, July 7-10). *Web-work-search system: Enhanced accessibility.* Paper presented at the Australian Society for Educational Technology International Education & Technology Conference (ASET 2002): Untangling the Web-Establishing Learning Links, Melbourne, Australia.

McKay, E., Martin, J., & Izard, J. (2005). *Cognitive awareness in vocational training programmes: Targeting successful outcomes for young people and those wishing to undertake vocational training.* Paper presented at the 3rd International Conference on Universal Access in Human-Computer Interaction, held at the 11th International Conference on Human-Computer Interaction (AC, UAHCI, HIMI, OCSC, VR, U&I, EPCE), Las Vegas, NV.

McKay, E., Thomas, T., & Martin, J. (2003). An interactive job seeking system for vocational rehabilitation. *Journal of Computer Assisted Learning, 19*(3), 396.

McKay, E., Thomas, T., & Martin, J. (2004, August 16-18). Work search prototype design: Human-computer interaction for vocational rehabilitation. In V. Uskov (Ed.), *Proceedings of the International Association of Science and Technology for Development: Computers and Advanced Technology in Education (CATE 2004)* (pp.167-172). Kauai, Hawaii.

Merrill, M.D. (2002a). Effective use of instructional technology requires educational reform. *Educational Technology, 42*(4), 13-16.

Merrill, M.D. (2002b). First principles of instruction. *ETR&D, 50*(3), 43-59. Retrieved January 11, 2006, from http://www.indiana.edu/~tedfrick/aect2002/firstprinciples-bymerrill.pdf

Merrill, M.D. (2002c). Pebble-in-the-pond model for instructional development. *Performance Measurement, 41*(7), 41-44. Retrieved March 10, 2005, from http://www.ispi.org/pdf/Merrill.pdf

Merrill, M.D. (2003). *Keynote address: Does your instruction rate 5 stars?* Paper presented at the eLearning Conference on Design and Development: Instructional Design - Applying First Principles of Instruction, Melbourne, Australia.

Okamoto, T., Matsui, T., Inoue, H., & Cristea, A. (2000, December 4-6). *A distance-education self-learning support system based on a VOD Server.* Paper presented at the International Workshop on Advanced Learning Technologies (IWALT 2000): Advanced Learning Technology: Design and Development Issues, Palmerston North, New Zealand.

Pedroni, L. (2004). *Robert Gagne (1916-2002).* My coach online. Retrieved December 12, 2005, from http://www.my-ecoach.com/idtimeline/theory/gagne.html

Preece, J. (1994). *Human-computer interaction.* Harlow, UK: Addison-Wesley.

Preece, J. (2002). *Interaction design: Beyond human-computer interaction.* Harlow, UK: Addison-Wesley.

Riding, R. (2002). *School learning and cognitive styles.* London: David Fulton.

Rogers, J. (1995, Spring). Work is key to recovery. *Psychosocial Rehabilitation Journal, 18*(4).

Section V

School Context

Chapter XVII

ActiveHealth: Enhancing the Community of Physical and Health Educators Through Online Technologies

Lori Lockyer, University of Wollongong, Australia

John Patterson, University of Wollongong, Australia

Gregg Rowland, University of Wollongong, Australia

Doug Hearne, University of Wollongong, Australia

Abstract

This chapter explores the perspectives of an instructional design team that designed and developed an online environment to facilitate the Australian physical and health educators' community of practice. The objective of the multidisciplinary design team was to determine what activities and supporting technologies would help invigorate senior members and initiate novice members to this well-established community. The chapter describes the community and the particular challenges it faces; details the design, development and implementation processes for the online environment and activities; identifies the issues addressed during the design and implementation process; and, analyses the experiences of the initial implementation. The authors hope that the instructional design principles derived from examining the challenges and successes for this particular community of practice will support designers and researchers working with other communities to address similar issues.

Introduction

This chapter explores the perspectives of an instructional design team comprising academics from the Faculty of Education at the University of Wollongong in New South Wales, Australia. The team was formed to design and develop an online environment that could facilitate the Australian physical and health educators' community of practice. The objective of the multidisciplinary design team was to determine what activities and supporting technologies would help invigorate senior members and initiate novice members to this well-established community.

The chapter describes the community and the particular challenges it faces; details the design, development and implementation processes for the online environment and activities; identifies the issues addressed during the design and implementation process; analyses the experiences of the initial implementation; and, defines the next stages of community development.

Background

Any profession is associated with stages, collectively referred to as the *professional* or *career lifecycle*. All professions have (at minimum) an induction phase to begin, and an expertise phase subsequent to reaching proficiency in the knowledge and skills base of the particular profession. These stages and the factors that influence them provide an important background when thinking about how professionals participate in their community of practice.

There are several models delineating various career stages in the teaching profession (Fessler, 1985; Steffy & Wolfe, 2001; Guskey, 2002). All models consider the lifecycle from the point of entry into pre-service teacher-education programs, through (variously named) phases of growth and renewal, to the final stage of exit.

Fessler's (1985) model considers the interaction of career-stage with a teacher's personal and organisational environment. The personal environment is comprised of individual disposition, family, positive critical incidents, crisis, cumulative life experiences, and avocational outlets. The organisational environment is comprised of professional and industrial organisations, regulations, management style, pubic trust, and societal expectations.

As teachers move from their *pre-service* and *induction* stages through *competency building* and into *enthusiastic and growing*, they are eager to develop skills, support their peers, and investigate and implement new practices and innovations. At these stages teachers often effectively participate in the community of practice. They may do this by actively seeking professional development opportunities; contributing to committee work in order to influence curriculum focus; creating and sharing teaching resources; supervising pre-service teachers during practice placements; and/or, acting as executive members of professional associations.

However, as teachers' organisational environments and personal situations move them through the stages of *career frustration,* to *career stability*, and on to a *wind-down* stage—involvement in the community of practice may plateau, diminish, or (at worst) be detrimental to the community of practice.

A supportive and nurturing organisational environment helps to sustain enthusiasm and facilitate teachers' progression towards a positive *wind-down* and *exit* stage (Woods & Lynn, 2001). On the other hand, a negative organisational environment can result in movement into the *frustration* stage, or can lead to burnout. Thus, it is important for the community of practice to support their members through difficult issues and to identify, design and implement activities and vehicles for revitalising involvement. Supporting members in the later stages of their careers is necessary for the sustainability of the community. That is, retaining experienced members provides for what Wenger (1998) refers to as *generational encounters*—the opportunity for interaction between newcomers and more experienced members.

In addition to the organisational challenges mentioned above, the demography of the teaching community may also be a factor contributing to the significant movement of members towards less active phases of their careers. Like their counterparts in other countries (such as the UK, U.S. and Canada), the majority of teachers in Australia are moving towards the *exit* stage (i.e., retirement or next career outlook). In 2001, the median age of the Australian teaching population was 43 years with 44% of teachers older than 45 years of age (Committee for the Review of Teaching and Teacher Education, 2003). This demographic is particularly indicative of Australian physical and health educators (PHE) and heightens the imperative of the community to tap into the wealth of experience of these members prior to their departure from the group.

Both the concept of the teaching career lifecycle, and contemporary calls for a professional learning that takes a broad, career-focused approach (Committee for the Review of Teaching and Teacher Education, 2003) highlight the importance of enhancing and sustaining the PHE community. These concepts provide the backdrop for understanding the context of the following case study.

Case Description

Context

The physical and health education teaching fraternity is a well-established community of practice in Australia. The community's reach extends to professionals employed in various public and private sector organisations who are interested in exercise, fitness, physical education, health promotion, and wellness. A core group includes high school teachers, teacher-educators (i.e., university-based academics), and the students they train to be PHE teachers (i.e., pre-service teachers).

Within the last 35 years, this core community has lobbied to have the importance of their discipline recognised as a key learning area and a mandatory component of secondary curricula across Australia.

Entry into the profession is in demand, with university entrance scores for physical and health education-specific programs often the highest among teacher-education courses.

Community members have organised themselves at national and state levels through various professional associations, and continually seek to address the challenges of their profession. Challenges for the community include calls for reform within the teaching profession, including national debate about teacher registration; calls for enhancement to quality teaching through the establishment of teaching standards and pedagogy reform; and, integration of information and communication technologies (ICTs) into the curriculum.

The Design Team

In 1999, an instructional design team began working to enhance this community of practice and to address these challenges through the construction of an online environment aimed at facilitating resource and idea sharing. It was envisioned that online technologies could provide opportunities for all members of the community to propose and contribute to activities—thereby addressing the suggested attributes of a professional learning community, including: supportive and shared leadership; collective creativity; shared values and vision; supportive conditions; and shared personal practice (Hord, 1997; Stuckey, Hedberg, & Lockyer, 2001).

This design team, all members of the Faculty of Education, consists of three subject matter experts (SME) and an educational technologist (ET). The educational technologist previously participated in the design, development and outcomes-related research of a range of CD-ROM and Web-based learning environments for both K-12 and university learners. Within the faculty she teaches across the range of pre-service teaching programs, in addition to teaching a postgraduate ICT in education specialisation program. Her health education experience is within health promotion and patient education contexts.

The SMEs, all former high school teachers, are teacher-educators within the pre-service physical and health education specialisation program. They have engaged in leadership roles within state and national PHE professional associations and have contributed to state PHE syllabus development and assessment. Their scholarship and research foci span the areas of PHE pedagogy, educational policy and teacher professional development.

These designers have collaborated with a technology team of graphic artists and programmers. This technology team is a research and development unit within the faculty, which has extensive experience developing educational software, particularly interactive CD-ROMs. In 1999 they had just recently moved into online environments, and this particular project provided an opportunity to explore the design and development of database-driven Web sites.

One subject matter expert and the educational technologist had previously worked together as co-lecturers and designed and implemented online collaborative learning within a health and health behaviour course within the pre-service PHE specialisation program in 1998 (Lockyer, Patterson, & Harper, 2001). This was the first time that "learning with" rather than "learning about" technology had been implemented in this or any of the faculty's pre-service programs. This initiative was implemented before institutional adoption of a learning management system, and thus a database-driven Web site was constructed to facilitate students' engagement in weekly collaborative tasks.

The Initial Idea: Resource Repository

While engaging in the predominately inquiry-based tasks for this health and health behaviour course, the pre-service teachers recognised the potential of Web-based resources to support teaching and learning activities. They became familiar with general education and PHE-specific Web sites (online clearinghouses) that categorised Web-based resources by curriculum areas. However, from the students' perspective, these resources were of limited use given their base in Canada, the United Kingdom or the U.S. Specifically, the curriculum categorisation and evaluation of the sites by practitioners had limited relevance to the Australian (and in particular, the PHE) teaching context.

At this stage Australian initiatives of online repositories for educational resources, such as EdNA (http://www.edna.edu.au), were just getting off the ground and therefore did not meet the needs of the pre-service teachers identified. The students suggested to the course lecturers (i.e., SME1 and the ET) that they would like to be involved in a faculty initiative to develop a PHE Web-resource clearinghouse with an Australian perspective.

The lecturers included two colleagues in the plan and thus formed the instructional design team who worked with these students to expand this initial idea. The educational technologist was particularly interested in developing this idea for the PHE community:

Research and evaluation studies focused on using technology to support education often involve small groups of "early adopters"—those teachers eager to try new things. These projects tell us little about what really works for the majority. Working with this PHE community, which extends across one of the largest education systems in Australia, means we had to design for a large dispersed group representing a vast range of both skills and interest in using technology. The experience and outcomes should be able to be applied to other communities and other contexts. [ET]

From their experience within the PHE community of practice, the SMEs saw that community members had traditionally participated in ideas exchange and professional development through collaborations within policy and syllabus consultation; curriculum and resource development; and practice teaching experiences for the pre-service teachers. Unfortunately, these activities had often been conducted on an ad hoc and irregular basis where individual members may not have had a sustained role or commitment. Thus, the SMEs believed that the online technologies might provide a structure to facilitate more consistent interaction among members. They each had different interests in developing an online environment for the PHE community:

Having been a member of the community for more than 30 years, it is stimulating to have a group of 1st year pre-service teachers approach their lecturers about an idea that can support PHE—it shows how quickly they are seeing themselves as professionals. Building on their ideas and excitement, the online environment can foster continuous innovation and develop into something that can make a difference for the profession. For me personally, it allows me to extend my boundaries in terms of use of IT and how it can be applied in a professional sense. [SME1]

Teachers sharing resources and ideas is nothing new—making that happen was part of my job when I was a physical and health education consultant for the state education department years ago. It was professionally motivating to get a group of teachers in a room to design materials. They'd go away, develop the resources by working with other teachers in their school and I'd collect, package and distribute the resources to all PHE departments in the region. But support for activities like that has declined over the years. A Web site might reignite the energy of those good old days for experienced teachers. [SME2]

Over the years, a number of both state-based and national PHE professional associations have emerged in Australia. Some teachers are part of one or more than one association—some do not belong to any. An online environment that is not specific to one association may be a vehicle for collaborative community activity that cuts across barriers of specific associations. [SME3]

Idea to Action

The initial phase of the project involved a needs assessment that elicited feedback from community representatives including pre-service teachers, practicing teachers, and teacher educators in a number of Australian universities. The needs assessment was used to check the initial ideas of the students and lecturers; to define the design of the Web-based environment; and to prioritise community activities that could be facilitated by the environment.

It was determined that the overall structure of the Web site would: (1) provide access to a repository of relevant teaching and learning resources; (2) include support for professional development and interchanges among community members and be a contact point between face-to-face activities; and, (3) act as an online gateway to the University of Wollongong Physical and Health Education academic program.

A primary goal of the needs assessment was to determine a name that could be used for the online environment—a name that would represent the diverse nature of this community of practice. A number of suggestions were presented to community representatives and, finally, *ActiveHealth* was born. The name and the identification of the overall Web site structure led the design team to begin work with the technology team to design and prototype the Web site.

The instructional design team made a deliberate decision that the main areas of the Web site would be open access—that is, registration to use the site would not be necessary. It was thought that, given the range of Internet experience and skill amongst community members, managing usernames and passwords in the initial stages of site development might be a barrier to use for some members.

Structuring the Resource Repository

Prioritising the development of a resource repository was seen as an opportunity to harness community member activity. Both pre-service and practicing teachers must stay in touch with current and emerging knowledge in physical and health education, and creating a collection of resources would support teachers in their day-to-day classroom practice. This activity was thought to be one that would particularly attract participation from those members in the *competency building*, *enthusiastic and growing*, and *career stability* stages.

Again, the idea of identifying, evaluating and sharing resources is not new for these experienced teachers. What is new is the technology to help support it. The key is to ensure resources are relevant and the technology is user-friendly. [SME2]

Members indicated that the resources most useful for the community are: reputable Web sites that provide information about the content covered with the physical and health education curriculum; Web sites specifically designed to support teachers and teaching practice; PHE lesson ideas; PHE assessment tasks; and online PHE learning activities.

An important design consideration was that the resources (developed for, or linked to the collection) should be perceived by community members to be of high quality and relevance to the state-based Australian PHE curricula. This led to two key design tasks:

1. **Curriculum review:** The SMEs reviewed all primary and secondary physical and health education curricula from each of Australia's states and territories to establish a set of categories and sub-categories. The establishment of this common language was designed to support the processes of tagging and searching for resources.
2. **Peer-review:** The instructional design team then developed a peer-review process for the identification and release of resources through the Web site.

With these two design tasks complete, the instructional design and technology teams defined the database structures and interfaces for the resource repository (Rowland, Lockyer, & Patterson, 2001).

Any community member may suggest a PHE Web site or teaching support site to add to the *ActiveHealth* collection (i.e., a link to an external URL). The database-driven site serves a resource suggestion form page on which the member is asked to add information about the resource. This information includes the resource title; the URL, a description of the resource, a suggestion of how it might fit into the PHE curriculum, and the *ActiveHealth* curriculum categories and subcategories. The member is also asked to identify themselves, their school or organisation, and their e-mail address.

Additionally, a community member may contribute a PHE lesson idea, assessment task or online learning activity that they have developed. In this case, the site serves a resource submission form page on which the member is asked to add information about the idea/task/activity. For example, the lesson idea information includes the lesson title, keywords, lesson overview, targeted year/grade, goal or purpose, time required, suggested number of participants, materials/equipment needed, procedure, discussion points, possible variations, how to evaluate, associated Web sites, and the *ActiveHealth* curriculum categories and subcategories. Again, the member is also asked to identify themselves, their school or organisation, and their e-mail address. Once a resource is submitted or suggested, the information is stored in the resources databases to await peer-review.

Community members, be they pre-service teachers, practicing teachers, or teacher-educators, can volunteer to review resources. Once authorised, reviewers are issued with an individual username and password so that when they access the *ActiveHealth* site, the database automatically provides recently received resources, review guidelines, and a review form to complete.

Following submission of a review, resources deemed appropriate are tagged in the database as available for circulation to *ActiveHealth* users. When a member wishes to access reviewed resources the site generates dynamic search, retrieve and view pages.

By 2001, the *ActiveHealth* site was functional and supported the process of storing, reviewing and sharing resources and ideas. However, it was necessary to implement a range of community activities that would help to develop the resource base.

Figure 1. ActiveHealth resource suggestion/submission and peer-review process

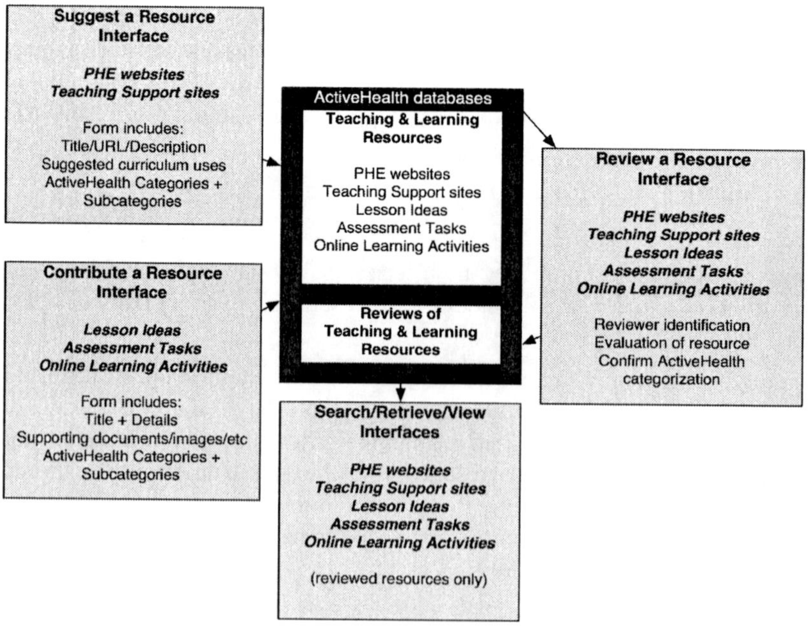

We knew, for this community, it was not a case of "if you build it, they will come." Using technology is not necessarily an everyday part of their life. So to ensure an initial base of resources, we needed to engage the community members in familiar and convenient activities to support resource contribution. [ET]

Community Activity: Resource Identification and Development

Given that development of such resources is often focused on teachers' traditional tendency toward face-to-face continuing education settings, the instructional design team worked with academic course coordinators, local schools, professional associations, technology companies, and the state government education authorities to establish opportunities for members of the PHE community to engage in resource development. Collaborative face-to-face activities included:

Teacher professional development workshops on:

- searching the Internet for curriculum-relevant Web sites;
- integrating Web resources into teaching and learning activities; and
- designing and developing online learning activities (e.g., WebQuests).

Pre-service university coursework tasks included:

- identifying and evaluating curriculum-relevant Web sites and teacher support sites;
- development of lesson ideas, assessment tasks and online learning activities; and
- individual teachers' evaluations and suggestions for improvement of the online learning activities created by pre-service teachers.

Resources identified, and products developed through these activities, were subsequently added to the *ActiveHealth* databases and then reviewed online by community members prior to general release to the community of practice.

The design team felt that involving pre-service teachers in the development of the *ActiveHealth* site was of particular importance. Not only did the initial idea come from this group, but also involvement would provide another opportunity to facilitate entry into the profession. Such projects involve collaboration with teacher-educators, other pre-service teachers and practicing teachers. This promotes, as Bruffee (1993) suggests, the opportunity to speak the language of their profession—and "speaking the language fluently defines membership in the community" (p. 130). Hence, the professional development experienced through the formal practicum of their university course is extended.

The pre-service teachers expressed a sense of pride to be significantly involved in the development of the Web site and specific activities that involved community member use of the site. They saw this as adding value to the usual coursework and practice teaching experience and that it added to their professional portfolio. [SME1]

Pre-Service Teaching Peer Support

The practice teaching component of the faculty's pre-service program was identified, by the instructional design team, as an opportunity to benefit from the affordances of the *ActiveHealth* Web site and its communication applications. While the school-based practice teaching model is an excellent example of the partnership among all community members, the effectiveness of its implementation has been a topic of debate and calls for reform (Ministerial Advisory Council on the Quality of Teaching 1998; Ramsey, 2000).

It was theorised that implementing a process of online peer support for students during their school-based practice teaching experiences might address some of the concerns raised by those calls for reform. As Naidu and Olsen (1996) suggest, online interaction between pre-service teachers could allow them to:

- share their practical learning experiences in order to benefit from those of others;
- bring together their varied practical experiences to develop a body of knowledge that is unique and relevant to their area of study;
- discuss unit/content material and their individual as well as collaborative notions of the meaning of content in light of their practical experiences;
- engage in individual and collaborative reflective thinking upon practice;
- develop a support network to facilitate ongoing sharing of information about theory and practice that is productive to the individual as well as the group; and
- move from a position of isolation and independent correspondence mode to a networked community of learners with the ability to electronically access other learners, tutors, lecturers, and also resources such as databases, catalogues, and so forth. (p. 268)

Since 2000, the instructional designers have worked to integrate the notion of online peer support for the pre-service practicum experiences. Final year students have supported each other during their concluding five-week practicum. Final year students have also supported second year pre-service teachers during their initial secondary school practicum (Lockyer, Patterson, Rowland, & Hearne, 2002; Hearne, Lockyer, Rowland, & Patterson, 2003, 2004).

Early Career Mentoring

The experience of facilitating online support during the pre-service teaching practicum was then extended to the beginning-teacher (*induction*) stage of the teachers' career lifecycle, with a mentoring initiative. The instructional design team brought together four professional associations and two educational authorities to develop a program in which experienced classroom teachers could mentor new professionals in their first two years of teaching.

Thereby, beginning-teachers can benefit from the insight and experience of their colleagues who are in the career cycle phases of *enthusiasm* and *stability*. These mentoring activities involve both face-to-face and online interactions and often focus on discussion topics of particular interest to beginning teachers—such as classroom management, assessment and professional responsibilities (Hearne, Rowland, & Webb, 2005).

With these specific community activities that involve use of online communication tools, username and password-protected subsections of the *ActiveHealth* Web site were created to develop a sense of privacy for members engaged in support and mentoring activities.

Successes and Challenges

The evolution of the *ActiveHealth* Web site has involved a number of iterative design, development and implementation cycles involving the instructional design and technology teams and a range of community representatives. Reflection on these cycles by the instructional designers helps to define both the successes and challenges encountered, and the strategies employed to facilitate success and meet those challenges.

While the "communities of practice" literature was in its infancy when the online environment for this PHE community was initially designed, the concepts found in that body of literature can now be applied to the analysis of the implementation of the *ActiveHealth* site.

Wenger, McDermott, and Snyder (2002) derive seven principles for cultivating community of practice from their previous experiences with a range of communities. The principles are:

1. *Design for evolution*
2. *Open a dialogue between inside and outside perspectives*
3. *Invite different levels of participation*
4. *Develop both public and private community spaces*
5. *Focus on value*
6. *Combine familiarity and excitement*
7. *Create a rhythm for the community.*

(Wenger, McDermott, & Snyder, 2002, p. 51)

These principles provided a framework with which the instructional design team could evaluate the design, development and implementation issues associated with *ActiveHealth.*

Design for Evolution

This principle considers the dynamic nature of communities in terms of their membership. The *ActiveHealth* environment was designed to be built in stages with members involved in different activities associated with each stage. The diversity of these activities, and the supporting online components, suggests a level of achievement.

However, there have been some limitations in this approach. Continued heavy reliance on the instructional design team to facilitate activities has meant that older activities receive less attention once newer ones are introduced. For example, the development of resources and recruitment of reviewers for the resource collection has slowed, due to the significant amount of time the designers have committed to developing the mentoring activities.

ActiveHealth was always envisaged as a "work in progress." The development process has shown us that consideration must be given, in the early stages, to the delegation of roles for implementation. It can't just fall to the instructional designers to facilitate ongoing activities while, at the same time, trying to design new activities. We need to expand the implementation team to keep all activities moving ahead. [SME1]

Open a Dialogue Between Inside and Outside Perspectives

Early in the design phase, attempts were made to gather perspectives on what technology structures and community activities would help to enhance the Australian PHE community of practice. A range of perspectives was gathered. The design team itself represented both inside and outside perspectives. The subject matter experts represented each type of PHE community member (having each been pre-service teachers, practicing school teachers, and practicing teacher-educators) and had been through various stages of the career lifecycle. The educational technologist and members of the technology team brought an outside perspective to the design. A range of meetings and workshops sought further insight into the insider perspective during the needs assessment stage of design.

Gathering such perspectives was successful in helping to outline design elements and prioritise activities. However, upon reflection there may not be appropriate representation of people from each of the career lifecycle stages—the site may cater more to some PHE community members than others.

Being teacher-educators we feel that we have a good balance in terms of inside/outside perspective. But, what has been particularly helpful to the design process has been the inclusion of consultative committees that have a range of expertise and years of teaching experience. [SME3]

Invite Different Levels of Participation

It has been argued that people have different levels of interest in their community of practice and thus should be encouraged to participate in different ways and at different levels (Wenger, McDermott, & Snyder, 2002). This is certainly exemplified in the development of the *ActiveHealth* site to support the PHE community. Pre-service teachers can elect to have limited involvement, by posting lesson ideas developed for their coursework assignments to the Web site. Those who are interested in taking a more active role can choose to participate in specific projects (e.g., volunteer to be a peer mentor, or to be mentored by a peer) or help lead a specific project (e.g., co-design the peer support sub-section of the site;

research the process or outcome of the peer support or early career mentoring activities). Similarly, teachers can have peripheral involvement through using resources on the site. In addition, they may be more actively involved by sharing their work and ideas through the resources area, acting as resource reviewers, attending workshops focused on resource creation, or acting as mentors for early career teachers.

I am happy with the different levels of involvement from community members—teachers at different career stages as well as teacher-educators. For the future I'd like to see involvement scale up—more members involved in more activities. [SME2]

Develop Both Public and Private Community Spaces

Wenger, McDermott, and Snyder (2002) suggest the need to "orchestrate activities in both public and private spaces that use the strength of individual relationships to enrich events and use events to strengthen individual relationships" (p. 59). The initial *ActiveHealth* design of open access was driven more from a usability intention than a deliberate attempt to be publicly inclusive. There was a concern that the need to register to contribute, and/or access community resources, would be a barrier to members in terms of both technical comfort and time. Contributors' and reviewers' names were associated with resources, as designers felt it was appropriate to acknowledge member participation—certainly teachers have a long history of sharing educational resources and ideas. However, it would be interesting to explore whether publication of their name on an open access site may have been a limiting factor in some members' participation in this community activity.

Certainly, private spaces did develop as specific activities (e.g., peer support and early career mentoring) included the use of communication tools and involved potentially more personal and sensitive information and idea sharing among members.

I believe the initial decision to enable access without registration to ActiveHealth by all PHE community members was the way to go given the nature of community. That principle of inclusivity has endured even in the closed spaces that are designed for specific professional development purposes—such as early career mentoring—where all participants can add and/or view postings in order to share ideas. [SME2]

Focus on Value

The basis of design of the *ActiveHealth* Web site, and the supporting community activities have always focused on adding value and benefiting the professional needs of the PHE teaching community. The *ActiveHealth* initiatives that have been implemented in "closed spaces"—such as the peer support and early career mentoring—have been evaluated and explicit positive outcomes for participants have been identified. However, the open access to the resource collection limits the opportunity for evaluation as it is impossible to understand the numbers, and range of members or others who may have used—but most importantly found value from—the resources.

I think we have learned a lot from the evaluation of the targeted community activities, such as peer support for pre-service teachers and early career mentoring, which are facilitated by ActiveHealth. While we are limited in the ways we can recruit potential participants in an evaluation study of the resources area, it is still doable and probably the time is right to understand what the impact has been in terms of dissemination. [ET]

Combine Familiarity and Excitement

The suggestion of creating opportunity for both familiar and exciting activities is based in the notion of the need to both comfort and challenge members. The *ActiveHealth* site and activity design may have leaned toward the familiar in the initial stages—that is, in its focus on the traditional interest of resource sharing amongst teachers. It could also be argued that the peer support for pre-service teachers and mentoring for early career teachers were also familiar activities of this community. However, the outcomes of these activities—such as mentors identifying their own learning from the activities, and all participants identifying a greater understanding of how technology can be used to support learning—suggests a level of excitement which may have been driven by the formalisation of the activities through the online environment.

In the early stages of development, it was important to implement activities that would be familiar to community members. Knowing that technology was going to form a greater part of a teacher's professional life we also needed to design a site that would motivate and enable take-up. [SME2]

Create a Rhythm for the Community

Wenger, McDermott, and Snyder (2002) advise that the rhythm of the community lies in the consistency of its interactions, and that this "is the strongest indicator of its aliveness" (p. 63). A brief examination of participation in the *ActiveHealth* Web site and its supporting activities indicates that the rhythm has been disjointed or inconsistent, as particular initiatives have seen more or less involvement over time. Of course it is important to remember that the Web site and the extent of its use are not the only indicators of the vibrancy of the community in its totality.

Again, it is hard for us to have a complete picture of usage of ActiveHealth by members as login is not required. So while there might be periods when there is limited contribution of resources to the site it does not necessarily mean community members are not using the resources already available within the site. [ET]

Principles

Designing for communities of practice is unique within the context of instructional design. The dynamic process of designing and implementing the *ActiveHealth* Web site, to support an existing community of practice, has helped the developers identify integral principles for design. They are:

1. Identify and remember the scope of the community
2. Create engagement through focused participation
3. Identify opportunities and foster involvement in leadership roles.

Identify and Remember the Scope of the Community

The subject matter experts on the design team were well aware of who is involved in the PHE community, and of the arrangements of both loose knit and formalised networks within the community. Initially, the design team may have considered the whole PHE community to be potential users of the *ActiveHealth* site—that is, the entire Australian physical and health education community including all geographical states, all professional organisations, all educational sectors, and all teacher-education institutions. However, in practice the majority of participation in *ActiveHealth* initiatives—both at the peripheral and active levels—was centred in New South Wales; the NSW chapters of the professional associations; the educational authorities of NSW; and, teacher-educators, pre-service teachers and graduates of the University of Wollongong. This limited participation is not necessarily a negative indicator for the Web site or its related activities, but may have provided a different set of opportunities if it was the original focus for design.

Create Engagement Through Focused Participation

Diverse members of the PHE community are all able to participate in *ActiveHealth* activities, because priority projects were identified and implemented that address the needs of members at various stages of their careers. The designers, when developing new initiatives for the site, look for opportunities to focus that development on topical concerns of various groups of PHE members.

For example, the resource collection was designed so it could address the context of, and/or challenges facing members at any particular time. Through 2002-2003, teachers participated in targeted workshops that developed resources to add to the *ActiveHealth* collection. These workshops were held at the same time as teachers were collectively dealing with the introduction of a new syllabus and were in the process of identifying new resources to support this syllabus.

Pre-service teachers can also participate in site initiatives developed with reference to their needs. Students, by contributing to the online resource collection, experience an added level of authenticity and value to what would otherwise be mere coursework assessment tasks.

They also have the opportunity to become peer mentors and support their less experienced colleagues, but can do so in a limited timeframe that does not impinge on the requirements of their own course.

These and other examples demonstrate the value of members being involved at different stages, at different levels, and for specific initiatives that are of interest and value to individuals, yet support the community as a whole.

Identify Opportunities and Foster Involvement in Leadership Roles

The most limiting factor for sustained growth of the *ActiveHealth* Web site and its supporting activities is the reliance on members of the design team for continued leadership. While, to a certain degree, there have been positive levels of participation in all activities, members have not self-identified to take on leadership roles for new or established activities. As such, members of the design team need to guide existing activities and at the same time attempt to initiate subsequent projects. A contributing factor may be that a teacher-education institution is the host of the Web site, and teachers tend to have loose connections to those institutions once they are not engaged in formal pre-service or professional development courses. The next challenge for the *ActiveHealth* design team is to build leadership roles out of the informal connections amongst the community.

Conclusion

This chapter has provided the perspectives of an instructional design team that has had five years of experience in the design, development and implementation of a Web site and supporting activities for the Australian physical and health education community. The experience of attempting to use online technologies to facilitate the next stages of development of this existing community has contributed to the team's understanding of communities of practice and has helped to identify some design principles that may benefit others working with communities that face similar issues and/or contexts.

Acknowledgment

The authors wish to acknowledge the editorial assistance of Ms. Elizabeth Patterson. The *ActiveHealth* Web site is developed by emlab, Faculty of Education, University of Wollongong (http://www.emlab.uow.edu.au/).

References

Bruffee, K.A. (1993). *Collaborative learning: Higher education, interdependence, and the authority of knowledge.* Baltimore: The Johns Hopkins University Press.

Committee for the Review of Teaching and Teacher Education. (2003). *Australia's teachers: Australia's future. Canberra: Commonwealth of Australia.* Retrieved September 29, 2005, from http://www.dest.gov.au/sectors/school_education/policy_initiatives_reviews/reviews/teaching_teacher_education/default.htm

Fessler, R. (1985). A model for teacher professional growth and development. In P.J. Burke & R.G. Heideman (Eds.), *Career-long teacher education* (pp. 181-193). Springfield, IL: Charles G. Thomas.

Guskey, T.R. (2002). Professional development and teacher change. *Teachers and Teaching: Theory and Practice*, *8*(3/4), 381-390.

Hearne, D., Lockyer, L., Rowland, G., & Patterson, J. (2003). An online mentoring practicum in physical and health education teacher preparation: Preliminary findings and future directions. In D. Lassner & C. McNaught (Eds.), *Proceedings of ED-MEDIA 2003 World Conference on Educational Multimedia, Hypermedia and Telecommunications* (pp. 1546-1553). Norfolk, VA: Association for the Advancement of Computing in Education.

Hearne, D., Lockyer, L., Rowland, G., & Patterson, J. (2004). Becoming a beginning teacher: An online mentoring experience for pre-service physical and health educators. In L. Cantoni & C. McLoughlin (Eds.), *Proceedings of ED-MEDIA2004 World Conference on Educational Multimedia, Hypermedia and Telecommunications* (pp. 4967-4972). Norfolk, VA: Association for the Advancement of Computing in Education.

Hearne, D., Rowland, G., & Webb, A. (2005). From surviving to thriving: The use of information and communication technology in an induction program for early career teachers in personal development, health and physical education. In P. Kommers & G. Richards (Eds.), *Proceedings of World Conference on Educational Multimedia, Hypermedia and Telecommunications* (pp. 2636-2643). Norfolk, VA: AACE.

Hord, S.M. (1997). Professional learning communities: What are they and why are they important? *Southwest Educational Development Laboratory, Issues about Change*, *6*(1), 1-9. Retrieved July 12, 2003, from http://www.sedl.org/change/issues/issues61.html

Lockyer, L., Patterson, J., & Harper, B. (2001). ICT in higher education: Evaluating outcomes for health education. *Journal of Computer Assisted Learning*, *17*(3), 275-283.

Lockyer, L., Patterson, J., Rowland, G., & Hearne, D. (2002). Online mentoring and peer support: Using learning technologies to facilitate entry into a community of practice. *Alt-J*, *10*(1), 24-31.

Ministerial Advisory Council on the Quality of Teaching. (1998). *Towards greater professionalism: Teacher educators, teaching and the curriculum*. Sydney: Department of Education and Training New South Wales.

Naidu, S., & Olson, P., (1996). Making the most of practical experience in teacher education with computer-supported collaborative learning. *International Journal of Educational Telecommunications*, *2*, 265-278.

Ramsey, G. (2000). *Quality matters: Revitalising Teaching: Critical times, critical choices; report on the review of teacher education.* NSW.

Rowland, G., Lockyer, L., & Patterson, J. (2001). Exploring on-line communities: Supporting physical and health education professional development opportunities. In N. Smythe (Ed.), *Proceedings of Apple University Consortium Conference* (pp 22-1-22-7). Sydney: Apple Computer Australia.

Steffy, B.E. & Wolfe, M.P. (2001). A life-cycle model for career teachers. *Kappa Delta Pi Record, 38*(1), 16-19.

Stuckey, B., Hedberg, J., & Lockyer, L. (2001) Professional development online: Doing IT pedagogically. In J. Price, D. Willis, N. Davis, & J. Willis (Eds.), *Proceedings of SITE 2001 Society for Information Technology & Teacher Education* (pp. 2439-2444). Norfolk, VA: Association for the Advancement of Computing in Education.

Wenger, E. (1998). *Communities of practice: Learning, meaning and identity.* Cambridge: Cambridge University Press.

Wenger, E., McDermott, R., & Snyder, W.M. (2002). *Cultivating communities of practice: A guide to managing knowledge.* Boston: Harvard Business School Press.

Woods, A.M., & Lynn, S.K. (2001). Through the years: A longitudinal study of physical education teachers from a research-based preparation program. *Research Quarterly for Exercise and Sport, 72*(3), 219-231.

Chapter XVIII

Creating CoPs During the Development of an Online Classroom-Based Simulation

Brian Ferry, University of Wollongong, Australia

Lisa Kervin, University of Wollongong, Australia

Abstract

The purpose of this chapter is two fold. First it reports on the research associated with the development and implementation of prototype versions of an online classroom simulation. It looks at how the use of these simulations helped to develop a community of practice among pre-service teacher users. Second, it reports on how a team of researchers, an instructional designer, programmers and graphic artists worked within a community of practice as the simulation software was created.

Introduction

It is widely accepted that instructional designers play a significant role in enhancing teaching and learning in universities, distance education and corporations. The purpose of this chapter is two fold. First it reports on the research associated with the development and implementation of prototype versions of an online classroom simulation. It looks at how the use of these helped to develop a community of practice among pre-service teacher users of the simulation. Second, it reports on how a team of researchers, an instructional designer, programmers and graphic artists worked within a community of practice as the simulation software was created.

The purpose of the simulated classroom was to enhance the initial practicum experience of pre-service teachers enrolled in their first-year of a primary teacher education degree. The pedagogical focus of the simulation was on the teaching of literacy skills in primary schools, skills that are considered one of the keys to success in schooling (Cambourne, 2001; Comber, Badger, Barnett, Nixon, Prince, & Pitt, 2001). Our research was conducted using five prototype versions of the simulation over a period of two and a half years; and to date it has involved more than 220 users (Kervin, Ferry, Carrington, Turbill, Cambourne, Hedberg, & Jonassen, 2005). Our research findings have consistently shown that pre-service teacher understandings of complex classroom situations associated with the teaching of literacy were enhanced by interaction with the software. In particular, the opportunities provided in the software to slow down or accelerate classroom events, revisit and reflect on critical decision points and replay events in the light of new understandings supported the pre-service teachers. These design affordances appeared to provide pre-service teachers with the time to think critically about complex teaching situations, which relied on their ability to identify and respond to the virtual children's experiences. Further, they were required to engage in dialogue and negotiation at key decision-making opportunities, as well as employ a range of indirect classroom strategies such as questioning, modelling and prompting when making decisions. Pre-service teachers have consistently reported that their experience with the simulation enabled them to appreciate the complex role of the teacher, specifically the impact of a subtle decision that experienced teachers made during lessons.

In addition, we report on how the research associated with each version of the simulation prototype software helped team members to more fully understand each other's role in developing and improving the simulation. Initially the instructional designer, content experts and researchers were leading the development process, while the other members were legitimate peripheral participants. Over time, the other members of the team developed into legitimate participants, and formed a viable community of practice as ways to support initial teacher education were examined. We describe the processes that we used to assist all members of the design team to enter the communities of practice and understand the context and purpose of the project.

A community of practice is defined as groups of people who accumulate and share their collective learning (Wenger, 2002). Lave and Wenger (1991) first used this term in relation to situated learning. In more recent years, the term "communities of practice" has typically been connected to knowledge management as it is a way to cultivate or nurture new knowledge. It focuses on the sharing of tacit knowledge within an organization. Throughout the project two distinct communities of practice emerged. The first involved the pre-service teachers

Figure 1. How we believe the CoPs interacted with each other during this project

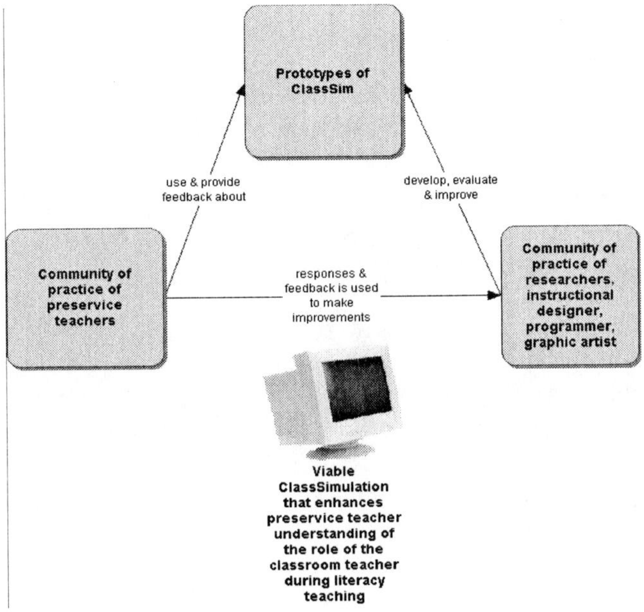

who engaged with the simulation software. The second community of practice included the design team as the software was developed. Individual members of one community of practice interacted with members of the other community in ways that assisted both communities to be more successful in their tasks. This process is represented in Figure 1.

Background

The development of a classroom simulation stemmed from both research-based and anecdotal-evidence claiming that many pre-service teacher education courses are not effective in preparing beginning teachers for their entry into the teaching profession. Several studies have criticised pre-service teacher education courses for presenting a fragmented and decontextualised learning experience (for example, Entwhistle, Entwhistle, & Tait, 1993; Ramsey, 2000). Such research asserts that learning experiences in pre-service teacher education often make it difficult for beginning teachers to retrieve knowledge from their university experiences when they are required to apply it in classroom situations. Pre-service teachers assert that this happens because there have often been minimal previous links between the theory and the practice (Bransford, Sherwood, Hasselbring, Kinzer, & Williams, 1990; Kervin & Turbill, 2003). Barth (1990) supports this view and argues that the teaching profession is better served when pre-service training is linked with actual classroom experience. He claims that, "seldom do these two worlds converge" (p. 118).

Ramsey (2000), in his review of teacher education in NSW, recommended that pre-service teachers receive quality classroom-based experience supervised by an accredited teacher mentor. He argued that providing more extensive classroom-based experience did not guarantee quality experience. Darling-Hammond (1999) also addressed this issue, and conceded that school-based practical experiences often consist of a series of isolated, decontextualised lessons prepared and implemented according to the requirements of the supervising teacher. Others such as Ramsey (2000) take an even stronger view and assert that at worst, the practicum can be an unsupported and disillusioning experience.

Danielson's (1996) research showed that classroom teachers typically make more than 3,000 non-trivial decisions each day. These findings pose serious challenges to pre-service teacher education. Other researchers have acknowledged that pre-service teacher learning needs to be organised in ways that allow pre-service teachers to regularly participate in the complex decision-making processes that teachers make in classroom settings (for example, Groundwater-Smith, Deer, Sharp, & March, 1996; Kiggins, 2001). However, as Ramsey (2000) reported, pre-service teachers' experience is often limited by a lack of regular access to quality classroom experiences.

This project was grounded within our belief that the development of a classroom-based simulation is one way to support the range of learning strategies incorporated within teacher education programs. The researchers in the team believed that a simulation had the potential to support existing programs by providing access to additional classroom experience within a virtual environment. Limited research is reported on simulations in teacher development, but advances in gaming software, particularly those which involve players creating worlds (e.g., The Sims), have demonstrated that it is possible to create a simulation that can support pre-service teachers' professional learning. The instructional designer, programmers and graphic designer soon explained that such a project was beyond the budget of this research project. However, they could create an environment that allowed users to participate in the creation of a virtual-classroom world, make decisions like a teacher, and then view and reflect on the effects of a multiplicity of classroom management decisions and teaching decisions. The challenge for the team was to combine our human resources (e.g., knowledge of classroom-based research in literacy teaching, initial teacher education, knowledge of the potential of the software and hardware) to create an effective online learning environment. We had to effectively use the financial and human resources available.

We decided to use a developmental approach to the research (Reeves, Herrington, & Oliver, 2005) (also known as "design research," "design experiment," or "formative research"). This design incorporates four phases characteristic of this approach, as depicted in Figure 2.

Figure 2. Development approach to research

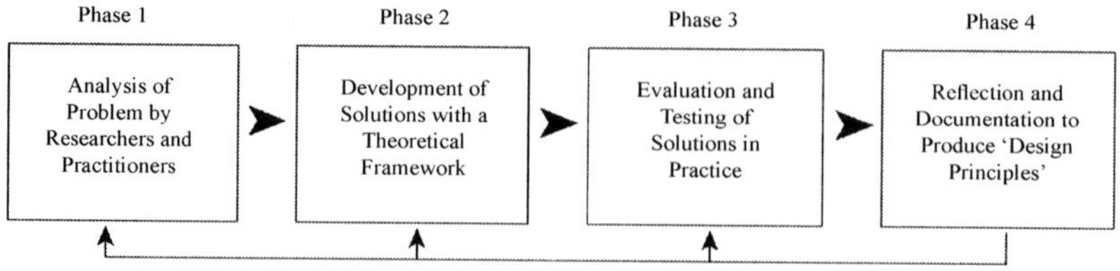

Phase 1: Analysis of the Practical Problem

The following research questions were devised to gain an understanding of the practical problems that the simulation needed to address.

1. What does the current research say about the planning and organization of literacy lessons in lower primary school classrooms?
2. How can pre-service teachers experience this knowledge in ways that encourage them to reflect on their current experience and access additional knowledge?
3. What design affordances could best support the development of a community of practice amongst users?

Members of the initial research team who had recent classroom experience and access to considerable classroom-based observation data addressed Question 1. In addition an extensive literature review on this topic provided direction for the software development.

To respond to Question 2, the researchers developed teacher scripts of classroom learning events, designed to depict the research from Question 1.

Additional information on this process has been previously reported (Kervin, Cambourne, Tubill, Ferry, Hedberg, Jonassen, & Puglisi, 2005). A trial of these scripts was held with a reference group of literacy experts, expert teachers and members of the design team. These different audiences suggested modifications. Storyboards of these events were then created in PowerPoint and were reviewed again by the reference group. These events were later used as an initial framework for the simulation design. At this stage all members of the design team met to discuss how this could be developed into an online environment, and the initial structure for the classroom simulation was developed. By this stage we had a shared understanding of the practical problem and possible approaches; however, we needed to develop possible solutions within a theoretical framework.

Phase 2: Development of Solutions within a Theoretical Framework

This challenge stimulated us to look for guidance from the literature. One of the most relevant articles we discovered was a review by Herrington, Oliver, and Reeves (2003). This review identified nine design elements of situated learning environments, and the challenge for us was to operationalize these principles in an online simulation. At the end of this phase, all members of the team had a shared vision of the goals of the software and how this focussed on an important educational problem. We were all developing an understanding of the knowledge that team members required to become legitimate participants in this develop-

Table 1. Operationalizing the nine design elements

Design Element	Initial Prototype	What we learned
Provision of authentic contexts that reflect the way that knowledge is used in real life	The kindergarten classroom within the simulation was developed from both the teaching experience and classroom-based research undertaken by team members. The literacy focus is responsive to the difficulties many pre-service teachers experience with the classroom application of abstract theory. The simulation prototype provides an opportunity for the students to operationalize this theory.	Collection of classroom artefacts (e.g., student work samples) adds to the authenticity of the software.
Authentic activities	Teaching and learning experiences incorporated within the simulation were collected from real classroom examples. The quality teaching framework (DET, 2003) was adopted to describe in detail what is happening in the classroom with specific attention on three targeted students.	Need to further trial the teaching and learning experiences with "real" kindergarten children to further develop and refine the virtual experience. Need to review the inclusion of student updates according to the targeted audience of first year pre-service teachers. Our trial has indicated that the quality teaching framework (DET, 2003) is difficult to understand for students working at this level (the need to focus more on input rather than providing an output became apparent).
Expert performances and modelling of process	The simulated kindergarten teacher provides a model of teaching practice. The user's decisions impacts upon the teaching and learning experiences offered, and the interaction of the teacher with students in the class.	The ability to critique the simulation teacher provides an opportunity for the user to comment and discuss what constitutes "effective" teaching practice.
Multiple roles and perspectives	The user is able to take on the role of the "teacher". Three targeted students within the classroom can be monitored.	Ability to monitor and track more students who are reflective of the diverse nature of classrooms. The initial plan for this project provided for the user to take on a selected role within the classroom. However, as our targeted audience are pre-service teachers, it is considered more meaningful to allow them access to take on only the role of the teacher.

continued on following page

Table 1. continued

Support for the collaborative construction of knowledge	Just-in-time support is included through summary sheets that feature links to core subject textbooks, mandatory policies (NSW), classroom artefacts and relevant web links.	Need to look to incorporate some type of forum, or a way to capture the user's personal journey throughout the simulation. This would provide an opportunity for discussion about the thinking space entries. The incorporation of this software within pre-service teacher training may change the role of a tutorial throughout use of the simulation.
Reflection so that abstractions and generalisations can be formed	The embedded thinking space provides opportunities for the user to reflect on what has happened in the simulated classroom, and the opportunity to plan, articulate and justify future decisions as they occur.	The first prototype offered the thinking space at decisive points throughout the running time of the simulation. The next version will have this embedded tool available throughout the whole time of the simulation, the user will be able to decide when they wish to access this tool.
Tools that enable tacit knowledge to be clearly articulated	The "Thinking Space" provides an opportunity for the user to articulate their understanding at decisive points.	Our trial of the prototype saw many users taking physical notes from the summary sheets. The thinking space did not allow the users to fully build upon their tacit knowledge. For the next version we plan to incorporate a "notebook" where the user will be able to cut and paste from "summary sheets" into a "notebook" that they can later print for their records.
Scaffolding and coaching by the teacher at critical times	Information about what the teacher is thinking is available to the user. These have been designed to allow the user to enter into the "mind" of a teacher and see why they make their decisions.	The ability to view the thoughts of the simulation teacher provides an opportunity for the user to enter into the meta-language of teaching, with specific attention to why such decisions are made within a classroom.
Authentic assessment of learning within the tasks	Discussions after using the simulation software provided some evidence of the connections the users made between the theory of their pre-service teacher education and what this may look like in the classroom.	This area is identified as a specific focus area for the next version of this software. In particular, we need to focus on how pre-service teachers learn, and what supports them in learning to be a teacher with particular emphasis on the connections they make.

ing community of practice. Table 1 summarises how we operationalized many of the nine design elements in the simulation. Specific screen captures will be presented to more fully illustrate these points.

Design of the Software

There are a range of powerful tools currently available in learning technologies which include: easier access, updating capability, scheduling of tasks, and flexible learning environments that collectively are referred to as rich Internet applications (RIAs). RIAs include rich-client technology, server technology, and development tools. Rich-client technology (for example, Flash player) provides all the benefits of the Web by keeping costs to a minimum (for example, automatic compression and loading of components on demand). In addition it provides features such as client scripting, high performance connectivity, and real-time server communication. Sever technology provides the mark-up languages to connect to the rich-client technologies. Development tools provide the ability to create the various pieces of an application.

ClassSim consists of a number of directories containing PHP (Hypertext Preprocessor), XHTML (Extensible HyperText Markup Language) and CSS (cascading style sheets) based pages. PHP is a widely used general-purpose scripting language that is especially suited for Web development and can be embedded into HTML. It is mainly focused on server-side scripting and can be used to collect form data, generate dynamic page content, or send and receive cookies. XHTML is an extension of HTML, and makes it relatively easy to introduce new elements or additional element attributes to Web pages. CSS provides a simple mechanism for adding style (e.g., fonts, colors, spacing, layout) to Web document-based pages.

The underlying storage system for the simulation consists of text files containing the "serialised" content of each user "session." This avoids the need for a database and associated complexities, and it simplifies backup and restore sessions. Each "session" consists of the data for a user's current progress through the site. This includes their current notes (from the "Thinking Space" embedded tool within the software) and where they've been. The data for each session is stored in PHP's "temporary" session management system, and is saved in a local directory.

Most of the pages within the simulation comprise of static XHTML with a PHP "header" that tracks the pages viewed by the user. This tracking of pages also includes a "history trail" of the major sections visited by the user. Many pages contain "triggers" for random events designed to simulate some of the random interruptions (e.g., messages for the teacher, student requests to go to the bathroom) that typically occur during a teaching session.

The layout and presentation of pages within the simulation are handled by the styling of elements of CSS. This leads to simplification of the XHTML source, and allows for quick changes to the look of each page without changing every file.

Each "session" consists of the data for a user's current progress through the site. This includes the user's current notes (from the "Thinking Space"), and tracks their journey. The data for each session is stored in PHP's "temporary" session management system, and is saved in a local directory.

Figure 3. Selection of teaching and learning experiences

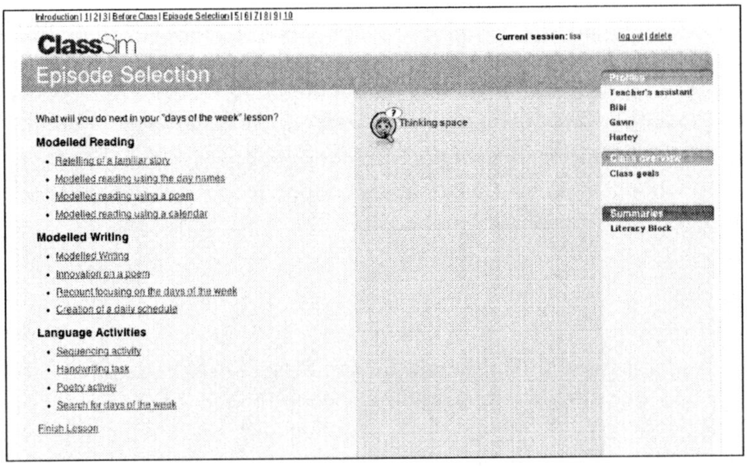

Pedogogical Focus

The focus of the developed simulation is the teaching of literacy in the early elementary school years. This is a curriculum area that beginning teachers find difficult to teach within the classroom. The ever-increasing profile of literacy within schools and the community was a key driver in this focus.

We acknowledge that the way language is taught in classrooms has changed considerably over past decades within Australian and international contexts. Teachers are requested to provide explicit teaching that also allow for opportunities for individual exploration of language processes. The terms "modelled," "guided" and "independent" are used frequently in current thinking about literacy teaching in the classroom (e.g., Crevola & Hill, 1998; Department of Education and Training, 2000). These three strategies are acknowledged as being "recursive," as "…teachers constantly return to them and apply them in new ways" (Department of Education and Training, 2000, p. 28). Teacher educators are challenged as they consider how this theoretical understanding can be best communicated to pre-service teachers in a way that is meaningful and representative of classroom reality.

The notion of a "literacy block" or "language workshop" containing "episodes" as a way to organise literacy time in the classroom has become increasingly common (Cambourne & Turbill, 1994; Crevola & Hill, 1998; Ivey, 2002). Crevola and Hill (1998, p. 14) state that "effective teaching is structured, and focused on the learning needs of each student in the class…" and "a literacy block provides for this regardless of a teacher's…previous level of training and expertise…" Classroom teachers are required to provide a "balanced" classroom literacy experience for all students. We believe that such "balance" comes about through the incorporation of modelled, guided and independent episodes within the classroom language experience. It is the theoretical understanding of a "literacy block," and the modelled, guided and independent teaching strategies that underpin the scenarios presented within the simulation software. The simulation we developed is focused on the concept of the "days-of-the-week" within literacy-based learning and teaching experiences. We believe this is a typical learning experience in a kindergarten classroom. The user is presented with a number of cycles within the simulation that they have to organise to best teach the literacy focus on the "days-of-the-week" in the virtual kindergarten classroom. In addition, the user is required to make decisions focused on classroom management and responses to individual students within the class. As decisions are made, the simulation allows access to a branching cycle, representative of a slice of time within the whole teaching period. Each cycle that the user engages with presents them with decisions related to that specific cycle. Figure 3 presents a screen capture of the teaching and learning episodes we constructed.

Three targeted students are represented in the simulation. The characteristics of the students are based on our own classroom teaching experiences and other research data gathered from classroom observations. They are described below.

Bibi is a refugee child from Afghanistan. She has been in Australia for two months, one month of which was spent in a detention centre. She has limited English, and listens intently to the teacher. Bibi has a friend called Mary who is also incorporated within the simulation story. The user is faced with a number of decisions related to this relationship.

Harley is medicated for attention deficit hyperactivity disorder (ADHD). He finds the classroom situation difficult, and is frequently not engaged during classroom lessons. If he is not medicated he tends to distract and annoy other children. The teacher is aware that Gavin is bullying Harley, and as such the situation is being monitored.

Figure 4 shows how the information about Harley is presented in the form of teacher notes to the user. The notes are based on the type of notes that teachers typically keep. It is designed to add authenticity to the simulation.

The simulation was developed to support the entry of pre-service teachers into the profession. To do this, experiences that grounded them within a classroom context, with opportunities for responsibility and control over decisions (typical to this context) are provided. We expected that the experience of using the simulation would help pre-service teachers to become effective legitimate peripheral participants during the practicum.

As such, the team decided it was important for the pre-service teachers to be able to record their thought processes as they decided what to do at each of the decision making points

Figure 4. Teacher notes on students

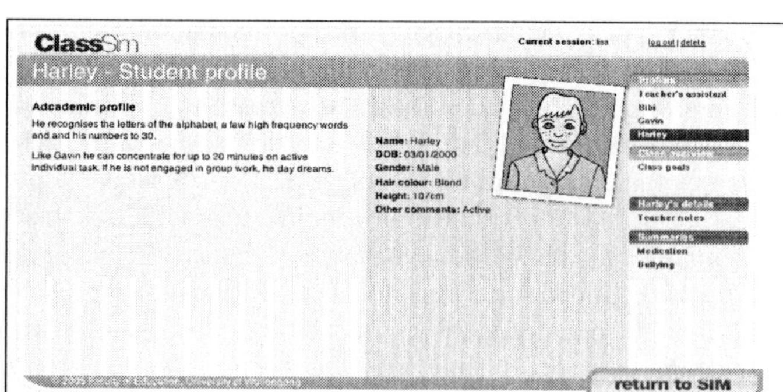

Figure 5. "Thinking Space"

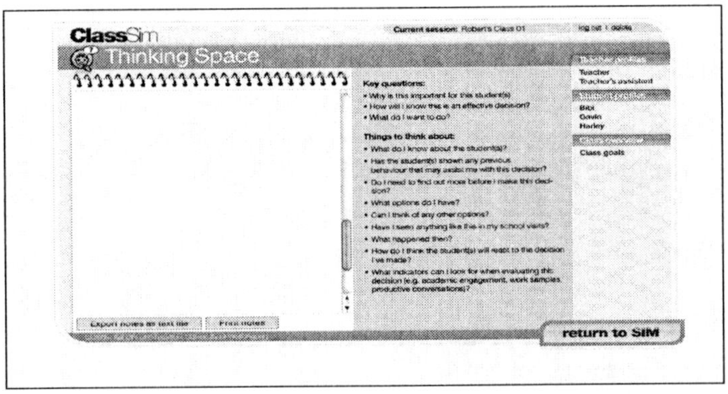

Table 2. Overview of software trials

Year	Student cohort	Number of students involved
2004	First year students enrolled in alternate KBC program	24
2004	Fourth year Bachelor of Education students	20
2005	First year student enrolled in alternate KBC program	24
2005	First year Bachelor of Teaching students	187
2005	Third year Bachelor of Teaching students	40

within the simulation software. An embedded tool, referred to as the "Thinking Space," supports this reflective process. This tool is available throughout the running time of the simulation to encourage users to plan and justify new decisions, reflect upon the consequences of previous decisions and above all, have the opportunity to "think like a teacher." This tool is represented in *Figure 5*.

Phase 3: Evaluation and Testing of Solutions

Five prototype versions of the simulation software have been tested in a trial with cohorts of pre-service teachers studying for a Bachelor of Teaching degree or the Bachelor of Education degree at the University of Wollongong, Australia. These trials are summarised in Table 2.

The software was made available to each of the pre-service teacher cohorts over a two-week period. During this time, the students used the simulation for two one-hour workshops (with no more than 20 other students in each session) with the researchers. The researchers conducted field notes and focus group interviews during these times. Audio and video footage was taken and analysed to add depth to the field note data. The simulation was available to all of the users outside these workshops through the provision of a URL and a password. A purposive sample of students was selected from each cohort to engage with individual semi-structured interviews before and after using the simulation. All data gathered was analysed using processes of data reduction, data display and conclusion drawing, and verification (Denzin & Lincoln, 2000). Constant comparative methods assisted researchers to determine issues and themes emerging from the data.

Outcomes for Users

Our data suggests that interaction with a classroom-based simulation is a feasible way to support and extend upon existing classroom-based experiences for pre-service teachers throughout their studies. Analysis of user interaction with the simulation highlights four key implications for its use in supporting pre-service teacher education.

1. The simulation emphasized the professional identify of teachers

   Participants have consistently commented that using the simulation enabled them to more fully understand the complex role of the teacher: *"I hadn't thought about many of the decisions the simulation provided, so for me it was a bit of a reality shock."* In particular, participants consistently identified the number and range of decisions that teachers have to make in the two-hour classroom block. One participant acknowledged that use of the simulation helped her *"...to understand the volume, complexity and consequences of the decisions made in the classroom."* Another participant stated: *"The classroom simulation helped to clarify my understanding of the work of a teacher."* Other participants made the following comments: *"...the role of a teacher doesn't stop in the classroom,"* another said the simulation was *"...eye opening,"* and another acknowledged *"it put me in the teacher's shoes to help me prepare and understand what is going to be expected of me as a teacher."*

   As the focus of this simulation was on the teaching of literacy within a kindergarten classroom, many participants have commented specifically on the complexity of the literacy classroom. One participant stated: *"The simulation has given an insight into the workings of a classroom and how a literacy block might operate."* The theoretical underpinnings of the simulation appeared to support the student cohorts in examining how this theory could look in practice through interaction with the virtual classroom environment. One participant acknowledged that the different theoretical underpinnings came together as he described the process he engaged with: *"...having to pick from modelled, guided and independent, also exemplified the structure of a lesson and the individual episodes within this structure."*

2. The simulation provided an opportunity for participants to "work" within a supported, authentic environment

   The design of the simulation drew upon the conditions for authentic learning environments as described by Herrington et al. (2003). Many participants identified that the simulation environment was authentic, with specific affordances supporting their movement through the scenarios. One participant stated: *"I feel that it was a realistic classroom setting with realistic students, teachers, parents and issues. It gave me an insight into what a real classroom setting will be like, and what sort of decisions I will be making throughout the day."* Likewise, another participant acknowledged the authentic context of the simulated environment, which *"...put me in the teacher's shoes to help me prepare and understand what is going to be expected of me as a teacher."*

Participants consistently identified the safety of the simulation environment as a positive affordance. One participant stated, *"It allowed me to experiment with various situations without experiencing any 'real' consequences if decisions I made weren't the best."* Another participant acknowledged *"I would hate to think that we had to practice on real children with real feelings so this was very good!"* Throughout the running time of the simulation participants are encouraged to take risks and make decisions. The navigational design of the simulation was such that participants were "forced" to make decisions at key points. One participant identified this design feature as a positive element of the simulation as it prepared her for classroom reality. She explained, *"...because the navigational arrows would ghost until you answered the question made me realise that daily choices needed to be made for the classroom routine to continue."*

Many participants identified the very positive opportunity not only to make decisions, but to also view the consequences of these, especially with regard to individual children. One participant stated: *"I realized I was in charge. I saw the impact each decision I made had on the class, the need to always be aware of the "needy" children (Gavin, Harvey and Bibi) and their affect on the class. The updates received helped keep me informed. I basically felt like I really was in charge of the class.*" Having this responsibility appeared to exemplify the role of the teacher and the range of considerations a typical teacher needs to make continually: *"...being placed in control of a class helped put things into perspective ...the variety of lessons and circumstances incorporated into the simulation helped me to understand that different students have different needs ... these needs come at various times and stages throughout the course of a lesson. It also opened my eyes to the amount of questions and decisions that a teacher has to make throughout the day."*

The simulation design enabled the participants to go back through their decisions, and change the decisions they had made to view alternate consequences. The majority of the participants identified this as a positive and supportive feature of the simulated environment. One participant stated: *"In my opinion, the best feature of the software is being able to continually go back and try a different pathway with a decision so you can actually see how this affects each child. Then you can determine which decision is the most beneficial for the entire class, not just the mainstream students."*

3. The simulation provided time (and permission!) for participants to think about the role of the teacher and the complexity of classrooms

The participants involved in research trials were all scheduled to use the simulation for two sessions, with access to the site at other times. This time allocation enabled all the participants to work through the software at their own pace. Our observational data showed that all participants appeared to be engaged throughout each of these sessions. What became increasingly interesting throughout each of the trials, was the way participants tended to use these sessions. During the first session of simulation use, participants were observed to work independently at their computer, systematically working their way through the scenarios. In the second session of use, participants still worked through the scenarios, but also established networks among their peers. They asked questions; posed problems they were facing; and discussed the possibilities.

Throughout their interaction with the simulation software, participants readily engaged in critique of the simulated teacher; identifying what was being done well, changes they would make, things they would do differently. One participant explained:

The simulation provided some experiences that the textbook cannot. The ability to make decisions regarding what to teach, how to teach, and in what order to teach it whilst contemplating students with difficulties, the class as a whole, noise levels, group formation and assistance from parents and aides forces the simulation user to put themselves into the position of a teacher and consider more of what their role as a teacher may take on.

The simulation appeared to support the participants in their pre-service teacher education. It provided them with an opportunity to make connections between the theory they had already been exposed to, and what this can look like in classroom practice. One participant acknowledged this as she explained: *"In the course so far, we have done a lot of theory, and as we have not experienced much, if any hands-on teaching, it created some fine examples that fitted in really well with the content being taught."* In addition, the simulation was seen by the participants as an additional practical classroom experience as *"...we also got a first hand look at lessons and the everyday running of a classroom, the types of things that happen within the classroom and the different situations we are put in as teachers."*

4. The simulation provided time for participants to reflect

The development of the "Thinking Space" provided the participants with a space to record and reflect upon their journey throughout the simulation. Participants used this facility to record and justify their decisions, and reflect upon consequences. They also used it to store information obtained from support material made available throughout the running time of the simulation. One participant described this tool as: *"...a feature that supported my decision making throughout the simulation ... it allowed me to write down the pros and cons of each decision, and as a result, make a more rational and informed choice."* Another participant described it as: *"somewhere where I could articulate and organise my thoughts, in trying to decide on which course of action to take."*

The simulation also provided an avenue for participants to explore what knowledge they had been exposed to in their pre-service teacher-education, and to identify future areas for professional learning. One participant described: *"Simulation has taught me that the role of a teacher doesn't stop in the classroom. We are always learning, continually upgrading our knowledge and researching, using various resources."*

Another participant identified that the simulation: *"... helped me to identify some issues that I will have to work on personally as a teacher, which is very helpful at such an early stage before habits become ingrained!"*

Phase 4: Documentation and Reflection to Produce Design Principles

Fostering a Community of Practice Through Use of the Simulation

Our data suggests that interaction with a classroom-based simulation is a feasible way to support and extend upon the existing communities among our pre-service teachers as they engage with a common, virtual classroom experience. The simulation supported users to "work" within the role of a teacher, identifying and responding to typical decisions. Further, the simulation encouraged the pre-service teachers to also acknowledge their preconceived ideas about the work of a teacher, and to reflect upon these as they developed new opinions and ways of thinking.

We believe that the conditions associated with the trials of the simulation supported the development of a community of practice amongst the participants. As each pre-service teacher engaged with the simulation, they showed that they were developing informed insights into the nature of classrooms and the work of a teacher. When they solved a problem, they often shared their experiences with peers—much like users of online games do. For example, when they encountered a decision point, pre-service teachers were able to talk with others about what they had done and the perceived implications. At other times they paused the simulation to discuss appropriate approaches to the emerging challenge. The provision of time to work with the software individually, and then collaboratively, positioned the pre-service teachers so that they could begin to argue their beliefs, and challenge conflicting positions in an informed way.

Fostering a Community of Practice among the Design Team

Each trial of the prototype was conducted in a multimedia computer laboratory that could accommodate twenty-four users. The programmers, graphic artist and instructional designer were located in the adjacent room, and could easily be called upon to fix "bugs," observe interactions, and make comments to researchers during the trial. The whole design team was involved in the trials, and all members were able to see the impact of their work on the users. After each trial, the data from thinking spaces, observer notes and follow-up interviews were collated and analysed as previously described. These were summarised and taken to a follow-up meeting with all team members. The follow-up meetings commenced with a brief presentation of the summary and then all members were free to contribute. At the end of each session, plans were developed for the design of the next prototype discussed.

Figure 6. Developing a community of practice within the design team

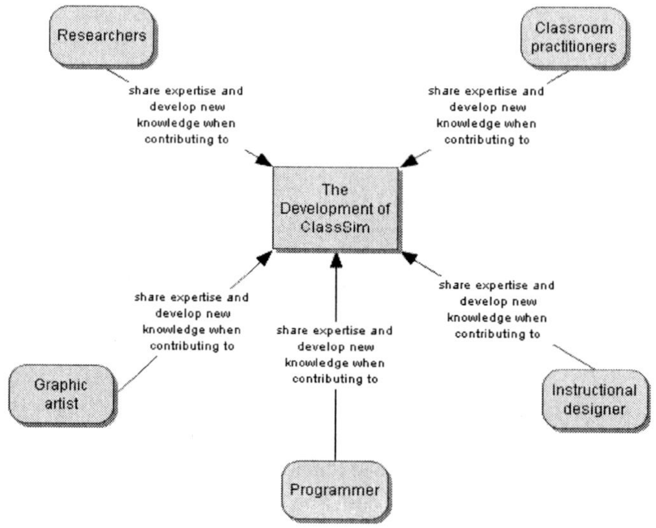

Figure 7. The importance of developing a viable community of practice in the design team

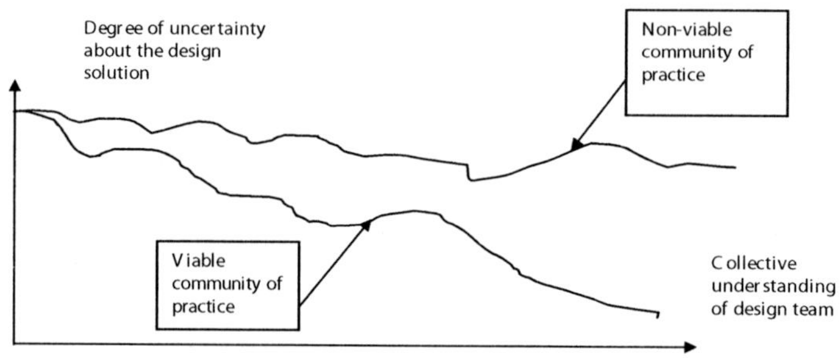

Most of the time was spent in clarifying our understanding of what the users learned and how the design features contributed to this learning. Open discussion about our future visions for the software assisted all members to appreciate the unique contribution that each member was making to this project, and to further clarify the short-term and long-term goals of the project.

Figure 6 is our conceptual diagram of how we think this process operated.

For example, during the second iteration of the simulation we debated about whether to include animated graphics and sound to reinforce key concepts about student response to user-selected actions. The instructional designer asked probing questions to elicit the purpose of these features, and how we thought this would enhance user understanding and conceptual development. The programmers and graphic artists then explained the process of developing these, and the form they would take. We then explored the strengths and weaknesses of the different options, finally selecting the simplest approach that could achieve our goals. This iterative process can be illustrated as shown in Figure 7.

As the collective understanding of the design team increases, the degree of uncertainty about the feasibility of design solution(s) decreases. We believe that a viable community of practice is needed for this to occur. If the community had not developed into a viable community of practice, then the outcome may have looked like the top line of the graph, where members of the community were still in a state of high uncertainty.

In our case, the community of practice was led by the instructional designer, whose role was more than the analysis of learning needs and systematic development of instruction. He organized and facilitated meetings so that all members of the design team were empowered to contribute to the community's understanding of the learning needs of the pre-service teachers, and the systematic development of the online simulation.

Conclusion

Our data illustrated that the simulation has the potential to develop pre-service teacher understanding of complex classroom situations associated with the teaching of literacy. The simulation provides an opportunity to slow down or accelerate classroom events, revisit and reflect on critical decision points, and replay events in the light of new understandings. This appeared to give pre-service teachers time to think about complex teaching situations, which relied on the teacher's ability to tune into children's experiences, engage with them in dialogue and negotiation, and utilise a range of indirect instructions such as questioning, modelling and prompting. Users reported that their experience with the simulation assisted them to make their practicum experience more focused by giving them the knowledge and experience to more fully appreciate the impact of subtle changes that experienced teachers make during lessons. At this stage of our research, we are confident that the design principles we operationalized, combined with our access to a large pool of authentic data, helped us design a simulation that contributed to the development of pre-service teacher understanding of the complex work of teachers in virtual and in real classrooms.

During this project, repeated use of the simulation motivated many of the pre-service teachers to develop into small communities of practice (Lave & Wenger, 1991) and to share their knowledge and experiences. They were involved in a process of interaction with others to produce and establish meaning among peers. From a situated cognition perspective, their learning occurred in a social setting through dialogue with others in the community (Lave, 1988). It becomes a process of reflecting, interpreting, and negotiating meaning among the participants of a community.

Our next challenge is to find ways to make the online design process accessible to others. This will allow other researchers to build on our efforts and extend the concept into other areas of professional education.

Members of the design team also formed a viable community of practice but it was for a different purpose. We feel that it was important that the following general principles were met in order for this community of practice to be viable:

1. Meetings were chaired by the instructional designer who provided opportunities for all members to share their knowledge and understanding.
2. The instructional designer communicated that the collective expertise of the team was important for the success of the project and that everyone's expertise was valued.
3. Design modification decisions were based on real data that team members had gathered. This involved members of the team working with the users of the simulation. There was no dispute over the authenticity of the data.
4. The research data was used to help members of the team to understand how interaction with the simulation assisted user learning.
5. As the project evolved, the instructional designer ensured that members could see that their expertise was having a positive impact on its success.
6. Team members received multiple opportunities to demonstrate and/or publish articles about their work.

We acknowledge that many of these conditions are not new, and are similar to those expressed by Wenger (2002). However, we believe that it is important that the leadership role of the instructional designer was a crucial factor in the success of this project. We conclude by stating that, in our experience, a community of practice does not just happen—it has to be formed. It is the responsibility of those empowered to lead such a community to ensure that the conditions that are conducive for the formation of such a community, are present and put into operation. The role of the instructional designer is seen as someone who leads the process of analysis of learning needs and goals and the development of a delivery system to meet those needs. This role also requires the instructional designer to lead a team that develops into a viable community of practice.

References

Barth, R.S. (1990). *Improving schools from within.* San Francisco: Jossey-Bass Publishers.

Bransford, J.D., Sherwood, R.D., Hasselbring, T.S., Kinzer, C.K., & Williams S.M. (1990). Anchored instruction: Why we need it and how technology can help. In D. Nix & R. Spiro (Eds.), *Cognition, education, multimedia: Exploring ideas in high technology* (pp. 115-141). Hillsdale: Lawrence Erlbaum.

Cambourne, B.L. (2001, November). What do I do with the rest of the class? The nature of teaching-learning activities. *Language Arts*, *79*(2), 124-135.

Cambourne, B., & Turbill, J. (1994). *Responsive evaluation: Making judgements about student literacy*. Melbourne: Eleanor Curtain Publishing.

Comber, B., Badger, L., Barnett, J., Nixon, H., Prince, S., & Pitt, J. (2001). *Socio-economically disadvantaged students and the development of literacies in school: A longitudinal study.* Three Volume Report, South Australian Department of Education, Training and Employment and University of Adelaide.

Crevola, C., & Hill, P. (1998). *ClaSS: Children's literacy success strategy: An overview*. Melbourne, Australia: Catholic Education Office.

Danielson, C. (1996). *Enhancing professional practice: A framework for teaching*. Alexandria, VA: Association for Supervision and Curriculum Development.

Darling-Hammond, L. (1999). Teacher education: Rethinking practice and policy. *Unicorn, 25(*1), 31-48.

Denzin, N.K., & Lincoln, Y.S. (2000). *Handbook of qualitative research* (2nd Ed.). London: Sage Publications.

Department of Education and Training. (2000). *Focus on literacy: Writing*. Sydney, Australia: Curriculum Support Directorate.

Entwhistle, N., Entwhistle A., & Tait H. (1993). Academic understanding and the contexts to enhance it: A perspective from research on student learning. In T.M. Duffy, J. Lowyck, & D.H. Jonassen (Eds.), *Design environments for constructive learning* (pp. 331-357). Heidelberg: Springer-Verlag.

Groundwater-Smith, S., Deer, C.E, Sharp, H., & March, P. (1996). The practicum as workplace learning: A multi-modal approach in teacher education. *Australian Journal of Teacher Education, 22*(2), 21-30.

Herrington, J., Oliver, R., & Reeves, T. (2003). 'Cognitive realism' in online authentic learning environments. In D. Lassner & C. McNaught (Eds.), *Ed-Media World Conference on Educational Multimedia, Hypermedia and Telecommunications* (pp. 2115-2121). Norfolk, VA: AACE.

Ivey, G. (2002, November). Getting started: Manageable literacy practices. *Educational Leadership, 60*(3), 20-23.

Kervin, L., Cambourne, B., Turbill, J., Ferry, B., Hedberg, J., Jonassen, D., & Puglisi, S. (2005). From classroom reality to virtual classroom: The role of teacher-created scripts in the development of classroom simulation technology. In P.L. Jeffrey (Ed.), *Proceedings of the 2004 Australian Association for Research in Education Conference*. Melbourne, Australia: AARE (Australian Association for Research in Education).

Kervin, L., Ferry, B., Carrington, L., Turbill, J., Cambourne, B., Hedberg, J., & Jonassen, D. (2005). Classroom simulation: Enhancing the learning experience for pre-service teachers. In M. Cooper (Ed.), *Proceedings of the 33rd Annual Teacher Education Association Conference* (pp. 244- 251). Centre for Professional Development, Griffith University.

Kervin, L., & Turbill, J. (2003). Teaching as a craft: Making links between pre-service training and classroom practice. *English Teaching: Practice and Critique, 2*(3), 22-34. Retrieved May 29, 2006, from http://education.waikato.ac.nz/research/files/etpc/files/2003v2n3art2.pdf.

Kiggins, J. (2001). *The knowledge building community project: A grounded theory of an alternative teacher education model.* Unpublished PhD thesis. University of Wollongong.

Lave, J. (1988). *Cognition in practice.* New York: Cambridge University Press.

Lave, J., & Wenger, E. (1991). *Situated learning: Legitimate peripheral participation.* Cambridge: Cambridge University Press.

Ramsey, G. (2000). *Quality matters revitalising teaching: Critical times, critical choices.* Report of the Review of Teacher Education in NSW. Sydney: NSW Department of Education & Training.

Reeves, T.C., Herrington, J., & Oliver, R. (2005). Design research: A socially responsible approach to instructional technology research in higher education. *Journal of Computing and Higher Education, 16*(2), 97-116.

Wenger, E. (2002). *Cultivating communities of practice.* Cambridge, MA: Harvard Business School Press.

Chapter XIX

Moving Toward the Digital Learning Environment: A Hong Kong Example of an E-Learning Management System

Kar-Tin Lee, Queensland University of Technology, Australia

Abstract

This chapter reports on a case study that examines the process of implementing an e-learning management system (ELMS) for learning science in secondary schools in Hong Kong. It describes the challenges, issues and problems associated with creating science content and then integrating it with both a diagnostic and an open-content marking tool. The study had two broad objectives: (1) to analyze and document the process of designing and implementing the ELMS and (2) to evaluate the overall impact of these practices. To achieve its purpose a team of instructional designers worked closely with content and technology experts to digitize science content for online delivery. The system facilitates timely and dynamic diagnosis of student weaknesses. It is argued that when teachers are actively involved in an implementation of a technology-rich environment, they begin to see the benefits of teaching science differently. Given the opportunity to use the online system, students also tend to take more responsibility for their own learning. Data from participants indicate that the ELMS provides added value to the teaching of science. Lessons learned from this case study should assist others who wish to implement similar systems in the future.

Introduction

A common observation amongst teachers in Hong Kong secondary schools is that there is a great demand for online content development, which needs to be linked to an efficient assessment mechanism in secondary science. In this chapter, experiences are shared to assist future efforts in implementing an e-learning management system (ELMS) in secondary schools for other curricula areas besides science. An account is provided of how a curriculum innovation was conducted in four secondary schools to establish a valid and reliable measuring tool for knowledge components and problem-solving skills when learning science. Information is also provided on how the use of engaging and cognitively demanding computer-based curricula could be applied to promote academic achievement among students who are currently not well served by the predominantly teacher-centred methods.

The case study incorporated a collaborative strategy, which leverages the wide range of expertise from a team of faculty instructional designers, science teachers, science experts, government school inspectors, and technology experts. It explored the process of expanding teachers' pedagogical practices to include the use of new models of online learning using an e-learning management system. This system includes the use of online assessment and profiling tools to monitor students' learning.

The objectives of the study were:

- To analyze and document the process of designing an ELMS to teach science content which incorporates tools for online assessment
- To provide science content that is mapped onto discrete skill outcomes
- To develop dynamic assessment systems that can provide detailed profiles of student learning
- To identify the challenges and issues that instructional designers face.

Partners involved in this study embraced the notion that learning environments where teachers could offer flexible and customisable opportunities to transform science instruction could provide windows on knowledge integration in the making (Barab & Luehmann, 2003). If curriculum materials could take advantage of new technologies, then these same technologies could be applied for innovative assessments (Linn, Davis & Bell, 2004, p. 7).

Analysis of data from this study could make an important contribution to the practice of instructional design. By applying theoretical constructs to the development of the online learning tools, the results from this research could be used to inform educators and policy makers about some of the considerations involved when designing online learning environments.

Background

In 1998, the Hong Kong government announced a five-year information technology (IT) plan to enhance the quality of education by incorporating IT into the school curriculum. At the same time, the government also embarked on an ambitious educational reform program. This program was aimed at generating new pedagogical practices in order to prepare students for the information society. Since then, numerous information and communications technologies (ICT) were appropriated for learning and teaching in Hong Kong schools, but their visions and understanding of how to use ICTs varied tremendously. During the five years in which ICT was implemented in schools, online learning environments (OLEs) or networked learning tools found increased use in schools. A closer look would, however, reveal that minimal thought had gone into the design of learning strategies to maximise the potential use of these tools apart from using them as a school Intranet. Even today it seems that the promise of OLEs is largely unrealised both in Hong Kong and internationally. Many teachers continue to use online learning environments as simple knowledge repositories (Jacobson & Spiro, 1995). If teachers believe that OLEs are little more than repositories of content, then their use of OLEs may be limited to this conception.

In the Hong Kong context there is a compelling need for more research on the implications of ICT on student learning processes. Since 1998, an unprecedented amount of funds have been invested in ICT, but it is obvious that the majority of this funding has been focused on the technology itself. Very little has been documented locally about how technological applications can enhance learning. Law, Yuen, Ki, Li, Lee, & Chow, (2000) stated that teachers, when given the opportunity to use ICT, only used the technology to teach the standard curriculum. Any interventions should provide plenty of opportunity for teachers to actively reflect on their own actions, to rethink their existing classroom practice, and to be more cognizant of individual student learning. More work is still needed in schools to assist teachers to adopt new pedagogical approaches, and to prevent teachers concentrating solely on the technical aspects (EMB, 2004).

To create new kinds of learning, the construction of learning environments ultimately depends on the beliefs and actions of those responsible for setting up the environment, particularly the underlying pedagogical philosophy of the teacher (Newhouse, Trinidad, & Clarkson, 2002). In order for students to learn with technology, Jonassen et al. (2003) contend that teachers must accept and learn a new model of learning. They argued that, first and foremost, teachers must relinquish at least some of their authority, specifically their intellectual authority. It was stated that, "if teachers determine what is important for students to know, how they should know it, and how they should learn it, then students cannot become intentional constructive learners" (Jonassen et al., 2003, pp. 13-14). It is their view that teachers must hand over some of their authority in their management of learning, and at the same time they must gain familiarity with the technology and assume new roles with different beliefs to those that they have traditionally pursued.

The most productive and meaningful uses of technology will not occur if technologies are used in traditional ways—as delivery vehicles for lessons (Jonassen et al., 2003). Rather, learners should use technologies to teach themselves and others. Meaningful learning will result when technologies engage learners in knowledge construction, not reproduction; conversation, not reception; articulation, not repetition; collaboration, not competition; and reflection, not prescription (Jonassen et al., 2003).

Besides using new technologies such as OLEs, and adopting new ways of teaching, teachers have had to contend with the push for changes in assessment. In 2001, the government's Curriculum Development Council, through its report entitled *Learning to Learn: The Way Forward in Curriculum Development* (EMB, 2001), stated the importance of assessment for learning, and expected that:

There should be a change in assessment practices, and schools should put more emphasis on assessment for learning, a process in which teachers seek to identify and diagnose student learning problems, and provide quality feedback for students on how to improve their work. (EMB, 2001)

It was also the government's intention to take advantage of the potential of online tools for assessment.

In response to this government thrust for more formative modes of assessment, the basic competency assessment (BCA) system (http://www.hkbca.edu.hk/index_eng.htm) was developed. Primary schools began to make use of it by mid-2003. It covered the three subject areas of Chinese language, English language, and mathematics. The student assessment system provided a resource bank through the Internet where teachers could develop and select the appropriate assessment tasks for their students. The BCA system (HKEAA, 2003) emphasized that schools must apply multiple modes of school internal assessments so as to effectively and fully understand the needs and progress of students.

Assessment methods used in Hong Kong schools have attracted continual criticism from educators and policy makers. Similar to the situation in many countries, the current science curriculum fails to prepare students to take advantage of new opportunities offered by ICT. Similar to the expectations of the BCA system, policy makers expected the science curriculum to be delivered in a significantly different way in order to facilitate teachers to fully engage students. This would also enable teachers to evaluate their students' ability to grasp more abstract concepts.

It is in this developing context of government initiatives that the project took place. Funding was sought from the government's Quality Education Fund (QEF) to develop an online assessment system for secondary science similar to the BCA for primary schools. The project focused on the use of ELMS. The project has allowed for assessment to be used as one of the most powerful ways of improving learning, simply by changing the assessment of the subject, which in turn affects the way students engage with the subject content (Black & Williams, 1998). The possible use of online assessment tools offered teachers many practical benefits, including fast test delivery and instantaneous feedback, automated intelligent marking, and profiling of group or individual performance.

The theoretical foundation for the study is framed within a socio-cultural perspective, specifically linked to reflections on learning environments (Jonassen & Land, 2000), while the ELMS used in this case study was modeled on Hall's (2001) broad definition for learning management systems. It is broadly defined as a system that organises and provides access to online learning services for students, teachers, and administrators. Within the ELMS, student progress is monitored through the following functions:

- Content development
- Classroom management
- Skills profiling
- Personalisation
- Report manager
- Intelligent marking and answer trainer.

While the ELMS enables learning opportunities, it is the teachers' careful planning and incorporation of instructional strategies that contribute to student interaction, growth and learning (Kirby, 1999). The development of the ELMS drew on research that had reported the alleged benefits of online learning environments (Cavanagh, Gillan, Kromrey, Hess, & Blomeyer, 2004; Goldberg & McKhann, 2000; Jones, Valdez, Nowakowski, & Rasmussen, 1995; Koschmann, 1994). Little research exists on how instructional design and styles of teaching, especially in an OLE, could influence student higher-order thinking. Several studies have demonstrated that OLEs can provide a venue for developing higher-order thinking in students (Jonassen, 2000; Valdez, McNabb, Foertsch, Anderson, Hawkes, & Raack, 2000), and are widely assumed to have a positive impact on student higher-order thinking and learning. Despite all the research, it cannot be assumed that the same teaching styles and approaches used in traditional classes will continue to work in an online classroom (Diaz & Cartal, 2000; Lee, 2005).

In order for readers to understand the context in which this project took place, the author will briefly explain the environment in which teachers work. Secondary school teachers remain steeped in the culture of setting and marking different forms of assessment, usually aimed at preparing students for high-stake examinations. Professional experience informs us that teachers often claim that they do not have the time to apply more formative assessment methods in their teaching. There is always the temptation to finish the syllabus and prepare for examinations. Time constraints prevent teachers from catering to individual learning differences or from developing ICT tools to enhance their classroom activities. There is simply no time to consider how evaluation of student learning in science could be done differently.

Due to heavy work demands, for teachers in Hong Kong schools to be able to devote more attention to individual students, they need to be provided with effective tools to collect and analyse data in order to adequately assess which difficulties confronted by students impact learning. For teachers to help individual learners, they need timely and rich information about each student's learning progress. When this information is on hand, the evaluation of learning is more likely to be based on how far along a student has progressed through the materials than on how they have done compared to others on a general exam (Tiene & Ingram, 2001, p. 199). A lot of time was devoted in this project to designing learning activities that could focus more on how the individual student had progressed. These activities identify weaknesses in a student's past performance to pinpoint areas for remediation, as opposed to merely recording how she or he has passed or failed in the high stakes exams.

Instructional design plays a significant role in the success of an online learning environment. In spite of the effort and resources spent in Hong Kong to date, it did not appear that many online learning environments had applied sound instructional design principles. Ideally, the ELMS would possess several characteristics:

- A means of accessing, generating, and sharing information
- Support learner articulation of knowledge and reflection on what they have learned
- Represent and simulate authentic, real-world problems and contexts
- Provide structure for student thinking
- Promote student control of learning decisions
- Integrate multiple learning perspectives. (Jonassen et al., 2003)

Case Description

Design Approach

A key issue when introducing new technological tools into the classroom is teacher time, which is often overlooked and underestimated. Substantial resources need to be made available for teachers in schools. The potential move to the use of Web-based tools as cognitive tools in classrooms clearly indicates a shift in how teaching and learning could occur in schools. It is very important for teachers to be competent in cognitive development, particularly as it relates to helping students gain mastery in specific content areas. A critical skill for teachers to develop is the capacity for intellectual empathy. Teachers need to be able to detect the extent and nature of each individual student's knowledge and competence in a subject, so that they may help that learner move ahead in developing independent mastery and lifelong learning skills.

For this project, the crucial element for success was to provide as much of the content as possible in the form of readily usable science content, developed from the Hong Kong curriculum. This content when integrated into the ELMS can be used to train and facilitate teachers to reflect on a clear vision of why ICT is being used, and how it can strengthen teaching and learning activities. At present, although the hardware infrastructure is mainly in place, most Hong Kong schools cannot afford to spend large amounts on software. They tend to focus on applications rather than development of content. This has led to a distressing lack of appropriate content that can be readily integrated into curricula and concurrently applied to gain monitoring and assessment data to inform teachers' practices. As Bransford, Brown, and Cocking (2000) asserted, good educational software and teacher-support tools, developed with a full understanding of principles of learning, have not yet become the norm. They cautioned that the use of technology to improve learning is never solely a technical matter. Teachers need to be more collegial, openly share their experiences, and avoid perpetuating their own private practice (Riel & Becker, 2002).

Through collaborative efforts with the technical experts, teachers, principals and science experts, a model for integration of content and assessment modes with ICT was developed.

This tool has helped teachers to move beyond computer operation, to ICT integration and the use of OLEs in a meaningful way. With careful attention to instructional design and facilitation of new ways of learning, this constructed learning space can become the locus of rich and satisfying experiences in collaborative learning. In this way, learners actively construct knowledge by learning together and are able to closely map their progress according to an extensive science skills framework. The learning environment can provide scaffolding support to augment what learners can do and reason about. Technology tools facilitate understanding through use of scientific visualisation and model-based learning (Bransford, Brown, & Cocking, 2000). In addition, the convenience and effectiveness of this new mode of learning will reinforce the formation of student lifelong learning and independent learning skills.

International and local policy papers (DEETYA, 2000; EMB, 2004; Teacher Training Agency, 1999) indicated that the effective application of technology in teaching would result in new organisational forms, and a strengthening of the principle of differentiation of teaching. It was vital for this project that this philosophy had the support of senior school administration. When given the opportunity, teachers had a key role to play within a collaborative and supportive framework. By defining the instructional strategies, curriculum objectives, student needs, and assessment strategies, the teachers had the opportunity to bring about changes in their daily teaching practice.

Pachler and Byrom (1999) stated that "the nature of assessment of and through ICT sits ill-at-ease with traditional educational paradigms of testing the retention, recall and understanding of knowledge by individual learners compared with the more skill- and application-based collaborative modes supported by and intrinsic to working with ICT … it seems therefore, that assessment paradigms will need to evolve in the light of emerging technologies and the learning objectives they predicate" (p. 127).

The successful completion of the project based on the current model allows other curricula content to be easily adapted for delivery. This model has been trialed for 18 months by the participating schools, teachers and students. This has increased the quality and efficiency of several school programs and how they are delivered to new and diverse communities of students. Expertise and experience gained from this project has allowed for dissemination of its success. This is one step closer to the acceptance of the fundamental need for the use of technologically-based learning to facilitate better access, improved quality of content, and closer monitoring of student learning for formal and informal assessment purposes.

Project Development and Implementation

The ELMS incorporates the use of two tools developed by Litespeed Pty Ltd: diagnostic tutorial assessment system (DTAS) and the intelligent content assessment marking (ICAM) system, which are described in detail in subsequent sections. Both these Web-based e-learning and diagnostic systems provide teachers with the facility to identify the strengths and weaknesses of students based on a comprehensive set of science skills. This is developed in conjunction with government science inspectors and science experts. The content is based on the Hong Kong science curriculum and emphasizes the learning of abstract science concepts.

The main objectives of the project were to:

- Provide teachers with science content that is mapped onto discrete skills outcomes (five topics of secondary two science were developed involving more than 175 major skill categories, which were further sub-divided into sub-categories)
- Provide principals and teachers with ELMS incorporating the DTAS and ICAM systems to develop dynamic assessment systems that can provide detailed profiles of student learning
- Collaborate with teachers to promote interactive secondary science content as well as to demonstrate the value of dynamic assessments for determining which difficulties impact learning most strongly
- Collect and analyze trend data via the ELMS to provide teachers with timely information to set meaningful and measurable goals for future learning.

Implementation and Processes

The project was conducted over a period of 18 months from July 2003 to December 2004. Before developing component lessons and questions, all parties involved had to engage in an exhaustive and iterative cycle of identifying the type of science problems that a student could or could not solve. Then the design team could focus on these problems to develop interactive component lessons. Great care was taken to design interactive materials to ensure that students achieve deeper mental interaction with the content. Through simulations, students could grapple with ideas, make decisions, and choose directions when given options to consider. The project produced substantial resources in the form of usable learning objects that were used to strengthen teaching and learning activities.

The project helped and motivated weaker students to grasp more abstract concepts of science. It also compelled the better students to look beyond the basics in an efficient manner. The creation of original secondary school content helped students to better understand their skills through engaging in interactive multimedia lessons. The DTAS and ICAM systems, when integrated with appropriate science content, enabled students to develop independent learning while being assessed diagnostically on their exact strengths and weaknesses. At the same time, teachers were also able to use the software and technology to significantly change their pedagogical practices and facilitate the learning process of students. With the ELMS, students can learn in and out of class from anywhere, anytime, putting the responsibility of learning into the students' hands.

The two Web-based assessment tools, DTAS and ICAM, were integral to the ELMS. ELMS is a fully featured system that offers a range of interactive lessons, tests and quizzes on aspects of the secondary two science syllabus. Most students access the system while at school, but some groups are also encouraged to access the system from home. The DTAS and ICAM were used to assess student learning and provide data for the diagnostic profiling system (DPS), which produced detailed individual student learning profiles. These tools mapped each essential science skill on to the DPS, so that teachers could closely evaluate student learning.

The partners in the project were faculty instructional designers from the Hong Kong Institute of Education; Litespeed Pty Ltd (a technology company from Singapore); science teachers, experts and inspectors; students from four secondary schools; and school principals.

The ELMS and its Component Tools

The entire e-learning environment comprised the following components shown in Figure 1:

- Multimedia lessons
- Assessment/diagnostic questions
- Diagnostic tutorial assessment system (DTAS)
- Intelligent content assessment marking engine (ICAM)
- Answer training database (training of answers by teachers)
- Diagnostic profiling system (DPS)
- Report manager (student profiles by individual or by group)
- Schools' database.

Each individual topic within the secondary two science curriculum was mapped onto discrete skills and tagged. The predict-observe-explain model (Kearney & Treagust, 2001) enabled students to structure their thoughts and promote their conceptual development (Duit & Treagust, 2003) in one or more of the following areas:

- Articulation/justification of their own ideas
- Reflection on their own and others' ideas
- Construction/negotiation of new ideas.

Constructive feedback was prepared for each topic area identified as "weak." Clear directions are then provided at appropriate stages during the learning cycle to guide students to revise and consolidate their weak areas through use of pop-up screens containing active links (Figure 2).

A typical student learning cycle depicting the inter-relationship of ICAM, DTAS and DPS is demonstrated in Figure 3. Research has highlighted the value of student collaboration. In this learning cycle, students worked in pairs or in small groups. This is more beneficial to learning than individual use (Underwood & Underwood, 1990, pp. 156-161). Group work not only facilitates the sharing of ideas, it provides opportunities for students to explain and have ideas validated as they help each other. Under these conditions, students are more likely to gain a higher sense of ownership of the learning process (Sandholtz, Ringstaff, & Dwyer, 1997).

Figure 1. Components of the e-learning management system

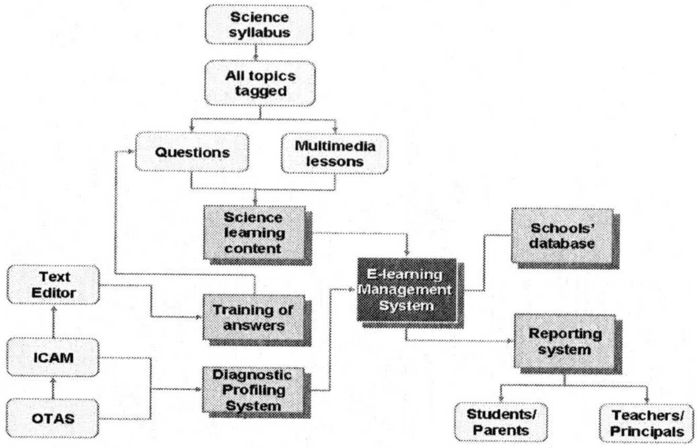

Figure 2. Recommendations guiding weak students to appropriate work

Recommended Lessons

- <u>Explain the need to respond to the environment using the sense organs.</u>
- <u>Describe briefly some defects of the eye.</u>
- <u>Understand the production and transmission of sound.</u>

<u>**Click here to test Your Weak Areas**</u>

What is DTAS?

The diagnostic tutorial assessment system (DTAS) is a tool developed by Litespeed Pty Ltd. It is an innovative tool, which intelligently identifies the specific strengths and weaknesses of individual students. Through each topic studied, students are automatically prompted to component lessons for remediation in weak areas. These lessons are Web-based, and aim to add value to the teaching and learning processes of students. By making learning more effective and efficient, learners are empowered to engage in self-learning through the Web on any topic within a subject. As no system is complete if lessons and test questions are mutually exclusive, DTAS instigates a complete learning cycle by replicating the teaching and learning processes while automating the performance feedback mechanism.

DTAS is used in class to supplement face-to-face teaching. It is also used at home for individual self-learning through repetition without the presence of the teacher. It provides opportunities for students to be independent learners and also offers an opportunity for schools to embark on and create an e-learning culture through learning and teaching via the Internet. Through this approach, students are exposed not only to quality content, but are also given the chance to experience knowledge acquisition in a different mode. This is an important process in the overall objective of the current education reform agenda.

Figure 3. Schematic of the learning cycle involving the use of DTAS, ICAM and DPS

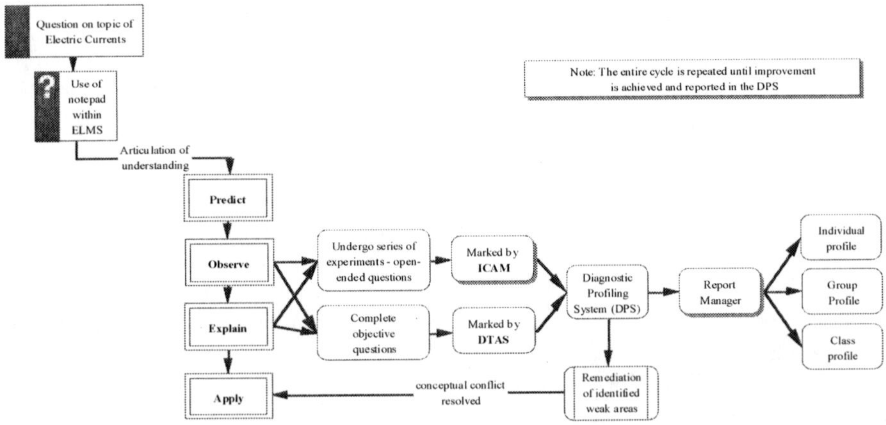

What is ICAM?

The intelligent content assessment marking (ICAM) system is a technology developed by Litespeed Pty Ltd. to mark open-ended content such as short and paragraph answers. This system classifies and groups students' answers—especially non-standard, creative answers—to facilitate immediate classroom discussions. With this engine, teachers can facilitate online learning. They are no longer constrained to conventional inputs such as multiple-choice and fill-in-the-blanks questions. This enables the online environment to mark thousands of open-ended answers instantaneously, and provide feedback to students as they learn.

ICAM is unique to this ELMS because it is the technology that enables the marking of open-ended questions for teachers. The system allows teachers to input model answers and refine the marking scheme based on subsequent answers entered by students. It uses two different modes to set model answers: the Answer Training Mode and the Student Training Mode.

Answer Training Mode

Open-ended questions are developed and set by teachers within the DTAS. This is the first step involved in training the system to mark answers. This mode allows the teachers to key in the model answers for each question in the first instance. The system is then able to provide a solution to this by using a technology called artificial neural cortex algorithm. With ICAM, the system is able to generate all possible variants of the model answer keyed in by the teacher.

Subsequently, teachers can train the system to allocate marks by identifying keywords in the students' answers. Teachers can also choose to put words in an exclusion list as well. As this technology lacks the human touch and can never be perfect, ICAM is only a tool for the teacher to use to save time and effort when marking open-ended answer scripts. The teacher allocates marks for up to 80% of the entire marking scheme. However, it is inevitable that there are still other creative ways of answering the question, which may not have been thought of by teachers. Students will always have a different way of responding to questions, although their message may be the same. The teacher's input is still vital, without it, the computer cannot eradicate the problem.

Student Training Mode

Other answers that are not identified by the system will require some manual marking on the part of the teachers. Teachers can reset the marking schemes simply by clicking on the selected student answer and dragging it to another mark allocation column. Subsequently this answer will be included for future marking.

The system can automatically tabulate all the marks of each student after the new marking scheme has been set and saved. In this manner, the teacher does not have to mark every script. All she or he has to do is to sieve out all the creative answers and allocate the marks that need to be rewarded for these answers.

Each student's answer will be profiled to allow the teachers to monitor the performance of each student. The profiling system for ICAM allows heads or coordinators of subject departments and teachers to gather real-time statistics of all students' performances through separate tests.

For instance, each developed question in science was structured in such a way that it would have a specific skill and sub-skills attached to it (Table 1). These codes are then used for monitoring within the system.

ICAM is then able to assess the students on their literal, interpretive or applied skills, and provide a profile with clear diagnostics of areas of weakness or strength. This is where the science teacher, experts and inspectors played a major role. The processes involved are in Table 2.

Before the trials began, individual members of the project team visited the schools on a weekly basis to ensure smooth operation. They also provided mutual support to teachers to ensure the technical infrastructure was stable. Once the system was running, usage data was continuously collected via DTAS and ICAM systems for subsequent analysis. Training sessions provided an introduction for the teachers and students to the science content and the formative assessment materials, using a one-to-one training method. A briefing gave teachers and principals an understanding of the rationale underpinning the project. Copies of the materials placed online, provided teachers with the opportunity to try the system in their own time. Once the teachers were ready, the project team members worked closely with the teachers in each of the trial schools to try out the system during their science classes and at home.

Each topic is trialed in the schools by rotation so that the answer database could continually grow and benefit the next group of students using the system. As indicated in earlier sections of this chapter, the answers were trained to become more intelligent, and would then be fed back into the system culminating in a more comprehensive set of possible answers

Table 1. An example of mapping of skill identification tags for profiling purposes

Unit No.	Unit Title	Skill ID	Skill Name
4	Energy (Forms of Energy)	LS1.04.01.01	Explain that energy is all around us and that we need energy to survive.
		LS1.04.01.02	Describe the various forms of energy as heat energy, light energy and sound energy.
		LS1.04.01.03	Describe the various forms of energy as kinetic energy such as potential energy, chemical energy and electrical energy
		LS1.04.02.01	Explain that these different forms of energy are found from different sources of energy-geothermal heat, solar, nuclear, tidal, fossil fuels and biomass fuel.
		LS1.04.02.02	Explain why some energy sources are non-renewable.

Table 2. Processes involved when setting questions using ICAM

Processes involved	Done by	Checked by
Question setting for each topic.	Science teachers.	Science experts and inspectors.
Comments are taken on board and questions are refined.	Science teachers.	Science experts and inspectors.
Develop content and design of multimedia lessons.	Instructional designers (pedagogical aspects) in conjunction with Litespeed (multimedia aspects).	Instructional designers.
Feedback on content and lesson design.	Science teachers, experts, inspectors and instructional designers.	

and variants. Table 3 demonstrates the rotation cycles of trialing in the schools in order to achieve maximum benefit.

By the time the topic "electricity" was trialed by School 2, the answers would have been trained by teachers in School 1. Similarly, by the time School 3 trialed the same topic, the teachers in School 2 would have trained the additional answers. As this cycle of events progresses, the answer database is continually expanded and being trained to resemble what the acceptable answers and marking scheme would be, if the teacher was marking the answers in person.

Table 3. Rotation of trials in schools

Topics	Rotation of schools completing each topic			
Electricity	School 1	School 2	School 3	School 4
Space	School 2	School 3	School 4	School 1
Acids and Alkalis	School 3	School 4	School 1	School 2

Facilitating Formative and Summative Assessment

The DTAS and ICAM tools engage students in a complete learning cycle of multimedia lessons, diagnostic tests, component lessons, and remediation activities (see Figure 3). Data collected with DTAS and ICAM are combined to reveal each student's degree of learning through the diagnostic profiling system (DPS).

At the system level, teachers are provided with the following:

- Instantaneous and meaningful feedback to students
- Removal of time lag for teacher feedback to students
- Significant reduction in marking load for teachers, freeing up time for them to focus on diagnostic and assessment strategies
- Provide historical records of student diagnostics—individual, class, or level
- Access to real-time statistics on student performance.

After the open-ended questions have been developed and set by teachers within the ELMS, the first step for "*training ICAM to mark*" is the answer training mode. This mode, as stated above, allows the teachers to key in the model answers for each question, which subsequently generates all possible variants keyed in by the teacher. Subsequently, teachers can train the system to allocate marks by identifying keywords in the students' answers, which sets the marking scheme. This is done by using the editing tool.

After the content and assessment items have been trialed by students, a second mode of answer training comes into operation—the student training mode. More creative answers not already in the system are dealt with here. The steps involved are shown in Table 4.

Once the answers have been marked, the system can automatically tabulate all the marks of each student after the new marking scheme (after Step 4 has been completed) has been set and saved. In this manner, the teacher does not have to mark every script. All she or he has to do is filter the creative or unacceptable answers and allocate the marks that need to be rewarded for correct or partially correct answers.

The student profiling system, DPS, collates each student's answer and allows the teachers to monitor the performance of each student. In addition to the teacher, coordinators or subject panels can gather real-time statistics of all students' performance. Since each skill is tagged, specific skills and sub-skills attached to the questions within topics can assist the teacher to more closely evaluate and assess the students on their literal, interpretive or applied skills. As

Table 4. Actions taken by teachers to train the answers

Steps	Action by Teachers
1	Teachers input model answers for each topic and allocate marking scheme.
2	Students complete the topics and input individual answers.
3	Teachers go over the answers from students and decide on the marking scheme for those answers not already in the system.
4	All answers are consolidated back into the system for future use.

and when needed, reports can be generated to provide a profile with clear diagnostics of areas of weakness or strength as depicted in the boxes in the right hand column (*Figure 4*).

Participants' Use of the Technologies

Student use: Students used DTAS and ICAM systems online at school or from home. Science content was delivered to allow teachers to teach, assess, diagnose and profile students' differing abilities. Students using DTAS and ICAM could engage in self-learning on the Web using their individual accounts. This made learning efficient as the degree of learning for each individual was monitored and assessed through the Diagnostic Profiling System (DPS) (Table 5).

The DTAS, ICAM and DPS facilitated the following:

- Animated multimedia lessons
- Diagnostic tests comprising different tests on individual topics studied
- Component lessons for remediation and to cater for difficulty levels to allow for differentiated learning. The DTAS identifies the specific strengths and weaknesses of the individual students and automatically prompts component lessons for remediation in

Figure 4. Strengths and weaknesses of each skill diagnosed for each student

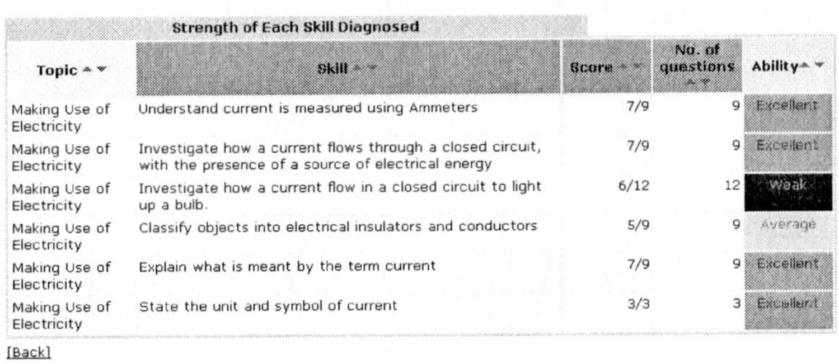

Strength of Each Skill Diagnosed

Topic	Skill	Score	No. of questions	Ability
Making Use of Electricity	Understand current is measured using Ammeters	7/9	9	Excellent
Making Use of Electricity	Investigate how a current flows through a closed circuit, with the presence of a source of electrical energy	7/9	9	Excellent
Making Use of Electricity	Investigate how a current flow in a closed circuit to light up a bulb.	6/12	12	Weak
Making Use of Electricity	Classify objects into electrical insulators and conductors	5/9	9	Average
Making Use of Electricity	Explain what is meant by the term current	7/9	9	Excellent
Making Use of Electricity	State the unit and symbol of current	3/3	3	Excellent

[Back]

weak concepts. The student is then prompted to undergo a re-test with simpler questions than the original set, which focus only on their weak concepts.

- The teacher could look up the DPS and provide each learner with individualised attention to allow for differentiated learning to occur.

Teacher use: Teachers using the system were provided with versatile teaching and learning tools that could be used to introduce lessons or reinforce teaching points. Aside from using the system as a complimentary resource tool to teach concepts, teachers benefited in the following ways:

- The lag-time for feedback on student performance was removed for each skill or topic to a negligible lag-time as compared to the current lag-time of several days of marking and time-consuming manual diagnoses of weak areas
- Marking load was considerably reduced which enabled teachers to teach, plan and conduct more activity-based lessons

Table 5. Using the ELMS: A student's perspective

Actions		Learning Model
What is current made of? Students **PREDICT** based on their existing knowledge.	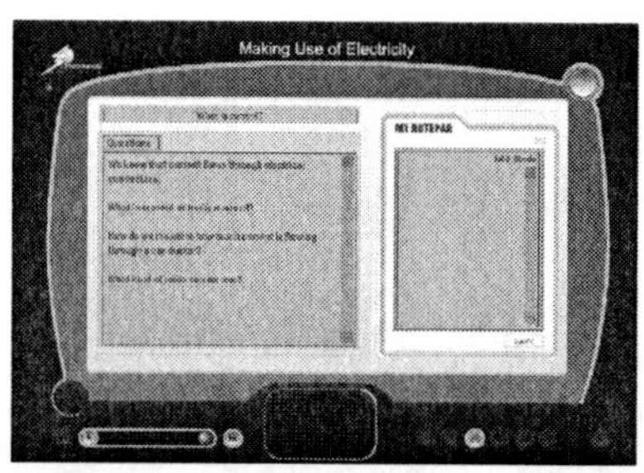	Articulation of understanding: Students are asked to type in what they think 'current' is, using the **notepad feature** within the ELMS. The content is saved for later comparison. **(1)**
	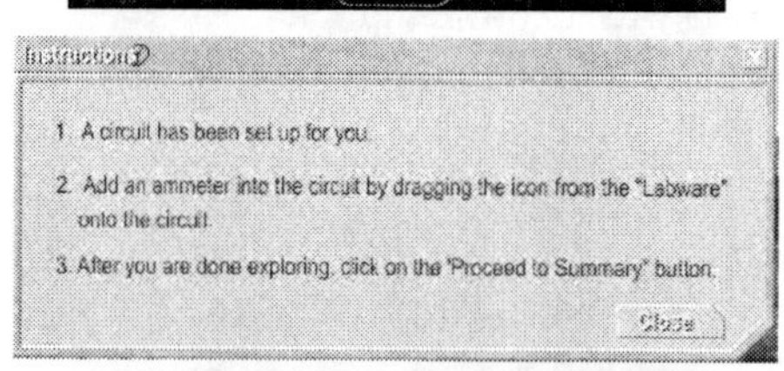	Instructions are given for students to explore.
A virtual experiment is set up for students to **OBSERVE** what happens		Students add an ammeter to the circuit.

continued on following page

Table 5. continued

Students can add from 1 up to 4 batteries and **CONTINUE TO OBSERVE** the change in readings on the ammeter.	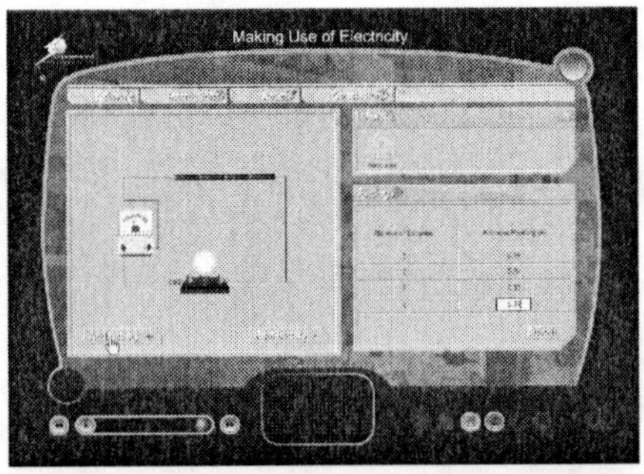	Observed readings on the ammeter are recorded in the table on the right.
Students are given many attempts to read the ammeter and input the readings until they get them all correct.	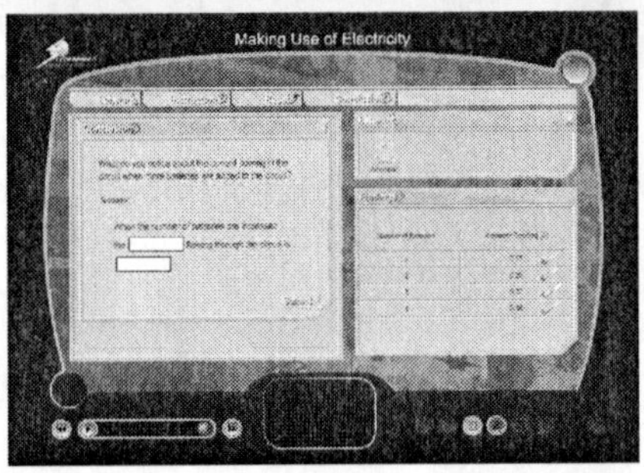	Once all readings have been entered students are asked to enter their answers in the '**Conclusion**' box on the right.

continued on following page

- Over a period of time, student profiles and historical records were maintained, thus enabling other teachers to see areas of strength and weakness of individual students or classes at any time of the year for each subject topic, to aid planning of future lessons or revision accordingly. This has eliminated the current practice where teachers are only able to know students' strengths and weaknesses after the tedious marking of several manual tests or exams
- Availability of the system as complementary tools to teach and diagnose the degree of learning and areas of weaknesses. The DTAS and ICAM systems allowed teachers to gather real-time statistics of the performance of students to suggest appropriate remediation for the areas of weaknesses identified
- Active participation in contributing to training the system to accept suitable answers – teachers can continually add, amend, edit or delete answers as appropriate.

Table 5. continued

Once all answers are correct, students are given a 'Summary' for consolidation	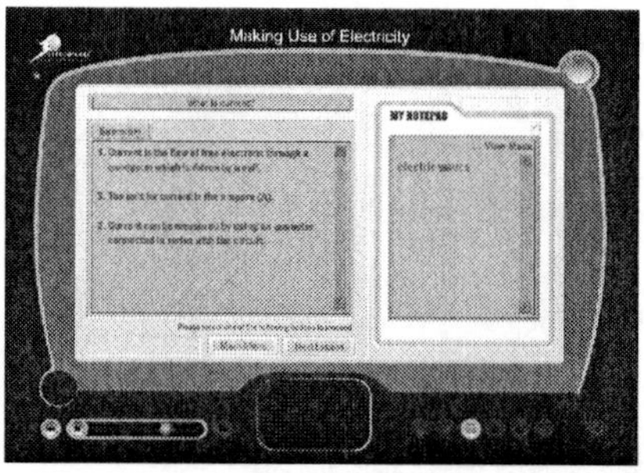	Presented with the summary information students can then **EXPLAIN** why their original concepts matched or mismatched the outcomes. **(2)**
	Students continue on to the next lesson where they **APPLY** what has been learnt or they can repeat the above topic.	
Start of the next cycle.	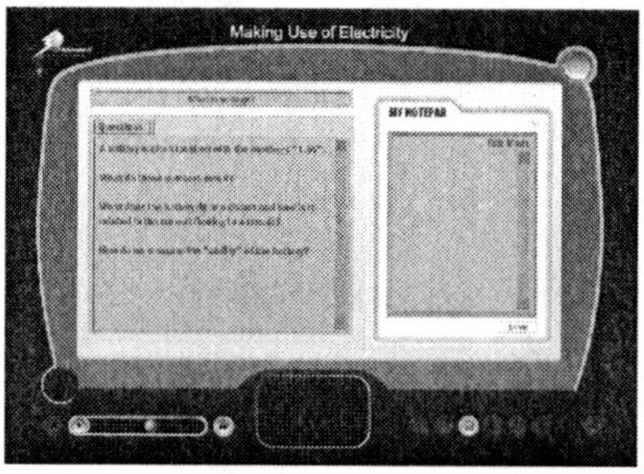	Students now APPLY the knowledge gained from the previous cycle described above.

Concept Maps for Non-Linear Learning

Games-based and scenario-based environments are used to introduce a certain degree of "play" into the assessment tasks. As Newton and Rogers (2001) point out, learning benefits accrue from how such properties (files work quickly, saves time and offers colourful graphics) are employed. Continuous assessment motivates and rewards students' continuous work. Instantaneous feedback allows students to self-assess and increases their interaction with the learning materials. Dori & Barak (2001) have also provided evidence that a combination of physical and virtual modeling supports the development of conceptual understanding. Figure 5 demonstrates one of the many topics where students interact with the content.

For each topic of study a concept map (Figure 6) was provided online in addition to the more linear progression of topics and tasks depicted by menus.

Figure 5. Students interact by moving weights and observing changes

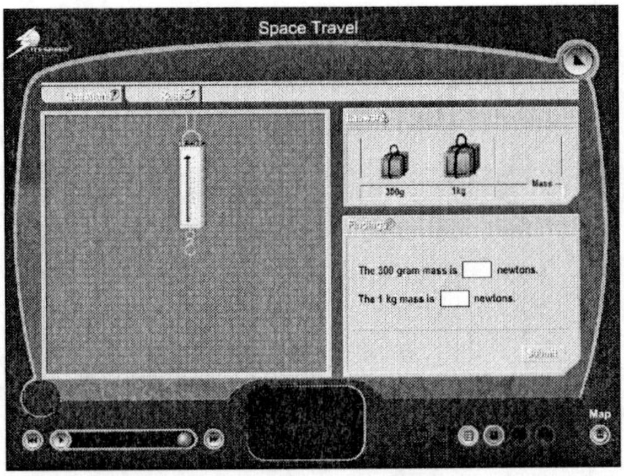

Figure 6. Concept map for the topic on electricity

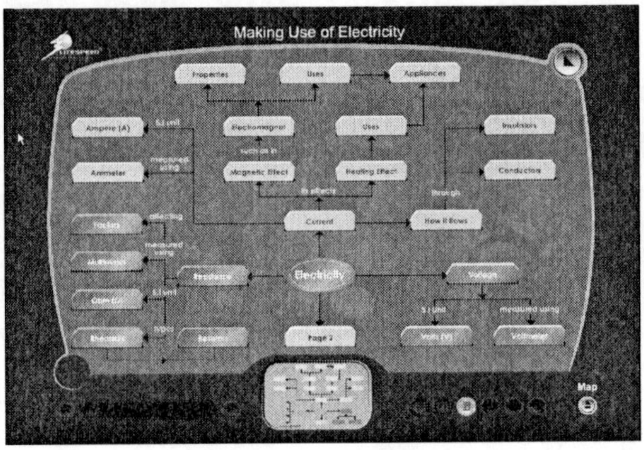

Challenges, Issues and Problems

Extensive human, information, learning, and technical resources are needed to produce and manage comprehensive OLEs. This section is devoted to the challenges, issues and problems encountered during the implementation of the ELMS in the four schools, and what steps were taken to resolve them. These challenges, issues and problems concurred with findings from other research studies (Becta, 2003; Britain & Liber, 2000; European Schoolnet, 2003; Specialist Schools Trust, 2005, July; Tanner & Jones, 2000) on the implementation of such learning environments in schools.

Challenge One: Extent of the Work to be Done

The entire secondary two science curriculum comprising five topics had to be developed with careful instructional design to convert them into interactive multimedia lessons accessible online for trialing in the schools. The intention was to map the science content onto discrete skills outcomes which were identified by codes recognised by the DTAS and ICAM systems so that individual student profiling could occur. As stated earlier, learning in this project is considered a constructive process (Duffy & Cunningham, 1996; Barab & Duffy, 2000; Duffy & Jonassen, 1992). Throughout the design stage all stakeholders expected that any content developed within the system would be goal directed. It was also an expectation that students would use the ELMS to construct an understanding to aid them in achieving their goal, that is, learning abstract scientific concepts. This goal should not be typically to "pass an exam," as this learning has little to do with being able to use the resources to function outside of the classroom (Honebein, Duffy, & Fishman, 1993); Bransford & Schwartz, 2001). Altogether, for the five topics there were over 175 skill identification tags (Table 1) that had to be incorporated within the software. This was a daunting task for all concerned.

Challenge Two: Unrealistic Expectations of Stakeholders

The development of content proved to be a great strain on the resources available. It was the expectation of the science inspectors that the content and assessment items had to be designed so that they would be able to enhance the learning of abstract and more advanced topics. They often required all content and questions to contain interactive elements that would provide a framework for prompting students' thinking. In discussions about these issues, there was not always agreement among the content writers, curriculum officers and the project team. Each stakeholder had a different expectation and it did not necessarily match those of the project team. At times, stakeholders did not fully understand the costs involved in designing the so-called "highly interactive content" that was capable of extending the learning of students. Each stakeholder held a different view of what "highly interactive" meant. For some, it meant having a lot of animations, while for others, it meant that the multimedia lessons must essentially test students and diagnose them on every aspect of their learning cycle. Some school principals anticipated the learning system to be just as good, if not better than the teaching that the teacher would do in a face-to-face situation, an unrealistic expectation. Others suggested that it should be commercial quality. This request came about due to past experience in other projects where teachers who were not multimedia developers had been asked to develop content, which turned out to be of poor quality.

To meet the above challenges, the project team had continual meetings with the stakeholders to arrive at an agreement on the design process that would be adopted. It was finally agreed that since teachers did not have the time to write these materials, suitable experts would be found to develop the content and would work with the project team and the technology partner to develop the interactive multimedia lessons to meet the deadline. Topics would be staggered and lessons would be uploaded at different times for schools to do the trial. A compromise was also arrived at to reduce the amount of interactive multimedia components for each topic. The funds were simply insufficient to support the huge number of multimedia items that were requested.

Issues

Firstly, in each of the schools the timetable was different and the scheduling for teaching the science topics were not the same from one school to the other. A lot of careful organisation and coordination had to be carried out so that the trials would go smoothly and data could be collected for analysis.

Secondly, teachers and principals were not willing to trial the online tools with classes that were of lower academic standards as they did not want the data collected to reflect the weaker students' profiles.

To solve the above two issues, trials had to be staggered and topics had to be uploaded at different times for different schools according to their schedule for teaching the relevant topics. As for the lower ability groups, principals and teachers were eventually persuaded to accept the view that the tools were in fact there to help at both ends of the spectrum, that is, the extension of the more academically able students as well as the weaker students. They were also informed that whatever data collected would be used judiciously and they would be consulted before any release of the results to government authorities.

Principals also had to be convinced to give teachers more of a free hand to trial the ELMS with students and not to be so concerned about school image and what results students were obtaining.

Problems

Developing interactive science content is not an easy task. Teachers and curriculum officers had very high expectations of what was to be produced. In view of the limited resources, the project team had to work under certain constraints and often measures had to be taken to restrict the amount of content that was requested for a topic or to limit the level of interactivity that teachers expected. An example of activities within an interactive lesson is shown in Figures 7a and 7b. Students could explore and predict the outcomes based on different scenarios presented.

The timeline was also a key problem. Teachers were always busy and it was not always possible to obtain their feedback on time. After the initial struggle, the team decided to outsource and found a panel of experienced science teachers who were commissioned to review all the content and provide feedback on schedule. A number of these teachers eventually became our content designers and writers, which considerably alleviated the workload of the actual teachers participating in the trials.

Extensive efforts had been made to solve the above issues and problems. A strict timeline had to be adhered to and by the fourth month after the commencement of the project, content had been developed and was ready for trialing in the schools. The first topic, "Electricity", was ready after three months preparation.

Although the partner schools were always very busy, they were very cooperative and the project team was able to successfully conduct the trials. Over the months, other topics were scheduled, these being "Space Travel" and "Common Acids and Alkalis." In each trial, the students completed a pre-test, studied the multimedia lessons and finally finished the

Figures 7a & 7b. Interactive lesson on electricity

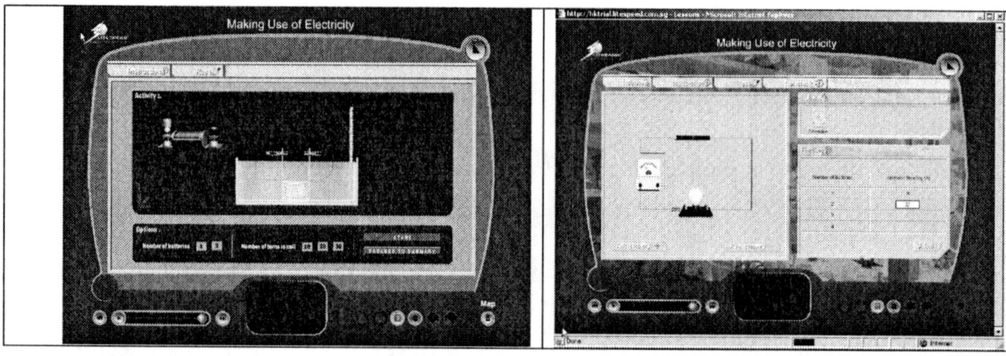

post-test. For the less able students who had not achieved the learning targets, the system directed them to the component lessons and subsequently retested them on the weak areas identified.

The teachers were also very dedicated to the project and invested an enormous amount of time to work with the project team and their students. Teachers gave up a lot of their spare time, usually in the evening or on weekends to participate in focus groups across the schools to train the answers within the ICAM system.

Preliminary Teacher and Student Feedback

It is not within the scope of this chapter to give a detailed analysis of teacher and student perceptions and attitudes to the ELMS. However, a presentation of some preliminary results will provide readers with a sense of how the project was received. Throughout the project both teachers and students were asked for feedback to allow progressive improvements to be made as each topic was developed and uploaded for trial. They were generally positive and always provided useful pointers as to how certain aspects might be improved.

It was found that 80% of students agreed that the e-learning platform enhanced their interest in learning science. Close to 82% of students also indicated that the system helped them to identify their weaknesses accurately. More than half revealed that the component lessons were helpful and did help them to revise what they had learnt in class and to prepare for tests. Students liked the instantaneous feedback that the system provided, although they felt that it was not always the case that all answers were marked correctly as they had anticipated. Students' responses also point to the fact that they recognise that it is they themselves who are able to change the parameters of learning within the system and then to see the effect of the change (Rogers & Finlayson, 2004).

For the schools where use of English was more of a challenge, they found the questions to be difficult. Students often tried to avoid the open-ended questions that required higher-level problem-solving skills in composing more comprehensive paragraph answers, which required them to explore issues and compare the results.

From the teachers' perspective, they were very pleased that all content and component lessons were developed for them thus saving them a lot of time. The DTAS and ICAM also greatly reduced their marking load thus freeing up time for them to focus more on exploring alternative teaching strategies. However, because the system was used for the first time in their respective schools, they had to assist with the training of the answers. For example they were required to input model answers into the answer training database and then adjust the marking scheme within the database. This was considered to be rather time consuming and demanding. But on the whole, they recognised that it was constructive and had potential.

Principles for the Future

Specific principles assisted with the continued adaptation process for the ELMS and these would be transferable to other instructional designers who undertake similar projects in future. When designing an ELMS, it is important to pay particular attention to the principles outlined below.

Firstly, an enormous amount of work needs to be done to convince teachers not to use the technology in traditional ways. Instructional designers and advocates of teaching technology have a responsibility to ensure that both technical skills and pedagogic skills are developed. Working to achieve this shift in mindset is significantly harder than solving the most difficult technical aspects of a system.

Secondly, teachers need to be drawn out of their own private spaces to be more collegial and openly share their experiences with others in their own school and with teachers in other schools, thereby establishing an open and active community of practice. Providing sufficient support to teachers and fostering a culture of peer-support are two strategies that may assist them to persevere beyond the initial weeks of frustration and uncertainty.

Thirdly, teachers as content experts played a crucial role in our study. It is extremely important that any sustained resistance to the new approaches diminishes through time. Teachers have to be convinced to engage wholeheartedly and be assured of senior administration support. It is the teacher who can either make or break the students' attitude to the use of the ELMS in terms of how the features and importance of its use are presented to the students and how seriously they handle the situation. Strategies to help teachers in this regard include providing explicit instructional guidance, within the environment itself, on the purpose of aspects of the environment and how to operate them, including specific guidance on how to guide students in their approaches to learning with the materials.

Fourthly, many students may experience problems with learning environments that focus on learner-centred tasks and activities. The willingness of the teacher to assist students to move toward a more self-motivated and less teacher-centred mode of instruction is crucial in increasing the degree of acceptance by students. The teacher must also be willing to give students the time and space to make mistakes and learn from them.

Conclusion

The experience from this project correlates with research findings, which indicate that technology-supported innovative classroom practices can help to change classroom teaching and learning (Kosma, 2003; Lee, 2002; Means, Penual, & Padilla, 2001; Schofield & Davidson, 2001). When teachers are already under extreme pressure and are then also required to collaborate with outside actors, they begin to see the potential use of the ELMS well beyond their normal expectations. Technology is then used differently and it is an accepted fact that their students will also use technology in another way. Both these changes in classroom practice demonstrate the possibilities of how curriculum can be delivered and how online technology can be used in more integrated ways to achieve desired learning outcomes.

As teachers moved to adopt learning settings that focused on student-centred rather than teacher-centred learning activities, the need for strategies to support and encourage learners became an important element in the design process. Teachers also acquired collaborative skills as a result of involvement in this project. Both teachers and senior administrators came to recognise the need to carefully and painfully plan, design and implement any form of online learning because the change of mindset is a gradual one. Teachers need a lot of hand-holding and scaffolding to facilitate them to adjust and accept cultural changes at the school level. Over time it may be possible for schools to use these tools to:

- Promote the value of using an ELMS with tools for closer monitoring of student learning
- Facilitate a meaningful and integrated approach to the use of OLEs
- Promote an entire school culture change.

A major contribution of the present study has involved the development of the ELMS and the DTAS and ICAM tools in order to assist teachers to teach science differently and to allow students to take responsibility for their own learning within a technology-rich learning setting. The study is innovative for the Hong Kong education system because no other system currently employs the use of the DTAS and ICAM tools. Significant issues and challenges remain but the successful implementation of the ELMS demonstrates that innovative ICT approaches can provide teachers and students with powerful collaborative capabilities, which support a range of learning activities within a classroom environment.

The study is also significant in that the entire ELMS has potential implications for the Hong Kong schools sector. Lessons learned from this project can be transferable to practice in other schools. With the continuous high levels of sponsorship from government for ICT integration in schools, there will be many schools that will be able to adopt such a system.

Finally, students using this system can have more autonomy over their learning processes and can in fact control their own rate of learning and how they sequence their learning. The ELMS has provided opportunities for students to take ultimate responsibility for making sense of learning activities and has provided teaching approaches that place the students in an intellectually challenging position. Further research should seek to explore the multiple uses of the ELMS and improve the design principles in order to achieve a higher degree of learner engagement and wholehearted participation by teachers, which are both paramount to learning success.

Note

When referring to government policies the term information technology (IT) is used because it is used within all Hong Kong government documents. In this chapter it is synonymous to the term information and communications technology (ICT) as used many other countries.

Acknowledgment

The author would like to acknowledge the support of the Quality Education Fund, Education and Manpower Bureau, Hong Kong SAR for the project. In addition the author thanks team members, principals, teachers, students and Litespeed, who contributed to the success of this project. This chapter has been significantly re-written from an initial draft presented at Ausweb 05.

References

Barab, S., & Luehmann, A. (2003). Building sustainable science curriculum: Acknowledging and accommodating local adaptation. *Science Education, 87*, 454-467.

Barab, S., & Duffy, T. (2000). From practice fields to communities of practice. In D. Jonassen & S.M. Land (Eds.), *Theoretical foundations of learning environments* (pp. 25-56). Mahwah, NJ: Lawrence Erlbaum.

BECTA. (2003). *Virtual learning environments in education: A review of the literature.* Retrieved August 15, 2005, from http://www.becta.org.uk/page_documents/research/VLE_report.pdf

Black, P.J., & Wiliam, D. (1998). *Inside the black box: Raising standards through classroom assessment.* London: King's College London School of Education.

Bransford, J.D., & Schwartz, D.L. (2001). Rethinking transfer: A simple proposal with multiple implications. *Review of Research in Education, 24,* 61-100.

Bransford, J., Brown, A., & Cocking, R. (Eds.). (2000). *How people learn: Brain, mind, experience, and school.* Washington, DC: National Research Council.

Britain, S. & Liber, O. (2000). *A framework for pedagogical evaluation of virtual learning environments. Report 41. JISC Technologies Application (JTAP) Programme.* Retrieved August 15, 2005, from http://www.jisc.ac.uk/index.cfm?name=project_pedagogical_vle

Cavanagh, C., Gillan, K.J., Kromrey, J., Hess, M., & Blomeyer, R. (2004). *The effects of distance education on K-12 student outcomes: A meta-analysis*. Jacksonville, FL: North Central Regional Educational Laboratory.

Department of Education, Training and Youth Affairs (DEETYA). (2000). *Learning for the knowledge society: An education and training action plan for the information economy*. Canberra: DEETYA

Diaz, D., & Cartal, R. (2000). Students' learning styles in two classes: Online distance learning and equivalent on-campus. *College Teaching*, *47*(4), 130-135.

Dori, Y., & Barak, M. (2001). Virtual and physical molecular modeling: Fostering model perception and spatial understanding. *Educational Technology & Society*, *4*, 61-74.

Duffy, T.M., & Cunningham, D.J. (1996). Constructivism: Implications for the design and delivery of instruction, In D.H. Jonassen (Ed.), *Handbook of research for educational communications and technology*. New York: Macmillan Library Reference USA.

Duffy, T.M., & Jonassen, D.H. (Eds.). (1992). *Constructivism and the technology of instruction: A conversation.* Hillsdale, NJ: Lawrence Erlbaum Associates.

Duit, R., & Treagust, D. (2003). Conceptual change: A powerful framework for improving science teaching and learning, *International Journal of Science Education*, *25*(6), 671-688.

Education and Manpower Bureau (EMB). (2001). *Learning for life, learning through life: Reform proposals for the education system in Hong Kong*. Hong Kong: Education Manpower Bureau, Education Commission.

Education and Manpower Bureau (EMB). (2004). *Information technology in education: Way forward.* Hong Kong: Hong Kong Special Administrative Region.

European Schoolnet. (2003). *Virtual learning environments for European schools: A survey and commentary.* Retrieved August 15, 2005, from www.eun.org/etb/vle/vle_report_restricted_2003.pdf

Goldberg, H., & McKhann, G. (2000). Student test scores are improved in a virtual learning environment. *Advances in Physiology Education*, *23*(1), 59-66.

Hall, B. (2001). *New technology definitions*. Retrieved August 15, 2005, from www.brandonhall.com/public/glossary/index.htm

Honebein, P., Duffy, T., & Fishman, B. (1993). Constructivism and the design of learning environments: Context and authentic activities for learning. In T. Duffy, J. Lowyck, & D. Jonassen (Eds.), *The design of constructivist learning environments: Implications for instructional design and the use of technology.* Heidelberg: Springer-Verlag.

Hong Kong Examination and Assessment Authority (The HKEA). (n.d.). *The Basic Competency Assessment (BCA) system*. Retrieved February 18, 2003, from http://www.hkbca.edu.hk/index_eng.htm.

Jacobson, M.J., & Spiro, R.J. (1995). Hypertext learning environments, cognitive flexibility, and the transfer of complex knowledge: An empirical investigation. *Journal of Educational Computing Research*, *12*(4) 301-333.

Jonassen, D., & Land, S. (2000). *Theoretical foundations of learning environments*. Hillsdale, NJ: Lawrence Erlbaum Associates.

Jonassen, D.H. (2000). *Computers as mindtools for schools: Engaging critical thinking.* Upper Saddle River, NJ: Merrill.

Jonassen, D.H., Howland, J., Moore, J., & Marra, R.M. (2003). *Learning to solve problems with technology: A constructivist perspective.* Upper Saddle River, NJ: Merrill/Prentice Hall.

Jones, B., Valdez, G., Nowakowski, J., & Rasmussen, C. (1995). *Plugging in: Choosing and using educational technology*. Washington, DC: Council for Educational Development and Research. Retrieved August 22, 2005, from http://www.ncrtec.org/capacity/plug/plug.htm

Kearney, M., & Treagust, D. (2001). Constructivism as a referent in the design and development of a computer program using interactive digital video to enhance learning in physics. *Australian Journal of Educational Technology, 17*(1), 64-79.

Kirby, E. (1999, Feb-Mar). *Building integration in online distance education course*. Paper presented at the SITE 999: 10th Society for Information Technology & Teacher Education International Conference, San Antonio, TX.

Koschmann, T.D. (1994). Using technology to assist in realizing effective learning and instruction: A principled approach to the use of computers in collaborative learning. *Journal of the Learning Sciences, 3*(3), 227-264.

Kozma, R. (Ed.). (2003). *Technology, innovation, and educational change: A global perspective.* Eugene, OR: International Society for Technology in Education.

Law, N., Yuen, H., Ki, W., Li, S., Lee, Y., & Chow, Y. (2000). *Changing classrooms: A study of good practices in using ICT in Hong Kong Schools.* Hong Kong: Centre for Information Technology in School and Teacher Education, University of Hong Kong.

Lee, K.T. (2002). Effective teaching in the information era: Fostering an ICT-based integrated learning environment in schools. *Asia-Pacific Journal for Teacher Education & Development, 5*(1), 21-45.

Lee, K.T. (2005). Teachers using an integrated learning environment to cater for individual learning differences in Hong Kong primary classrooms. *Technology, Pedagogy and Education, 14*(3), 373-391.

Linn, M., Davis, E., & Bell, P. (Eds.). (2004). *Internet environments for science education.* Mahwah, NJ: Lawrence Erlbaum Associated.

Means, B., Penuel, W., & Padilla, C. (2001). *The connected school: Technology and learning in high school.* San Francisco: Jossey-Bass.

Newhouse, C., Trinidad, S., & Clarkson, B. (2002). *Quality, pedagogy and effective learning with information & communications technologies (ICT): A review of the literature.* Perth: Western Australia Department of Education.

Newton, L., & Rogers, L.T. (2001). *Teaching science with ICT.* London: Continuum.

Pachler, N., & Byrom, K. (1999). Assessment of and through ICT. In M. Leask & N. Pachler (Eds.), *Learning to teach using ICT in the secondary school* (pp. 125-146). London: Routledge Falmer.

Riel, M., & Becker, H. (2000). *The beliefs, practices and computer use of teacher leaders.* Irvine: University of California

Rogers, L., & Finlayson, H. (2004). Developing successful pedagogy with information and communication technology: How are science teachers meeting the challenge? *Technology, Pedagogy and Education, 13*(3), 287-305.

Sandholz, J.H., Ringstaff, C., & Dwyer, C.D. (1997). *Teaching with technology: Creating pupil centered classrooms.* New York: Teachers College Press.

Schofield, J., & Davidson, A. (2002). *Bringing the Internet to school: Lessons from an urban district.* San Francisco: Jossey-Bass.

Specialist Schools Trust. (2005, July). *Harnessing new technologies – a response from the Specialist Schools Trust.* UK. Retrieved 27 May, 2006, from http://www.schoolsnetwork.org.uk/content/articles/4884/harnessingtechnologyresponse2005.doc.

Tanner, H., & Jones, S. (2000, September). *Using ICT to support interactive teaching and learning on a secondary mathematics PGCE course.* British Educational Research Association (BERA) Annual Conference, Cardiff University. Retrieved August 15, 2005, from http://www.leeds.ac.uk/educol/documents/00001628.htm.

Teachers Training Agency. (1999). *Ways forward with ICT.*UK: School of Education, Communication & Language Sciences, University of Newcastle upon Tyne.

Tiene, D., & Ingram, A. (2001). *Exploring current issues in educational technology.* New York: McGraw-Hill Higher Education.

Underwood, J., & Underwood, G. (1990). *Computers and learning: Helping children acquire thinking skills.* Oxford: Blackwell.

Valdez, G., McNabb, M., Foertsch, M., Anderson, M., Hawkes, M., & Raack, L. (2000). *Computer-based technology and learning: Evolving uses and expectations.* Retrieved August 22, 2005, from http://www.ncrel.org/tplan/cbtl/toc.htm.

About the Authors

Michael J. Keppell is an associate professor and head of the Centre for Learning, Teaching and Technology (LTTC) at the Hong Kong Institute of Education. He has been the director of three innovative educational technology units over the last 12 years and has worked as an instructional designer on over 200 technology-enhanced initiatives in areas as diverse as coal mining, medicine and teacher education. His expertise lies in his ability to combine the operational and development tasks of educational technology with the academic study of curriculum, instructional design and evaluation. His current research interests at the institute focus on technology-enhanced authentic learning environments, blended learning, peer learning, problem-based learning and learning-oriented assessment.

* * *

Sue Bennett is a senior lecturer in the Faculty of Education at the University of Wollongong, Australia. She is an active member of the Centre for Research in Interactive Learning Environments, a research group which focuses on investigating the integration of technology to support learning in a wide variety of learning settings. Sue's research interests include learning designs and learning objects, interactive whiteboards in the classroom, and case-based learning. Bennett teaches subjects on interactive multimedia and Web design to on-campus and distance students.

Jenny Bird is an educational designer at the Teaching and Learning Centre, Southern Cross University, Australia. She has a long history as a staff developer, an educational designer, a curriculum developer and a writer of distance education materials. She has a particular interest in curriculum design and development, and teaches *Curriculum Design in Higher Education* in the Graduate Certificate of Higher Education (Learning and Teaching) through the TLC. Her research interests lie in issues related to the profession of flexible learning designers/developers and the flexible delivery of programs.

Gwyn Brickell is a lecturer in the Faculty of Education at the University of Wollongong (Australia) with a teaching focus on ICT and science education. His professional interests are in instructional design, implementation and evaluation of digital technologies for educational purposes. He has a background of 22 years teaching in secondary schools (in NSW, Canada and the U.S.) in the curriculum areas of science and computing studies. His current responsibilities include leading the training and development of pre-service teachers for mathematics and science teaching in secondary schools.

Christine Brown was seconded from the Faculty of Education to Flexible Learning Services as acting manager in 2003. Part of her responsibility was the completion of a major CD-ROM based project (*Ridgeline*) in conjunction with the Interactive Multimedia Lab and emLab in the Faculty of Education. Within Flexible Learning Services, Brown engaged with more than 20 projects as a designer between 2003 and 2005. In addition, she provided academic mentoring and production guidance to teaching staff nominated for University of Wollongong and National Teaching Awards. She now works primarily as an educational/academic developer, liaises strategically with the Faculty of Science, and coordinates the Teaching Innovation and Evaluation Unit within CEDIR.

Katy Campbell, PhD, is associate dean, Faculty of Extension at the University of Alberta, Canada. Dr. Campbell's research program and publications focus on three areas: the socio-cultural process of learning design, the lifeworld of the designer, and the faculty experience of design as transformative practice. These main threads are framed by a feminist epistemology of ethical, relational knowing, and from a critical theory perspective. From within these frameworks Dr. Campbell explores, in her research, teaching, and instructional design practice, issues of inclusivity in learning design and practice (especially related to gender issues). She has authored the text *E-ffective Writing for E-learning Environments* (2004, IGI) and serves on several editorial boards.

Beth Cavallari is acting director of the Teaching and Educational Development Institute (TEDI) at the University of Queensland, Australia. Her career spans 30 years in primary and secondary school teaching, computer educational consultancy and Instructional Design and Headship of the Educational Resources Unit of the TEDI. As acting director of TEDI, she provides leadership in the areas of e-learning, educational resource development and problem-based learning. She is currently involved in implementing a range of university-wide e-learning initiatives and has been actively involved in managing the university-wide introduction of online learning management systems.

Tang Buay Choo is an instructional designer with the Institute of Technical Education, Singapore. She has many years of experience in the professional development of teaching staff and leaders in the application and development of educational technologies. Before joining ITE, she was a head of department (Information Technology & Media Resources) in a primary school, senior IT instructor with the Educational Technology Division of the Ministry of Education, part-time tutor with the National Institute of Education and Educational Technologist, training manager with private organizations that develop e-learning and CD-ROM based learning resources.

Susan Crichton is an assistant professor in the Faculty of Education at the University of Calgary, Alberta, Canada. She is in the specialization of educational technology, working on issues of online learning and teacher preparation (specifically as it relates to online learning). She has been involved in international work (CIDA and Asian Development Bank). Prior to coming to the university in fall 2001, Crichton lived in a small community in the West Kootenays in British Columbia, Canada for 23 years where she developed a program for returning adult students and at risk youth that was supported by distributed learning. Her interests include appropriate technology and issues of equity of access and social justice as they impact the sustainability of rural communities.

Brian Ferry is associate professor and associate dean graduate at the University of Wollongong, Australia. His research interests include the use of online simulations in initial teacher education, alternative approaches to initial teacher education, and science education. He began his career as a teacher in an isolated rural primary school and later moved to secondary schools before becoming an academic.

Cathy Gunn works in academic development specializing in technology-facilitated learning. She has contributed to, and managed change at all levels within a large research university since the early 1990s. Research and teaching interests span a range of topics including organizational change, evaluating innovations, information technology in education and the psychology of learning. Gunn has many publications reflecting this breadth of experience, and is currently serving as president of The Australasian Society for Computers in Learning in Tertiary Education (ascilite). She has a PhD in computer-based learning research and an MSc in human-computer interaction from Heriot-Watt University in Scotland.

Doug Hearne is a lecturer in the Physical and Health Education Program in the Faculty of Education, University of Wollongong and president of the New South Wales branch of the Australian Council for Health, Physical Education and Recreation. His major teaching responsibilities are within physical and health education (PHE) curriculum and pedagogy. Hearne's research interests include: PHE teacher preparation; online mentoring in teacher preparation; PHE curriculum implementation; and the place of professional teaching standards in teacher preparation and professional learning.

Richard F. Kenny, PhD, is an associate professor with the Center for Distance Education at Athabasca University (Canada), where he teaches learning theory and instructional design. He has a PhD in instructional design from Syracuse University and over 30 years of experience in education, having taught at both the K-12 and university levels. He has also worked as an instructional designer at the school system level and in university distance education. Dr. Kenny's current research interests encompass three areas: instructional design and change agency; the design and development of online learning to foster problem-solving and critical thinking; and mobile learning applications and strategies.

Lisa Kervin is a lecturer in the Faculty of Education, University of Wollongong, Australia. She has taught across the primary grades and has been responsible for both the literacy and numeracy curriculum areas within schools. She has been employed in consultancy roles within New South Wales education systems. Kervin graduated in July 2004 with a PhD and her thesis was concerned with the professional development of teachers in literacy. Her current research interests are related to the literacy development of children, the use of technology to support student learning and teacher professional learning.

Myint Swe Khine was an associate professor and coordinator of the Master Degree Program at the Learning Sciences and Technologies Academic Group, National Institute of Education, Nanyang Technological University, Singapore. He received his master's degrees from the University of Southern California (USA) and University of Surrey (UK), and Doctor of Education from Curtin University of Technology (Australia). He has co-authored and published books which include *Studies in Educational Learning Environments: An International Perspective* (World Scientific), *Engaged Learning with Emerging Technologies* (Springer-Verlag), and *Technology-rich Learning Environments: A Future Perspective* (World Scientific).

Coco Kishi has managed instructional technology projects and taught multimedia production courses at the University of Texas at Austin (USA) for over 10 years. Kishi initiated the Faculty And Student Teams for Technology (~FAST Tex) program, based on the successful practice of assigning students to work on faculty projects in her courses. As a senior systems analyst for the Division of Instructional Innovation and Assessment, Kishi coordinates new media research and development of campus instructional technology projects, as well as faculty and student training and support services in media technologies at the University of Texas at Austin.

Samuel Ng Hong Kok is the divisional director of educational design and technology at the Institute of Technical Education (ITE), overseeing the pursuit, development and implementation of innovative educational designs and solutions with learning technologies among the lecturers in ITE Colleges. He has been chiefly responsible for the development and implementation of the 5-year institution-wide IT master plan which has created an IT-based teaching and learning environment for students and teaching staff to engage in flexible and independent learning. Ng received a BSc (Hons.) in electrical and electronic engineering from Loughborough University of Technology, UK (1988) and Master of Business in information technology from the Royal Melbourne Institute of Technology, Australia (1994).

Sarah Lambert joined the Flexible Learning Services production unit of the Centre for Educational Development and Interactive Resources (CEDIR) in 1999. As project manager for the unit she has worked in project teams (approximately 30 client projects per annum), managed production processes and streamlined the project management procedures of multiple parallel multimedia projects. From 2002 her position shifted to the newly formed Learning Design Unit, which focuses on ensuring the educational quality of the products. Within CEDIR, Sarah has managed the Faculty Service Agreement Program that matches production resources with teaching priority projects in each faculty.

Kar-Tin Lee is a professor and head of the School for Mathematics, Science and Technology Education, Queensland University of Technology, Australia. She has wide experience in the design, development, implementation and evaluation of technology-mediated and online learning materials. Since 1995, she has been a lead investigator in research and development projects sponsored by government, university and industry partners. She has initiated, directed, and co-developed several high profile, successful e-learning solutions for education (tertiary and school sectors) in the Asia-Pacific region. Her research interests include e-learning and pedagogy and how the design and development of pedagogically sound teaching and learning resources for online delivery can impact or enhance learning. A key element in all her projects has been the successful generation of ideas to help schools to engage in successful change processes in order to change and sustain the change.

Pamela Pai Wan Leung has been teaching at the Hong Kong Institute of Education since 1995. Her areas of specialization include Chinese linguistics and teaching and learning of the Chinese language. Prior to her teacher-education employment, she taught at primary, secondary and tertiary levels in Hong Kong and Australia. She received a BA (Chinese language and literature) from The Chinese University of Hong Kong, an MA (applied linguistics) and MPhil (linguistics) from The University of Sydney and a PhD (education) from Griffith University, Australia. Her PhD study focused on how pre-service teachers learn to become teachers of Chinese in Hong Kong. Currently, she is involved in research on classroom instruction, learning-oriented assessment and collaborative professional development in teaching supervision.

Min Liu, EdD, is a professor of instructional technology at the University of Texas at Austin (USA). She has been teaching new media related design, production, and research courses over 15 years. Her research interests center on the impact of new media technology on learning and the design of engaging and interactive learning environments for all age groups. She publishes widely in leading IT research journals and serves on a number of editorial/manuscript review boards of IT research journals. She is also active in professional organizations such as AACE, AERA, and ISTE. She has directed and managed both CD-ROM and Web-based development projects, including award-winning ones.

Lori Lockyer is director of the Digital Media Centre, Director of Educational Development in the Graduate School of Medicine and teaches in the Information and Communication Technologies in Learning Program within the Faculty of Education, University of Wollongong. Her academic and professional career has spanned disciplines of educational and social history, information sciences, health education, cancer prevention and care, and educational technologies. She designed and researched the Faculty of Education's first implementation of Web-based collaborative learning in pre-service education which led to the establishment of the *ActiveHealth* Web site to support the physical and health education community.

Jacqueliné McDonald is a senior lecturer in the Distance and e-Learning Centre at the University of Southern Queensland, Australia. She is a teacher, online educator and a practicing instructional designer. She has designed training and distance education, blended learning materials for on-campus, national and international learners. Her research interests include instructional design, hybrid/blended learning, communities of practice, amd interaction and engagement in online learning. She has written a number of journal articles and presented at international and national conferences. She holds a master's degree in flexible learning and is researching online interaction as a doctoral student at USQ.

Elspeth McKay, PhD, MACS(Snr), is a senior lecturer in HCI Research at RMIT University, Australia. Dr. McKay investigates how individuals interpret text/graphics since gaining her PhD in communication science and IS at Deakin University, Australia. She has a bachelor's degree in business, with distinction (business IS), a graduate certificate of applied science (instructional design), and a graduate diploma of education (computer studies). She identified that not all individuals cope effectively with graphical learning. McKay's research interests include specialist e-learning shells implemented through Rich Internet Apps, interactive dynamics of Web-mediated knowledge mediation, ontological strategies of learning design with asynchronous Web-enabled frameworks, and development of enhanced accessibility through touch screen technologies.

Jennifer Martin, PhD, is an associate professor in social work at RMIT University, Australia. Martin has research and practice experience in conflict prevention, management and resolution. She has a Bachelor of Social Science, a Bachelor of Social Work, a Master of Social Work and a graduate certificate in developmental child psychiatry. Much of her academic and direct practice work is in multidisciplinary teams. She has developed a model for effective multidisciplinary collaboration. Her research interests include conflict prevention, management and resolution, mental health, and multidisciplinary and cross-cultural communications. She is a practicing mediator and forensic consultant.

Terry Mayes is currently a research professor at Glasgow Caledonian University, Scotland. He has experience as both researcher and practitioner in learning technology. He was director of research in the Institute for Computer-Based Learning at Heriot-Watt University, Edinburgh, from its formation in 1990. His early work with teaching machines was followed by 14 years as a lecturer in psychology at the University of Strathclyde, during which period he researched cognitive aspects of learning. Since the mid-1980s he has worked extensively on the development of interactive learning through technology. During the late 1990s, Mayes led collaborative projects funded through the UK Research Councils involving research on the educational potential of vicarious learning. He is currently chair of the Scottish Funding

Council/Quality Assurance Agency Steering Group on the Enhancement Theme of Flexible Delivery. He has published widely on human aspects of learning technology.

Patricie Mertova is a research fellow in the Educational Development and Flexible Learning Unit in the Faculty of Law, Monash University, Australia. Her background is in the areas of linguistics, translation, cross-cultural communication and foreign languages. She has an interest in discourse across a broad range of disciplines and settings. Apart from her strong linguistic background and interests, she also has expertise in educational theory and research.

Chris Morgan is a lecturer and educational designer at the Teaching and Learning Centre, Southern Cross University, Australia. He has a 20-year span of work as a curriculum designer, staff developer and instructional designer in a variety of educational contexts. Morgan's research and publication interests are in the area of student assessment. He has written two international texts on the subject in recent years, including *Assessing Open and Distance Learners* (Kogan Page, 1999) and *The Student Assessment Handbook* (Routledge US, 2004). He regularly consults with universities and industry on assessment issues.

Meg O'Reilly is a lecturer and educational designer at the Teaching and Learning Centre, Southern Cross University. O'Reilly has extensive experience in providing academic staff development, curriculum development and educational design for innovation and flexibility in teaching, learning and assessment. She has co-authored two international texts with colleague, Chris Morgan, and now teaches *The Scholarship of Teaching in Higher Education* unit in the Graduate Certificate in Higher Education (Learning and Teaching). Her doctoral studies involve action research to investigate how academic staff might improve their assessment practices online through critical reflection and transdisciplinary collaboration.

John Patterson is a professor and deputy vice chancellor (operations) at the University of Wollongong, Australia. Patterson was formerly the dean of the Faculty of Education (1993-1999). Before becoming a teacher educator in 1974 he taught physical education in secondary schools and was also a primary school teacher. Having held significant positions on state and national advisory councils and professional associations, Patterson has led policy change in areas of teacher competencies, teacher registration, physical and health education curriculum change, and the selection of pre-service teachers. His research interests include physical and health education, policy development in education, and information technology and education. He led the establishment of the *ActiveHealth* Web site.

Stephen Quinton is currently working with the Division of Humanities and the School of Information Systems at Curtin University as a researcher in knowledge networks and e-learning systems. He is involved in several research projects that focus on the application of emergent information and communications technologies (ICT) to support the design of advanced learning environments. Other research interests include the identification of learner preferences, needs, and attitudes to provide customised learning solutions. The intended practical outcome of all research activities is to demonstrate how individualised learning approaches supported by advanced technologies can enhance the learner's capacity for creative thinking and knowledge innovation.

Suzanne Rhodes has been managing projects and instructional design teams for 10 years with a focus on online and hybrid environments. She is a senior systems analyst for the University of Texas at Austin's Division of Instructional Innovation and Assessment and manages the Faculty And Student Teams for Technology (~FAST Tex) program. ~FAST Tex pairs faculty and students to develop technology-based projects to enhance teaching and learning. Prior to this, she worked as an instructional design lead and project manager for Human Code/Sapient. She has a Master of Arts in curriculum and instruction, specializing in instructional technology (University of Texas at Austin).

Gregg Rowland teaches physical and health education within the Faculty of Education at the University of Wollongong, Australia. He holds a PhD in professional development and education policy. Rowland has an extensive background in pedagogy and the use of information and communication technology for teaching physical and health education. Rowland has been a member of the *ActiveHealth* project team and is leading projects that provide online mentoring opportunities for undergraduate students whilst involved in their practicum experiences and for early career physical and health education teachers.

Richard. A. Schwier, EdD, is a professor of educational communications and technology at the University of Saskatchewan (Canada), where he coordinates the graduate program in educational technology. He is the principal investigator in the Virtual Learning Communities Research Laboratory, which is currently studying the characteristics of formal online learning communities. Dr. Schwier's other research interests include instructional design and social change agency.

Lalen Simeon is a lecturer in the Faculty of Business at Pacific Adventist University, Papua New Guinea. Her teaching focuses on ICT use in teaching and learning with pre-service primary school teachers. Since completing her academic studies, majoring in Information Technology, Training and Education at the University of Wollongong, her research focus has been in developing effective ICT training programs for different groups of employees, students and women's groups in developing countries such as Papua-New Guinea.

Len Webster is the faculty director for IT, flexible learning and multimedia as well as director of the Educational Development and Flexible Learning Unit in the Faculty of Law, Monash University. His experience includes research in teaching and learning in higher education with a special interest in narrative inquiry research methods. As an educational theorist, Dr. Webster has sought to link educational theory with learning and research models to provide educationally sound learning environments. Recently this work has been recognized in an award made to Dr. Webster by the Australian Society for Computers in Teaching and Learning for his co-creation of the online interactive environment "*InterLearn*."

Index

O

P